Soups

In this section you will find a great variety of soups, from clear consommes, creamy vegetable soups and delicately flavoured iced soups to thick meat and vegetable soups and chowders, which are sufficiently filling and nutritious to be served as a meal in themselves. You will also find rich party soups and continental fruit soups, not to mention the numerous nourishing everyday soups.

They are all interesting to make as well as tasty and nearly all are simple to prepare. If you are an imaginative cook, you can turn them into at least twice this number by your own original additions and variations.

If you are not already a convinced soup-maker I hope this section will inspire you to become one, because what can be more warming on a cold winter's night than a bowl of richly-flavoured and aromatic steaming home-made soup? Soup also has its place in summer when appetites are jaded. A light iced concoction can revive the spirits and make the perfect beginning for a summer party menu.

Shrimp Bisque (see p. 32)

STOCKS

Chicken Stock for Consomme

1 boiling chicken with giblets
2 peeled and sliced onions
4 stalks of celery
2—3 carrots
1 thin sliver of lemon rind
1 bay leaf
6—8 sprigs of parsley
1 sprig of tarragon (or large pinch dried tarragon)
1 small sprig of thyme (or large pinch dried thyme)
6 peppercorns
1 level teaspoon salt (or more if needed)

1. Put a cleaned and cut-up boiling chicken into a large pan with sliced vegetables. Add the herbs, lemon rind and seasoning. Cover with water, and bring slowly to the boil. Then cover pan and simmer for 2 hours until all the flavour is in the soup.

2. Strain and allow to cool. When cold, skim fat from the top and use the stock for chicken consomme or other soups requiring strong chicken stock. The stock can also be stored in the deep freeze.

Ordinary Chicken Stock

1 cooked chicken carcass
giblets, if available
1 onion, sliced
2 carrots, sliced
2 stalks of celery
1 bay leaf
1 sprig of thyme (or 1/8 teaspoon or
     large pinch dried thyme)
6 sprigs of parsley
6 peppercorns
1 level teaspoon salt
1 chicken cube (if necessary)

1. Put the broken-up chicken carcass and bones into a pan with any available giblets and any leftover chicken meat or skin. Add the vegetables and herbs. Cover with water, and add pepper and salt. Bring to the boil slowly, and simmer for 1–2 hours, or until well flavoured. If not sufficiently well flavoured add a chicken cube and cook for a few more minutes.

2. Strain and allow to cool. If not using at once store in the refrigerator, boiling it up daily, or in a deep freeze.

1 game carcass with any meat
     attached
2 onions sliced
2 carrots sliced
2–3 stalks of celery
6 sprigs of parsley
1 sprig of thyme (or 1/8 teaspoon or
     large pinch dried thyme)
1 bay leaf
6–8 peppercorns
½ teaspoon salt

Game Stock

1. Put the carcass of the game bird into a pan with the sliced vegetables, herbs and seasoning. Cover with water and bring slowly to the boil. Then skim off any scum that rises to the surface, and simmer until well flavoured and reduced in quantity.

2. Strain and use or freeze for later use.

White Bone Stock

2 pounds raw veal knuckle bones
1 chicken carcass and giblets
2 onions, peeled and sliced
2 carrots, peeled and sliced
3 stalks of celery
1 bay leaf
6 sprigs of parsley
1 small sprig of thyme (or 1/8 teaspoon
**   or large pinch dried thyme)**
2 level teaspoons salt
6 peppercorns
1 small piece of mace
3 quarts water
rind of ½ lemon

1. Get butcher to chop the raw veal bones and chicken carcass into small pieces. Put these into pan of water with vegetables, herbs and seasoning. Bring to the boil and skim frequently for about half an hour. Add 1 cup cold water and skim again. Then add lemon rind and simmer for 2 hours.

2. Strain through muslin and sieve. Then allow to cool. Remove the fat from the top. Use at once, keep in covered bowl in refrigerator or freeze.

Creole Soup (see p. 10)

Fish Stock

½—1 pound fish back-bones and skins
1 onion sliced
2 small carrots sliced
2 stalks celery
6 sprigs of parsley
1 bay leaf
1 sprig of thyme
2½ pints water
½ pint white wine or cider (optional)

1. Use back-bones from white fish—sole, turbot or halibut preferably—and the skins if available. Put these in a pan with the sliced onion, carrot, celery, herbs and water. Add the white wine or cider if available. Then add salt and pepper. Bring very slowly to the boil and simmer for 30—40 minutes until the liquid has reduced and is well flavoured.

2. Strain and cool. Use at once or freeze for later use.

Rich Brown Beef Stock

2—3 pounds veal bones
2—3 pounds meaty beef bones
(including a bone with marrow)
2 pounds of lean beef—in one piece for
boiled beef or cut into pieces
3—4 onions unpeeled or 2 onions and 2
leeks
4 carrots
4 stalks of celery
10 peppercorns
a few mushroom stalks or peelings
2 bay leaves
8—10 sprigs of parsley
1 sprig of thyme (or 1/8 teaspoon
or 1 large pinch dried thyme)
5 quarts water
2 level teaspoons salt

1. Get butcher to break bones. Put them into a pan with the beef and a little beef marrow or good dripping. Heat the pan, and as the bones and meat brown, stir and keep from burning. Remove and keep warm while browning the vegetables. Return the bones and meat to pan, and cover with water. Add herbs, salt, pepper, and mushroom peelings or stems if available.

2. Bring to the boil. Skim frequently during the first hour. Then cover pan and simmer for 2—3 hours, by which time the stock should be well flavoured and a good brown colour. (If the meat is a large piece and is to be used as boiled beef this can be removed after 2 hours, and the stock simmered without it for remaining cooking time.)

3. Strain the stock and allow to cool. Then skim off the fat, which will form a crust on top. If the stock is not required for a day or two, do not remove fat until just before using, as it acts as a protective seal. Keep in a refrigerator or deep freeze.

---

3 medium onions, unpeeled
3 medium carrots, peeled
2 leeks, white part only
4—5 stalks of celery
1 small turnip, peeled
1 level tablespoon butter or oil
2—3 quarts water
6 peppercorns
1 bay leaf
4—6 sprigs of parsley
1 sprig of thyme (or 1/8 teaspoon
or large pinch dried thyme)

Vegetable Stock

1. Cut up the vegetables and brown these until golden in either a little butter or oil. Add water, herbs and seasoning. Bring to the boil, and simmer 1½—2 hours, by which time the stock should be well flavoured.

2. Strain and cool. Use for soups or sauces calling for vegetable stock.

Mixed Household Stock

2 pounds mixed raw or cooked beef,
veal and/or chicken bones and
possibly a ham bone
1½ pounds of onions, carrots, celery,
chopped
a little oil
1 bay leaf
6 sprigs of parsley
1 sprig of thyme
a few mushroom stalks or peelings
6—8 peppercorns

Stock made from mixed raw and cooked bones, either beef, veal, chicken, or ham but not mutton or pork, as these have a rather strong flavour

1. Brown the raw bones and the vegetables in a little hot oil. Then add the cooked bones, herbs, mushroom peelings. Add water to cover and bring to the boil. Then simmer for 1½—2 hours until reduced and well flavoured.

2. Strain and cool, allowing the fat to set in a solid crust on top. Use this stock quickly or keep in a freezer. If keeping in a refrigerator for a day or two re-boil every day to keep it from becoming sour.

VEGETABLE SOUPS

Spring Soup

A delicious soup full of fresh spring vegetables, enriched with egg yolk and cream (Serves 4–6, hot)

4 young carrots
2–3 young leeks according to size (or
   8–10 spring onions)
1½ oz butter
¾ oz flour
1½ pints chicken stock (or water and
   chicken cubes)
4 oz cauliflower flowerets
2–3 tablespoons peas
2–3 tablespoons young green beans
a little sugar
2 level tablespoons mixed parsley,
   chervil, mint and thyme

LIAISON
¼ pint cream
2 egg yolks

1. Peel and dice the carrots. Wash the leeks or spring onions thoroughly and cut the white part into slices. Melt the butter and cook these vegetables gently in a covered pan for 5–6 minutes without allowing to brown. Sprinkle in flour, mix thoroughly, then add stock. Blend well until smooth and bring to the boil, stirring constantly. Cook for a few minutes before adding cauliflower flowerets, peas, sliced beans and sugar. Simmer for 15 minutes. Add the herbs, and cook for a few more minutes, to draw out flavour of the herbs. Season to taste.

2. Make the liaison by mixing the cream with the egg yolks. Take a few spoonfuls of the hot soup and mix well with the cream and egg yolk mixture before straining it back into the soup, stirring constantly. Reheat, being very careful not to allow soup to boil as this causes egg to curdle and spoils the texture of the soup.

3 oz dried haricot or soup beans
2–3 tablespoons olive oil
1–2 cloves garlic crushed
1 medium onion, sliced
2 slices bacon
1½–2 pints brown or vegetable stock
1 stalk celery, finely sliced
1 leek, white part only cut into
   match-like shreds
2 small carrots, shredded
2–3 oz chopped cabbage
1–2 small courgettes, cut in strips
1 small can or 3–4 fresh tomatoes
1 level teaspoon tomato purée
6–7 green beans, chopped
2–3 level tablespoons peas
2 oz macaroni, broken into pieces
2 level taplespoons chopped mixed
   parsley
majoram, oregano, and basil

GARNISH
¼ pound grated Parmesan (or other
   hard cheese)

Minestrone

A richly varied vegetable soup originally from Italy, garnished with grated Italian cheese (Serves 6–8, hot)

1. Soak the beans overnight in cold water. Then drain and put them in a pan with 2 cups slightly salted water. Put the lid on the pan, and bring to the boil. Then simmer for 2 hours until tender.

2. In another pan heat the oil, and cook the garlic, onion and diced bacon until golden brown. Add to the bean pot, with the stock, celery, leek, and carrots. Cook together for 20 minutes. Then add finely sliced cabbage, courgettes, chopped tomatoes, tomato purée, green beans, peas, macaroni and chopped herbs. Cook for 15–20 minutes more.

3. Season to taste, and serve with plenty of grated cheese in a separate bowl.

Soupe au Pistou

2 oz butter
1 large onion or 3 leeks, sliced
3 potatoes, sliced
2–3 large ripe tomatoes, peeled and
    chopped (or 1 small can)
2½–3 pints stock
chopped parsley
a pinch of oregano
1 cup sliced green beans
2–3 tablespoons vermicelli
2–3 cloves garlic
several sprigs of fresh basil (1
    teaspoon dried basil)
2 slices tomato, grilled or fried

GARNISH
grated cheese

A type of minestrone, but with the addition of garlic, which gives a strong and unmistakable taste. (Serves 6–8 hot)

1. Melt the butter, and cook the onion or leeks and potatoes for 5–6 minutes without browning. Add the tomatoes. Pour on stock and bring to the boil. Add herbs, seasoning, beans and vermicelli. Cook over a low heat until all are tender.

2. Meanwhile prepare a garlic paste: Crush the garlic and mix with the basil and 2 slices of grilled or fried tomato. Pound all together to make a smooth paste, adding a little of the juice from the soup to moisten.

3. Add this mixture to the soup just before serving and mix well. Serve hot, with grated cheese in a separate dish.

Green Pea Soup

1 oz butter
1 small onion (or several young green
    onions) finely chopped
1 head of lettuce, washed and sliced
½ pound fresh or frozen peas
1¾–2 pints chicken stock
sugar to taste
1 sprig of mint (or ½ teaspoon
    dried mint)

GARNISH
4–6 tablespoons double cream
1 teaspoon fresh (or dried chopped)
    mint
fried bread or bacon croutons (see
    garnish section)

Creamy pea soup delicately flavoured with a touch of mint (Serves 4–6, hot)

1. Melt the butter and soften the onion and lettuce for 4–5 minutes without browning.

2. Measure ½ pound of peas, and add 6 ozs to the soup pan, reserving the remainder as garnish. Add stock, salt, pepper, sugar to taste, and mint. Cover pan with lid and cook gently until tender, about 20 minutes.

3. Put soup into electric blender, first removing mint stalk, and blend until smooth; or put through moulie or fine sieve.

4. Meanwhile, cook the remaining peas in a little boiling salted and sugared water. Drain and divide among soup cups.

5. Re-heat the soup, and adjust seasoning to taste. Pour into soup cups, add a tablespoon of cream to each cup, sprinkle with chopped mint and serve with fried bread croutons or bacon croutons.

Purée of Turnip Soup

½–¾ pound sliced young turnips
2 medium sliced potatoes
1 small onion, sliced
1½ oz butter
¾ oz flour
1¼ pints white or chicken stock
½ pint milk
1 level tablespoon chopped parsley
    (or ½ teaspoon paprika)

GARNISH
bacon croutons (see garnish section)

Turnips and potatoes cooked in butter and puréed with white stock (Serves 4–6, hot)

1. Melt the butter and cook the turnips, potatoes and onion gently until they are tender, 20–30 minutes. Sprinkle in the flour and blend thoroughly. Pour on the stock and mix well before bringing to the boil. Reduce the heat and simmer for 15 minutes.

2. Put soup into the electric blender and blend until smooth. Re-heat, adding more seasoning, if necessary, and the milk.

3. Sprinkle with parsley or paprika on top, and serve bacon croutons separately.

Creole Soup

1½ oz or 2 tablespoons butter, oil or
    bacon fat
4—5 ounces chopped pepper
1 onion, chopped
1 oz flour
1 teaspoon tomato purée
4 large ripe tomaotes (or 1 small
    can tomatoes)
1½ pints stock
1 bay leaf, 4 sprigs of parsley,
    sprig of thyme, tied together
a pinch of cayenne pepper
1/8 teaspoon paprika pepper
1/8 teaspoon sugar
1 teaspoon vinegar
1—2 teaspoons grated fresh horseradish
    (or ½ teaspoon dried horseradish)

GARNISH
1 tablespoon chopped parsley
garlic croutons (see garnish section)

*A spicy tomato and pepper soup, suitable for winter meals (Serves 4, hot—
see picture, p. 6)*

1. Melt butter, oil or bacon fat. Cook the peppers and onions gently for
5—6 minutes without browning. Stir in flour and blend well; add tomato
purée, chopped, de-seeded fresh or canned tomatoes, stock, bay leaf,
herbs and seasoning. Bring to the boil, stirring constantly. Then reduce heat
and simmer for 30—35 minutes.

2. Remove the bay leaf and herbs, and adjust seasoning. Add freshly
grated or dried horseradish and vinegar. If soup is not a good enough colour
a little more tomato purée can now be added. Serve hot, sprinkled with
chopped herbs and garlic croutons.

Pea Pod Soup

4—5 handsful of young pea pods
1 medium onion (or 3—4 shallots)
    finely chopped
1½—2 pints chicken or veal stock
    (or cubes and water)
3—4 sprigs of parsley (or 1 tablespoon
    dried parsley)
1 sprig of fresh mint (or 2—3 pinches
    of dry mint)
1 oz butter
¾ oz flour
sugar to taste

GARNISH
4—6 tablespoons whipped cream
1 tablespoon finely chopped mint

*An unusual soup made from young tender pea pods, which can be served
hot or chilled (Serves 4—6)*

1. Shell peas and wash pods, reserving peas for future use. Put pods into a
pan with the onion, stock, parsley and mint. Bring to the boil and simmer
until tender, about 20 minutes. Then press the pulp from the pea pods
through a nylon sieve or moulie.

2. Melt butter, and blend in the flour. Add the purée from pods and then
the liquid in which they were cooked. Blend carefully. Bring to the boil, and
add salt, pepper and sugar to taste.

3. Serve hot or chilled with a spoonful of whipped cream on top of each
cup and sprinkled with chopped parsley.

Potage Solferino

3 leeks, sliced
2 small young carrots, thinly sliced
2 medium or 3 small potatoes
1½ oz butter
1 small clove garlic crushed (or shake
    of garlic powder)
4 ripe tomatoes (or 1 small can
    tomatoes)
1 tablespoon chopped parsley
1/8 teaspoon or a large pinch
    chopped basil
½ bay leaf
¼ teaspoon sugar
1½—2 pints stock or water
1 teaspoon tomato purée

GARNISH
1 ripe tomato, peeled, seeded and
    chopped (or 3—4 tablespoons
    potato dice cooked in boiling
    salted water)
1 tablespoon chopped parsley

A delicious tomato and vegetable soup (Serves 4—6, hot)

1. Melt the butter and cook the leeks, carrots and potatoes gently for 5—6
minutes, stirring constantly to prevent browning. Add the garlic.

2. If using fresh tomatoes, dip them into boiling water for 10 seconds,
then into cold. Peel and chop, and add to soup with herbs and seasoning.
Pour on stock or water, and bring soup to a boil. Then reduce heat and
simmer for 20—30 minutes or until the vegetables are tender. Remove bay
leaf.

3. Put soup through a fine moulie or electric blender, and blend until
smooth. Re-heat, adding the tomato purée, and adjust seasoning to taste.

4. Serve hot, garnished with the chopped flesh of one peeled and seeded
tomato or potato dice cooked in a little boiling water. Sprinkle with
chopped parsley.

French Onion Soup

Strongly flavoured brown onion soup, garnished with French bread and cheese, and browned in the oven or under grill (Serves 4—6, hot)

1½—2 oz butter
4—5 medium onions, peeled and
    finely sliced
1—2 cloves garlic, crushed
¼ teaspoon sugar
1 oz flour
2 pints vegetable stock (or water)
¼ pint white wine (optional
1 bay leaf
3—4 sprigs of parsley
1 sprig of thyme
a pinch of nutmeg
4—6 slices French bread (long flute or
    yard of bread type)
3—5 tablespoons grated mixed Gruyere
    or Emmentaler and Parmesan cheese
    or other strong hard cheese

1. Melt the butter, and add the onions and garlic and a sprinkling of sugar. Brown slowly, stirring constantly to prevent burning. Sprinkle in the flour and brown this slightly. Add the stock or water, and the wine if using any—otherwise add the equivalent amount of water. Bring to the boil, stirring constantly. Add herbs and seasoning, and simmer for 20—30 minutes.

2. Meanwhile, cut the French bread into slices and put into the oven to dry and brown slightly.

3. Remove bay leaf from soup. Put the slices of bread into the oven-proof soup bowls or a large tureen. Pour the soup over the bread, sprinkle thickly with cheese and put into a hot oven for 15—20 minutes or under grill for 7—10 minutes to brown the cheese.

Spinach Soup

4—5 handsful fresh spinach (or 1
   package frozen spinach)
1½ oz butter
1 onion, finely chopped
¾ oz flour
1¾ pints white or vegetable stock (or
   water and 2 chicken cubes)
3—4 sprigs of parsley (or 1 tablespoon
   dried parsley)
1 bay leaf
a squeeze or two of lemon juice
¼ teaspoon powdered mace
¼ pint cream

GARNISH
2 hard-boiled eggs, sliced
paprika
or
fried bread croutons or bacon croutons
   (see garnish section)

A quickly made spinach soup garnished with hard-boiled egg slices (Serves 4—6, hot)

1. Wash the spinach thoroughly if using fresh spinach, drain and shake off excess water. Melt butter, and cook the onion and spinach gently until the spinach has softened and become limp, without browning. If using frozen spinach allow block to unfreeze completely during this process. Sprinkle in flour and blend smoothly. Add the stock (or water and cubes). Bring soup to the boil, stirring constantly. Then add parsley, bay leaf and seasoning. Reduce heat and simmer for 10—12 minutes. Do not overcook as this spoils the green colour and fresh flavour. Remove the bay leaf.

2. Put soup through a fine moulie, or blend until smooth in an electric blender. Re-heat, adding a little lemon juice. Adjust seasoning and add the mace. Stir in the cream just before serving.

3. Garnish with slices of hard-boiled egg in each cup sprinkled with paprika, or alternatively with fried bread or bacon croutons.

Watercress Soup

A creamy green watercress soup garnished with watercress sprigs and croutons (Serves 4–6, hot)

2 bunches fresh watercress
1½ oz butter
1 potato, sliced
1 small onion, finely chopped
½ oz flour
1¼ pints white or chicken stock (or water)
3–4 sprigs of parsley
1 bay leaf
¾ pint milk
1/8 teaspoon mace
a little green colouring (optional)

GARNISH
watercress sprigs
4–6 tablespoons cream
fried bread croutons (see garnish section)

1. Wash and pick over the watercress, discarding any yellow leaves. Reserve enough green top-sprigs to make the final garnish, and chop the remaining cress roughly. Melt the butter and cook the potato and onion together for 2–3 minutes before adding the chopped watercress. Continue cooking for 3–4 minutes, stirring constantly to prevent browning. Sprinkle in flour and blend well. Add stock and blend together before bringing to the boil. Add herbs and some seasoning, reduce heat, and simmer until the potato is tender, about 20 minutes.

2. Remove bay leaf. Put soup into electric blender and blend until smooth, or put through a fine moulie or sieve. Return soup to pan and re-heat gently. At the same time heat milk in a separate pan. When almost at boiling point, pour into watercress mixture—this makes texture of soup lighter and more delicate. Adjust seasoning, adding mace and a little green colouring if desired.

3. Serve with a spoon of cream in each cup and the reserved watercress sprigs on top. Fried bread croutons are also excellent with this soup.

2 large onions, finely sliced
2 slices of bacon, chopped
½ oz butter
4—6 ripe tomatoes (or 1 small can tomatoes) chopped
1 level tablespoon tomato purée
2—3 strips of lemon rind
1½—¾ pints chicken stock
1 level teaspoon sugar
1 level tablespoon parsley
1/8 teaspoon or 1 large pinch of thyme
½ teaspoon basil

GARNISH
1 level tablespoon chopped mixed parsley and basil
fried garlic croutons (see garnish section)

French Tomato Soup

Tomato soup flavoured with bacon, lemon and herbs, and served with garlic croutons—a winter soup (Serves 4—6, hot)

1. Heat the bacon pieces in a pan. When the fat has run, add the butter. When it has melted, add the onions and cook gently for 5—6 minutes until tender and golden brown. Add the tomatoes and tomato purée, lemon rind, stock, salt, pepper, sugar and herbs. Bring to the boil. Then simmer for 20 minutes or until tomatoes are tender.

2. Put soup through a moulie or blend in electric blender. Adjust seasoning and serve hot, sprinkled with chopped parsley and basil and with fried garlic croutons.

1 onion, sliced
2 small carrots, sliced
1½—2 oz butter
1 potato, peeled and sliced
1 oz flour
1 level teaspoon tomato purée
¾ pound sauerkraut
1½—2 pints brown or household stock
1 level tablespoon chopped parsley
1 level teaspoon chopped chervil

GARNISH
sour cream

Russian Sauerkraut Soup

Strongly flavoured Russian soup containing sauerkraut and garnished with sour cream (Serves 4—6, hot)

1. Melt the butter, and cook the onion and carrots until golden. Then add the potato. Stir in flour, and when smooth, add the tomato purée and sauerkraut. Cook for a few minutes, stirring constantly. Then add the stock and the herbs.

2. Bring to the boil, and simmer for about 40 minutes. Season to taste, and serve hot with a spoonful of sour cream in each soup cup.

Cauliflower Soup

A white soup flavoured with cauliflower and sprinkled with cheese (Serves 4–6, hot)

1 medium cauliflower
1 bay leaf
1 onion, chopped
1 medium potato, sliced
1½ oz butter
½ oz flour
2 pints milk
¼ pint cream
1 large pinch of mace

GARNISH
1 level tablespoon chopped
   chervil
grated cheese

1. Divide well washed cauliflower into flowerets, and cut the hard stalk and leaves into small pieces. Cook the cauliflower in boiling salted water with bay leaf for 4–5 minutes to lightly cook and to remove any strong flavour. Drain and rinse under cold water. Reserve ¼ of small flowerets for garnish.

2. Meanwhile, melt the butter, add the onion and potato, and cook gently for 5–6 minutes, stirring to prevent browning. Sprinkle in flour, and blend smoothly. Then pour in milk, and mix well before bringing to a boil. Add the cauliflower, then reduce heat, and simmer gently until potatoes and cauliflower are just tender.

3. Put the soup into an electric blender and blend until smooth, or put through a fine moulie. Return to pan and re-heat, adding the reserved cauliflower flowerets. Add seasoning and the cream.

4. Sprinkle with chopped chervil and serve grated cheese separately.

Leek and Potato Soup

4 leeks
2 medium potatoes
1½–2 oz butter
1 oz flour
1½–1¾ pints white, chicken or
   vegetable stock (or water
   and cubes)
3–4 sprigs of parsley
1 bay leaf
1 large pinch grated nutmeg
   (or powdered mace)
½ pint creamy milk

GARNISH
½ level tablespoon chopped chives
   (or 1 level tablespoon chopped
   parsley)
cheese croutons (see garnish section)

Leeks and potatoes blended into a creamy soup (Serves 4–6, hot)

1. Slice the white parts of the leeks and wash well in salted cold water. Peel and slice the potatoes finely. Melt the butter and add the potato and drained leeks. Cook gently for 5–6 minutes, stirring to prevent sticking and browning. Sprinkle in flour. When thoroughly mixed, add stock (or water and cubes). Add herbs and seasoning. Bring to the boil, stirring constantly. Then lower heat, and simmer for 25–30 minutes or until vegetables are tender. Remove the bay leaf.

2. Blend the soup in an electric blender or put through a fine moulie. Re-heat and adjust seasoning. Put the milk into a separate pan, and bring to just below boiling point before adding it to the soup.

3. Sprinkle with chives or chopped parsley in each soup cup, and serve cheese croutons separately.

Chervil Soup

An interesting and unusually flavoured soup, liked by devotees of herbs (Serves 4–6, hot)

2 young carrots, finely sliced
1 small potato, finely sliced
1½–2 pints chicken or white stock
3 sprigs of parsley
1½ oz butter
1 oz flour
1 large pinch of mace or a pinch of
   nutmeg
2–3 oz fresh chervil
¼ pint cream

GARNISH
fried bread croutons (see garnish
   section)

1. Put carrots and potato in a pan with stock and parsley sprigs, and simmer until tender, 15–20 minutes.

2. Melt butter and stir in flour. When smooth, strain stock on to flour and butter, and mix well.

3. Blend the potato and carrots in electric blender and add to soup. Mix well. Then bring to the boil, stirring constantly. Simmer for a few minutes, adding salt, pepper and mace or nutmeg.

4. Just before serving add the chopped chervil and cream. Re-heat but do not boil, as this destroys the delicate flavour of chervil.

5. Serve with fried bread croutons.

Lettuce Soup

Light summery soup, suitable to serve either hot with croutons or cold (Serves 4—6, hot or cold)

2—3 heads lettuce
1½ oz butter
1 small onion or 6—8 young green onions, finely chopped
1 oz flour
1¼—1½ pints chicken stock (or water and cubes)
¼ teaspoon sugar
3—4 sprigs of parsley (or 1 level tablespoon dried parsley)
2 sprigs of mint (or 1 level teaspoon chopped mint)
½ pint creamy milk

GARNISH
4—6 tablespoons double cream
1 teaspoon finely chopped mint or parsley
fried bread croutons (or brown bread and butter)

1. Chop the well washed lettuces coarsely. Melt butter and soften the lettuce and onion gently in a covered pan for 5—6 minutes without browning. Sprinkle in the flour and blend smoothly before adding the stock and seasoning. When smooth, bring to the boil, stirring constantly. Reduce heat and simmer for 15 minutes, having added salt, pepper, sugar, parsley and mint.

2. Put soup into electric blender and blend until smooth, or put through moulie or fine sieve.

3. Re-heat soup in clean pan. Meanwhile, heat the creamy milk in another pan and add when on the point of boiling—this lightens the texture of the soup. Adjust seasoning to taste.

4. If serving hot, pour into soup cups and put a large spoonful of cream on top of each cup. Sprinkle with chopped parsley or mint. If serving cold, chill thoroughly, adding a little more seasoning. Serve in soup cups with a spoon of whipped double cream on top, and sprinkle with chopped herbs as above.

5. If serving hot serve with fried bread croutons; if cold, with brown bread and butter.

Parsley Soup

A nourishing and deliciously different green soup (Serves 4—6, hot)

3—4 oz fresh chopped parsley
1½ oz butter
1 onion, chopped
1 stalk celery, chopped
1 oz flour
1½—2 pints vegetable or white stock
a pinch of nutmeg
½ bay leaf

GARNISH
4—6 tablespoons double cream
a sprinkling of paprika
fried bread or bacon croutons (see garnish section)

1. Coarsely chop the parsley including the stems, which are full of flavour.

2. Melt the butter, and cook the onion and celery gently for a few minutes without browning. Sprinkle in flour and mix well. Pour on stock and bring slowly to the boil, blending smoothly. Add the chopped parsley and salt, pepper, nutmeg and bay leaf. Simmer for 25 minutes.

3. Remove the bay leaf. The soup can be served as it is, blended in an electric blender or put through a moulie.

4. Re-heat soup, pour into soup bowls and serve with a spoonful of cream in each bowl, a sprinkling of paprika, and fried bread or bacon croutons.

Parsnip Soup

An unusual soup, popular with those who like the rather sweet taste of parsnips (Serves 4, hot)

1½ oz butter
½—¾ pound peeled and finely sliced parsnips
1 onion, chopped
½ oz flour
1½—1¾ pints vegetable or white stock (or water and cube)
3—4 sprigs of parsley
1 small bay leaf
a pinch of thyme
a pinch of nutmeg
¼ pint cream

GARNISH
1 tablespoon chopped parsley
fried bread croutons (see garnish section)

1. Melt the butter, and cook the onion and parsnips gently for 5—6 minutes with a lid on the pan, to soften without browning. Remove from heat, and sprinkle in flour. Then blend well. Pour on stock, mix well, and add herbs and seasonings. Bring to the boil, and simmer for 20—30 minutes until the parsnips are tender. Remove bay leaf.

2. Put soup into electric blender, and blend until smooth, or put through moulie. Return soup to pan, adjust seasoning and re-heat, adding cream.

3. Serve in soup cups sprinkled with chopped parsley and with fried bread croutons.

Green Bean Soup

Delicious and unusual light soup of green beans (Serves 4—6, hot)

1. Melt the butter and cook the onion and garlic for 5—6 minutes in a covered pan. Add the flour and blend in smoothly. Pour on stock and mix well. When smooth, bring to the boil, stirring constantly. Add salt and pepper.

2. String the beans and cut in slanting slices or break in half depending on their size. Add to the soup, with dried savory, and cook for 25 minutes or until beans are tender.

3. Strain the soup, reserving a few pieces of bean for garnish (keep warm). Put remaining soup and beans through a moulie or blend until smooth in electric blender.

4. Re-heat soup, adjust seasoning to taste and add a little green colouring if required.

5. Serve hot with a spoon of whipped cream on each cup, and sprinkled with finely crumbled crispy fried bacon.

1—1½ oz butter
1 medium onion (3—4 shallots)
    finely chopped
1 clove garlic, crushed
1 oz flour
1½—1¾ pints chicken or veal stock
1 pound french beans
1 level teaspoon chopped or dried
    summer savory
a little green colouring if required

GARNISH
4—6 tablespoons whipped cream
2 slices bacon

CREAM SOUPS

Cream of Asparagus Soup

The Queen of cream soups, whether made from green or white asparagus (Serves 4, hot)

1. If using fresh asparagus, wash, scrape and trim it. Remove tips for garnish. If using canned asparagus, merely remove tips and drain off liquid, reserving it for making soup.

2. Chop the asparagus stalks and put in a pot with chopped onion. Add parsley sprigs, 1¼—1½ pints of chicken stock (or water and chicken cubes), and the liquid from can if canned asparagus is used. Add a little salt and pepper. Cover pan with lid and simmer for 10—15 minutes or until the asparagus is tender.

3. Put into electric blender and blend until smooth, or through moulie or fine nylon sieve.

4. Melt butter and add the flour. Stir until smooth, and cook for a minute or two. Remove from heat and strain in the blended asparagus liquid. Blend smoothly, bring to the boil, stirring constantly, and simmer for a few minutes. Adjust seasoning to taste, and add some mace.

5. Meanwhile, in a small pan cook the reserved tips for about 5—7 minutes in a little hot stock or water, until tender. Strain liquid into soup and divide tips into soup cups equally.

6. Make liaison: Mix egg yolks and cream well. Add a few spoonfuls of hot soup and mix well before straining into soup, stirring constantly. Re-heat soup gently without allowing it to boil.

7. If soup is not a good colour, a little green colouring can be added, but great care must be exercised as it can easily be overdone. Serve soup hot with fried bread croutons.

1 pound asparagus, green or white (or
    equivalent amount of canned
    asparagus)
1 onion, finely chopped
3—4 sprigs of parsley
1¼—1½ pints chicken stock (or water
    and chicken stock cubes)
1½ oz butter
1 oz flour
1 large pinch mace
a little green colouring, if necessary

LIAISON
2 egg yolks
¼ pint double cream

GARNISH
fried bread croutons (see garnish
    section)

Cream of Mushroom Soup

2 oz butter
1 onion, chopped
½–¾ pound sliced mushrooms
1½ oz flour
1¼ pints chicken or white stock (or
    water and 2 cubes)
1 bay leaf
3–4 sprigs of parsley
1/8 teaspoon or large pinch mace
¾ pint creamy milk

GARNISH
chopped parsley or chives
fried bread croutons (see garnish
    section)

Creamy mushroom-flavoured soup (Serves 4–6, hot)

1. Melt the butter and cook the onion for 4–5 minutes to soften. Then add the mushrooms, cover pan and cook for 5 more minutes. Sprinkle in the flour, and stir until smooth. Pour on the stock, and mix well. Add bay leaf, parsley and mace. Season with salt and pepper. Bring to a boil, and simmer for 10–15 minutes.

2. Remove bay leaf. Put soup through a fine moulie or into an electric blender and blend until smooth. Re-heat, adding the heated milk. Adjust seasoning to taste.

3. Sprinkle with chopped parsley or chives, and serve with fried bread croutons.

Cream of Tomato Soup

1½ oz butter
1 large onion, chopped
1 carrot, chopped
1 stalk celery, sliced (or 1 level
    teaspoon dried celery)
1 oz flour
1 level tablespoon tomato purée
1 pound of fresh ripe tomatoes (or
    1 medium tin tomatoes)
¾ pint vegetable stock (or chicken
    stock)
1 level teaspoon sugar
¼ teaspoon paprika
1 bay leaf
3–4 sprigs of parsley
a sprig (or a good pinch) of thyme
1 pint milk

GARNISH
4–6 tablespoons double cream (or
    sour cream, if desired)
1 tablespoon chopped parsley (or
    chives)
cheesy croutons (see garnish section)

A fairly thick, creamy tomato soup served with cheesy croutons (Serves 4–6, hot)

1. Melt the butter and cook the onion, carrot and celery gently for 5–6 minutes to soften without browning, stirring frequently. Sprinkle in the flour, and mix well. Then stir in the tomato purée and the chopped tomatoes. Add the stock, and the sugar, salt, pepper, paprika and herbs. Bring to the boil, stirring constantly. Reduce heat, and simmer for about 30 minutes. Remove the bay leaf.

2. Put the soup through a fine moulie, or blend until smooth in an electric blender. Re-heat soup. In a separate pan heat the milk to just below boiling point and add to the soup mixing thoroughly. Adjust seasoning to taste.

3. Serve with a spoonful of cream on top of each soup cup, a sprinkling of herbs, and cheesy croutons.

Cream of Curry Soup

1½ oz butter
1 large onion, chopped
1 sour cooking apple, peeled and
    cored
1½ teaspoons curry powder or paste
    (or more if desired)
½ oz flour
1 tablespoon rice
1½–2 pints chicken stock (or water
    and cubes)
1 level teaspoon sweet chutney
1 teaspoon coconut
1 bay leaf
3–4 sprigs of parsley
1 slice lemon
¼ pint single cream

GARNISH
1 level tablespoon chopped parsley (or
    paprika)
lemon wedges
4–6 tablespoons plain boiled rice

Creamy soup with a delicious curry flavour (Serves 4–6, hot)

1. Melt the butter, and cook the onion and apple gently for 5–6 minutes to soften without browning. Stir in curry powder or paste and cook for 1 minute. Remove from heat and sprinkle in flour. Blend well. Then add rice, stock, chutney and coconut. Bring to the boil, stirring constantly. Reduce heat. Add seasonings, herbs and slice of lemon. Cover pan, and simmer for 15–20 minutes to cook the rice.

2. Remove bay leaf and lemon. Put soup into electric blender and blend until smooth. Re-heat, adjust seasoning, and just before serving stir in cream.

3. Sprinkle with chopped parsley or paprika, and serve lemon wedges and plain boiled rice separately.

Cream of Corn Soup

Creamy potato and sweetcorn soup sprinkled with chives or parsley (Serves 4–6, hot)

1½ oz butter
1 onion, chopped
1 medium potato, finely sliced
6–8 oz or medium can sweetcorn
1½ pints milk
1 bay leaf
3–4 sprigs of parsley
1/8 teaspoon or a large pinch of mace
1 chicken stock cube

GARNISH
4–6 spoons double cream
1 level tablespoon chopped chives or parsley (or a sprinkling of paprika)
fried bread croutons (see garnish section)

1. Melt the butter, and cook the onion and potato gently with a lid on the pan for 5 minutes, shaking the pan occasionally to prevent sticking. Add 1 cup of the sweetcorn. Stir well. Then add the milk, bay leaf, parsley, salt, pepper and mace. Bring to simmering heat, add a chicken stock cube and cook until vegetables are tender.

2. Put soup into electric blender and blend until smooth, or put through moulie.

3. Return soup to the pan with the remaining sweetcorn (which if fresh should be simmered until tender in salted water). Re-heat soup until nearly boiling, and adjust seasoning.

4. Serve in soup cups with a spoonful of cream in each cup, a sprinkling of chopped chives, parsley or paprika, and fried bread croutons.

Curried Sweetcorn Soup

Made in the same way as Cream of Corn Soup, but with curry flavouring (Serves 4–6, hot)

1. Using the recipe for Cream of Corn Soup (see above) add 1 level dessertspoon of curry powder to the onion and potato mixture, and cook with those ingredients. If using canned sweetcorn use mixed corn and pimento rather than the plain sweetcorn.

2. Garnish the soup with paprika.

Cream of Carrot Soup

2 oz butter
½ pound sliced young carrots
1 large onion, finely sliced
½ clove garlic
1 tablespoon rice
3—4 sprigs of parsley (or 1 level
    tablespoon dried parsley)
thinly peeled rind from ½ orange
1½—1¾ pints chicken or white
    stock
a large pinch of sugar
juice of ½ orange

LIAISON
2 egg yolks
¼ pint single cream

GARNISH
finely grated rind of ½ orange
2 teaspoons chopped parsley

*Delicious orange-coloured soup with delicate flavour of carrot and orange
(Serves 4—6, hot)*

1. Melt the butter and add vegetables, crushed garlic and rice. Mix well over gentle heat for 5 minutes without browning. Add the parsley, orange rind, stock, sugar and seasonings. Bring soup to the boil. Then lower heat, and simmer for 30—40 minutes, or until vegetables are tender.

2. Put soup into electric blender and blend until smooth, or put through moulie. Return to pot, and re-heat, adding orange juice.

3. If soup is not thick enough, add cream and egg yolk liaison: Mix the egg yolks and cream well. Put a few spoons of hot soup into the liaison. Then strain back into soup, stirring constantly. Re-heat soup without allowing to boil.

4. Serve in soup cups, sprinkled with grated orange rind and parsley.

Almond
Cream Soup

A very delicately flavoured almond and chicken soup (Serves 4, hot or cold)

1 small potato, finely sliced
3—4 spring onions, finely
    sliced (or 2—3 slices of ordinary
    onion)
3—4 stalks celery, finely sliced
1¼ pints chicken or white stock
3—4 oz almonds
1 small bay leaf
3—4 sprigs of parsley
1 oz butter
½ oz flour
a pinch of mace
4—5 tablespoons double cream

1. Put the potato, onions and celery in a pan with the stock, bay leaf and sprigs of parsley. Simmer gently with lid on until the potato slices are tender.

2. Meanwhile, pour boiling water on the almonds, allow to stand for a few minutes, drain and pop almonds out of their skins. Reserve 10—12 whole almonds for garnish, and chop or finely grind the remainder. This can be done in an electric blender but a little stock should be added to liquify slightly. Add this paste to the pan, and cook for another 20 minutes.

3. Remove the bay leaf and sprigs of parsley. Pour soup into the electric blender and blend slowly until smooth. Strain through a fine sieve.

4. Melt the butter, add the flour and stir until smooth off the heat. Add the strained soup slowly, stirring until smooth. Bring to the boil, stirring constantly. Add salt, pepper and mace, being careful not to overpower the light almond flavour.

5. Cut the remaining almonds into slivers, brown lightly in a cool oven, and sprinkle with a little salt.

6. Add a spoonful of cream to each soup cup, and at the last moment sprinkle with the crisp brown almonds. The soup can also be served chilled.

Cream of Celery Soup

Creamy celery and potato soup garnished with croutons or bacon croutons (Serves 4—6, hot)

1 slice bacon
1½—2 oz butter
½—¾ pounds chopped celery or
   celeriac
1 large onion, chopped
1 potato, sliced
½ oz flour
¾ pint water (or white stock)
1 bay leaf
several sprigs of parsley
a pinch of thyme
1¼ pints milk

GARNISH
4—6 tablespoons single cream
paprika
fried bread croutons or bacon croutons
   (see garnish section)

1. Chop the bacon and put in a pan with the butter. Cook gently for a few minutes. Then add the celery, potato and onion. Cook together for 4—5 minutes, stirring constantly to prevent browning. Sprinkle in the flour and blend smoothly. Add the stock or water, mix well, and bring to the boil. Reduce the heat, add bay leaf, parsley sprigs and thyme. Simmer for 20—30 minutes, or until the vegetables are tender.

2. Put soup through fine moulie or into electric blender and blend until smooth. Re-heat gently. In another pan heat the milk, and when nearly boiling add to soup pan with seasoning to taste.

3. Serve with a spoonful of cream, a dusting of paprika in each soup cup, and fried bread croutons or bacon croutons separately.

Cream of Potato Soup

A creamy potato and onion soup made with milk (Serves 4—6, hot)

1½ oz butter
3—4 medium potatoes, finely sliced
2 medium onions, finely sliced
1—2 stalks celery, finely sliced
1 pint boiling water
1 bay leaf
3—4 sprigs of parsley
a pinch of thyme
1/8 teaspoon or large pinch mace
    or nutmeg
¾ pint milk

GARNISH
4—6 tablespoons double cream
1 tablespoon chopped chives or
    parsley
fried bread croutons or cheesy
    croutons (see garnish section)

1. Melt the butter and cook the potatoes, onions and celery very gently, stirring frequently, without allowing them to brown, for about 5—6 minutes. Add the boiling water and stir well. Add herbs, salt and pepper, mace or nutmeg. Bring to the boil. Then reduce heat, and simmer gently with lid on pan for about 30—40 minutes, or until the vegetables are tender. Stir from time to time to keep vegetables from sticking and browning.

2. Remove bay leaf. Then put soup through fine moulie or into electric blender, and blend until smooth. Re-heat. Then add the milk which has been heated until nearly boiling in a separate pan—this lightens the texture of the soup. Adjust seasoning.

3. Serve with a spoonful of cream in each cup, a sprinkling of chopped chives or parsley, and fried bread croutons or cheesy croutons.

Cream of Brussels Sprout Soup

An unusual green winter soup with a delicious nutty flavour (Serves 4—6, hot)

2 oz butter
1 onion, chopped
1 potato, chopped
1 pound washed and trimmed
    Brussels sprouts, chopped
¾ oz flour
1½ pints white stock (or water
    and chicken cubes)
2 bay leaves
3—4 sprigs of parsley
1/8 teaspoon or large pinch mace
½ pint single cream or milk

GARNISH
4—6 oz of cooked chestnuts, broken
    into pieces
1—1½ oz butter
seasoning

1. Melt the butter, and cook the onion and potato for 2—3 minutes. Then add the chopped sprouts, and cook for a further 5 minutes, stirring constantly. Sprinkle in the flour and blend well. Then pour on stock. Stir until well mixed and smooth. Then bring to the boil, stirring constantly. Reduce the heat, add the bay leaves, parsley sprigs and seasoning. Cover and simmer soup for about 20 minutes, or until vegetables are tender; but not overcooked, as this would give the soup an unpleasant flavour.

2. Remove bay leaves. Then put the soup through a moulie, or into an electric blender and blend until smooth. Adjust seasoning, and re-heat soup, adding at the last moment a cup of hot cream or creamy milk.

3. Sprinkle with pieces of cooked chestnut, fried in butter until golden brown.

Cream of Chicken Soup

Creamy chicken-flavoured soup enriched with egg yolks and cream, and garnished with cooked chopped chicken (Serves 4—6, hot)

1 small onion, chopped
2 stalks celery, sliced
4—5 button mushrooms, sliced
1½ oz butter
1 oz flour
1½—2 pints well-flavoured chicken
    stock
1 small bay leaf, 2—3 sprigs of parsley
    tied together
1/8 teaspoon or large pinch mace
3—4 oz chopped cooked
    white chicken meat

LIAISON
2 egg yolks
¼ pint single cream

GARNISH
1 level tablespoon chopped
    tarragon or 1 tablespoon
    chopped parsley

1. Melt the butter, and cook the onion, celery and mushrooms gently with lid on for 5—6 minutes without allowing to brown. Sprinkle in flour, and mix well. Pour in stock, and blend until smooth. Bring soup to the boil, stirring constantly, and then reduce heat. Add the herbs and seasoning. Simmer gently for 20—30 minutes.

2. Remove herbs and put soup through a fine moulie or blend until smooth in an electric blender. Return soup to pan and re-heat, adding the chopped chicken meat. Adjust seasoning.

3. Make the egg and cream liaison: Mix the egg yolks and cream together thoroughly. Add a few spoonfuls of hot soup to this. Mix thoroughly, and then strain back into the soup, stirring constantly. Do not allow the soup to boil or the egg will curdle.

4. Serve hot in soup cups sprinkled with chopped parsley or tarragon.

Cream of Artichoke Soup

1 pint water
1 teaspoon lemon juice
1 bay leaf
3—4 sprigs of parsley
½ teaspoon salt
pepper and mace to taste
1 pound peeled and sliced Jerusalem
 artichokes
1½ oz butter
1 onion, finely sliced
1 stalk celery, finely sliced
1 oz flour
1 pint milk

LIAISON
2 egg yolks
¼ pint single cream

GARNISH
1 tablespoon chopped parsley
fried bread croutons (see garnish
 section)

A creamy, warming winter soup, delicately flavoured with Jerusalem artichokes, and served with crisp golden fried croutons (Serves 4—6, hot)

1. Put the water, lemon juice, bay leaf, parsley sprigs and seasoning into a pan and add the finely sliced artichokes. Bring to a boil, and simmer until tender, about 10—15 minutes.

2. Melt the butter and cook the finely sliced onion and celery slowly with lid on pan until soft. Do not allow to brown. Sprinkle in flour, and blend well.

3. When artichokes are tender strain the liquid on to the onion mixture and blend well. Remove bay leaf and parsley sprigs. Mix in artichokes, and bring to a boil, stirring constantly. Put soup through a moulie or fine sieve, or blend thoroughly in an electric blender until creamy.

4. Return to pan and re-heat. At the same time, in another pan heat the milk to just below boiling point. Pour into artichoke soup and whisk together (adding hot rather than cold milk. This makes the soup lighter and more delicate).

5. Make the liaison, by mixing the egg yolks and cream thoroughly. Add a few spoonfuls of hot soup, mix well; then strain the liaison into soup, stirring constantly.

6. Re-heat soup, being careful not to boil it or the egg will curdle. Sprinkle with chopped parsley and serve with fried bread croutons.

Cream of Chestnut Soup

1 pound fresh peeled chestnuts (buy
 2 pounds to produce this amount)
 or 1 large can chestnut purée
 (unsweetened)
1½ oz butter
1 large onion, sliced
2 small carrots, sliced
1 stalk celery, sliced
2—2¼ pints ham, chicken or brown
 stock (or water and bouillon cubes)
1 level tablespoon chopped parsley (or
 3—4 sprigs of parsley)
a pinch of thyme
1 bay leaf
a pinch of nutmeg
½ pint single cream

GARNISH
2—3 cooking apples
2 oz butter
1 teaspoon sugar
1 level tablespoon chopped parsley

A richly-flavoured chestnut soup, served with fried apple-ring garnish (Serves 4—6, hot)

1. If using fresh chestnuts, prepare as follows: Make a small slit in the top of each nut and place in a well-greased pan in a moderate oven for 10—15 minutes to loosen both outer and inner skin. Remove both skins. If using canned chestnut purée, add to the soup after the vegetables have been cooked.

2. Melt the butter, and add the onion, carrots and celery. Mix well over gentle heat before adding the chestnuts. Cover the pan, and cook for 3—4 minutes, shaking the pan occasionally. Add the stock, herbs and seasoning and simmer for 20—30 minutes, or until the chestnuts and vegetables are tender.

3. Remove the bay leaf, put soup into electric blender and blend until smooth, or put through a fine moulie. Return to pan, and re-heat soup. Season to taste. Add the cream just before serving or put a spoonful of cream in each soup cup.

4. Make apple-ring garnish by peeling and coring 2—3 cooking apples and cutting into rings. Melt butter and fry the apple slices until golden brown on each side, sprinkling the slices with a little sugar.

5. Float 1—2 slices of apple in each soup cup and sprinkle with chopped parsley.

Cream of Barley Soup

6—8 oz pearl barley
1 onion, sliced
1 carrot, sliced
2 stalks celery, sliced
1 bay leaf
3—4 sprigs of parsley (or 1 level
    tablespoon chopped parsley)
1½—2 pints chicken or veal stock
chicken carcass or ham bone, if
    available
¼ pint cream

GARNISH
1—1½ tablespoons chopped parsley
fried bacon croutons (see garnish
    section)

Mildly flavoured creamy soup (Serves 4, hot)

1. Wash pearl barley and soak overnight if possible, otherwise cover with boiling water, and soak for 2 hours.

2. Put vegetables into pan with drained barley, herbs and stock (or cubes and water). If a chicken carcass or a ham bone is available it can be added to the soup at this stage. Cover pan with lid, and cook gently until barley is tender, about 1½—2 hours.

3. Discard bones and herbs. Then set aside the barley and strain soup through sieve, or blend soup and barley in electric blender.

4. Re-heat soup and adjust seasoning. Add the cream just before serving. Sprinkle with chopped parsley and serve with bacon-flavored croutons.

White Onion Soup

1½—2 oz butter
3—4 onions, finely sliced
1 oz flour
1½—2 pints hot milk
1 bay leaf
4 sprigs of parsley
¼ teaspoon mace

LIAISON
2 egg yolks
¼ pint single cream

GARNISH
fried bread croutons (see garnish
    section)

Creamy white onion soup enriched with cream and egg yolks, a warming winter soup (Serves 4—6, hot)

1. Melt the butter and cook the onions very gently with a lid on the pan until tender, stirring frequently to prevent browning, about 10 minutes. Remove from heat and sprinkle in flour. When well mixed in, add the milk and blend well. Bring to the boil, stirring constantly. Add the bay leaf, parsley, salt, pepper and mace. Simmer soup for 15—20 minutes, stirring frequently to prevent it sticking to the bottom of the pan.

2. Make liaison: Mix the egg yolks into the cream. Add several spoonfuls of hot soup to this mixture and when blended strain back into the soup, stirring constantly. Re-heat, without boiling or the egg will curdle.

3. Serve hot with fried bread croutons.

White Vegetable Soup

1 onion or the white part of
    2 leeks (well washed)
2 young carrots
2 stalks celery
1½ oz butter
1 oz flour
1½—2 pints milk
1 level tablespoon chopped parsley
a pinch of dried thyme and
    powdered bay leaf
1/8 teaspoon or a large pinch mace
3—4 oz peas (fresh or frozen)
2—3 oz of green beans
2—3 oz sweetcorn

LIAISON
2 egg yolks
¼ pint cream

GARNISH
1 level tablespoon chopped parsley
fried bread croutons (see
    garnish section)

A creamy soup full of tender vegetables, served with fried croutons (Serves 4—6, hot)

1. Peel and cut the root vegetables into short strips or dice. Melt the butter and cook these vegetables until tender without browning, about 5—6 minutes. Sprinkle in flour and mix well, add the milk and blend well. Slowly bring to the boil. Then reduce heat, and simmer for 10—12 minutes. Add herbs and seasoning.

2. Meanwhile, cook the peas, beans and corn in boiling salted water until just tender, 7—10 minutes. Drain and rinse under cold water. Add to the soup. Heat together for 5 minutes. Adjust seasoning and add liaison.

3. Make liaison: Mix egg yolks and cream well. Add a few spoonfuls of hot soup and stir well. Then strain back into the hot soup, stirring constantly. Re-heat soup but do not boil, or egg will curdle.

4. Serve hot in soup cups, sprinkled with chopped parsley and with fried bread croutons.

CHICKEN, TURKEY & GAME SOUPS

Chicken Noodle Soup

Clear chicken soup with noodles and chopped parsley (Serves 4–6, hot)

1½–2 pints of well-flavoured clear chicken stock (or water and cubes)
3 tablespoons fine noodles
1 tablespoon finely chopped parsley

1. Bring the stock to the boil, add the noodles, stirring constantly, and boil slowly for about 15 minutes or for time stated on package of noodles. Stir frequently to prevent noodles from sticking. Add seasoning to taste.

2. Serve hot in soup cups liberally sprinkled with finely chopped parsley.

Italian Stracciatella

*Clear chicken soup with addition of beaten egg and cheese
(Serves 4–6, hot)*

2 large or 3 small eggs
2–3 oz of grated Parmesan or other hard, well-flavoured cheese
2 pints well-flavoured clear chicken stock
1 level tablespoon chopped parsley
1 glass white wine (optional)

1. Beat the eggs well with a little salt and pepper, and stir in the grated cheese.

2. Strain the chicken stock into a pan, having removed any traces of fat. Bring to the boil, skimming if necessary, and when boiling fast pour in the cheese and egg mixture slowly with one hand, whisking the soup with the other hand. Allow the soup to continue cooking gently for a few minutes.

3. Then serve at once sprinkled with chopped parsley. A little white wine can be added to the soup if desired.

Chicken Giblet Soup

A light chicken flavoured broth garnished with cooked chicken livers and herbs. This is a good soup to make when using a chicken or chickens for another dish or preparing several chickens for the deep freeze (Serves 4–6, hot)

2 sets chicken giblets
1 large onion
2–3 carrots
2–3 stalks celery
chicken skin and carcass (if available)
2 pints water
4–5 parsley stalks, 1 sprig of thyme, 1 bay leaf tied together
6 peppercorns
chicken cube (optional)
1 oz butter
¾ oz flour

GARNISH
½ oz butter
2 chicken livers
1 tablespoon chopped parsley

1. Wash the chicken giblets, removing the livers. Reserve these for garnish.

2. Peel and slice the onion, carrots and celery. Put these into a pan with the giblets—and any skin or carcass from the chicken. Add the water, herbs, peppercorns and some salt. Bring slowly to the boil, skimming off any scum that rises to the top. Reduce heat, and simmer for 1–1½ hours until the vegetables are tender and the giblets well cooked. Taste soup: if not well flavoured a chicken cube can be added. (Remove skin and carcass, or strain soup into another pan.)

3. Melt the butter and blend in the flour. Strain on to the chicken stock, blend thoroughly and bring to a boil, stirring constantly. Cook for a few minutes.

4. Cook the chicken livers gently in 1 tablespoon butter for about 5–8 minutes depending on their size. Chop livers roughly and divide between soup cups before pouring on hot soup. Sprinkle with chopped parsley.

Turkey and Chestnut Soup

A delicious soup made from the remains of the Christmas Day turkey and chestnut stuffing (Serves 4–6, hot)

carcass of one cooked turkey
2–3 tablespoons or more of leftover chestnut stuffing (or 4–5 tablespoons canned chestnut purée)
2 onions, sliced
2–3 carrots, sliced
2–3 stalks of celery, sliced
several sprigs of parsley
1 bay leaf
2–2½ pints water
½ oz butter
½ oz flour

GARNISH
5–6 chestnuts
1 level tablespoon chopped parsley

1. Remove the remaining chestnut stuffing from the cold turkey and reserve. Take off any pieces of turkey meat which can be used as a garnish. Break up the turkey carcass and put into a large pan with sliced onions, carrots, celery and herbs. Cover with water and simmer until well flavoured. Avoid boiling hard as this makes stock cloudy. Strain.

2. Put the chestnut stuffing into the electric blender with ½ pint of turkey stock and blend until smooth. Turn into a pan and add the remaining 1½ pints stock, seasoning and the turkey meat. Cook together for a few minutes. If the soup is too thin, blend the butter and flour together to make a paste, add to the soup in small pieces, and stir until thickened.

3. Bring to the boil, and serve hot with a few cooked chestnuts, fried in butter and broken into pieces, and sprinkled on top with chopped parsley.

Chinese Chicken Soup

Light chicken soup with mushrooms, spring onions, beaten egg and chicken shreds cooked in boiling soup (Serves 4—6, hot)

4—5 spring onions
6 small mushrooms, finely sliced
2 pints of strongly-flavoured clear chicken stock
3—4 oz shredded white chicken meat
2 beaten eggs
2 teaspoons soy sauce

1. Finely slice the white part of the spring onions and reserve the green part for garnish. Heat the chicken stock until boiling. Add the mushrooms and onions, and cook for 2—3 minutes. Add the shredded white chicken meat.

2. Beat the eggs until frothy with a little salt and pepper.

3. Stir the soup well. Then pour the beaten egg steadily into the soup, stirring constantly, so that it remains in shreds. Allow to cook for a minute or two to set egg. Add soy sauce to taste and serve in soup bowls, sprinkled with the finely chopped green parts of the spring onions.

Mock Bouillabaise (see p. 33)

Game Soup

2 pints of well-flavoured game stock
    (made from carcass and meat
    of any game available)
1 onion, diced
2 small carrots, diced
2 stalks celery, sliced
1 bay leaf, 1 sprig of thyme,
    3—4 sprigs of parsley, tied
    together
1 level tablespoon redcurrant or
    other sharp jelly
1 small glass port (or sherry)
3—4 oz diced cooked game (if
    available)
a dash of lemon juice

GARNISH
1 level tablespoon chopped parsley
fried bread croutons (see garnish
    section)

Game stock with cooked vegetables and additions of sherry and sharp jelly (Serves 4—6, hot)

1. Put strained stock into a soup pot, having first skimmed off the fat. Add the herbs and diced raw vegetables, and cook these in the simmering stock until they are tender. Avoid boiling the soup as this makes the stock cloudy. Add the redcurrant or other sharp jelly, and let dissolve. Remove herbs and add port (or sherry) and the diced cooked game if available. Heat through. Season to taste, and add a dash of lemon juice.

2. Sprinkle with chopped parsley, and serve with fried bread croutons.

Pheasant Soup

1 pheasant carcass
2—2½ pints water
1 onion, sliced
2 carrots, sliced
2 stalks celery, sliced
4 sprigs of parsley
1 small bay leaf
3—4 peppercorns
4—6 mushrooms, finely sliced
3—4 oz cooked peas
3—4 oz diced cooked pheasant meat
1 small glass sherry (or port)
1 tablespoon chopped parsley

A clear soup made with pheasant carcass, garnished with pheasant meat, mushrooms and vegetables (Serves 4—6, hot)

1. Break the carcass into pieces and put into pan with the water, onion, carrots and celery. Add the herbs and some seasoning. Bring to a boil, and simmer for 30 minutes to 1 hour, until it is well flavoured. Strain through a fine sieve.

2. Add the mushrooms to the soup and cook for a few minutes. Add the peas and pheasant meat, and heat through. Just before serving, add the sherry (or port) and serve hot, sprinkled with chopped parsley.

Chicken and Ham Soup

Clear chicken soup, with a garnish of finely shredded lean ham and cooked peas (Serves 4—6, hot or cold)

1½—2 pints of clear chicken stock (or consomme)
1 glass white wine
2 slices of mild ham
3—4 ounces lightly cooked fresh peas
1 level teaspoon chopped (or ½ level teaspoon dried) tarragon
1 tablespoon chopped parsley
¾—1 ounce gelatine for cold soup

1. If serving hot, heat the clear chicken stock, adding at the last minute a glass of white wine, the shredded ham which has had all the fat removed, the lightly cooked green peas and herbs. Serve hot. Sprinkle with chopped parsley.

2. If serving cold and using chicken stock which is not already jellied, put gelatine to soak in ¼ pint of stock. When it has swollen, heat gently and add to the heated stock. Skim off any grease carefully, add the white wine and let cool in a bowl. When it is on the point of setting, add the shreds of ham and the peas, and spoon into soup cups. Chill well and serve garnished with chopped parsley or watercress leaves.

White Fish Chowder, see right

FISH SOUPS

Clam Chowder

A traditional American chowder which is a delicious meal in itself (Serves 4, hot)

3—4 quarts clams in shells, preferably hard backs (or ½—¾ pint of chopped canned clams)
¾ pint water
1—1½ inch cube of fat salt pork (or 2 slices of fat bacon)
1 onion, finely sliced
4—6 oz diced potato
1 bay leaf
1 level tablespoon parsley
1/8 teaspoon or large pinch thyme
½—¾ pint chicken stock if using canned clams; reduce to ¼ pint if using raw clams
¾ pint canned tomatoes
½ green pepper, seeded and diced
1 oz butter
paprika

1. If using fresh clams, scrub the shells well and wash carefully in several changes of cold water. Put into a soup pot and pour over ¾ pint water. Cover the pot tightly and bring to a boil slowly. When boiling point is reached remove from heat and leave for a minute. Strain through muslin (to catch any sand) and reserve juice. Cool clams, remove from shells, and chop. If using canned clams, merely chop, drain and reserve liquid.

2. Chop the fat salt pork or fat bacon, and heat gently until fat melts and the bacon is crisp. Remove any crisp pieces of pork or bacon and reserve.

3. Cook the onion gently in fat for 4—5 minutes without browning. Add the potato, bay leaf, parsley and thyme. Pour on the stock, heat gently to boiling point and cook for 10 minutes, adding seasoning to taste. Add the tomatoes and green peppers. Cook for 5—7 minutes.

4. Add the chopped clams and their liquid, and cook for long enough to heat through thoroughly without boiling. Add crispy pieces of bacon. Just before serving, stir in the butter. Place in soup plates and sprinkle with paprika.

5. Serve with plain water biscuits which can be crumbled into the chowder if desired.

White Fish Chowder

A substantial thick soup of fish and potatoes, which can make a meal in itself (Serves 4—6, hot)

1 pound fresh cod, haddock or halibut, filleted
head, skin and bones of fish
¾ pint water
2 onions, 1 sliced, 1 chopped
1 carrot, sliced
1 bay leaf
3—4 sprigs of parsley (or 1 level tablespoon dried parsley)
1 small cube of fat salt pork (about 1 inch) or 2—3 slices of fat bacon
4—6 oz diced potatoes
¾ pint milk
1/8 teaspoon or 1 large pinch ground mace or nutmeg
1 level tablespoon chopped fennel
1 level tablespoon chopped parsley
1 oz butter

1. Wash the fish skin, head and bones in cold water, and put into a pan with ¾ pint of water. Add 1 onion, carrot, bay leaf, parsley sprigs, salt and pepper. Bring slowly to the boil, skimming as necessary. Reduce heat, and simmer for 15—20 minutes. Strain, and reserve liquid for chowder.

2. Chop the fat salt pork or bacon, and cook slowly until the fat melts. Remove the crispy pieces of bacon, and reserve for garnish.

3. Chop the second onion and add to the hot fat. Cook gently until tender. Then add the diced potatoes and the fish stock. Cook for 5—6 minutes before adding the fish chunks. Then simmer until the potatoes are tender and the fish cooked, about 10 minutes.

4. Bring the milk to nearly boiling point and add to the fish mixture with seasoning and herbs. When ready to serve, stir in the butter, and serve at once.

Shrimp Bisque

A rich party soup with flavour of shrimps or prawns, heightened by the addition of sherry or brandy (Serves 4—6, hot—see picture, p. 4)

2 pounds prawns or shrimps
1¼ pints chicken stock
1½ oz butter
1 onion, sliced
1 carrot, sliced
1 stalk celery, sliced
2 tablespoons rice
1 bay leaf
3—4 sprigs of parsley (or 1 level
   tablespoon dried parsley)
a squeeze of lemon juice
1/8 teaspoon or large pinch ground
   mace
½ pint double cream
3 tablespoons brandy or sherry

1. Remove the shells from the shrimps, and wash in cold water. Reserve ¼ pound shrimps for garnish. Put the shells into a pan with the stock, and simmer gently for 20 minutes.

2. Melt the butter, and cook the onion, carrot and celery for 4—5 minutes to soften. Add the rice, the shrimps, roughly chopped, the herbs, lemon juice and seasoning. Cook together for a minute. Then strain over the stock. Bring to the boil, and simmer for 20 minutes.

3. Remove the bay leaf. Put the soup into electric blender and blend until smooth or put through a moulie or sieve.

4. Return soup to pan, add the reserved ¼ pound of shrimps. Re-heat and adjust seasoning. Add the heated cream, and just before serving, add the brandy or sherry.

Moules Marinière

A succulent mussel soup, eaten from deep soup plates. It is extremely filling and can be used as a main course (Serves 4, hot)

1. Wash the mussels and scrub thoroughly to remove weed or sand. Knock or scrape off barnacles. Remove the beards. Examine mussels carefully, and if any are not tightly closed discard immediately, as they are poisonous if not alive when cooked. Soak the mussels in plenty of cold water, as they will expel any sand from inside the shells during soaking process.

2. Meanwhile, chop the onion or shallots, peel and chop the carrot and slice celery. Crush the garlic and add to the pan with wine, water, 1 tablespoon of chopped parsley, the bay leaf, thyme and ground black pepper. Bring to the boil, and then simmer for 6—8 minutes.

3. Drain the mussels and add to the pan. Cover tightly with a lid and simmer for 6—8 minutes, shaking the pan frequently to make sure that all mussels are covered by liquid. Remove from heat as soon as the mussels open their shells.

40—50 mussels fresh and unopened
1 onion or 4—5 shallots
1 carrot
1 stalk celery
1 clove garlic
8 liquid oz white wine
8 liquid oz water
2 level tablespoons chopped parsley
1 bay leaf
a pinch of thyme
1 oz butter
¾ oz flour

4. Strain off liquid and reserve. Remove mussels from pan and carefully remove half of each shell. If serving for a party, carefully remove the inner part of gristly beard; otherwise, each diner can do this for himself at the table. Put the half shells holding the fish into a deep dish and keep warm.

5. Put cooking liquid into a pan. Blend the butter and flour into a paste, and add to the liquid. Bring slowly to the boil, whisking constantly. Add the second tablespoonful of chopped parsley. Adjust seasoning, and pour over the mussels.

6. Serve in deep soup plates.

Lobster Bisque

A party soup with a rich and never-to-be forgotten flavour (Serves 6, hot)

1. Split the freshly boiled lobster down the back with a sharp knife and remove the intestine, which looks like a long black thread down the centre of the back. Also remove the stomach sac from head and the tough gills. Crack the claws, remove the meat and add this to the back meat. If the lobster is female and there is red coral or roe: reserve this for garnish. Also reserve the greenish curd from the head.

2. Break up all the lobster shells and put into a pan with the fish stock. Add the onion, carrot, celery, herbs, salt and pepper. Cover the pan and simmer for 30—45 minutes.

3. Meanwhile, cut the lobster meat into chunks. Pound the coral roe with 1 oz butter to use as garnish and to colour soup.

4. Melt 1½ oz butter in a pot, stir in the flour until smoothly blended, cook for a minute or two before adding the strained lobster stock. Blend until smooth and then bring to the boil, stirring constantly. Reduce heat, and simmer for 4—5 minutes before adding the lobster meat. Remove herbs. Add the mace or nutmeg, and adjust seasoning. Lastly, add ½ pint of hot cream and the sherry (or brandy).

5. Serve in soup cups with a piece of the coral butter in each cup and sprinkle with paprika.

1 large freshly boiled lobster (or 2 small, preferably female, lobsters)
2—2½ pints fish stock
1 small onion, sliced
1 carrot, sliced
2 stalks celery, sliced
1 bay leaf, 3—4 sprigs of parsley, tied together
2½ oz butter
1¼ oz flour
1/8 teaspoon or large pinch mace or nutmeg
½ pint cream
2—3 tablespoons sherry (or brandy)

Mock Bouillabaisse

True bouillabaisse, a rich fish soup originating from the Mediterranean area, requires special fish not readily available, but a delicious imitation can be made. This is a very filling soup, and as it is fairly complicated to make it is only worth preparing for a large number of people (Serves 6—8, hot—see picture, p. 29)

1. Heat the oil in a large pan. Add the onions, leeks, carrots and garlic. Cook slowly until golden brown, stirring frequently to prevent burning.

2. Add the fish, which should be boneless and cut into chunks. Add the peeled, chopped tomatoes (or canned tomatoes), bay leaf, fennel, saffron, thyme, parsley, orange zest, fish stock or water, salt and pepper. Cover the pan, and cook for 15—20 minutes.

3. Then add the shellfish, leaving the shrimps whole, but cutting the clam or lobster meat into chunks (canned minced clams and canned lobster meat can be used). Bring to the boil, and cook for 6—8 minutes. Then add lemon juice and wine. Re-heat for a few more minutes, and adjust seasoning.

4. While the soup is cooking, cut the French bread into ½-inch slices and put into a warm oven to bake hard. Mix the softened butter with a crushed clove of garlic, add pepper and salt. Spread this paste on to the bread slices.

5. Put a slice of bread into the bottom of each soup cup or plate. Carefully spoon the pieces of fish and shellfish into the soup cups, dividing equally; then spoon over the broth, sprinkle with chopped parsley and serve at once.

4 liquid oz olive oil
2 medium onions, chopped
2 leeks, chopped
2 carrots, chopped
1—2 cloves of garlic, crushed
2 lbs mixed fish: flounder, whiting, halibut, perch, red mullet, haddock, eel
4 ripe tomatoes (or small can tomatoes)
1 bay leaf
1 level tablespoon chopped fennel
a pinch of saffron soaked in boiling water
1 sprig of thyme
4—5 parsley stalks chopped
2—3 thinly peeled pieces of orange zest
¾—1¼ pints fish stock or water
4—6 oz shrimps, clams, and lobster meat
1 teaspoon lemon juice
8 liquid oz white wine

GARNISH
6—8 slices of French bread
1 oz butter
1 clove garlic, crushed
1 tablespoon chopped parsley

1 pound filleted white fish

STOCK
skin, bones and heads of several fish
2 pints water
2 onions
1 carrot
several sprigs of parsley (or 1
tablespoon chopped parsley)
1 bay leaf
1 sprig (or 1/8 teaspoon chopped)
thyme
6 peppercorns
¼ teaspoon salt

SOUP
1½ oz butter
1 onion, finely chopped
2 small carrots, finely sliced
2 leeks, sliced
1 stalk celery, sliced
1 clove garlic, crushed
1 oz flour
1 tablespoon tomato purée
8 liquid oz sieved tomatoes
sugar and mace or nutmeg to taste
1 level tablespoon chopped parsley and
fennel
3—4 oz peeled fresh (or canned) shrimps
or flaked cooked (or canned)
salmon

GARNISH
paprika
garlic croutons (see garnish section)

Pink Fish Soup

A very filling and attractively coloured fish soup, which can be used as a main course for a family lunch (Serves 6, hot)

1. Skin and fillet fish if not already prepared. Cut the fish into bite sized chunks, and put in refrigerator while making stock.

2. Wash the skin head and bones of fish and put in pan with 5 cups water, peeled and quartered onions, and carrot, herbs, peppercorns and salt. Bring to the boil. Then lower heat, and simmer gently for 20—30 minutes. Then strain and reserve stock for soup.

3. Melt butter. Add the onion, carrots, leeks, celery and garlic, and cook gently for 5—6 minutes with lid on pan, until they are tender. Sprinkle in the flour and blend well. Add the tomato purée and tomatoes, stirring until well mixed. Add seasoning and herbs, cover pan and cook gently for 10—15 minutes. Pour in the fish stock, add the fish chunks, bring the soup to the boil and simmer for 10 minutes.

4. Add the shrimps, or flaked cooked salmon or canned salmon. Heat through and adjust seasoning. Sprinkle with paprika, and serve with garlic croutons.

2—2¼ pints strong beef stock
12—16 oz mixed vegetables (fresh, left-
over or frozen—include chopped
onions and celery, diced carrots,
peas, haricot beans, cut french
beans, corn, okra and tomatoes,
not marrow, cabbage or potatoes)
1 pound crab meat (claw or white
meat)
claws and pieces of whole crabs if
available (either raw or cooked)

Maryland Crab Soup

A hearty, highly flavoured sea food favourite (Serves 4—6, hot)

1. Heat the stock in a large soup pot. Add the vegetables and seasoning, and simmer for 1 hour.

2. Add the crab meat and the crab claws and pieces (if available) 30 minutes before serving. Simmer gently, to heat through and allow flavours to blend.

3. Serve hot in large soup bowls, with bread and butter or hard crusty rolls and butter as accompaniment.

CONSOMMES

Consomme Madrilene

*Clear tomato-flavoured
chicken consomme
(Serves 4—6, hot or cold)*

1. Chop the tomatoes and put into an enamel or heat-proof glass pan. Add well-flavoured jellied chicken stock, which has been skimmed to remove fat. Add chopped lean raw beef, sherry or white wine, herbs, sugar and seasoning.

2. Beat the egg whites until frothy but not stiff. Add to the soup pan with the finely crushed egg shells. Bring the soup very slowly to the boil, whisking thoroughly the whole time. When the soup is just reaching boiling point and is rising up in the pan, stop whisking, remove pan from heat to allow the egg white crust to subside, then leave pan on a very low heat for 30—40 minutes.

3. Put a piece of clean cloth over a fine sieve and strain soup carefully, allowing the egg white crust to slide on to the cloth. Pour soup through this filter again, by which time it should be clear. Adjust seasoning.

4. Prepare garnish: Dip 1 large tomato into boiling water for the count of ten and then in cold water. Remove skin and seeds, and cut the tomato flesh into strips. Add to soup just before serving. If serving cold, allow to cool, and set in refrigerator. Then stir with a fork. Serve in chilled soup cups with lemon quarters and cheese straws.

1 pound ripe tomatoes
2 pints well-flavoured, clear jellied
   chicken stock
½ pound chopped lean beef
2 liquid oz sherry (or white wine)
1 level tablespoon parsley
1 level teaspoon basil
a pinch of sugar
2 egg whites and shells of two eggs

GARNISH
1 large tomato peeled and cut into
   strips, if hot
lemon quarters and cheese straws (see
   garnish section) if cold

Tomato Consomme Madras

A most unusual cold soup of consomme flavoured with curry and tomato and garnished with lemon mayonnaise and chives (Serves 4–6, cold)

2 10 oz cans of jellied condensed consomme
1 small bottle of tomato juice cocktail, with tabasco or Worcestershire sauce added
1 teaspoon curry powder (or paste)
a few drops lemon juice
2 tablespoons fresh mayonnaise
grated lemon rind to taste
1–2 teaspoons lemon juice
1 tablespoon double cream, whipped
1 teaspoon chopped chives

1. Heat the consomme very slightly to dissolve it. Add the tomato juice and the curry powder (or paste). Mix in thoroughly. Add a little lemon juice.

2. Pour into the soup cups and allow to chill.

3. Mix the mayonnaise with grated lemon rind and juice. Add the whipped cream. Put a spoonful of this mayonnaise on to the centre of each cup of jellied soup and sprinkle with chopped chives. Serve with brown bread and butter.

Consomme a La Princesse

Clear consomme garnished with diced cooked chicken and asparagus tips (Serves 4–6, hot)

2–3 tablespoons asparagus tips
1 small cooked chicken breast
1½–2 pints clear chicken or beef consomme
a little sherry (optional)
1 level tablespoon finely chopped parsley

1. Cook the asparagus tips, if fresh, in boiling water; if canned, rinse and heat in a little of the liquid from the can. Dice the white chicken meat.

2. Heat the clear chicken or beef consomme. Add a little sherry if desired, the asparagus tips and the chicken dice, and heat through.

3. Serve hot with the asparagus and chicken divided between soup cups. Sprinkle with finely chopped parsley.

Clear Beet Consomme

Clear ruby red consomme with highly individual flavour heightened by garnish of sour cream (Serves 4—6, hot or cold)

1½—2 pints clear jellied brown or
  chicken stock
2—3 small well-coloured cooked
  red beetroots
1—2 teaspoons onion juice
juice of approx half a lemon

GARNISH
4—6 tablespoons sour cream
piroshki (see garnish section)
1 lemon cut in quarters or sixths

1. First prepare clear jellied stock. Either chicken or brown stock may be used, or use canned jellied consomme to make equivalent quantity. Put 1½—2 pints of stock or consomme into pan with the grated peeled beetroots, the onion juice (made by squeezing small pieces of cut onion in a garlic press) and some seasoning if necessary, although the stock should be well flavoured.

2. Bring the soup slowly to a moderate heat and let it cook very gently for 30—40 minutes or until the soup is well flavoured and coloured by the beetroots. Do not let it boil as this makes the soup a muddy brown colour instead of a rich red.

3. Strain soup through a double layer of clean cloth. Add enough lemon juice to sharpen the flavour and adjust seasoning. If serving hot, re-heat to just below boiling point and serve with a garnish of sour cream, handed separately, and with piroshki. If serving cold, put into a clean bowl and chill in refrigerator. Mix with a fork before serving with lemon quarters and sour cream.

Poor Millionaire's Consomme I

Delectable combination of sherry-flavoured consomme, topped with black or red caviar and cream (Serves 4—6, cold)

2 cans of condensed consomme (or
 1¼ pints well-flavoured home-made
 consomme)
1½ tablespoons sherry
a squeeze of lemon juice
1 small jar of caviar (black or red)
1 small carton of sour cream or fresh
 thick cream made sour with lemon
 juice
a pinch of onion or garlic powder
 (optional)
paprika or ½—1 teaspoon chopped
 chives

GARNISH
cheese straws (see garnish section)
lemon quarters

1. Heat the jellied or canned consomme very slightly until it just dissolves. Add the sherry and a few drops of lemon juice to sharpen flavour. Pour into the soup cups allowing space at the top for the garnish, then chill until thoroughly set.

2. Place a large teaspoon of caviar in a mound on top of each cup of jellied soup.

3. Mix salt, pepper, onion or garlic powder (if liked) and paprika into the sour cream, and spoon this mixture over the caviar.

4. Sprinkle the top with paprika or chopped chives, and serve with cheese straws and lemon quarters.

Consomme Julienne

Clear soup with a garnish of strips of cooked vegetables (Serves 4—6, hot)

1½—2 pints clear beef consomme
2 small carrots
2—3 sticks celery, white part only
1 leek, white part only
½ pint stock
1½—2 tablespoons sherry

1. Prepare the vegetables by cutting into even, match-like strips. Put into a pan, and cover with a little stock and seasoning. Cook gently until just tender. Drain, reserving the stock for use in another soup or sauce.

2. Heat the clear consomme and add a little sherry. Add the julienne of vegetables, and serve hot.

Beef Consomme

Clear, strongly-flavoured beef soup which can be served hot or cold and jellied (Serves 6—8, hot or cold)

1. Cut the lean beef into small pieces and put into a pan with the rich brown stock, which has been specially made with bones, vegetables, herbs and seasonings.

2. Beat the egg whites until frothy but not stiff. Wash the egg shells, crush them into the whites and add all this mixture to the soup pan. Heat the soup gently while whisking the egg white mixture into it with a wire whisk using a backward beating movement. When just reaching boiling point remove whisk and allow soup to rise in the pan. Then remove quickly from heat, and when it subsides again continue to cook on a very low heat for 35—45 minutes to allow meat juices and flavour to blend into soup.

3. Put a piece of muslin or a clean cloth over a fine sieve and strain the soup through this, allowing the egg-white crust to slide on to the cloth. Pour the soup back through this filter and if necessary repeat a second time to make soup completely clear. Add sherry and seasoning if necessary, and serve hot or chilled.

1 pound of lean beef
4 pints rich beef stock made from raw bones and meat
2 egg whites
egg shells of two eggs
3—4 tablespoons sherry

Poor Millionaire's Consomme II

Tomato-flavoured chicken consomme, chilled and garnished with fresh shrimps (Serves 4—6, cold)

1. Heat the jellied chicken stock or canned consomme gently with the peeled, seeded, chopped tomatoes, seasoning (if necessary) and lemon rind. Simmer for 20—30 minutes or until the soup is well flavoured and coloured. Strain and cool.

2. If the soup is not a clear red add a little food colouring. Add lemon juice and adjust seasoning.

3. Chill in a bowl in refrigerator. When set break up slightly with a fork and spoon into soup cups.

4. Garnish with freshly cooked shrimps. Canned or frozen shellfish can be used but may need to be soaked in a little French dressing to improve the flavour. Decorate with lemon curls.

1—1½ pints of chicken consomme (or clear chicken jellied stock)
3—4 ripe red tomatoes, peeled, seeded and chopped
2 thin strips of finely pared lemon rind
a little red vegetable colouring (if needed)
1 teaspoon lemon juice
24—36 peeled freshly boiled shrimps
4—6 thin slices lemon

Consomme Royale

Clear consomme served with a garnish of Royale custard (Serves 4—6, hot)

1. First make Royale garnish. Beat the whole egg and the egg yolks well together. Mix the cream with 3—4 tablespoons consomme. Add a good pinch of salt, pepper, mace and the chervil if available. Add the eggs to this creamy mixture, and mix well together. Butter the sides of a baking pan or a fire-proof dish or bowl and pour in the custard. Cover tightly with foil, and stand it in a pan of hot water which should reach half way up the sides of the baking pan or dish. Cook in a slow oven (300°F) until the custard is set, 15—20 minutes or more. Let cool. Turn out cold custard and cut into slices. Cut slices into small shapes—diamonds, crescents, stars etc.—and use as garnish for soup.

2. Heat the clear consomme, add seasoning to taste and sherry. Pour into soup cups. Add the Royale garnish and serve hot.

1½—2 pints clear beef consommé or canned consommé
2 tablespoons sherry

ROYALE GARNISH
1 whole egg
2 egg yolks
¼ pint cream
3—4 tablespoons consommé
a pinch of mace
1/8 teaspoon or large pinch, chopped chervil

Pre-heat oven to 300°F Mark 2

Creamy Consomme Philadelphia

A wonderful light creamy mixture of consomme and cream cheese (Serves 4–6, cold)

2 10 oz cans condensed consomme
2 small or one medium packet of cream cheese (Philadelphia if available)
a few drops tabasco
a few drops onion juice (or garlic juice, or powder)
1–2 tablespoons cream
1–2 tablespoons sherry

GARNISH
2–3 teaspoons chopped chives or a sprinkling of paprika
hot garlic bread (see garnish section)

1. Reserve just over a quarter of one can of consomme for garnish. Put remainder into electric blender with the cream cheese, tabasco, onion or crushed garlic, salt and pepper to taste. Blend gently until smooth, adding a little cream if necessary.

2. Taste and adjust seasoning. Pour into soup cups and chill, covered with paper or foil to prevent garlic odor getting into refrigerator.

3. Heat the remaining consomme until just melted but not hot. Add sherry. Allow to cool and when the soup is set, spoon a thin layer of this garnishing mixture on to each cup and chill again. When set, sprinkle with chopped chives or a little paprika.

4. Serve cold with hot garlic bread.

Variation
Creamy Shrimp Consomme

Shrimp-flavoured creamy consomme chilled soup (Serves 4–6, cold)

1. Use same ingredients as above adding 1½–2 tablespoons to blender, and using two full cans of consomme.

2–4 tablespoons shrimps

2. The garnish in this case is 3–4 whole shrimps to each cup and a sprinkling of chopped parsley or paprika.

Variation
Creamy Curry Consomme

Curry-flavoured creamy consomme (Serves 4–6, cold)

1. Use same ingredients and method as first recipe, but add 1½–2 teaspoons curry powder or paste to the blender and also a squeeze of lemon juice.

1 teaspoon curry powder (or paste)
a squeeze of lemon juice
lemon slices

2. Garnish with very thin slices of lemon.

Variation
Creamy Tomato Consomme

Tomato-flavoured creamy consomme (Serves 4–6. cold)

1. Use same ingredients and method as first recipe, but add 1–1½ tablespoons tomato purée to mixture in blender and also a squeeze of lemon juice.

1–1½ tablespoons tomato purée
a squeeze of lemon juice
1–2 tomatoes, sliced (or shredded)
1–2 teaspoons chopped parsley (or chives)

2. Garnish with slices of peeled, sliced tomato or thin strips of tomato flesh, with seeds removed, and a little chopped parsley or chives.

SOUPS WITH A DIFFERENCE

Eastern Avocado Soup

2—3 avocados, rather over-ripe
1¼ pints tomato juice
1½—3 teaspoons curry powder (or paste)
2—3 teaspoons lemon juice
½ pint chicken stock
1 small carton natural yoghurt
½ pint cream

GARNISH
1 level tablespoon chopped chives (or 1 tablespoon chopped nuts)
lemon quarters
brown bread and butter or water biscuits

A lightly curried and tomato-flavoured avocado soup: a useful way to use rather over-ripe avocados (Serves 6, cold)

1. Peel and remove seeds from avocados. Put in an electric blender, adding a can of tomato juice, 1½—3 teaspoons of curry powder, according to taste, and stock. When blended, add lemon juice, yoghurt, and salt and pepper to taste. Blend again.

2. Chill in refrigerator until just before serving, when the lightly whipped cream should be stirred into the soup, leaving a streaky appearance.

3. Sprinkle with chopped chives or chopped nuts, and serve with lemon quarters and brown bread and butter or water biscuits.

Danish Apple Soup

1½ pounds cooking apples
2 pints water
6—8 strips of thinly pared lemon rind
juice of half a lemon
¼ pound sugar
¾—1 tablespoon cornflour
¼ pint double cream

GARNISH
grated lemon rind, if hot
thin slices of lemon, if cold

Lemon-flavoured apple soup—delicious served chilled on a hot summer night, but also good hot (Serves 4—6, hot or cold)

1. Wash and quarter apples removing cores and peel. Put into a pan with water and thinly pared lemon rind. Cook with lid on pan until the apples are soft, about 20—25 minutes.

2. Strain the liquid from the pan. Put apple pulp through a fine sieve or moulie, or blend until smooth in an electric blender, adding the liquid gradually and mixing well with the sugar and lemon juice.

3. Mix the cornflour with a little cold water. Add a few spoonfuls of hot soup, and mix well before adding to the soup. Bring soup to the boil, and cook for 4—5 minutes to cook cornflour.

4. Stir in cream just before serving, and sprinkle top of each soup cup with finely grated lemon rind. If serving cold, add the cream when the soup is cold and serve with a thin slice of lemon on top of each soup cup.

Danish Mushroom Soup

1—1½ oz butter
1 onion, finely sliced
½ pound sliced white mushrooms
1 oz flour
1¾ pints or 2 cans clear beef stock or 2 cans consomme
1 level tablespoon chopped parsley
1 level teaspoon chopped tarragon
¼ pint cream
3 tablespoons sherry

Party soup with a deliciously different flavour (Serves 4—6, hot)

1. Melt the butter, and cook the onion gently with lid on pan for 3—5 minutes, without browning. Add mushrooms, and cook for a minute or two more. Sprinkle in the flour. When blended, add the stock or canned consomme. Bring slowly to the boil, stirring constantly, and simmer for 10—15 minutes. Add seasoning.

2. Just before serving add herbs, cream and sherry. Serve at once.

Iced Avocado Soup

Creamy luxurious soup for a summer dinner party (Serves 6, cold)

2—3 ripe avocados
3 teaspoons lemon juice
1 teaspoon onion juice
a dash of tabasco
1¼ pints chicken stock
1 small carton yoghurt (natural)
1/8 teaspoon or a large pinch nutmeg
¼—½ pint double cream
1—2 level teaspoons chopped fresh dill
   or a few fresh tarragon leaves

GARNISH
cheese straws
   (see garnish section)
or rolls of brown bread and butter
   sprinkled with chopped walnuts

1. Peel avocados. Reserve a quarter of one avocado to use as garnish; sprinkle it with lemon juice and cover it with a plastic wrap to prevent browning. Mash the remaining avocado with 2—3 teaspoons lemon juice. Make onion juice by crushing small pieces of onion in a garlic press or squeezing through a fine sieve. Add this juice and a dash of tabasco to the avocado.

2. Put all these ingredients into electric blender and add the chicken stock by degrees, blending slowly. When smooth add the natural yoghurt. Blend again, and when thoroughly mixed add salt, pepper and nutmeg to taste.

3. Add half the cream to the soup, stirring it in only partially to give a marbled appearance to soup. Pour into soup cups and chill.

4. Just before serving beat remaining cream and cut the ¼ of avocado into thin slivers. Slide these into soup cups. Put a spoonful of whipped cream into each cup and sprinkle top with chopped fresh dill or a few tarragon leaves.

5. Serve with hot cheese straws or rolls or brown bread and butter sprinkled with chopped walnuts.

Danish Beer Soup

A very unusual soup, suitable for breakfast on cold mornings (Serves 4, hot)

6—7 slices rye or pumpernickel bread
¾ pint water
¾ pint brown ale or beer
grated rind and juice of 1 small lemon
sugar to taste

GARNISH
whipped cream, or milk

1. Crumble the rye or pumpernickel bread and soak in water overnight or for at least 3—4 hours. Add the ale or beer and bring to the boil, stirring constantly. Then simmer until the bread disintegrates into a thickish brown soup.

2. Blend in electric blender with lemon rind and juice, and sugar to taste. Re-heat, and serve with whipped cream on top, or milk to thin slightly.

Vichyssoise

A creamy and delicately flavoured cold party soup, made with leeks and potatoes (Serves 4—6, cold)

3 medium leeks
2 oz butter
1 medium onion, finely sliced
3 medium potatoes, finely sliced
1½ pints chicken stock
1/8 teaspoon or a large pinch mace
1 bay leaf
½—¾ pint cream

GARNISH
1 level tablespoon chopped chives
brown bread and butter, or crisp
   melba toast

1. Wash the white part of leeks carefully, slice finely and wash again to remove any clinging sand or earth. Melt the butter and add the leeks, onion and potatoes. Turn in the butter over a low heat until all are coated in butter. Cover the pan and cook very gently without allowing to brown, as this will ruin colour and flavour of soup. Stir and shake pan from time to time until the vegetables are soft. Pour on the chicken stock and add salt, pepper, mace and bay leaf. Simmer gently for 20 minutes.

2. Remove bay leaf. Pour soup into electric blender and blend until smooth, or put through fine moulie. Then pour through sieve into a bowl to cool.

3. Add the cream and adjust seasoning, then chill.

4. Sprinkle with chopped chives, and serve with brown bread and butter or crisp melba toast.

Hot Avocado and Prawn Soup

Unusual and quickly made party soup (Serves 4—6, hot)

1 small onion, finely chopped
2 stalks celery, finely chopped
¾—1¼ pints well-flavoured chicken
   stock
1 small bay leaf
a blade or pinch of mace
3—4 sprigs of parsley
2—3 avocados (according to size)
2—3 oz peeled prawns

GARNISH
½ pint double cream
chopped chives or paprika
slivers of fresh avocado

1. Put the onion and celery into the stock with the bay leaf, mace, sprigs of parsley and a little seasoning. Simmer for about 15 minutes to flavour stock. Strain and reserve stock.

2. Peel and remove seeds from avocados, and chop the flesh roughly. Put into electric blender, and blend slowly while adding the stock. When quite smooth, return to pan and heat very gently, adding the prawns. Do not allow to boil, as this will spoil flavour and texture of soup. Adjust seasoning.

3. Whip the cream slightly and add a spoon of cream to each soup cup. Sprinkle top with paprika or chopped chives, and add a few thin slivers of another avocado as party garnish.

Creamy Cucumber Soup

Delicately flavoured cucumber soup, suitable for a dinner party (Serves 4—6, hot)

2—3 medium cucumbers
4—5 spring onions (or 3 shallots)
   chopped finely
1½ oz butter
1 oz flour
1¾ pints chicken stock or white stock
   (or water and cubes)
1/8 teaspoon or large pinch mace
a pinch of sugar
1 level tablespoon chopped parsley
1 level teaspoon chopped dill
a little green colouring (if necessary)
2 egg yolks
¼ pint double cream

GARNISH
1 teaspoon chopped dill
fried bread croutons (see garnish
   section)

1. Peel and quarter the cucumbers, remove and discard seeds. Cut into small dice. Reserve 4—5 tablespoons of cucumber dice to use as garnish: sprinkle these with salt, and let stand for 20 minutes before washing and draining. Melt the butter and cook the onions (or shallots) very gently for 5 minutes to soften without browning. Add the larger amount of cucumber dice and cook gently for 2—3 minutes, stirring frequently.

2. Sprinkle in flour, blend smoothly before adding stock. Bring to a boil, stirring constantly. Add herbs and seasonings, then simmer gently for 15 minutes or until vegetables are tender.

3. Put soup into electric blender and blend until smooth, or put through moulie. Return to pot and re-heat. Add a little green colouring and adjust seasoning to taste.

4. Make liaison: mix the egg yolks and cream well, add a few spoonfuls of hot soup, and mix well before straining into soup, whisking constantly. Heat soup gently, but do not boil, as this causes the egg yolk to curdle.

5. Just before serving add the raw, drained cucumber dice, and sprinkle each soup cup with a little chopped dill. Serve with fried bread croutons.

Avgolemno Soup

Traditional Greek light lemon flavoured soup (Serves 4—6, hot or cold)

1. Heat the strongly-flavoured chicken stock in a pan. When boiling, add rice and cook for 12 minutes or until rice is cooked.

2. Meanwhile, beat the eggs well with the lemon juice, until frothy. Take the soup pan off the heat and allow to cool slightly before adding 4—5 tablespoons hot stock to egg mixture. Stir in well.

3. Pour the stock and rice into the top of a double boiler. Strain the egg mixture into the stock, and stir in well. Stir over gentle heat while the soup thickens. Do not boil, or the eggs will curdle.

4. When soup is creamy, add the lemon rind and adjust seasoning. If serving hot, pour into soup cups, put a spoonful of cream into each and sprinkle with chopped parsley. If serving cold, allow soup to cool, add the slightly whipped cream, then chill before serving.

2 pints strong chicken stock
2 tablespoons rice
2 eggs or 3 egg yolks
1 large or 2 small lemons
4—6 tablespoons double cream
chopped parsley

Yoghurt, Shrimp and Cucumber Soup

½ large cucumber, peeled and diced
½ pint natural yoghurt
¾ pint chicken stock
½ pint tomato juice
1 clove garlic, crushed
1—2 teaspoons lemon juice
1 teaspoon chopped dill or fennel
3—4 oz cooked shrimps
1 large tomato, peeled, and diced
2 tablespoons diced green pepper
½ pint cream

GARNISH
1 teaspoon chopped dill or fennel, or
   paprika
French bread and butter, or garlic
   bread (see garnish section)

Unusual summer cold soup made with yoghurt, tomato juice, chicken stock and shrimps (Serves 4—6, cold)

1. Peel and dice the cucumber. Sprinkle with salt and leave covered for at least 20—30 minutes. Then drain and rinse with cold water. Put the yoghurt, stock, tomato juice and crushed garlic into an electric blender and blend slowly until smooth, adding pepper, lemon juice and chopped dill or fennel when soup is well mixed.

2. Add the drained diced cucumber and shrimps, the diced tomato and diced pepper. Stir in cream, adjust seasoning and chill thoroughly.

3. Sprinkle with chopped dill or fennel or paprika, and serve with French bread or garlic bread.

Peanut Soup

Creamy golden-coloured nut-flavoured soup (Serves 4—6, hot)

1 oz butter
1 small onion, finely chopped
3 oz of freshly roasted peanuts (or
   1½ oz peanut butter)
½ oz flour
1½—2 pints stock
¼ teaspoon Worcestershire sauce
a dash of chili sauce
a good squeeze of lemon juice

GARNISH
paprika
fried bread croutons (see garnish
   section)

1. Melt the butter and cook the onion gently for 2—3 minutes to soften. If using peanut butter, add this and then the flour. If using whole peanuts blend in an electric blender with one cup of stock and add to onions after the flour. Stir in the stock and mix well until smooth. Bring to the boil. Then reduce heat, and simmer for about 20 minutes, stirring constantly to prevent soup from sticking to bottom of pan.

2. Add Worcestershire sauce, chili sauce, lemon juice, salt and pepper.

3. Serve hot with a garnish of paprika and fried bread croutons.

Iced Tomato and Cucumber Soup

A refreshing summer soup made with tomato juice, cucumber and seasonings (Serves 4—6, cold)

1 cucumber, peeled and diced
2 cans (about 16 oz each) or 1½ pints
   tomato juice
1—2 teaspoons onion juice
1—1½ teaspoon Worcestershire sauce
¼ teaspoon sugar
2—3 teaspoons lemon juice
a dash of tabasco

GARNISH
3—5 tablespoons sour cream
4—6 slices lemon
1 level tablespoon chopped chives
brown bread and butter

1. Peel and dice the cucumber. Sprinkle with salt and leave covered for at least 20—30 minutes. Drain and rinse with cold water.

2. Put tomato juice into bowl and add the onion juice (made by crushing small pieces of onion in a garlic press). Add Worcestershire sauce, sugar, lemon juice, salt and pepper and a dash of tabasco.

3. Add the diced cucumber to tomato soup and ladle into soup cups. Chill thoroughly.

4. Garnish with a spoonful of sour cream and a thin slice of lemon or a sprinkling of chopped chives in each cup. Serve brown bread and butter separately.

Gazpacho

A traditional iced Spanish uncooked soup (Serves 4—6, cold)

4—6 large ripe red tomatoes
4—6 spring onions or 1 medium onion
1—2 cloves garlic
1 medium cucumber
1 green pepper
1 thick slice brown bread
¾ pint iced water
3 tablespoons good quality olive oil
1½ tablespoons wine vinegar
1 tablespoon lemon juice
1 tablespoon chopped mixed parsley,
   basil, marjoram
a few ice cubes

GARNISH
fried garlic croutons (see garnish
   section)

1. Remove skins from tomatoes by dipping in boiling water for a count of 10, then in cold water, thus loosening skins. Chop tomatoes coarsely, removing hard cores. Reserve 2—3 tablespoons for garnish. Slice the white parts of spring onions or chop medium onion. Crush garlic, and mix with onions and tomatoes. Peel and dice cucumber, sprinkle with salt and let stand for 20—30 minutes, then wash well and drain. Add half to tomato mixture and reserve remainder for garnish. Remove stalk, pips and veins from green pepper and slice finely. Add three-quarters to soup and reserve rest for garnish. Soak the bread in half the iced water until really soft.

2. Put the tomato mixture into electric blender. Add olive oil, vinegar, lemon juice, the softened bread and some salt and pepper. Blend until smooth and strain if necessary through a coarse sieve.

3. Add the reserved vegetables to the soup, and chill thoroughly. Just before serving, add enough of the remaining iced water to thin to a desired consistency. Adjust seasoning, sprinkle with herbs and serve with a few small ice cubes in each soup cup and with fried garlic croutons.

Cherry Soup

A bitter-sweet rich red soup, good for summer (Serves 4–6, hot)

1½ pounds sweet red cherries (or canned equivalent)
1½–1¾ pints water
½ cinnamon stick (or ¼ teaspoon ground cinnamon)
3–4 slivers of orange or lemon rind and juice of half an orange or lemon
8 liquid oz wine
1 level tablespoon cornflour
sugar to taste

1. Pit the cherries and put about three-quarters of them into a pan. Cover with the water and add the cinnamon and lemon or orange rind, which must be very finely pared, and the juice of half an orange or lemon. Cover the pan and simmer gently until the cherries are tender. Remove cinnamon stick.

2. Put the soup through a fine moulie or into an electric blender and blend until smooth. Add red wine.

3. Add the cornflour to cold water and mix until smooth. Add a little hot soup to the cornflour mixture and pour this back into the soup, stir in well then bring to the boil and cook for 4–5 minutes. Add the reserved cherries for the last few minutes to heat through.

4. Add sugar to taste and serve hot with water biscuits which can be crumbled into the soup if desired.

Cranberry and Orange Soup

A delicious cold fruity soup for summer (Serves 4–6, cold—see picture, p. 59)

1 pound of fresh cranberries (or canned equivalent)
¾ pint of light chicken stock (or water)
12 liquid oz white wine
2–3 pieces of lemon rind
pared rind of a ripe orange
½ cinnamon stick
2–4 oz sugar to taste
juice of two oranges
juice of ½ lemon
1 oz gelatine (if soup is to be jellied)

GARNISH
4–6 slices or orange

1. Wash the cranberries if fresh. Put into a pan with chicken stock (or water) and white wine. Add the pieces of lemon and orange rind and the cinnamon stick. Simmer for about 10 minutes, until the cranberries have softened.

2. Put the fruit and juice through a fine nylon sieve or the fine moulie after removing the cinnamon stick. Sweeten to taste and add the orange and lemon juice. (If using canned cranberries it may not be necessary to add any sugar as these are usually sweetened.)

3. This soup can also be served jellied if two envelopes of gelatine are softened in a little stock or water and then added after the soup has been sieved. It will then be necessary to re-heat the soup for a few minutes while blending in the gelatine.

4. Serve chilled or jellied with a thin slice of orange as a garnish.

Cold Buttermilk Soup

A very refreshing cold soup (Serves 4–6, cold)

2 large eggs
grated rind and juice of 1 lemon (or vanill extract)
2 oz sugar
1¾ pints buttermilk
¼ pint double cream

GARNISH
grated rind of half a lemon or
2 tablespoons chopped and lightly browned almonds

1. Beat the egg yolks, lemon rind and juice (or vanilla) with the sugar until light and frothy. Beat the buttermilk, and stir into the egg yolk mixture.

2. Beat the egg whites stiff, adding a pinch of salt. Then whip the cream. Carefully fold the egg whites into the cream. Add this to the egg yolk and buttermilk. Do not blend too thoroughly but leave it rather lumpy in texture.

3. Ladle into soup cups. Then chill thoroughly, garnish with finely grated lemon rind or chopped almonds, and serve plain biscuits separately.

MEAL-IN-A-SOUP

½—¾ pound dried black beans
1 ham bone or some ham meat minus
    fat
2—2½ pints water
2 medium onions, sliced
4—5 stalks celery, sliced
2—3 carrots, sliced
1 bay leaf, 5—6 sprigs parsley, 1
    sprig thyme, tied together
2 cloves
¼ teaspoon mustard powder
a pinch of cayenne pepper
stock or milk

GARNISH
2 hard-boiled eggs
4—6 slices lemon or 2—3 oz chopped
    ham
fried bread croutons (see garnish
    section)

Black Bean Soup

A thick, filling winter soup, served by itself or with slices of bread and cheese (Serves 4—6, hot)

1. Wash beans in several changes of cold water then cover with cold water and soak overnight. Drain and put beans into a large thick pan. Add water, ham bone or pieces of ham, cover the pan and cook for 2 hours. Add the onions, celery and carrots, the herbs, cloves, mustard and cayenne pepper. Re-cover pan and cook for another 1—1½ hours or until beans are tender.

2. Remove the bone and herbs. Put the soup through a fine sieve or blend in electric blender. Re-heat soup and if too thick add enough stock or milk to make a good texture. Adjust seasoning.

3. Serve hot. Garnish with slices of hard-boiled egg and lemon slices or chopped ham and fried bread croutons.

7 oz split peas
2—2½ pints water
1 ham bone
1 onion, chopped
2 stalks celery, chopped
1 bay leaf
1 level tablespoon parsley (or 1 large
    tablespoon dried parsley)
¼ teaspoon sugar
1/8 teaspoon ground pepper
1 oz butter
½ oz flour
a little mint

GARNISH
4—6 tablespoons cream
3—4 oz chopped ham (or 2—3
    slices of bacon chopped and fried
    crisply)
fried bread croutons (see garnish
    section)

Ham Flavoured Pea Soup

Thick pea soup made with dried peas and ham stock, garnished with chopped ham, a meal in itself (Serves 4—6, hot)

1. Start making this soup the day before it is required, as the split peas need to be soaked for 6—8 hours in cold water after being washed in several changes of cold water.

2. Next day wash the ham bone, and remove and discard any surplus fat. Put into a large pan with the split peas and the water in which they have been soaking. Add the onion, celery, bay leaf, parsley sprigs, sugar, black pepper and a little salt, remembering that the ham bone is likely to be salty. Cover and bring the soup to the boil. Then simmer gently, until the peas are tender. Stir from time to time to prevent peas from sticking. This may take 1—2 hours.

3. Remove bay leaf and bones. Then put soup into electric blender and blend until smooth, or put through moulie.

4. Melt butter in rinsed out pan, stir in flour, and when blended pour on soup. Stir until smoothly blended, then bring to a boil, stirring constantly. Simmer for a few minutes. Adjust seasoning, and add mint and a little more water if soup is too thick.

5. Serve hot with a spoon of cream on top of each serving and a garnish of chopped ham or fried bacon bits, or fried bread croutons.

Tripe Soup

Traditional soup, somewhat simplified for modern kitchens, based on old-style Philadelphia pepper pot soup (Serves 6, hot)

½ pound cooked honeycomb tripe
1¼—1½ pints chicken or white stock
2 potatoes, chopped
2 onions, chopped
2—3 stalks celery, chopped
1½ oz butter
¾ oz flour
1 level tablespoon chopped parsley
1 level teaspoon marjoram
a pinch of thyme
a pinch of cayenne pepper

GARNISH
1 oz butter
¼ pint cream
fried bread croutons (see garnish
    section)

1. Buy ready cooked tripe or canned tripe, and cut into small cubes. Cook gently in the chicken or white stock for about 1 hour, with pepper and salt if necessary.

2. Meanwhile, cook the potatoes, onions and celery in melted butter in tightly-covered pan until tender, shaking to prevent sticking and burning, about 12—15 minutes. Then blend in the flour until smooth.

3. When the tripe is cooked, strain the liquid into the vegetables and stir to mix in well. Bring slowly to the boil, stirring until smooth. Add the tripe and the chopped herbs and cayenne pepper. Simmer together for a few minutes. Adjust seasoning. Add some butter and cream just before serving.

4. Serve hot with fried bread croutons.

Cock-a-Leekie Soup

*A rich chicken broth with rice and vegetables, a meal in itself
(Serves 6—8, hot)*

1 small boiling chicken
1 onion
2 carrots
1 stalk celery
6 peppercorns
1 bay leaf
1 sprig of thyme (or a large pinch
    of dried thyme)
6—8 sprigs of parsley
1 sprig of tarragon (or a large pinch
    of dried tarragon)
4—6 leeks, white part only
2 carrots, sliced
1½ tablespoons rice
1 level tablespoon chopped parsley

1. Put the chicken in water with 1 onion, 2 carrots and 1 stalk of celery. Add peppercorns, herbs and salt. Simmer for 1½—2 hours or until the chicken is really tender. Remove chicken and strain stock, which will be reserved for soup.

2. While chicken cooks, wash and slice white part of leeks and soak in salted water to remove grit. Then drain well. Put leeks and carrots in a pan and add 2½ pints of stock from cooked chicken. Cook for 10 minutes. Then add rice and continue cooking for 10—15 minutes.

3. Add some meat from the cooked chicken to the soup with the chopped parsley. Re-heat and serve hot with wholewheat bread and butter. Remaining chicken can be used for another dish.

Chicken Gumbo

1 large or 2 smaller onions, chopped
1½ oz butter or bacon fat
1 can (15 oz) tomatoes
½ green pepper, seeded and chopped
1 small can (10 oz) okra (or ready-
    cooked okra)
1½ tablespoon rice
1½—2 pints strongly-flavoured chicken
    stock made with whole chicken
6—8 oz chopped cooked chicken
1 level tablespoon chopped parsley
1 level teaspoon chopped tarragon
2—3 oz cooked sweetcorn
    (optional)

GARNISH
fried bread croutons (see garnish
    section)

A well-flavoured chicken soup rich with vegetables and rice (Serves 4—6, hot)

1. Melt the butter or bacon fat in a soup pot and cook the onion gently for 5—6 minutes with the lid on until tender but not brown. Add the chopped tomatoes, chopped pepper, okra and rice. Pour in stock and mix thoroughly. Add salt and pepper if necessary. Cover the pan and simmer until the vegetables are tender, about 20—30 minutes.

2. Adjust seasoning and add the chopped cooked chicken and herbs. If available, 2—3 ounces of cooked sweetcorn can also be added. Re-heat and serve hot.

3. This soup can be served on its own as a main course and then it is nice to serve fried bread croutons or thick bread and butter with it.

1 large onion, chopped
1 carrot, chopped
1—2 stalks celery, chopped
1 medium sour cooking apple
1½—2 oz butter (or oil)
1 level tablespoon curry powder (or paste)
¾ oz flour
1 level tablespoon tomato purée
1½—2 pints stock
1 bay leaf
3—4 sprigs of parsley
a pinch of thyme
1 tablespoon desiccated coconut
1 teaspoon sugar
2 teaspoons lemon juice
3—4 tablespoons cooked rice

GARNISH
4—6 slices of lemon
paprika

Mulligatawny Soup

A fairly thick curry soup with cooked rice, garnished with lemon (Serves 4—6, hot)

1. Melt butter or oil and add the onion, carrot, celery and apple, stir well and cook gently for 5—6 minutes. Add the curry powder or paste, and cook for a few more minutes. Add the flour, mixing well, and cook for a few minutes to brown slightly. Add the tomato purée and the stock. Blend well before bringing slowly to the boil. Reduce the heat. Add herbs, seasoning, coconut and sugar. Simmer for 30—45 minutes with lid on pan.

2. Remove bay leaf, then blend soup in electric blender or put through fine moulie. Return to pan, add rice and adjust seasoning. Re-heat, adding lemon juice just before serving. (If preferred the rice can be served separately.)

3. Serve hot with a slice of lemon and sprinkled with paprika.

Cabbage Soup

A very filling vegetable soup garnished with sliced cooked sausages (Serves 4–6, hot)

½—¾ pound green cabbage (or 2 cups of shredded green cabbage)
1 large onion, chopped
2 small leeks, white part only, sliced
2 carrots, sliced
1 potato, sliced
2 slices fat bacon
1 level tablespoon flour
1½ pints brown stock (or water and cubes—ham stock can be used, if not too salty)
1 tablespoon chopped parsley
1 bay leaf
a pinch of nutmeg
1 teaspoon of chopped dill or 1 teaspoon dill seeds

GARNISH
3—4 frankfurters
fat for frying
fried bread and bacon croutons (see garnish section)

1. Slice and wash the green cabbage, put into a pan of boiling salted water, and cook for 5 minutes. Then drain and rinse under cold water.

2. Meanwhile, chop the bacon and heat over gentle heat until the fat runs. Then add the onion, leeks, carrots and potato, and stir over heat for a few minutes. Sprinkle in flour, and blend well before adding stock (or water and cubes). Add parsley, bay leaf, salt and pepper. Bring to the boil. Then reduce heat, and simmer for 10 minutes before adding cabbage. Cook for 20 minutes more, or until the vegetables are tender but not mushy.

3. Adjust seasoning, and add nutmeg and chopped dill, or a few dill seeds. Remove bay leaf.

4. For garnish, either fry frankfurters and cut in slices, putting a few slices into each serving, or prepare fried bread and bacon croutons to serve separately.

Yellow Pea Soup

7–8 oz split yellow peas
2 pints water
1 ham bone
2 onions, sliced
3–4 oz chopped celery or celeriac
2 carrots, sliced
1 small potato, sliced
1 bay leaf, several sprigs of parsley, 1
    sprig of thyme, tied together
3–4 oz chopped ham
1 tablespoon parsley

GARNISH
fried bread croutons (see garnish
    section)

Thick ham-flavoured yellow pea soup, very filling, garnished with chopped ham (Serves 6–8, hot)

1. Wash and soak the split peas overnight if not using a quick cooking variety. Drain and put into a pan, with 2 pints water, the ham bone, vegetables, bay leaf, parsley, thyme and some salt and pepper. Bring to the boil. Then simmer for 1½–2 hours or until peas and vegetables are tender.

2. Remove the ham bone and herbs, and put the soup into electric blender and blend until smooth. Measure soup and bring it up to the required quantity with water or stock. Taste and adjust seasoning. Re-heat, adding the chopped ham.

3. Sprinkle with chopped parsley, and serve with fried croutons.

Scotch Broth

A very filling meaty soup full of vegetables and pearl barley (Serves 6—8, hot)

1½—2 oz pearl barley
1½—2 pounds neck or breast
    of mutton or lamb
2½—3 pints water
½ teaspoon salt
1/8 teaspoon pepper
1 bay leaf
2 large onions, one to add whole, the
    other diced for garnish
1 clove
3 carrots, one sliced for the soup,
    2 diced for garnish
4 stalks celery, 2 whole for
    the soup, 2 diced for garnish
½ small turnip, diced for garnish
1 leek, sliced for garnish
1 tablespoon chopped parsley

1. Soak barley for several hours, preferably overnight, in cold water.

2. Remove as much fat as possible from the lamb or mutton and put into a soup pot with the water and the drained barley. Add salt and pepper, the bay leaf, herbs, a whole onion stuck with a clove, a sliced carrot and 2 stalks of celery. Bring slowly to the boil and simmer for 1½ hours, skimming off the fat and scum occasionally.

3. If time allows let soup cool and skim off fat; if not, skim carefully while hot, removing the bay leaf and celery and carrot as far as possible.

4. Add the diced vegetables and cook for 20—30 minutes or until they are tender. Adjust seasoning of soup and if too much liquid has evaporated add a little extra to make up quantity. Remove the bones, leaving the meat in the soup. Re-heat and serve hot sprinkled with chopped parsley.

Lentil Soup

7—8 oz red lentils
1 large or 2 smaller onions, chopped
2 small carrots, chopped
2 stalks celery, chopped
1oz butter or bacon fat
1 ham bone
1 bay leaf 4—5 sprigs of parsley, 1
**   sprig of thyme, tied together**
a little sugar
1 level teaspoon tomato purée

GARNISH
fried bread croutons (see garnish
**   section)**
chopped cooked sausages
2—3 oz chopped ham
1 tablespoon chopped parsley

Thick winter ham-flavoured soup, served with hot sausages or chopped ham and fried croutons (Serves 4—6, hot)

1. Wash the lentils several times. Then cover with cold water and soak for 4—6 hours or overnight. If used unsoaked the cooking time has to be considerably increased as does the amount of water used, as it evaporates during cooking.

2. Cook the onion, carrots and celery in the melted butter for 5—6 minutes to soften. Then add the drained lentils and the ham bone. Add the bay leaf, parsley sprigs, thyme, pepper and a little sugar. Bring to a boil. Then cover and simmer until tender. This will take at least 2 hours or longer, depending on the type of lentils.

3. Remove the herbs, and put soup through a moulie or into the electric blender and blend until smooth, adding tomato purée. If the soup is too thick at this stage, bring it up to the required quantity with stock or water. Adjust seasoning, adding salt if necessary.

4. Serve hot with fried bread croutons, chopped cooked sausages or chopped ham. Sprinkle with chopped parsley.

Borsch or Russian Beet Soup

3 medium beetroots
1 onion, sliced
2 carrots, shredded
½ small turnip, shredded
½ small parsnip, shredded
2 stalks celery, sliced
2½ pints well-flavoured brown or
**   household stock**
1 bay leaf
3—4 sprigs of parsley
½ small cabbage, shredded
1 tablespoon tomato purée
1 teaspoon lemon juice
1 tablespoon mixed chopped
**   parsley, dill and basil**

GARNISH
6 tablespoons sour cream
3—4 cooked frankfurters or other
**   sausages**

A rich red beet soup thick with vegetables and very filling, a meal in itself (Serves 4—6, hot)

1. Peel and cut two of the beets into thin, short strips. Place in soup pot with onion, carrots, turnip, parsnip and celery. Cover with stock, and add herbs and seasoning. Cook gently without boiling for 30—35 minutes.

2. Meanwhile, wash the cabbage and drain thoroughly. Add cabbage and tomato purée to the soup. Simmer until cabbage is tender but not over-cooked.

3. While the soup cooks, grate the remaining beetroot into a small pan, cover with a cup of hot stock and add the lemon juice to make the beet juice run. Heat gently for a few minutes but do not boil as this will ruin the good red colour. Strain this juice into the soup, adjust seasoning and add the chopped herbs.

4. Serve hot with a spoonful of sour cream and hot slices frankfurter or other cooked sausage in each soup plate. (This soup improves by being made a day before being served and re-heated carefully.)

Cheese Soup

1½ oz butter
2 slices of bacon, chopped
1 large or 2 small onions, chopped
2—3 stalks celery, chopped
3 oz fresh white breadcrumbs
1½—2 pints stock or consomme
a pinch of cayenne pepper
1 bay leaf, 3—4 sprigs of parsley, tied
**   together**
2—4 oz Parmesan or other strongly
**   flavoured hard cheese**
a pinch of dry mustard

OPTIONAL GARNISH
2 egg yolks
¼ pint cream
fried bread croutons (see garnish
**   section)**
paprika

Delicious cheesy thick soup (Serves 5—6, hot)

1. Cook bacon, onion and celery gently in melted butter stirring frequently until the onions are golden brown. Add the fresh bread crumbs and mix well before adding the stock or consomme. Add seasoning, cayenne pepper, bay leaf and parsley sprigs. Bring the whole mixture to the boil, stirring constantly. Cover and simmer for about 20 minutes. Remove the bay leaf and parsley.

2. Add the cheese and mix well. A little dry mustard can also be added. This soup can be made richer by adding a mixture of egg yolks and cream if preferred.

3. Sprinkle with paprika and serve hot with croutons.

Kidney Soup

Rich, filling, meaty soup, served with fried croutons to make a hearty winter meal (Serves 4—6, hot)

3 lamb kidneys or ½ pound ox kidney
salted water to cover kidneys for
   soaking
1—1½ oz butter or oil
2 onions, chopped
2 carrots, sliced
2 stalks celery, sliced
¾ oz flour
1 level tablespoon tomato purée
2 pints beef or brown stock
1 teaspoon Worcestershire sauce
several sprigs of parsley, 1 sprig
   thyme, 1 bay leaf, tied
   together
1 cup sliced mushrooms
a dash of tabasco or chili sauce
a little gravy mix, beef bouillon or
   soy sauce
1—2 tablespoons sherry
1 tablespoon chopped parsley

GARNISH
fried bread croutons (see garnish
   section)

1. Remove the skin and cores from kidneys and cut into small pieces. Put to soak for a few minutes in cold, slightly salted water to remove any strong flavour. Drain.

2. Melt the butter and cook the onions, carrots and celery for a few minutes, stirring well. Add the kidney and cook for 6—7 minutes to brown all the ingredients lightly. Sprinkle in flour and mix well. Add the tomato purée, stock and Worcestershire sauce. Bring to the boil slowly, stirring constantly. Add herbs and seasoning. Then cover pan and simmer for about 45 minutes or until the kidney and vegetables are tender. Remove herbs.

3. Just before the end of the cooking time add the sliced mushrooms and a dash of tabasco or chili sauce. Adjust seasoning, and if soup is not a good colour, add a little gravy mix, beef bouillon or soy sauce.

4. Just before serving, add the sherry and sprinkle with chopped parsley. Serve with fried croutons.

Fresh Corn Chowder

A filling creamy chowder with corn, potato, pepper and celery all blended together (Serves 4—6, hot)

2 potatoes, peeled and diced
10—15 oz or can fresh corn
1¼ pints salted water
½ green pepper, seeded and chopped
1½ oz butter or bacon fat
1 onion, chopped
2 stalks celery, chopped
1 oz flour
¾ pint milk
1 bay leaf, 3—4 sprigs parsley, tied
   together
1/8 teaspoon mace or nutmeg
¼ pint cream

GARNISH
1 tablespoon chopped parsley
fried bread croutons or cheesy
   croutons (see garnish section)

1. Pre-cook the diced potatoes together with the fresh corn in 1¼ pints of lightly salted water until tender, or about 6—8 minutes. Then strain carefully, reserving ¾ pint of the water for chowder.

2. Melt the butter or bacon fat and cook the pepper, onion and celery for 6—7 minutes, until golden brown. Sprinkle in the flour and blend thoroughly. Then add the ¾ pint of reserved potato water. Mix this in thoroughly and add the milk, bay leaf, parsley sprigs, salt, pepper and mace or nutmeg. Bring to the boil and cook for 2—3 minutes.

3. Add the potato and corn, remove from heat, and allow the flavours to blend for at least 10—15 minutes. Then remove herbs. Re-heat chowder, and adjust seasoning. At the last minute add the cream, and re-heat without boiling.

4. Sprinkle with chopped parsley or paprika, and serve with fried bread croutons or cheesy croutons.

QUICK CANNED SOUPS

Quick Tomato Consomme

Canned consomme and tomato juice combined to make a jellied soup (Serves 4–6, cold)

¾ pint jellied chicken consomme
¾ pint tomato juice
1 level teaspoon tomato purée
1/8 teaspoon sugar
1 teaspoon lemon juice
½ oz gelatine
¼ pint extra consomme (or water)
4 tablespoons white wine
red vegetable colouring (if needed)

GARNISH
4–6 lemon slices
1 bunch watercress
cheese straws or garlic bread (see
   garnish section)

1. Put the canned consomme, tomato juice, tomato purée and sugar into a pot with lemon juice and bring slowly to the boil.

2. Put gelatine into a small pan with a little water and when it has swelled dissolve over gentle heat. Remove hot soup from heat and add gelatine.

3. Strain soup through muslin and a fine sieve. Adjust seasoning. When almost cold, add the white wine and the additional consomme or water. If the colour is not good, add a little vegetable colouring.

4. Pour into soup cups and let chill. Decorate the top of each cup with a lemon slice or a little watercress. Serve with cheese straws or garlic bread.

Two-Tone Tomato and Chicken Soup

Canned jellied chicken consomme and tomato consomme, chilled and mixed (Serves 4–6, cold)

2 cans chicken (or beef) consomme
½ can of tomato juice
1 level tablespoon tomato purée
a little lemon juice
a little sugar
¾ oz gelatine
1–1½ oz sherry

GARNISH
4–6 slices of lemon or several
   watercress sprigs

1. Mix 1 can of chicken consomme with ½ can of tomato juice and the tomato purée. Add ½ oz gelatine to a little of this mixture and allow to swell. Dissolve over very low heat and then add to the rest of the tomato consomme along with the lemon juice, sugar and seasoning. Mix thoroughly and allow to chill.

2. Add ¼ oz gelatine to the other can of consomme, allow to swell and then heat gently to dissolve. Add the sherry and allow to set separately from the first consomme.

3. Just before serving, spoon some of each consomme into each soup cup, alternating them so that it looks attractive. Serve with lemon slices or watercress sprigs.

Tomato and Horseradish Soup

1 can of condensed tomato soup
1 can stock (or water)
1 teaspoon fresh horseradish (or
   ¼ teaspoon dried horseradish)
1 level teaspoon tomato purée
1 level tablespoon chopped parsley
1 level teaspoon basil
½ teaspoon sugar

GARNISH
4 tablespoons double cream
1 level tablespoon chopped parsley
cheese croutons (or cheese straws)
   (see garnish section)

A way of making canned tomato soup taste home-made (Serves 4, hot)

1. Pour the soup into a pan and add a can of stock or water. Add the horseradish, tomato purée, parsley, basil, sugar, salt and pepper. Bring to the boil and serve with a spoonful of cream in each cup and a sprinkling of chopped parsley on top.

2. Serve with cheese croutons or cheese straws.

Boula

A party soup made by combining canned green turtle and pea soup (Serves 4–6, hot)

¾–1¼ pints of green turtle soup
¾–1¼ pints of green pea soup (if using condensed soup, use equal quantities of soup and water)
3 tablespoons sherry
4–6 tablespoons double cream
cayenne pepper

GARNISH
cheese straws (see garnish section)

1. Heat the canned soups together gently, blending thoroughly. Add seasoning and sherry just before serving.

2. Serve in soup cups with a large spoonful of whipped cream on each one, and sprinkle a little cayenne pepper on top of the cream. Serve at once with cheese straws.

Iced Tomato Soup Louise

Delicious, original, tangy cold tomato and cheese soup (Serves 4–6, cold)

1 can of condensed tomato soup
1–2 cans milk
½ pound ricotta (or cottage) cheese
a little grated onion
1 teaspoon grated horseradish
lemon juice to taste
a little sugar

GARNISH
4–6 tablespoons whipped cream
chopped chives or paprika
cheese straws (see garnish section)

1. Blend the canned soup with the milk and cheese. Add the grated onion, horseradish, lemon juice, sugar and seasoning. Blend again until smooth.

2. Chill well. Serve in soup cups with a spoonful of whipped cream in centre of each cup and sprinkled with chopped chives or paprika.

3. Serve with cheese straws.

Canned Corn Chowder

A quickly made, filling corn chowder, which can be flavoured with curry if desired (Serves 4, hot)

1 small can of corn and pimento mixed
1 can of condensed chicken or celery soup
1 level teaspoon of onion powder or de-hydrated onion
a pinch of sugar
1 level teaspoon of curry powder (optional)
½–¾ pint milk
½ chicken cube
2–4 liquid oz cream
½ oz butter

GARNISH
1 level tablespoon chopped parsley

1. Mix the can of soup with the can of mixed corn and pimento. Add the onion powder or dehydrated onion, salt, pepper, a pinch of sugar and, if desired, 1 teaspoon curry powder.

2. Heat together, adding the milk and the chicken cube. Cook gently for 5–6 minutes without boiling. Just before serving, add a little cream and put a small lump of butter on top of each soup cup. Sprinkle with chopped parsley, and serve with plain bisucits.

Cranberry and Orange Soup (see p. 48)

Cold Asparagus Soup

A delicious quick soup made from cans (Serves 4, cold)

1 can of condensed asparagus soup
milk
1 can green asparagus tips
1 carton natural yoghurt
a little lemon juice
a few drops of tabasco
2 liquid oz double cream
paprika

GARNISH
cheese straws (see garnish section)

1. Blend the condensed asparagus soup with the liquid from the can of asparagus tips using enough milk to fill the soup can.

2. Stir in the yoghurt, or blend in an electric blender. Add a little lemon juice and a few drops of tabasco.

3. Stir in the asparagus tips and serve chilled with a spoonful of whipped cream in each cup. Sprinkle with paprika and serve with cheese straws.

Baked Bean and Tomato Soup

Tomato and baked bean soup garnished with crisp fried bacon (Serves 4–6, hot)

1 8 oz can baked beans in tomato sauce
1 can condensed tomato soup
1 can tomato juice
1 can water
1 level tablespoon tomato purée
¼ teaspoon sugar
1 tablespoon chopped parsley

GARNISH
2–3 slices bacon

1. Put half a can of baked beans in pan with tomato soup, tomato juice, water, tomato purée and seasonings. Heat together gently, adding the chopped parsley. When well mixed and hot put into electric blender and blend until smooth.

2. Return to pan and heat, adding the remaining beans. Serve hot with the bacon, which has been fried until crisp, sprinkled on top.

Orange and Canned Tomato Soup

Tomato soup flavoured with orange, which gives a delicious fresh flavour (Serves 4, hot)

1. Remove the rind from the orange and lemon with a potato peeler. Cut into match-like strips. Put these into boiling water for 1 minute, then drain and rinse with cold water.

2. Put can of soup in a pan with stock or water, add sugar, salt and pepper and heat, stirring until smooth. For the last few minutes add the orange and lemon rind and lastly the juice of the orange and ½ lemon.

1 orange
½ lemon
1 can of condensed tomato soup
1 can stock or water
a little sugar

Mock Crab Bisque

A delicious, quickly made party soup for unexpected guests (Serves 4—6, hot)

1. Mix the cans of soup in an electric blender, slowly adding the milk or cream.

2. Put into a pan and heat without boiling. When really hot, add the canned crab meat or shrimps and re-heat, adding the sherry and butter at the last minute.

3. Serve hot with a spoonful of double cream in each cup and sprinkled with chopped parsley or paprika.

1 can tomato soup
1 can green pea soup
1 can milk or single cream
1 small can of crab meat or shrimps
2—3 tablespoons sherry
½ oz butter

GARNISH
3—5 tablespoons double cream
1 level tablespoon chopped parsley
or sprinkling of paprika

Canned Pea Soup with Bacon

A delicious way of making canned pea soup taste home-made (Serves 4–6, hot)

1 can of condensed pea soup or two cans of ordinary pea soup
1 can of water or milk if using condensed soup
2 slices of bacon
3–4 tablespoons cooked peas
3–4 tablespoons double cream
1 level tablespoon chopped mint

GARNISH
fried bread croutons (see garnish section)

1. Chop the bacon slices, and cook gently until crisp. Add the pea soup and a can of water or milk. Stir over gentle heat until smooth. Then add the cooked peas. Heat to boiling point.

2. Pour into heated soup cups and put a spoonful of double cream into the centre of each one. Sprinkle with chopped mint and serve at once with fried bread croutons.

10 GARNISHES

Bacon Croutons

(For 4)

2 slices bacon
2 large slices white bread cut into
    cubes
oil
pepper

1. Remove rinds from bacon slices and chop the bacon finely. Put into a dry frying pan and cook slowly to extract fat, then cook until crisp and golden. Remove bacon bits and reserve.

2. Add enough oil to bacon fat to cook the diced bread in same way as fried bread croutons (see p. 63). When golden brown, remove and drain. Add the bacon bits with pepper and serve hot.

Cheese Croutons

(For 4)

2—3 slices white bread
1 oz butter (approximately)
a little mustard or vegetable extract
3—4 tablespoons grated Italian cheese
cayenne pepper

1. Toast bread slices on one side only. Allow to cool. Then butter the reserve side and spread with a little mustard. Sprinkle thickly with the grated cheese, and with a little salt and pepper.

2. Grill or toast until cheese is melted and browned. Sprinkle with cayenne pepper. When slightly cooled cut into squares or fingers. Serve hot.

Fried Bread Croutons

(For 4)

1. Remove crusts from slices of bread and cut the bread into small cubes. Heat enough oil in frying pan to come at least half way up the sides of the bread cubes while cooking. When the oil is hot, add the butter. When this has melted and is foaming, add all the bread cubes at once.

2. Cook over a moderate-to-hot flame and stir constantly to ensure that the cubes brown evenly. When golden brown, place on kitchen paper to drain. Remove from pan when slightly less brown than the final colour you want as they continue to cook for a few seconds, because of the hot oil.

3. Season with salt and pepper, and onion powder, if this will improve the soup for which the croutons are intended. Keep hot and serve separately.

2 large slices white bread
oil
½ oz butter
onion powder (as desired)

Garlic Croutons

(For 4)

1. Crush the garlic. Cut the crusts off bread slices and cut into cubes. Heat the oil. When hot add the bread cubes and cook, stirring constantly. When cubes start to turn colour add the garlic and mix well. When cubes are golden brown, remove and drain.

2. Sprinkle with salt and pepper and a touch of cayenne pepper, and serve hot.

1 clove garlic or ¾ teaspoon dried or
**   powdered garlic**
3 slices white bread
oil
cayenne pepper

Garlic Bread

1. Cut a long French loaf into slanting slices without quite cutting through the bottom of loaf. Soften the butter and mix in the crushed garlic and seasonings. Spread this mixture between the slices. Close the loaf and wrap in foil.

2. Put into medium oven to heat through for about 10 minutes. Then open the foil and allow the bread to crisp for about 2 minutes.

1 long French loaf
1½–2 oz butter
1–2 cloves garlic
salt and pepper to taste
1 teaspoon oregano (optional)

Cheese Straws

Light cheesy straws which go well with a variety of soups (For 4)

1. Cut the butter into the flour which has been sifted into a bowl. Blend well. Add the grated cheese, dry mustard, pepper, cayenne pepper, and salt if necessary. Shape the paste into a ball, wrap well and refrigerate for at least 10 minutes.

2. Roll out paste on a floured board and cut into strips or rounds. Bake in a hot oven for 10 minutes or until golden brown and crisp.

¼ pound of butter
4 oz plain flour
4 oz grated cheese
1/8 teaspoon mustard
cayenne pepper and salt to taste

Pre-heat oven to 400°F Mark 5

Sausage or Hamburger Balls

A filling addition which makes soup into a meal (Serves 6, hot)

1 thick slice of white bread without
   crusts
¼ pint cold water
½ pound of sausage meat or ground
   raw beef
1 small chopped onion
1 clove garlic
½—1 oz butter
1 level tablespoon chopped parsley
1/8 teaspoon or a large pinch thyme
   and oregano
1 teaspoon Worcestershire sauce
2 teaspoons tomato sauce
a dash of tabasco
1 beaten egg

1. Soak the bread in cold water. Put the sausage meat or ground beef into a bowl. Squeeze the water from the bread and add to the meat. Mix with a fork.

2. Chop the onion and crush the garlic. Melt the butter and cook onion and garlic gently until golden brown, about 6—7 minutes. Add this to the meat together with parsley, thyme, oregano and the sauces. Add seasoning to taste and enough of the beaten egg to hold the mixture together. Mix thoroughly.

3. Take the mixture by large teaspoonsful and roll into balls. Cook these in boiling stock or soup for about 15 minutes, or roll in seasoned flour and fry gently in butter or oil for about the same length of time.

4. Add to any meat or vegetable soup as a filling garnish.

Piroshki for Beet Soups

(For 4)

1 oz butter
1 small onion finely chopped
4—6 mushrooms
2 tablespoons cooked rice
1½ tablespoons cooked chopped
   ham
1 level tablespoon chopped parsley
1 small packet of frozen puff pastry
   (thawed)
1 beaten egg
Pre-heat oven to 425°F Mark 7

1. Melt butter and cook finely chopped onion for 2—3 minutes to soften, then add mushrooms and cook for 4 more minutes. Add cooked rice and ham. Season with salt and pepper, and add chopped parsley. Cool before using.

2. Roll out the puff pastry into a long strip about 1½ inches in width or wider if larger piroshki are desired. Using a 1½ inch cutter, cut out as many rounds as possible.

3. Put a teaspoon of the cooled filling into the centre of each pastry circle. Moisten the edges and press together to form a crescent shaped pie or piroshki. Brush the top with beaten egg and bake in a hot oven for 10—15 minutes until golden brown and crisp. Serve hot with beetroot soup.

4. Other ingredients can be used in piroshki such as smoked salmon, diced chicken, or small quantities of left-over meat.

List of additional Garnishes

1. Chopped parsley
2. Other chopped herbs
3. Chopped chives or young green
   onion tops
4. Watercress sprigs
5. Slices of lemon
6. Olives, sliced
7. Yogurt
8. Shreds of orange rind
9. Shreds of lemon rind
10. Slices of cucumber
11. Cooked shrimp
12. Browned almonds or peanuts
13. Rice plainly boiled or colored
    with turmeric or paprika
14. Popcorn
15. Crumbled bacon bits
16. Whipped cream
17. Sour cream
18. Crumbled potato chips
19. Grated cheese
20. Grated nutmeg
21. Paprika
22. Slices of avocado
23. Sliced cooked sausages
    or frankfurters
24. Chopped cooked ham
25. Canned devilled ham
26. Cooked noodles
27. Alphabet noodles
28. Hard-boiled eggs, sliced or
    sieved
29. Royale custard (see p. 39)

Meat Dishes

Most families eat meat once a day, and with ever-rising prices the cook must make the best possible use of every piece she buys. In this chapter you will find recipes for every sort of meat dish from really delicious party dishes such as Fillet of Beef Wellington to everyday family favourites like Irish Stew and Scotch Mince Collops.

For both party and everyday occasions I have tried to include unusual and interesting dishes and there are many continental and Eastern recipes in this section. Plain mince is far from being the only way to serve a pound of minced beef, and pork or lamb chops can be prepared in a variety of exotic and tasty ways.

Offal — liver, kidneys, tripe and sweetbreads, for example — are often neglected because it can be a little more difficult to prepare them attractively. I have given some delicious ways of cooking offal which should appeal even to those who do not normally like it.

The last part of the chapter tells you how to use up leftovers — it is remarkable what can be achieved with a little ingenuity, and some of these dishes are quite good enough for a dinner party.

BEEF: PARTY DISHES

Roast Beef and Yorkshire Pudding

*Classic roast of rolled sirloin with the traditional accompaniment of
Yorkshire pudding and roast potatoes (serves 8, hot)*

1. Prepare batter: sift flour into mixing bowl; add salt; make hollow in
centre; add eggs and a little milk. Stir and draw flour into centre gradually
until smooth. Add remaining milk. Beat well. Let stand for 30 minutes.

2. Melt dripping in roasting pan. Place roast in pan, baste well and roast
for 15 minutes per pound, basting every 15 minutes.

3. Peel potatoes. Boil for 5 minutes, drain and scratch with fork to make
crisp. After 15 minutes put in pan with meat to cook for about 45 minutes.
After 30 minutes, pour off about 2–3 tablespoons of the fat drippings
from meat into small open roasting tin. Reheat, add batter and place at
top of oven until well-risen and brown, about 30 minutes.

4. When roast is cooked, place on heated dish with potatoes and Yorkshire
pudding, and keep warm. Pour off all clear fat, and make gravy with juices
in roasting pan, adding stock. Stir and scrape well to loosen all meaty
brown bits, and season to taste.

5. Serve with horse-radish sauce.

4 pounds boned and rolled sirloin
½ pound plain flour
½ teaspoon salt
2 large eggs
1 pint milk
¼ pound dripping for roasting
2 pounds potatoes
½ pint horse-radish sauce

Pre-heat oven to 450°F Mark 8

Beef Burgundy

*A traditional and classic French dish with a truly wonderful flavour and
aroma of wine, meat and vegetables (serves 4–6, hot)*

1. Cut the meat into large pieces. Melt the dripping or oil in a thick
casserole. Brown the meat quickly on both sides. Take out and keep
warm. Cut the bacon into small pieces and put into the hot fat with
onions, mushrooms and a pinch of sugar. Brown all over. Remove onions
and mushrooms, and put in a serving dish to keep warm. Add flour to the
bacon and brown slightly. Return meat to casserole.

2. Heat the brandy and wine together and bring to boil. Set alight, pouring
over the meat while flaming. Add enough stock almost to cover the meat.
Add a few bits of parsley, sprig of thyme, and bay leaf, and season. Cover
the casserole and cook for about 2 hours. After 1 hour add onions and
mushrooms, and cook for another hour.

3. Add the meat to the vegetables in the serving dish. Boil up sauce to
reduce the quantity a little, and pour it over the meat. Serve with mashed
potatoes and large croutons of fried bread.

1½–2 pounds braising beef
2 tablespoons oil or dripping
4–5 rashers of fat bacon
8–12 pickling onions
12 button mushrooms
a pinch of sugar
½ oz flour
3–4 tablespoons brandy
¼ pint Burgundy or red wine
½–¾ pint beef stock
parsley, sprig of thyme and bay leaf

Pre-heat oven to 325°F Mark 3

Tournedos Rossini

*Juicy steaks on fried bread, garnished with paté,
mushrooms and a rich sauce (serves 8, hot)*

2½ pounds beef fillet (cut into 1—1½
   inch thick slices)
1 tablespoon dripping (or oil)
2 tablespoons chopped onions
1 rasher bacon
2 teaspoons flour
1 teaspoon tomato purée
8 large mushrooms
1 pint beef stock (or water and beef
   cube)
2—3 liquid oz red wine (if available)
1 teaspoon chopped parsley and thyme
6—7 oz butter
½—¾ pint oil
8 slices white bread
1 can pate de foie gras

Pre-heat grill

1. First make sauce: Melt dripping. Add onion and diced bacon. Cook
to golden colour slowly. Stir well. Add flour and cook until just turning
light brown. Add tomato puree, chopped mushroom stems, stock, wine,
salt and pepper. Bring to boil and simmer for 15 minutes. Now add
parsley and thyme and cook a few more minutes. Strain through fine sieve
into sauceboat ready to serve, and keep warm.

2. Put mushroom tops in a buttered dish, with a small pat of butter and
salt and pepper on each. Cook in oven for 10 minutes.

3. Cut bread into rounds the same size as the tournedos. Heat oil and add 1
tablespoon of butter. When foaming, fry bread until golden brown on
both sides. Drain and keep warm.

4. Melt 4 oz of butter in large frying pan. When foaming, cook tournedos
4—6 minutes each side, according to taste. (Or brush with melted butter
and grill 5—8 minutes each side.)

5. Place tournedos on the fried bread. Top each with a slice of pate and a
mushroom. Garnish with watercress and serve with chips and a green
vegetable.

Beef Salad Nicoise

*A rich mixed salad of beef, tomatoes, onions, lettuce, celery,
hard-boiled eggs, cucumbers and peppers, decorated with
anchovies and olives (serves 8, cold)*

8 slices rare cold roast beef
1 small cucumber
8 ripe tomatoes
2 green peppers
2 small chopped onions or 24 spring
   onions
3 lettuce hearts
3 stalks white celery
3 hard-boiled eggs (optional)
16 anchovy fillets
12 green olives
12 black olives

DRESSING
5 tablespoons best wine vinegar or
   lemon juice
15 tablespoons best olive oil
1 large teaspoon French mustard
¼ teaspoon sugar
2 cloves crushed garlic

1. Prepare the ingredients for the salad; cut the slices of beef into thin strips; slice the cucumber, salt and allow to stand for 10 minutes, then wash and drain in cold water; quarter and seed the tomatoes; seed and slice peppers; wash and chop onions or top spring onions; break up and wash the lettuce and discard outer leaves; wash and chop celery; hard-boil eggs. Soak the anchovies in milk for 10 minutes to remove salt and drain. Pit the olives.

2. Arrange lettuce leaves round a large salad bowl or dish. Put the ingredients into the bowl in layers reserving the anchovies and olives for the top. Arrange the top layer carefully with an eye to colour. Now make a lattice design over the whole top with the anchovies putting an olive in the centre of each lattice alternating the colours.

3. Mix all the ingredients for the dressing together and spoon over the whole salad. Serve cold with garlic bread or French bread and butter.

Beef Strogonoff

A delicious dish of strips of steak cooked with onions, mushrooms and soured cream (serves 4, hot)

Do not start to cook this dish until you are ready to eat it. It can be cooked in a chafing dish at the table.

1—1½ pounds fillet of beef
1—2 onions
8—10 medium sized mushrooms
2 oz butter
¼ pint soured cream
a grating of nutmeg

1. Cut beef fillet into strips about 2½ inches long and ½ inch thick. Slice the onions and mushrooms finely. Melt 1 oz of butter in a frying pan and cook the onions slowly until they are golden brown. Remove from pan and keep warm. Add a little more butter. Cook the mushrooms for about 5 minutes and add them to the onions.

2. Melt the remaining butter. When foaming put in about half the strips of steak and fry quickly for about 4 minutes, until they are brown on all sides. Remove and repeat with the remaining steak.

3. Replace all meat and vegetables in the pan, shake over heat adding salt, pepper and nutmeg. Lastly, add the soured cream, heat until it nearly boils and serve immediately with plain boiled rice.

Beef Tartare

A classic dish of succulent raw meat (serves 4, cold)

1 pound best sirloin, rump or fillet
   steak
4 large rings raw onion
4 raw egg yolks
4 anchovy fillets
2 teaspoons capers
fresh horse-radish if available (optional)
4 quarters lemon
freshly ground black pepper

1. Buy and mince the steak as near to serving time as possible, as the meat becomes dark in colour if left standing. Only add pepper to the meat.

2. Shape the meat into 4 equal sized cakes, and make a depression in the centre of each with a spoon. Place an onion ring round this depression and put an egg yolk into the centre of each.

3. Serve with a few capers and curled anchovy fillets, a few chives or fresh horse-radish, if available, and Rye bread and butter, or French bread and lemon quarters.

Chilli con Carne

A simple, easy-to-prepare supper party dish with a spicy, exotic flavour (serves 4–6, hot)

1½ pounds minced beef
¾–1 oz bacon fat
1 onion
1–2 cloves garlic
1–1½ pints canned cooked red
   kidney beans
1 pound tomatoes
6–7 liquid oz beef stock
¾–1 tablespoon chilli powder
1 bay leaf
¾ teaspoon sugar

1. Melt the bacon fat, add chopped onion and crushed garlic and cook for 5 minutes. Add the meat and cook for another 2–3 minutes.

2. Mix in canned beans together with the tomatoes (peeled and chopped) the stock, chilli powder, bay leaf, sugar and salt and pepper.

3. Cover the pan with a lid and cook slowly for about 1 hour.

Silver Baked Steak

Steaks cooked with onions, mushrooms, green peppers and mixed herbs in a foil parcel, to seal in all the flavour (serves 4, hot)

4 large sirloin, or T-bone
   steaks
oil
1 clove garlic (optional)
1 medium onion
3—4 oz chopped mushrooms
1 small green pepper
4—5 small tomatoes (or 1 tablespoon
   tomato puree)
1 tablespoon mixed herbs
1 oz butter
chopped parsley

Pre-heat oven to 350°F Mark 4

1. Beat steaks to tenderize and brush over with oil, crushed garlic and black pepper. Leave for at least 1 hour.

2. Meanwhile, cut 4 squares of foil large enough to wrap one steak in each. Chop onion, mushrooms, green pepper and tomatoes and cook for a few minutes in a little oil. Add salt and pepper to season.

3. Heat grill, and grill steaks for about 1—2 minutes on each side, or fry for same length of time. Put each steak on the centre of a foil square. Pile the tomato and onion mixture on top of each steak and sprinkle with herbs. Then fold foil over to seal. Bake in oven for 15 minutes for rare steak, 20 minutes for medium and 25—30 minutes for well done steak.

4. Open them, serve on the foil with a pat of butter rolled in chopped parsley on top of each.

Beef Pancakes in Tomato Sauce

Light French-style pancakes filled with meat and mushroom stuffing and grilled in tomato sauce with cheese topping (serves 4—6, hot)

PANCAKE BATTER
8 oz plain flour
salt and pepper
2 eggs
2 egg yolks
1 pint milk
½—¾ oz butter

FILLING
1—2 oz butter
1 onion
2 oz mushrooms
¾—1 oz flour
½ pint beef stock
8—12 oz cooked minced beef
a pinch of mace or nutmeg
1 tablespoon Worcestershire sauce

TOPPING
1 can condensed tomato soup (or
   tomato sauce)
3—4 tablespoons grated cheese
¾—1 oz melted butter

1. Make the pancake batter: Sift the flour with the salt and pepper into a bowl. Make a hollow in the centre with a wooden spoon, drop in the eggs and 3—4 tablespoons of the milk. Mix these well together before gradually adding the flour, adding more milk as the mixture thickens. When the mixture is smooth and like thick cream, beat for about 5 minutes. Stir in the melted butter and half the remaining milk. Cover bowl with a cloth and keep in a warm place for at least ½ hour before cooking.

2. Make the filling: Melt the butter and cook the finely chopped onion for 3—4 minutes until it is soft, add the mushrooms, chopped finely, and cook for a few minutes. Add the flour and then the stock. Bring slowly to a boil stirring all the time. Add the meat, parsley, mace, Worcestershire sauce and seasoning. Keep warm until pancakes are cooked.

3. Make the pancakes: Thin the pancake batter with remaining milk until it is like thin cream. Grease a 5—6 inch frying pan or pancake pan with oil. When hot pour out any extra oil. Pour in enough batter to just coat pan and cook until golden brown on one side. Turn over and cook on other side. Pile the pancakes up in a clean cloth, as they are made and keep warm. Allow 2—3 per person.

4. Put a tablespoonful of filling or more on each pancake and roll up. Arrange them down the centre of a dish. Heat a can of condensed tomato soup adding seasoning and spoon this over the pancakes. Sprinkle the top with grated cheese and melted butter, and put under a pre-heated grill for 3—5 minutes until the cheese is browned and the pancakes thoroughly hot.

Braised Beef with Olives

Unusually aromatic braise of beef with green olives as a final touch (serves 6—8, hot)

2—2½ pounds braising meat
2—3 tablespoons oil
2—3 rashers bacon
2 onions
2—3 carrots
2 cloves garlic
½ oz flour
½ pint red wine
½ pint stock
1 tablespoon chopped parsley
1 teaspoon chopped thyme
1 large pinch chopped marjoram or
    oregano
1 bay leaf
12—20 green olives
4 tomatoes peeled, seeded and
    quartered

Pre-heat oven to 350°F Mark 4

1. Heat some of the oil in a frying pan. Cut meat into large pieces and cook on both sides for 1—2 minutes until browned. Put into a casserole. Fry the bacon for a minute then remove and add to the meat. Then fry chopped onion and sliced carrot with the crushed garlic for a few minutes, until brown. Add flour and cook again for a minute.

2. Heat the wine in a small pan and when hot set alight to burn off the spirit. Add to the onion mixture with the stock and bring to a boil. Add herbs and pour over the meat. Add seasoning and cover casserole tightly.

3. Cook in moderate oven for 1 hour. Then add olives and tomatoes and season to taste. Cook again for 20—30 minutes and serve with boiled spaghetti or other pasta and a green salad.

Anchovy Steaks

Juicy grilled steaks, served with anchovy butter to give an extra dimension for a dinner party (serves 4, hot)

4 large, tender steaks (sirloin or rump
    steaks)
oil
1 clove garlic
1½—2 oz butter
1—2 tablespoons anchovy paste
a squeeze of lemon juice

Pre-heat grill

1. Brush steaks with oil and crushed garlic. Leave for an hour at least, longer if possible, to marinade.

2. Cream the butter until soft. Add the anchovy paste gradually, using more or less paste according to personal taste. Add the lemon juice and ground black pepper. Make into 4 balls or pats. Put in refrigerator to chill.

3. When the grill is very hot, put steaks under and cook for 3—6 minutes on each side, depending on the thickness of the steaks and on personal taste.

4. When ready, put a pat of anchovy butter on each steak and serve at once with grilled tomatoes, chips and a green salad.

Pepper Steaks

Tender steaks with a peppery coating, and a wine and brandy sauce (serves 4, hot)

4 large sirloin steaks (1 inch thick)
2 tablespoons peppercorns
3—4 tablespoons of oil
2—3 oz butter
¼ pint white wine
2 tablespoons brandy (optional)
a little lemon juice

Pre-heat grill

1. Press the crushed peppercorns well into the steaks, using a wooden spoon.

2. Heat the oil in a pan and add half the butter. When foaming, fry steaks for 4—6 minutes on each side or longer if preferred. Add remaining butter, if needed. Remove to heated dish to keep warm.

3. Add wine and brandy to the juices in the pan, and lemon juice. Bring to a boil, season with salt and pepper and pour over steaks. Serve at once. (The pepper may be scraped off before adding the sauce, if preferred.)

Beef Olives or Boneless Birds

Thin slices of tender steak, with bacon and breadcrumb stuffing,
and braised in a mushroom and onion sauce (serves 8, hot)

1. Make stuffing by mixing breadcrumbs, herbs, and seasoning together. Add beaten eggs and melted butter.

2. Cut beef into slices about 4 inches square allowing 2 slices each. Beat the slices of beef and season with a little salt and pepper. Cover centre with half a rasher of bacon, then a spoonful of stuffing. Roll each slice up neatly and tie with thread.

3. Brown beef olives quickly on all sides in hot oil or dripping in a frying pan. Remove and keep warm. Now fry chopped onions for a few minutes, add mushrooms and cook for 5 minutes without browning. Add beef stock and bring to the boil.

4. Pack beef olives into an ovenproof casserole, pour over onion sauce mixture and add bay leaf. Cover tightly and cook slowly in oven for 1½–2 hours or until beef is tender. Remove the threads before serving. Thicken sauce if necessary with a teaspoon of cornflour mixed to a paste in cold water and boiled in the sauce for 2–3 minutes.

2½–3 pounds rump steak or topside
4–5 oz white breadcrumbs
4 tablespoons chopped parsley
1 tablespoon mixed chopped thyme
**   and marjoram and lemon rind**
2 eggs
½–¾ oz butter
8 rashers streaky bacon
6 tablespoons oil (or dripping)
2 onions
6 oz chopped mushrooms
¾ pint strong beef stock
1 bay leaf
cornflour (optional)

Pre-heat oven to 350°F Mark 4

Fillet of Beef Wellington

An unusual way of cooking steak, wrapped in pastry to seal in the
flavour (serves 4, hot)

1. Heat oil or dripping in oven. Rub the fillet over with cut piece of garlic and season with pepper. Roast for about 20–25 minutes. Allow to cool. Re-set oven to 450°F for pastry.

2. Melt the butter, cook the finely chopped onion and mushrooms for 5 minutes until the onion is soft. Add brandy, seasoning and herbs, then allow to cool.

3. Roll out the puff pastry thinly on floured board, to a size that will completely cover the beef. Lay cooled meat in centre, spoon the mushroom and onion mixture over the top. Brush the edges of the pastry with water. Fold over the top and pinch together to make a pattern. Fold the pastry carefully over the ends to seal. Decorate with leaves made from left-over pastry. Brush the whole surface with beaten egg, to glaze, and bake in hot oven for 20–30 minutes until the pastry is browned.

4. Cut in slices to serve.

1 fillet of beef, 2–2½ pounds
3–4 tablespoons oil or dripping
1 clove garlic
1½ oz butter
1 tablespoon mixed herbs
1 onion
3–4 oz mushrooms
2 tablespoons brandy
1 packet puff pastry
1 egg

Pre-heat oven to 400°F Mark 6

BEEF: EVERYDAY DISHES

Beef Hedgehog

Unusual meat roll covered with mashed potatoes, onions and mushrooms (serves 4—6, hot)

1 pound minced beef
½ pound ham (or bacon)
4—6 tablespoons oil
1 small onion
1 oz flour
½ pint strong beef stock (or water and cube)
2 oz fresh breadcrumbs
1 egg
2 tablespoons ketchup (or 1 tablespoon soy sauce)
2 level tablespoons chopped mixed herbs, mainly parsley
2 pounds old potatoes
1 oz butter (or margarine)
¼ pint milk
12 small button mushrooms
12 pickling onions

Pre-heat oven to 375°F Mark 5

1. Mix the minced beef and chopped ham in a bowl.

2. Heat 2—3 tablespoons of oil in a fairly large pan. Cook the finely-chopped onion with the lid on the pan for 5 minutes. (If using bacon, chop and cook for a few minutes before adding the beef). Add the beef and ham. Mix in the flour and blend well. Add stock and bring to the boil stirring all the time. Cook for a minute or two. Then cool slightly. Add the breadcrumbs, then the beaten egg and sauce. Mix well, adding herbs and seasoning to taste.

3. Butter a loaf tin or oval baking dish well and turn the meat mixture into it. Cover with a lid or foil, and bake for about 1 hour.

4. Peel and boil the potatoes, drain and dry before mashing. Beat in butter and enough milk to make a dryish mixture. Season well and keep warm.

5. Heat 2 tablespoons of oil and cook the baby onions for about 10 minutes sprinkling with a little sugar to help browning. Remove and keep warm. Add the button mushrooms to the pan and cook these for 3—4 minutes.

6. When the beef roll is cooked, turn onto an ovenproof dish, reserving any juice to make gravy. Coat the meat roll all over with an even layer of mashed potato, and mark with a fork. Press the onions and mushrooms into the potato in rows to represent the hedgehog's spines. Then return the roll to the oven for 15 minutes or until golden brown. (If in a hurry this can be done more quickly under the grill.)

Great Granny's Beef Mould

Traditional meat mould with hot mustard sauce (serves 4—6, hot)

1 pound minced steak
½ pound bacon
3 oz fresh breadcrumbs
grated nutmeg
1 tablespoon Worcestershire sauce
1 egg
1 oz butter
1 oz flour
½ pint milk
1½—2 teaspoons English mustard (or more if strong flavour is liked)
1 dessertspoon white wine vinegar
a dash of tabasco

1. Mince the beef and bacon and add to the breadcrumbs together with seasoning and Worcestershire sauce. Mix together with beaten egg.

2. Put into well-greased mold, covering mold with double layer of greaseproof paper or foil. Tie on tightly, and steam for 2 hours.

3. Make mustard sauce: Melt butter. Remove pan from stove, and add flour and milk. Bring to the boil, stirring constantly. Boil for 2 minutes. Add mustard, mixed with vinegar and a dash of tabasco, and seasoning to taste.

4. Turn out meat mould and serve with mustard sauce over, or separately, whichever is preferred.

Spaghetti with Meat Balls

Boiled spaghetti served with delicious savoury meat balls and tomato sauce (serves 4, hot)

- 1 pound minced steak
- ½ pound spaghetti
- 2 oz butter
- 2 small onions
- 2 tablespoons finely chopped parsley, thyme and marjoram
- 2 cloves garlic
- 2–2½ oz fresh white breadcrumbs
- ½ oz flour
- 1 medium sized can tomatoes
- 2 teaspoons tomato puree
- ½ pint stock
- 1 tablespoon mixed herbs
- 4–6 oz grated parmesan cheese

1. Bring a large pan of water to the boil. Add salt. Curl in spaghetti and bring to boil stirring constantly, simmer for 10–15 minutes until done but still firm. Drain and wash with hot water, drain again. Melt ½ oz butter and toss spaghetti in this with black pepper. Keep warm.

2. Mix together the minced beef and 1 chopped onion. Add chopped herbs and crushed garlic clove, together with breadcrumbs. Season well with salt and black pepper. Shape mixture into small meat balls. Melt ½ oz butter and fry meat balls until brown. This takes 5–7 minutes.

3. To make tomato sauce: Melt 1 oz butter and cook 1 sliced onion and 1 crushed garlic clove for 5 minutes. Mix in flour. Add tomatoes and puree, stock and herbs, with seasoning. Bring to the boil and simmer for 10–15 minutes.

4. Strain sauce and add meat balls. Heat through and serve with the spaghetti. Serve the grated parmesan separately.

Bobotee

2 pounds minced beef
2 thick slices white bread
½ pint milk
¾ oz butter
3 onions
2 tablespoons curry powder (or paste)
1 teaspoon sugar
juice of a lemon
10 almonds
3 eggs
2 liquid oz strong beef stock
2 bay leaves
4 tablespoons chopped parsley

Pre-heat oven to 350°F Mark 4

A delicate curry of minced beef (serves 8, hot)

1. Mince the meat fairly coarsely. Soak the bread in some of the milk, squeeze until dry retaining the milk.

2. Fry the chopped onions in butter. Add curry powder or paste, and fry for another minute. Add the meat, sugar, salt, lemon juice and slivered almonds. Beat the eggs, and add half to the meat mixture. Whisk the other half into the milk. Now mix the soaked bread into the meat mixture thoroughly. Add stock.

3. Put the meat mixture into a buttered fireproof dish and smooth top. Pour the egg and milk mixture over and add two bay leaves. Cook in oven for 30—40 minutes or until set.

4. Remove from oven. Decorate top with chopped parsley and serve with plain boiled rice and chutney.

Beef and Macaroni Stew

1 pound minced beef
½ oz butter or tablespoon oil
2 onions chopped
1 clove garlic
1 small green pepper
1 large can tomatoes
4 oz uncooked macaroni
1 tablespoon chopped parsley and thyme
¾ teaspoon salt
a large pinch of pepper
4—6 liquid oz stock or water

A savoury family stew of beef and macaroni, with onions, tomatoes and herbs (serves 4, hot)

1. Melt butter or oil. Add meat and brown gently all over for about 10 minutes. Add onion, garlic, chopped pepper, tomatoes, macaroni (broken into small pieces), seasoning, and half the herbs and stock.

2. Mix in well and cook in covered pan, stirring occasionally for about 20—30 minutes until the macaroni is soft. Add more stock if necessary.

3. Sprinkle the remaining herbs on top, and serve.

Caribbean Corned Beef Kebabs

Chunks of corned beef wrapped in bacon, grilled on skewers with chunks of banana and pineapple and served with risotto and gravy (serves 4, hot)

4 thick slices canned corned beef
2 medium onions
1½ tablespoons oil
½ pound rice
1¼ pints beef stock (or water with
    cube)
1 orange
1—2 oz butter
2 liquid oz pineapple juice
1 teaspoon Worcestershire sauce
1 level teaspoon cornflour
8 rashers bacon
2 bananas
12 pineapple chunks (fresh or canned)
8 button mushrooms
4 bay leaves

Pre-heat oven to 350°F Mark 4
Pre-heat grill

1. Make risotto first: Cook 1 finely chopped onion in oil for 5 minutes without browning. Add the rice and cook for another 2—3 minutes. Now add ¾ pint of stock and seasoning, and stir well. Cook in oven for about 30 minutes until all the stock is absorbed. Grate about half the orange rind over the rice, and mix in the juice of the orange with 1 teaspoon of melted butter. Pack into a buttered cake tin and keep warm in oven.

2. For the gravy, cook 1 finely chopped onion in ½ pint of stock for about 15 minutes. Add pineapple juice, Worcestershire sauce and the remaining grated orange rind, without pith. Mix cornflour with 1 tablespoon cold water until smooth, add to gravy and boil for 1 minute to thicken.

3. Cut each slice of corned beef into 4 chunks and wrap each in half a slice of bacon. Arrange 4 skewers alternately with banana and pineapple chunks, mushrooms and half bay leaves. Brush well with melted butter and grill (or barbecue) for 10 minutes, turning all the time.

4. Turn the rice mould onto a warmed serving dish. Lay the kebabs on top or alongside and serve the gravy separately.

Boiled Beef and Carrots

A traditional way of cooking beef with the additional aroma of dumplings made with herbs (serves 6, hot)

3—4 pounds topside or round of beef
1 large onion stuck with 2 cloves
8—10 medium carrots
2 small turnips
3 celery stalks
4—6 small onions whole
6 peppercorns
1 bay leaf
some parsley stems
a sprig of thyme
4 oz suet (or butter)
½ pound plain flour
1 teaspoon baking powder
¼ teaspoon salt
2 tablespoons chopped parsley
1 tablespoon mixed thyme and
   marjoram

1. In a large pan put the beef, the large onion, the peppercorns, herbs, enough water to cover the meat and a little salt. Bring to the boil slowly, remove any scum that rises to the surface, put lid on pan and simmer for 1 hour.

2. Peel and quarter the carrots and turnips lengthwise. Remove herbs and the single onion from the pan, and add the carrots, turnips, celery and small onions. Simmer for another hour.

3. Make dumplings: Sift flour with baking powder and ¼ teaspoon of salt. Mix in finely-shredded suet, herbs, and pepper. Mix in water to make a light dough. Divide into pieces about size of small walnut, rolling between hands. Drop dumplings into boiling liquid around meat, cover pan and cook them for about 15—20 minutes.

4. Serve on a large dish with vegetables and dumplings, and serve the gravy in a sauceboat separately.

Greek Meat Balls in Avgolemno Sauce

Delicately flavoured meat balls in a light sauce made with egg yolks and lemon (serves 4, hot)

1 pound finely minced lean beef
1 onion
1 clove garlic
1 oz ground rice
2 tablespoons parsley
1 large pinch ground coriander seed
1 egg
3 egg yolks
2 lemons
¼ pint water or chicken stock

1. Have the meat minced twice. Mix meat in a bowl with the finely chopped onion and crushed garlic. If you have a liquidizer, these ingredients can be mixed for a few minutes at a high speed. Return to the bowl. Mix in the ground rice, herbs and seasoning and the well-beaten egg. The mixture should now be beaten to a very smooth paste with a wooden spoon or by hand.

2. Roll the meat paste into balls the size of walnuts and simmer in lightly salted water for about 20 minutes.

3. While meat balls are cooking, prepare the Avgolemno sauce. Beat the egg yolks until light and fluffy, then add the juice of 2 lemons and 5 liquid oz of water or ¼ pint chicken stock slowly. This can be done with an electric mixer. Heat the sauce in a double saucepan and cook until thickened. Do not let mixture boil. If not using at once, keep warm with the lid on the double saucepan.

4. Drain the meat balls, submerge them in the sauce and warm through gently. Sprinkle grated rind of one lemon over the top and serve with plain boiled rice or pasta.

Scotch Mince Collops

A family dish of minced beef garnished with golden fried bread triangles (serves 4–6, hot)

1 pound best minced steak without
    added fat
¼ pint oil
1 large or 2 small onions
1 level taglespoon flour
1 tablespoon Worcestershire sauce
2 tablespoons chopped parsley
3–4 slices of white bread
½ oz butter
1 tablespoon chopped parsley

Pre-heat oven to 350°F Mark 4

1. Heat 1 tablespoon oil. When hot, not smoking, add meat and fry gently, turning constantly with a spoon until all the meat has turned from red to light brown. Add the finely chopped onion and the flour, and cook again for a few minutes before adding 8–10 liquid oz of water, Worcestershire sauce, parsley and salt and pepper. Put into a covered ovenproof dish and cook in a moderate oven for 45 to 60 minutes.

2. Cut the crusts from the slices of bread and cut into triangles. Heat the remaining oil, add the butter, when foaming put in the bread triangles and fry until golden brown on both sides. Drain and keep hot.

3. When the meat is cooked remove lid, sprinkle top with parsley and arrange the fried bread triangles round the edge and across the centre of the meat. Serve at once, otherwise the fried bread may become soggy.

Lasagne al Forno

A delicious pasta dish with alternate layers of meat sauce and cheese, baked until golden brown (serves 4, hot)

½ pound Lasagne
1 pound raw minced beef
3 tablespoons oil
2 onions
1½ oz flour
3 tablespoons tomato puree
½–¾ pint beef stock
1 level teaspoon oregano
¼ pound curd or cream cheese
6 oz Mozzarella cheese
4 tablespoons Parmesan cheese

Pre-heat oven to 375°F Mark 5

1. Buy the Lasagne verde (green) preferably and cook it in boiling salted water for 15 minutes or according to instructions on package. Drain well and rinse in cold water to prevent sticking.

2. Prepare meat sauce: Heat oil and cook sliced onion until golden brown. Add minced beef and saute for 5–6 minutes stirring all the time. Add flour, mix well. Then add tomato puree and stock. Add pepper, salt and oregano. Bring to the boil, simmer for 45 minutes.

3. Butter an ovenproof dish. Put a layer of Lasagne at the bottom. Then put a layer of meat sauce and another layer of Lasagne. Then a layer of cheese using ½ Mozzarella and ½ curd cheese. Then Lasagne, sauce, more Lasagne, then cheese etc. finishing with a layer of sauce.

4. Sprinkle the top thickly with grated Parmesan. Bake for 20–30 minutes until golden brown on top.

Beef

A traditional British dish of tasty steak and kidney, covered with light crisp pastry (serves 4–6, hot)

1½ pounds rump steak (or other good braising steak)
½ pound ox kidney
4–5 tablespoons flour
¼ teaspoon salt
a large pinch of pepper
a large pinch of mace (or ground nutmeg)
1 mild onion or 2–3 shallots
8–12 mushrooms
1 level tablespoon chopped parsley
1 level teaspoon mixed chopped thyme and marjoram
¼ pint red wine or beer
¼–½ pint water or beef stock
1 tablespoon Worcestershire sauce
1 bay leaf
½–¾ pound block of frozen puff pastry
1 egg

Pre-heat oven to 375°F Mark 5 for meat, to 425°F Mark 7 for pastry

Steak and Kidney Pie

1. Cut the meat into 1 inch cubes and cut up kidney into smaller pieces, having removed fatty core. Put flour into bowl with salt, pepper and mace. Roll meat and kidney well in flour mixture. Pack into pie dish, putting a funnel in centre to hold up pastry. Scatter in chopped onion or shallots, mushrooms and herbs. Then pour in beer or red wine mixed with stock or water. Add Worcestershire sauce and bay leaf.

2. Cover dish with foil or lid, and cook gently in moderate oven for 1½ hours until meat is tender. Remove bay leaf and add more seasoning and liquid, if necessary, and let cool.

3. Roll out pastry. Put rim of pastry around dish then moisten this with water. Lay remaining pastry on top. This should overlap the dish slightly. Press the edges together with fork and then cut off extra pastry with a sharp knife. Make hole over funnel. Decorate around it with pastry leaves and flowers. Brush pastry all over top with a beaten egg to glaze, but do not let glaze drip over cut edge as this deters rising.

4. Put into hot oven, 425°F and cook for 30 minutes until well risen and a rich brown.

5. The meat can be cooked the day before, or deep frozen in this state. The pastry must not be added until after defrosting.

One of the simplest and quickest but most delicious ways of serving steak (serves 4, hot)

4 grilling steaks about 1½ inches thick
6–8 medium onions
3–4 tablespoons oil
½ level teaspoon sugar
1–1½ oz butter
2–3 tablespoons chopped parsley

Pre-heat grill

Steak and Onions

1. Heat the oil and add the thinly sliced onions. Cover pan over moderate heat for 6 minutes, then remove lid, add salt, pepper and sugar, continue cooking stirring constantly until the onions are crisp and brown, about 5 minutes. Drain and keep warm.

2. When grill is hot and while onions are cooking, brush the steaks with oil, put under grill, allowing 4–6 minutes each side if liked rare, or 7–9 minutes if liked medium. Brush frequently with oil. Season when partly cooked.

3. Arrange on hot serving dish. Surround with onions, put a pat of butter rolled in parsley on each steak, and serve at once.

Cheeseburgers

A popular quick snack with a difference (serves 4, hot)

1. Cook chopped onion in hot oil until soft for about 4 minutes. Add chopped mushrooms, cook for another 2–3 minutes. Add to the steak, herbs and chutney. Season and mix well.

2. Divide into 8 round flat cakes, brush with oil, and grill for 5–6 minutes on each side.

3. Put a slice of cheese on top of each beefburger, and grill for another 2 minutes.

4. Put into slit-open rolls and eat at once.

1 pound minced steak
1 onion
1½–2 tablespoons oil
2–3 oz mushrooms
1 teaspoon mixed herbs
2 teaspoons chutney
4 slices cheese cut in half
8 hamburger rolls

Pre-heat grill

Mediterranean Beef

*A simple, but aromatic stew which can be prepared well in advance
(serves 4–6, hot)*

1½–2 pounds braising beef
4 rashers bacon
1 small can tomatoes or 6 tomatoes
2 onions
¼ pint red wine
2 cloves garlic
2 level teaspoons rosemary
1 bay leaf
5–10 juniper berries

Pre-heat oven to 250°F Mark ½

1. Cut the meat into even-sized pieces. Put the meat in a casserole and cover with the bacon cut into pieces.

2. Add the peeled and sliced tomatoes, the sliced onion, wine, crushed garlic, chopped rosemary, bay leaf, crushed juniper berries and seasoning. Cover with lid and cook in oven for 3–4 hours until meat is tender.

Carbonnade of Beef

*Casserole of braising beef cooked in ale or beer and topped with
crisp toast soaked in gravy (serves 4, hot)*

1½ pounds beef suitable for braising,
    cut into large pieces
2 tablespoons oil
2–3 medium onions
1 clove garlic
1 level tablespoon flour
½ pint of brown ale or beer
parsley, thyme, bay leaf
a pinch of nutmeg, sugar
4–6 slices of French loaf (or 4–6
    2 inch squares of crustless bread)
French mustard

Pre-heat oven to 325°F Mark 3

1. Heat oil and brown meat on both sides quickly. Remove and add sliced onions and brown these. Pour off any excess fat. Add crushed garlic and then flour. Pour ½ pint of hot water onto beer or ale and add to pot, bring to the boil, adding herbs, nutmeg, sugar and seasoning.

2. Return meat to casserole. Cover with tightly fitting lid. Cook slowly for 1½–2 hours.

3. Before serving put in the slices of bread, which have been spread thickly with French mustard, allow to soak up oil from top of casserole and some gravy.

4. Return casserole to oven without lid for another 15 minutes, when bread should be a good brown.

Moussaka

*Traditional Greek dish of meat with aubergine and tomatoes topped
with cheese sauce and crisp breadcrumbs (serves 4, hot)*

1 pound minced beef
1 large or two small aubergines
7 tablespoons oil
1 large onion
1 clove garlic
1 tablespoon Worcestershire sauce or
    ketchup
1 tablespoon chopped parsley
1 tablespoon tomato puree
4–5 ripe tomatoes (or small can
    tomatoes)
3 medium potatoes
1 oz butter
¾ oz flour
½ pint milk
1½–2 oz grated cheddar cheese
onion powder
½ teaspoon French mustard
1 egg
1 tablespoon dried breadcrumbs
    or crushed biscuits

Pre-heat oven to 400°F Mark 6

1. Slice aubergine. Sprinkle well with salt and leave for 30 minutes. Cook chopped onion and crushed garlic in 2 tablespoons oil until soft. Add meat and cook until it changes colour. Add Worcestershire sauce, parsley and tomato puree. Put into baking dish to keep warm.

2. Skin tomatoes by dipping in boiling water for 10 seconds and then into cold, and then peel and slice. Peel and slice potatoes. Drain liquid from aubergine, wash in cold water and dry. Heat 3–4 tablespoons oil. Fry aubergine slices until brown on both sides. Drain on paper towel. Then put in layer over meat and season with pepper. Put tomato slices on top of aubergine and season. Fry potato slices in remaining oil until brown and place over top of tomatoes.

3. Make cheese sauce: Heat butter and stir in flour. Add milk and stir until it boils. Add seasoning, mustard and half the cheese. When dissolved, cool slightly and mix in egg yolk. Beat egg white and fold into sauce. Pour sauce over top of Moussaka.

4. Sprinkle top with grated cheese and dried breadcrumbs, and cook for 20–25 minutes in oven until top is well browned.

LAMB : PARTY DISHES

Stuffed Crown Roast of Lamb

*A highly decorative party roast with a delicious
stuffing (serves 6—8, hot)*

1. Buy prepared crown roast, allowing 16 ribs to make a nice size roast. Cover tips of rib bones with foil to prevent burning and crumple some foil into centre of crown roast to preserve shape while roasting.

2. Heat 2—3 tablespoons of oil in roasting pan and when hot put in crown roast. Baste with hot fat before putting in oven. After 10 minutes reduce heat to 350°F and cook for 25 minutes per pound of meat. Season with salt and pepper, and baste every 15 minutes.

3. Meanwhile prepare stuffing: Boil rice. When cooked and drained, mix in the cooked peas, corn and red and green peppers. Cook the chopped onion gently in the butter until golden brown. Add to rice along with lightly browned almonds and the raisins which have been soaked in a little sherry. Lastly add seasoning and herbs.

4. When crown roast is cooked, remove from oven. Put on serving dish and remove foil. Fill the centre with rice stuffing. Decorate the chop bones with paper or foil frills and serve crown roast with a green vegetable and gravy made with the roasting juices and redcurrant jelly. Carve down between bones allowing 2 per person.

crown of lamb, allowing at least 2 ribs
   per person
oil for roasting
4—5 oz rice
3—4 oz cooked peas
3—4 oz cooked corn
2 oz chopped cooked red and green
   sweet peppers
1 large onion
1½—2 oz butter
1 oz almonds skinned, sliced
2—3 oz raisins
2—3 tablespoons sherry
chopped mixed herbs

Pre-heat oven to 450°F Mark 7

Lamb Kebabs on Saffron Rice

*Kebabs of tender lamb, onions, mushrooms, pepper, tomatoes and
pineapple, served on a bed of flavoured saffron rice (serves 4, hot)*

1. To make saffron rice, first put a pinch of saffron to soak in 2—3 tablespoons of hot water. Cook rice slowly in 1 oz of butter or 2 tablespoons oil until slightly brown, stirring all the time. Remove from heat. Add boiling stock, saffron water, salt, pepper and a little onion salt. Cook with lid on over a low heat for 20—30 minutes until liquid is completely absorbed by rice. Then add parsley. Turn into a buttered cake pan and press in firmly. Keep warm.

2. Cut meat into even-sized chunks and marinade in 3—4 tablespoons of oil. Peel onions and cook for a few minutes in boiling water. Then drain and cool. Cut the stems off the mushrooms, pepper into squares, removing seeds, and tomatoes in half. Drain pineapple chunks.

3. Thread various kebab ingredients onto 4 skewers and brush all over with oil. Sprinkle with salt and pepper, and a little garlic powder if liked. Cook under grill for 10—15 minutes until meat is tender and thoroughly cooked. Brush with oil from time to time while grilling. (This grilling can be done on a barbecue or charcoal grill.)

4. When meat is cooked turn rice onto a hot plate and lay the kebabs on top. Serve with tomato, barbecue or brown sauce, and a salad.

1—1½ pounds lamb cut into small
   chunks
8 oz long grain rice
a large pinch of saffron
5—6 tablespoons oil or 2½—3 oz butter
1—1¼ pints boiling stock or water
½ teaspoon salt
a large pinch of pepper
onion salt
1 teaspoon chopped parsley
16 small onions
12 button mushrooms
1 green or red sweet pepper
4 small tomatoes
12 chunks pineapple

Pre-heat grill

Californian Stuffed Breast of Lamb

*Unusual orange flavoured stuffing turns cheaper cut of lamb
into a party dish (serves 4, hot)*

1. Make stuffing: Melt butter and cook onion and celery slowly until soft without browning. Mix into breadcrumbs, adding raisins and sugar and grated rind of 2 oranges and 1 lemon. Now add juice of lemon and beaten egg. Season with salt and black pepper. Add sections of 2 oranges. Mix well and stand for a few minutes before using.

2. Flatten out the boned breast of lamb and dust over with garlic powder. Spread orange stuffing evenly over meat about ¼ inch thick. (Any left over can be cooked separately in a buttered dish). Roll meat up tightly and tie in three or four places with white string, and roll in seasoned flour.

3. Warm the oil or dripping in a roasting pan in the oven. Add the rolled breast of lamb and baste well. Cook for 1½ hours, basting every 15 minutes. For the last 10 minutes turn up the oven to 400° F Mark 6 to brown outside of roll.

4. When meat is tender and cooked through remove and keep warm on a serving dish. Pour away excess fat, reserving juices, add teaspoon of flour, mix well then add stock and grated rind and juice of 1 orange. Bring to the boil, season and serve.

3 pounds breast lamb, boned
2–2½ oz butter
2 chopped onions
3–4 stalks chopped celery
3 oz fresh white breadcrumbs
2–3 oz raisins
½ teaspoon sugar
3 oranges
1 lemon
1 egg
garlic powder
2 level tablespoons flour
oil (or dripping)
½ pint stock

Pre-heat oven to 350°F Mark 4

Barbecued Stuffed Leg of Lamb

Leg of lamb stuffed with rice, dried fruit and nuts, and cooked
on a spit over a charcoal barbecue grill or ordinary grill (serves 6—8, hot)

1. Chop the onion and mix with the chopped soaked dried apricots, chopped raisins and dates. Add chopped nuts, rice, parsley, marjoram, lemon rind and juice, salt and pepper and enough stock to moisten. Fill this stuffing into the cavity left by the removal of the bones. Sew up the slits.

2. Cut the garlic into slivers and insert these into small shallow slits cut into the surface of the lamb with the point of a sharp knife. Put the lamb onto the rod of the spit, spoon the oil over the surface and season well with salt, pepper and barbecue spice, or barbecue sauce.

3. Cook for about 1½ hours or until the meat is tender and browned, basting with oil and seasoning when necessary.

4. Make a sauce with the liquids from the lamb and some stock and seasoning.

1 leg of lamb weighing 3 pounds after removal of bone
1 onion
3—4 oz dried apricots
2 tablespoons raisins
2 tablespoons chopped dates
2 tablespoons chopped nuts
4 tablespoons cooked rice
2 level tablespoons chopped parsley
1 level teaspoon chopped marjoram
a little lemon rind, and juice
a little strong stock
1 clove garlic
oil

Roast Rack of Lamb with Anchovies

Roast lamb with an unusual flavour of anchovies (serves 4, hot)

1. Trim the rack of lamb or best end of neck by exposing the last inch of the bones and scraping these clean. Score the fat of the lamb in a trellis pattern and rub in the crushed clove of garlic and the black pepper.

2. Drain anchovies of oil, soak in milk for 10 minutes, rinse carefully and dry.

3. Heat oil in a roasting pan. When smoking put in the meat, baste with hot fat and cook in oven for about 30—40 minutes, according to size and personal preference. Baste every 10 minutes. After 15—25 minutes place anchovy fillets in a criss-cross design over the fat of the meat and continue cooking.

4. When cooked, remove and keep warm while the roasting liquid is skimmed and heated with the stock to make gravy. Serve with potatoes and a green salad.

1 rack of lamb or 1 best end of neck
   with 8—9 bones
1 clove garlic
black pepper
1 can of anchovy fillets
a little milk
2—3 tablespoons oil
½ pint of brown stock

Pre-heat oven to 400°F Mark 6

Lamb Chops Princess

Lamb chops, egged and crumbed, and fried in butter, garnished with asparagus tips, and served with mushrooms and Madeira flavoured sauce (serves 4, hot)

8 lamb chops
1 oz flour
1 large or 2 small eggs
2—3 oz fresh white breadcrumbs
16—20 fresh asparagus tips (or can of
    green asparagus tips)
3½—4 oz butter
1½—2 oz chopped mushrooms
¾ oz flour
½ pint brown stock
1 teaspoon chopped parsley
¼ pint Madeira or sherry

1. Dip each chop into flour and beaten egg. Then press in breadcrumbs all over surface. Heat 2—3 oz butter in a frying pan until foaming. Fry chops for about 4 minutes on each side until the crumbs are golden brown and crisp, and chops tender. Keep warm.

2. Cook asparagus tips in boiling salted water until tender. Then drain and toss in ½ oz of melted butter. (If using canned asparagus tips, drain and heat gently in hot butter.) Keep warm.

3. To make sauce: Melt 1 oz butter and cook chopped mushrooms for 3—4 minutes. Mix in ¾ oz flour and cook for 1 minute before adding stock, parsley and Madeira. Bring to boil and simmer for 10—15 minutes. Strain through a fine sieve or strainer, and add salt and pepper to taste.

4. Arrange chops on a hot dish with a bunch of asparagus tips for each. Serve sauce separately, very hot.

Turkish Stuffed Aubergines

Aubergines stuffed with meat, pine nuts, raisin and rice stuffing, baked in tomato flavoured stock (serves 4, hot)

1 pound of lean lamb
4 medium or 8 small aubergines
3 teaspoons salt
1 oz butter
1 onion
4 oz rice
2 tomatoes (or 1 tablespoon tomato puree)
2 level tablespoons chopped parsley
2 level tablespoons pine nuts (or chopped walnuts)
1 oz raisins
juice of 1 lemon
3–4 tablespoons oil
½–¾ pint stock
2–3 tablespoons tomato puree
2 tablespoons browned breadcrumbs

Pre-heat oven to 425°F Mark 7

1. Cut the aubergines in half lengthwise and score flesh deeply without piercing skin. Sprinkle with salt and leave for at least 30 minutes.

2. Heat butter and cook finely chopped onion for 3–4 minutes. Add rice and cook for another 3–4 minutes. Add finely chopped meat and stir for a few minutes over the heat. Stir in chopped tomatoes (or tomato puree), chopped parsley, nuts and raisins, lemon juice and seasoning.

3. Squeeze the juice from the aubergines and wash them in cold water. Drain well and dry thoroughly. Heat oil and cook cut side of the aubergines until they are brown and fairly soft. Scrape flesh from skins and add to meat mixture. Stir in well adding about 6–7 liquid oz stock, or as much as will moisten the mixture. Put this mixture into aubergine skins and lay them in a fireproof dish.

4. Mix the remaining stock with 2–3 tablespoons of tomato puree, and season. Pour this sauce around the edge of dish, and cook in oven for 20 minutes. Then turn the oven down to 325°F (Mark 3), and cook for another 40 minutes. During the last 15 minutes sprinkle with browned breadcrumbs.

Stuffed Courgettes

Stuffed courgettes baked with tomatoes, and served with yoghurt and grated lemon rind (serves 4, hot)

1 pound minced lamb
8–12 small courgettes
1½ tablespoons oil
1 onion
1 clove garlic
2 tomatoes (or 1 tablespoon tomato puree)
4–5 tablespoons cooked rice
2 tablespoons chopped parsley
1 level teaspoon chopped marjoram
1 oz raisins
6 ripe tomatoes (or 1 small can tomatoes)
1 lemon
a touch of garlic salt
1 level teaspoon chopped basil
2–3 teaspoons chopped parsley
5–6 tablespoons stock
1 carton of yoghurt for garnish

Pre-heat oven to 350°F Mark 4

1. Cut a small slice off the stalk end of each courgette and scoop out inside with an apple corer or spoon. Cook the skins in boiling salted water for 3–4 minutes and drain. Put the chopped pulp into a bowl with a good sprinkling of salt and leave for ½ hour. Then wash well in cold water and drain.

2. Heat oil, and cook chopped onion and crushed garlic until soft, about 4 minutes. Add meat and drained courgette pulp, and cook, stirring frequently, until the meat is slightly browned. Add 2 skinned and chopped tomatoes (or puree), cooked rice, parsley, marjoram, and raisins, and season to taste. Put this mixture into courgette skins but do not fill more than ¾ full to allow for expansion of rice.

3. Slice 6 tomatoes if fresh (or chop if canned). Put half in a layer on bottom of the casserole. Place stuffed courgettes on top in rows. Heat the remaining tomatoes with lemon juice, herbs, and 2–3 tablespoons of stock. Add seasoning and a pinch of sugar. Spoon this sauce over the courgettes. Cover casserole and cook in oven for about 45 minutes until courgettes are tender. If the sauce appears dry add more stock.

4. Just before serving mix yoghurt with grated lemon rind, and spoon over the dish. Serve with plain boiled rice, or noodles.

(This method and stuffing can also be used with sweet peppers or aubergines. A can of condensed tomato soup can replace the sauce to save time).

Lamb Curry

*Lean lamb cooked in curry sauce with traditional accompaniments
(serves 4, hot)*

1½ pounds lean lamb
2 tablespoons oil
1 large onion
2 stalks of celery
1 tablespoon curry powder
1 teaspoon curry paste
½ oz flour
½ pint stock
1 apple
1 oz raisins
1 large tablespoon chutney
1 bay leaf
2 tablespoons shredded coconut
juice of ½ lemon
2 teaspoons jam or jelly

1. Cut the meat into cubes and brown quickly all over in oil. Put into a casserole and keep warm. Cook the finely sliced onion and celery in the hot oil for 2—4 minutes. Add curry powder and paste, and cook for 2 minutes. Add flour and cook for 1 minute. Stir in the warmed stock and stir until smooth. Bring to the boil and cook for 2—3 minutes. Add peeled and diced apple, raisins, chutney, salt and bay leaf. Pour over meat, and cook over gentle heat for 1 hour, stirring occasionally. By this time the meat should be tender.

2. While meat is cooking pour 2—3 liquid oz of boiling water over the coconut and let stand for 30 minutes. When the meat has been cooking for 50 minutes add strained juice of coconut to the meat with the lemon juice and jam or jelly. Continue cooking for 10 minutes.

3. When cooked, serve with plenty of plain boiled rice, chutney, quartered lemon, shredded coconut, sliced bananas, grated cucumber in yoghurt and fried poppadums.

Lamb Parcels

Slices of boned lamb, wrapped in pastry with onion, garlic, mushrooms, ham, tomato puree, herbs and sherry, and baked in the oven (serves 4, hot)

2 racks or best ends of neck of lamb
   with bones and excess fat removed
2 tablespoons oil
1 onion
½ clove garlic
1 oz butter
3—4 oz chopped mushrooms
2—3 oz chopped ham
1 tablespoon tomato puree
1 tablespoon chopped mixed herbs
1 tablespoon sherry or brandy
1 packet frozen puff pastry
1 beaten egg

Pre-heat oven to 425°F Mark 7

1. Cut each rack or best end of neck into 4 slices, roll each slice neatly and fix with a toothpick. Brush with oil and season with pepper. Heat the grill and grill the lamb until partially cooked allowing 3—4 minutes on each side depending on thickness of lamb. Remove from grill and allow to get completely cold.

2. Meanwhile, cook chopped onion and crushed garlic for 2—3 minutes in butter. Add chopped mushrooms and ham. Stir in tomato puree and cook for a few seconds before adding herbs, sherry and seasoning. Let cool.

3. Roll out the puff pastry until large enough to cut into 8 pieces, each piece large enough to cover a lamb roll completely. Put a small spoonful of mushroom mixture on the centre on each piece of pastry. Lay a lamb roll on top, and spread the remaining mushroom mixture on top of the lamb. Fold pastry over to make a neat parcel of each slice, sealing edges with beaten egg. Brush parcels well with beaten egg, and bake in a hot oven for 20—30 minutes until pastry is brown and well risen.

4. Serve with spinach and chips and a rich brown sauce. (The parcels can be prepared ahead of time and glazed with egg just before baking in oven.)

Persian Lamb and Apricot Pilau

*Cubes of tender lamb cooked slowly in oven with onion, apricots,,
raisins, cinnamon and herbs, served with rice and decorated with
almonds (serves 4—6, hot)*

1½—2 pounds lean lamb
4 oz butter
1 onion
2 oz seedless raisins
6—8 oz dried apricots
¼ teaspoon ground cinnamon
¼ teaspoon chopped thyme
1 pound long grain rice
2 tablespoons almonds

Pre-heat oven to 325°F Mark 3

1. Melt half the butter in pan and cook onion until soft and golden brown. Add meat cut into cubes and brown all over slowly. Add raisins and halved apricots. Sprinkle with cinnamon, thyme, salt and pepper. Pour over cold water to barely cover the meat. Cover and cook gently in oven for about 1½ hours.

2. When meat is tender, if there seems to be too much liquid, boil up to reduce quantity.

3. Boil the rice in usual way for 10—12 minutes or follow the instructions on package and drain well. Melt remaining butter and stir into rice before drying it over gentle heat.

4. Arrange rice and meat in layers in a casserole. Bake in moderate oven for 15—20 minutes. Peel, shred and lightly brown almonds in oven. Sprinkle on top of dish and serve hot.

Indian Curried Lamb Chops

*Cold fried lamb chops, coated with jellied curry sauce
Garnished with tomato, cucumber and lemon slices
(serves 4, cold)*

8 best end of neck or rib lamb chops
3 oz butter
8 oz long grain rice
1 small can clear consomme
1 oz gelatine
2 onions
1 level tablespoon curry powder (or paste)
½ oz flour
¾—1 pint stock
1 teaspoon shredded coconut
1 teaspoon redcurrant jelly
a little lemon juice
1 lemon
1 tomato
1 hard boiled egg (optional)
1 cucumber

1. Trim the bones of the chops and scrape clean. Melt 1½ oz of butter and fry the chops for about 4 minutes on each side. Lay out on a dish, put a baking sheet on top with a weight, and let cool. Cook the rice and let cool. Dissolve 1 level teaspoon of the gelatine in the consomme and let cool.

2. Melt 1½ oz of butter and cook sliced onions until soft and golden. Add curry powder and cook for 1 minute. Add flour, cook 1 minute, add stock and bring to boil. Add coconut and simmer for 15 minutes. Now add jelly and lemon juice, and cook for a few minutes. Strain sauce, return to pan and add remaining gelatine. Dissolve it adding salt and pepper to taste and allow to cool.

3. Place cold chops on a wire cake rack and spoon the setting curry sauce over one side of the chops. Leave to set. At this stage the chops can be decorated with pieces of lemon and tomato (or cold hard-boiled egg white cut into shapes). The decorations are kept in place by the consomme which is now spooned over each chop. Leave to set.

4. Arrange the cold rice in the center of a dish, stand the chops around, bones upwards. These can be decorated with paper frills if available. Chop any remaining jellied consomme and arrange around the edge. Decorate the dish with slices of lemon, tomato and cucumber.

Baked Stuffed Mushrooms

Large flat mushrooms sandwiched together with savoury meat stuffing and baked wrapped in bacon (serves 4, hot)

½ pound minced lamb
1½ oz butter
1 small onion
1½—2 oz fresh breadcrumbs
½ clove garlic
1 tablespoon parsley
1—2 teaspoons chopped capers
a pinch of mace (or nutmeg)
1 egg
16 large flat mushrooms
8 rashers of bacon
2—3 tablespoons mixed brown breadcrumbs and grated cheese

Pre-heat oven to 350°F Mark 4

1. Heat 1 oz butter, and cook chopped onion and crushed garlic for 4—5 minutes. Add minced meat, and cook for another 7—8 minutes, stirring constantly. Mix in breadcrumbs, parsley and capers, and season well with salt, pepper and mace. When it has cooled slightly add enough beaten egg to moisten mixture without making it at all runny.

2. Remove stems from mushrooms level with base. Chop stems and add to stuffing mixture. Divide stuffing into 8, mold over mushroom caps and lay the other 8 mushroom caps on top, pressing firmly together. Wrap each mushroom sandwich in a strip of bacon and place in buttered fireproof dish.

3. Spoon ½ oz of melted butter over mushrooms, cover with foil, and bake in oven for 20—30 minutes. After 15 minutes remove foil and sprinkle breadcrumb and grated cheese mixture over dish. Cook for another 10—15 minutes and if necessary brown under grill.

Lamb Chops on Ratatouille

Lamb chops baked in a savoury mixture of onions, garlic, sweet peppers, tomatoes and herbs, until tender and aromatic (serves 4, hot)

4 large loin chops or 8 small best end
  or rib chops
2—3 tablespoons oil
2 onions
2 cloves garlic
2 small or 1 large green sweet pepper
1 small can tomatoes or 4—5 fresh
  tomatoes
1 teaspoon tomato puree
1 teaspoon chopped parsley
1 teaspoon mixed basil, thyme and
  marjoram
a little sugar

Pre-heat oven to 350°F Mark 4

1. Heat oil and cook the chops quickly on each side until light brown. Drain and keep warm.

2. Slice the onions and crush garlic, and cook for 2—3 minutes in hot oil. Add the seeded and chopped pepper, the canned or fresh peeled and chopped tomatoes, and tomato puree. Stir in herbs, seasoning and sugar and cook together until thoroughly heated. (Or you can use a can of Ratatouille, also well heated.)

3. Put a layer of the Ratatouille in the bottom of a fireproof dish or casserole. Lay the chops on top. Cover the chops with the remaining Ratatouille, and cook in a medium oven for 20 minutes or until chops are tender.

4. Serve with potatoes or spaghetti.

LAMB: EVERYDAY DISHES

Danish Blue Lamb Chops

Grilled lamb chops, covered with creamed blue cheese and glazed under the grill (serves 4, hot)

8 loin or best end of neck lamb chops,
   1 inch thick
oil
3–4 oz Danish blue or Roquefort cheese
2 tablespoons thick cream
a clove garlic or garlic powder
   (optional)

Pre-heat grill

1. If using best end of neck chops trim and scrape the rib bones. Brush chops with oil and sprinkle with black ground pepper (and garlic powder or crushed fresh garlic if this is liked). Leave for a couple of hours if possible before grilling.

2. Mix the cheese and the cream and mash well together to form a paste.

3. Grill chops 5–6 minutes on each side. Remove from heat and spread cheese mixture on one side of each chop. Replace under heat until cheese is light brown and bubbling.

4. Serve with mashed or baked potatoes and a salad.

Lamb or Mutton Savoury

Simple hot savoury lamb mixture finished with tomatoes and hot cheese topping (serves 4, hot)

1 pound of cold cooked lamb or
   mutton
1 onion
2—3 oz butter
2 teaspoons chopped parsley
¼ teaspoon chopped thyme
1 teaspoon Worcestershire sauce
2 large tomatoes
2 tablespoons dried breadcrumbs
2 tablespoons grated parmesan or
   strongly flavored cheese

Pre-heat oven to 400°F Mark 6

1. Mince or chop the lamb or mutton finely. Chop the onion and cook in 1—1½ oz of butter, until light golden brown. Add the meat and mix well, adding the chopped herbs and Worcestershire sauce, and salt and pepper to taste.

2. Butter 4 scallop shells or gratin dishes and divide the mixture evenly between them. Smooth down and put 2—3 slices of tomato on top of each. Sprinkle the top with mixed breadcrumbs and cheese. Dot the top with the remaining butter in small pieces.

3. Cook in a hot oven for about 15 minutes. If the top of the scallops are not brown and crisp, finish off under a hot grill for a few minutes.

Durham Lamb Cutlets

Deep fried cutlet shaped patties of savoury lamb mixture (serves 4, hot)

½ pound of cold cooked lamb
1 small onion
½ oz butter
½ pound mashed potato
1 tablespoon chopped parsley
1 teaspoon tomato puree
3—4 tablespoons flour
1 egg
5—6 tablespoons white breadcrumbs
fat for deep frying

1. Mince or chop meat very fine. Chop onions finely and cook in melted butter until golden brown. Add mashed potato and meat to onion. Then add chopped parsley and tomato puree, and salt and pepper to taste. Cook all together for a few seconds.

(cont.)

2. Turn mixture onto a plate to cool. Then divide into 8 equal sized portions and shape into cutlet shapes. Roll each in flour, then dip into beaten egg until coated all over. Now roll in dried breadcrumbs.

3. Heat fat to 360–390° F in a deep fat frying pan. When smoking slightly, put 3–4 cutlets into frying basket and lower into hot fat. Cook until cutlets are a rich brown. Drain on paper towel and keep warm while frying remaining cutlets.

4. Arrange in an overlapping circle around a hot dish, and serve with vegetables and a brown or tomato sauce.

Braised Lamb Shanks

*A rich casserole of cheaper cuts of lamb which can be prepared
well in advance (serves 4, hot)*

4 lamb shanks
2 tablespoons oil
2 large onions
1 clove garlic
¾–1 oz flour
½–¾ pint stock or water
½ pint ale or beer
2 carrots
2–3 stalks celery
1 small tablespoon vinegar
1 small tablespoon Worcestershire sauce
1 bay leaf
2 tablespoons chopped parsley and
   thyme
1 tablespoon chutney
4 tomatoes

Pre-heat oven to 325°F Mark 3

1. Heat oil and brown lamb shanks all over. Put into casserole and keep warm.

2. Cook chopped onion and crushed garlic for a few minutes until light brown. Remove from heat, add flour and stir in well. Cook for another minute. Then add stock or water and ale. (If not using ale or beer, increase the quantity of stock.) Add sliced carrots and celery, vinegar, Worcestershire sauce, herbs and bay leaf. Bring to the boil, stirring all the time. Then cover the casserole and cook in oven for about 1½ hours or until lamb is tender.

3. If the braise is to be served the same day, put the peeled tomatoes, cut in slices, into the pot 15 minutes before the end of cooking, together with chutney. If keeping until next day, add tomato and chutney just before reheating for half an hour in moderate oven. Serve with plain boiled rice or mashed potatoes.

Turkish Kofte in Tomato Sauce

Light meat balls with tomato sauce and sour cream or yoghurt (serves 4, hot)

1 pound minced fresh mutton or lamb
¼ pint cider (or light white wine)
2 slices stale white bread
1 large onion
2 tablespoons chopped parsley
1 level teaspoon chopped thyme
1 level teaspoon lemon rind
2 teaspoons paprika
2 eggs
2—3 tablespoons seasoned flour
4 oz butter
1 medium onion
1 clove garlic
1 cup peeled and chopped tomatoes
   (or canned tomatoes)
1 level teaspoon basil
½ pint soured cream or plain yoghurt

Pre-heat oven to 350°F Mark 4

1. Pour cider over bread, leave for some minutes to soak. Put the minced meat in large bowl with finely chopped or minced onion, 1 tablespoon chopped parsley, thyme, lemon rind, 1 teaspoon paprika, and salt. Squeeze cider out of bread and put bread into meat mixture. Beat this mixture by hand, adding the beaten egg gradually. This beating should take 7—10 minutes and gives the meat balls their light texture. Take 1 tablespoon of mixture at a time and roll in either wet or oiled hands to shape into rounds. Then cover with seasoned flour.

2. Melt 2½ oz butter in a frying pan. Brown meat balls in butter, then put into an ovenproof dish. Pour over tomato sauce and bake for 30—40 minutes.

3. To make sauce: Melt 1½ oz butter, and cook sliced onion and crushed garlic for 5—6 minutes. Add tomatoes, 1 tablespoon chopped parsley, basil, seasoning, 1 teaspoon paprika and cider from the soaked bread. Heat together to boiling point and pour over the meat balls.

4. Serve with soured cream or yoghurt spooned over meat dish and a sprinkling of chopped parsley on top.

Lamb Stuffed Dolmas

*Economical dish of cabbage leaves stuffed with meat filling and
tomato sauce which looks attractive and tastes delicious (serves 4, hot)*

1 pound lean minced lamb
8—12 medium sized green cabbage
   leaves
1—1½ oz butter
1 onion
½ oz flour
2 tablespoons tomato puree
1 tablespoon chopped parsley
6—7 oz cooked rice
a large pinch of mixed spice
¾—1 pint stock
2 tablespoons seasoned flour
¾—1 pint tomato sauce or brown gravy

Pre-heat oven to 350°F Mark 4

1. Put cabbage leaves into a pan of boiling salted water and cook for 2—3 minutes. Drain, rinse in cold water and let dry.

2. Heat butter and cook lamb and finely chopped onion until lamb is brown. Sprinkle in flour and stir well. Add tomato puree, chopped parsley, rice, mixed spice, seasoning and about 4 liquid oz of stock. Bring to boil and cook for 5 minutes. Then cool slightly. Put a spoonful on centre of each cabbage leaf and roll up neatly, tucking in ends to hold in stuffing while cooking. Roll in seasoned flour and place in a casserole, packing them tightly together. Pour over 8—10 liquid oz of stock to half cover the Dolmas.

3. Put lid on casserole and cook for 45 minutes until tender, adding more stock if necessary, and serve with a tomato sauce or brown gravy.

Navarin of Lamb or Mutton

*A hearty winter dish of lamb or mutton with lots of vegetables,
in a well-flavoured sauce (serves 4, hot)*

1½—2 pounds breast or shoulder of
   lamb or mutton
1½ tablespoons oil
½ oz flour
2 tablespoons tomato puree
1—1½ pints water
1 clove garlic
1 tablespoon mixed herbs
4 onions
4 carrots
2 small turnips
3—4 stalks celery
4—6 potatoes

1. Cut the meat into fairly big even-sized pieces. Heat oil, brown meat quickly all over. Add flour, brown this slightly. Add tomato puree, water and crushed garlic and bring to boil. Sprinkle in herbs and seasoning. Cover pan and simmer gently for 45 minutes.

2. Meanwhile prepare the vegetables. Peel onions, cut in quarters, peel carrots and slice. Peel turnips and quarter, and slice celery. Peel the potatoes and cut into thick slices.

3. Take a little of the fat from the top of the stewing meat and brown the vegetables in this. When the meat has been cooking for 45 minutes, add vegetables, but reserve potatoes to add later. When the vegetables have been cooking for about 30 minutes, add the sliced potatoes and cook for another 30 minutes.

4. Skim all fat from the top of the stew, and check seasoning before serving.

Lamb Hot Pot

*Budget casserole for the family, with tender meat and tasty
vegetables (serves 4, hot)*

1—1½ pounds lean lamb neck
   chops or shoulder slices
2 tablespoons oil
2 onions
4 potatoes
2 carrots
2 stalks celery
1 small can of tomatoes (or 3—4
   tablespoons tomato puree)
3 oz mushrooms
¾—1 pint water or stock
2 tablespoons herbs
1 bay leaf

Pre-heat oven to 350°F Mark 4

1. Heat oil, brown chops or slices quickly on both sides. Put into deep casserole and keep warm.

2. Cook thickly sliced onion, carrot, celery and potatoes in oil for a few minutes. Add drained tomatoes, or tomato puree, and mushrooms. Pour over meat. Moisten with ¾—1 pint of water or stock. Sprinkle herbs over top, add bay leaf and seasoning, and put in oven for about 1 hour, or until meat is tender.

Roast Lamb with Rosemary

*A simple roast of leg or shoulder with a strong aromatic flavor
(serves 6, hot)*

1 small leg or shoulder of lamb
1 clove garlic
fat for roasting
2 tablespoons dried rosemary leaves
     (or 2 sprigs fresh rosemary)
¼–½ pint of stock

Pre-heat oven to 425°F Mark 7

1. Cut the garlic into small slivers and with a sharp knife push these slivers into fatty parts of the meat, near the bone. Sprinkle the lamb with seasoning.

2. Heat fat in roasting pan. Put in meat. Baste with hot fat and cook for 15 minutes at 425°F. Then reduce heat to 375°F Mark 5 for the rest of the time, allowing 20 minutes per pound.

3. During last 45 minutes add rosemary, allowing it to flavour meat. When meat is cooked put onto serving dish. Make gravy with juices from roasting pan adding stock, but strain out rosemary leaves.

Curate's Lamb

A delicious variation for a simple budget meal (serves 4, hot)

2 breasts lamb (boned)
1 package sage and onion stuffing (or
     apple and lemon stuffing)
1 small can mushrooms
1 small can condensed mushroom soup
1 teaspoon Worcestershire sauce

Pre-heat oven to 425°F Mark 7

1. Prepare stuffing from instructions on package. Drain and add mushrooms.

2. Halve breasts of lamb, and place them in layers with stuffing mixture, with the two thicker pieces of lamb at the bottom and top. Tie with string to hold meat together during cooking. Place in an ovenproof dish, and cook in oven for 40 minutes.

3. Add Worcestershire sauce to heated soup, and pour over as a sauce. (An orange flavoured brown gravy can be used instead, if preferred.)

Irish Stew

*Cheaper cuts of lamb cooked slowly with onions and potatoes to
make a succulent stew (serves 4, hot)*

1½–2 pound middle neck or shoulder
     chops of lamb
4 medium potatoes
2–3 medium onions
1 tablespoon chopped parsley
¼ teaspoon chopped thyme
1 small bay leaf

1. Trim excess fat off chops, and cut potatoes and onions into quarters or thick slices.

2. Place meat and vegetables in a thick stew pan in layers, starting and ending with a layer of potatoes and sprinkling herbs and seasoning on each layer. Add ¾–1 pint water. Cover tightly with lid or foil.

3. Simmer stew over a gentle heat (or cook in low oven, 250°F. Mark ¾) for 2–2½ hours. Shake the pan from time to time to prevent the stew from sticking. Towards the end of the cooking time check the liquid in the pan. The consistency should be thick and creamy but not dry, so add a little more liquid if necessary.

(Sometimes 4 carrots and 1 turnip are added to this stew but this would not be accepted in Ireland as a true Irish stew.)

PORK, HAM & BACON: PARTY DISHES

Hawaiian Pork Chops

*Pork chops marinaded then baked with an unusual combination of
vegetables and fruit (serves 4, hot)*

4 pork chops
1 green pepper
1 medium sized onion
4 stalks white celery
2—3 tablespoons oil
½ oz butter
4 slices pineapple
½ pint chicken or veal stock
a little paprika
MARINADE
1 clove garlic, crushed
grated rind of half an orange
8 liquid oz soy sauce
2 liquid oz sherry or port
1/8 teaspoon grated fresh ginger
½ bay leaf, crushed

Pre-heat oven to 350°F Mark 4

1. Mix the marinade ingredients together with seasoning and pour over the
pork chops. Leave for at least 1 hour.

2. Remove seeds from pepper and cut 4 rings and chop the rest. Chop the
onion and the celery, mix the chopped vegetables together.

3. Remove the chops from marinade and dry on paper towel. Heat oil
and add butter and when foaming put in the chops and brown on both
sides, this takes about 2—3 minutes each side. Put them into an ovenproof
dish with a lid. Put a slice of pineapple on each chop and a spoonful of the
chopped vegetables. Mix the stock with the remaining marinade and pour
round the chops in the dish. Replace the cover and bake in a moderate
oven for about 1 hour. If the meat looks as if it is becoming dry add a
little more stock.

4. During the last 5 minutes put the pepper rings on top of the pineapple.
Just before serving dust each pineapple ring with paprika.

Stuffed Pork Chops

*Pork chops split and stuffed with apple, celery and lemon
stuffing and cooked in barbecue sauce (serves 4, hot)*

4 good sized pork chops
1½ oz butter
1 onion
1 stalk celery
1 apple
4 oz fresh breadcrumbs
3 tablespoons chopped parsley, thyme
    and a little sage
grated rind of ½ lemon
a few drops lemon juice
1 small egg
2—3 tablespoons oil
BARBECUE SAUCE
1 onion
1 clove garlic
1 tablespoon oil
1 level teaspoon flour
1 small can tomatoes
½—¾ pint brown stock
1½ tablespoons vinegar
1½ tablespoons Worcestershire sauce
1 tablespoon tomato chutney
1 level tablespoon sugar
1 teaspoon lemon juice
1 tablespoon chopped parsley and
    thyme
a large pinch of celery salt

Pre-heat oven to 350°F Mark 4

1. Make the barbecue sauce: Heat oil and cook chopped onion and
crushed garlic for 3—4 minutes to soften. Then remove lid and brown
slightly and add the flour and brown a little. Add canned tomatoes and
½ pint stock. Bring to boil. Add all other ingredients, cook for 15 minutes.
Strain and set aside.

2. Make stuffing: Cook chopped onion and celery in butter. Add to
breadcrumbs together with chopped apple, herbs and grated lemon rind.
Bind mixture with beaten egg, and dash of lemon juice, and if too dry add
a little milk or stock.

3. Make a cut in centre of the side of each pork chop, being careful to
make a pocket without piercing top or bottom surface of meat. Push
stuffing into pocket. Sew up the slits in the chops and then dry them.
Brown on both sides in a little hot oil. Then remove and put into ovenproof
dish.

4. Spoon over a little barbecue sauce thinned with a little extra stock.
Cook in oven for about 1 hour. Take out and remove threads, and serve
with barbecue sauce and boiled potatoes.

Sweet and Sour Pork

*Cubes of pork fried in a light batter and served with a sweet
and sour sauce (serves 4, hot)*

1½ pounds lean pork cut in small
   cubes
2 tablespoons oil
3 onions
2 carrots
2 tablespoons sweet pickle chutney
1 small can pineapple chunks
   (drained)
4 liquid oz pineapple juice
2 tablespoons soy sauce
4 liquid oz stock
1½ tablespoons sugar
1½ tablespoons vinegar
2 level tablespoons cornflour
2 eggs
2 level teaspoons flour
oil for deep frying

1. Make sauce: Heat oil, fry sliced onion and carrots until golden brown, about 10 minutes. Add chutney, pineapple chunks and juice, soy sauce, stock, sugar, vinegar and salt. Cover pan and cook slowly for 15 minutes. Mix 2 teaspoons cornflour with a little cold water. Add to sauce and heat again almost to boiling point, stirring all the time for 5—6 minutes. Season. Keep hot.

2. Heat oil and fry meat cubes until golden brown. This should take 3—4 minutes. Drain on paper towel.

3. Beat eggs, add flour and remaining cornflour and mix well. Re-heat fat until it will cook a bread cube in 20 seconds. Coat the pork pieces with the egg mixture and fry until golden brown, 1—2 minutes.

4. Drain and serve with plain boiled rice, pouring sauce over top.

Baked Glazed Ham

*Small ham baked in a honey, mustard and sugar glaze, served
with pineapple slices (serves 4—6, hot)*

2—3 pound canned ham
1½—2 tablespoons honey
grated rind of 1 orange
1 level teaspoon dry mustard
3 tablespoons brown sugar
4 liquid oz cider (or pineapple juice)
1 small can pineapple rings
½ oz butter
a dusting of sugar
6—8 canned sweet cherries

Pre-heat oven to 400°F Mark 6

1. Scrape jelly off canned ham and reserve. Place in baking tin.

2. Melt honey, spread over surface of ham. Mix orange rind, mustard, and brown sugar together and sprinkle over surface of meat. Pour cider (or pineapple juice) over ham. Add jelly from ham and baste very gently over ham without disturbing sugar coating. Bake for 30 minutes, basting after 15 minutes.

3. Melt butter in frying pan. Sprinkle pineapple slices with sugar and brown in butter on both sides. Serve around ham with cherries in the centre of each ring.

4. Use liquid from baking tin to make sauce, adding water and a squeeze of lemon if too sweet.

Danish Roast Stuffed Pork Fillet

*Roast tender pork with apple, lemon and prune stuffing, and
cream gravy, poached apples and redcurrant jelly (serves 4, hot)*

2 pork fillets weighing 1—1½
   pounds each
2 cooking apples
12 cooked stoned prunes
1 teaspoon grated lemon rind
a little lemon juice
2 tablespoons oil
½ oz butter
½ pint stock
1 tablespoon cream
2 apples
3—4 teaspoons redcurrant or cranberry
   jelly

Pre-heat oven to 450°F Mark 8

1. Split the fillets lengthwise without cutting completely in half. Beat the meat to flatten and tenderize it. Peel, core and dice cooking apples. Mix them with prunes and lemon rind together with seasoning, and spread half the mixture on each tenderloin. Sprinkle with a little melted butter and lemon juice. Roll each loin up like a Swiss roll, and tie in several places.

2. Pre-heat oil in roasting pan. Put loins in oven and baste. Brown the outside of meat for 10—15 minutes. Reduce heat to 375°F Mark 5 and cook for 50 minutes, basting frequently. When cooked and tender, remove.

meat for carving. Pour off excess fat and make gravy with residue and stock, adding cream at the last minute.

3. Carve the pork into slices for serving, and place on a hot serving dish. Surround the meat with a garnish of apples, peeled, halved, cored and poached in light syrup, with a teaspoonful of redcurrant or cranberry jelly in the center of each.

Normandy Pork Chops

Pork chops braised with carrots and sauce, and topped with caramel apple rings (serves 4, hot)

4 pork loin chops
1½ tablespoons oil
5 medium carrots
2 celery stalks
2 medium onions
1 clove garlic
½ oz flour
1 tablespoon tomato puree
¼ pint red wine or cider
½–¾ pint stock (or water and cube)
½ teaspoon chopped thyme
1 tablespoon chopped parsley
1 bay leaf
3 medium cooking apples, cored and peeled
1 level tablespoon brown sugar
2–3 oz quartered mushrooms

Pre-heat oven to 350°F Mark 4

1. Brown chops on both sides in hot oil, about 2 minutes on each side. Place in an ovenproof dish with lid and keep warm.

2. Fry chopped onions, crushed garlic, carrots, and celery cut into strips, until golden brown. Stir in flour, add tomato puree and stock. Bring gently to the boil stirring all the time. Add wine, or cider, and herbs. Pour vegetable mixture over chops and replace lid on dish. Bake in oven for 40 minutes.

3. Meanwhile, cut the apples into rings. After 20 minutes add mushrooms and stir these well into sauce. Lay apple rings in an overlapping layer all over dish. Sprinkle with brown sugar and finish cooking with the lid off dish.

African Savoury Pork

An unusual dish of diced pork cooked with onions, garlic, tomatoes, and chilli-flavoured sauce, and served with peanuts, cheese and noodles (Serves 6 hot)

**1—1½ pounds lean pork
2 large onions
1—2 tablespoons peanut oil
1 clove garlic
1—2 teaspoons lemon juice
3 large ripe tomatoes (or 1 small can tomatoes)
1—2 chillies (or ¼ teaspoon tabasco or chilli sauce)
1—2 teaspoons sugar
1 tablespoon Worcestershire sauce
10—12 oz raw noodles
4—6 oz grated cheddar cheese
2—3 oz salted peanuts**

1. Dice pork. Cook pork and chopped onions together in oil until golden brown. Add garlic and lemon juice. Stir well.

2. Skin and chop tomatoes; seed and chop chillies. Add them to mixture, with sugar, Worcestershire sauce, pepper and a little salt. Simmer gently for 20—30 minutes or until pork is tender and thoroughly cooked.

3. Meanwhile, cook noodles in plenty of boiling salted water for 10—15 minutes until tender. Drain, rinse with hot water. Allow to dry slightly.

4. When pork is cooked and just before serving, mix in cheese and peanuts. Check seasoning. Serve the pork mixture and noodles together in one large dish, or serve the noodles separately.

Chinese Baked Spare Ribs

Tasty spare ribs cooked with spicy marinade (serves 4—6, hot)

**3—4 pounds pork spare ribs
½ clove garlic
2 liquid oz soy sauce
2 liquid oz sherry
2 tablespoons honey
1/8 teaspoon ginger**

Pre-heat oven to 350°F Mark 4

1. Crush garlic, mix ingredients together, add seasoning. Pour mixture over spare ribs. Leave to marinate overnight or longer, turning as often as possible.

2. Bake spare ribs for 1¼—1½ hours, basting every 15 minutes with marinade. The ribs should be well browned and meat tender.

3. Serve with rice and salad.

PORK, HAM & BACON: EVERYDAY DISHES

Ham Mousseline

A light mousse of ham, cream and eggs (serves 4, hot)

8–10 oz minced ham
1 oz butter
¾ oz flour
6–8 liquid oz milk
3 eggs
ground nutmeg or mace
6–8 liquid oz cream
1 tablespoon chopped parsley

1. Pound the minced ham until really fine, or liquidize. Add a white sauce made with the butter, flour and milk; cook for a few moments. Let cool.

2. Separate egg yolks from whites. Mix yolks with cream and add to ham, with parsley, salt, pepper and nutmeg or mace. Beat the egg whites until stiff, fold into the meat mixture and put into a buttered dish large enough to allow it to rise.

3. Place this dish, with a buttered paper tied over the top, into the top of a steamer and steam for 1¼ hours.

4. It can then be served either in the same dish, or after a few moments turned out onto a warmed flat plate, with a cheese sauce and buttered spinach or green peas.

Sunday Double Decker Sandwich

Simple supper dish of layered bacon, tomatoes and cheese (serves 4, hot)

1. Remove crusts and toast bread on one side only. Spread untoasted side with butter. Halve bacon rashers and lay on bread. Grill until bacon is cooked and then spread with mustard, if desired.

2. Slice tomatoes and place slices on top of bacon. Brush with a little melted butter and grill for a few minutes. Sprinkle onion over tomato and grill for another minute.

3. Cover tomato with cheese. (Make sure tomatoes are thickly covered.) Grill until cheese bubbles. Pile one on top of another to make 4 sandwiches and grill again until top layer of cheese is well browned. Serve at once.

8 rashers of bacon
8 slices white bread
2—3 oz butter
2 teaspoons mustard
4 large tomatoes
1—2 chopped onions
6—8 oz grated cheese

Pre-heat Grill

Savoury Pork Fillet

A light, fully-flavoured pork dish, quick to prepare (serves 4, hot)

1. Cut fillets in slices and lightly brown in oil until golden brown all over, about 4—5 minutes, sprinkling on paprika. Remove from pan and place in a flameproof dish. Cook quartered mushrooms for 2—3 minutes in the oil and add to pork slices.

2. Pour over the tomato sauce, season, and cook for about 10—12 minutes over gentle heat.

3. Spoon over soured cream, decorate with a sprinkling of parsley, and serve with potatoes.

2 pork fillets
1—2 tablespoons oil
1 level teaspoon paprika
10—12 mushrooms
1 small can tomato sauce (or 3—4 tablespoons tomato puree, a little onion and 4—6 tablespoons stock)
3—4 tablespoons soured cream
a little chopped parsley

Ham Toasts

A light savoury mixture of ham and eggs, quick and easy to make (serves 4, hot)

8—10 oz minced ham
2 teaspoons chutney (optional)
4—6 eggs
2 tablespoons cream
a pinch of cayenne pepper
4 large slices bread
2 level teaspoons mustard
1½ oz butter
1 tablespoon chopped parsley

1. Mix the minced ham with the chutney. Beat eggs with cream, and stir into ham. Add salt, pepper, and cayenne pepper to taste.

2. Toast the bread, remove crusts and spread with butter and mustard. Keep warm in an ovenproof dish.

3. Melt remaining butter and when foaming pour in ham and egg mixture. Cook as if making scrambled eggs. When mixture thickens spoon onto toast. Sprinkle top with chopped parsley and serve at once.

Belgian Ham and Celery Rolls

Celery hearts, rolled in ham and baked in delicious cheese sauce (serves 4, hot)

4 large slices lean ham
1 large can or 2 medium cans celery
    hearts (allowing 1 celery heart per
    person)
1 oz butter
¾ oz flour
½—¾ pint milk
4 oz grated cheddar cheese
½ teaspoon French mustard
2 tablespoons dried breadcrumbs

Pre-heat oven to 350°F Mark 4

1. Drain canned celery hearts. If they are very large cut in half. Wrap each in a slice of ham, and put ham and celery rolls in buttered fireproof dish.

2. Make cheese sauce: Melt butter, remove from heat, stir in flour and add milk. Bring to the boil, stirring all the time. Add 3 oz of the grated cheese, mustard and seasoning, and stir over heat until cheese has melted.

3. Pour sauce over ham and celery rolls. Sprinkle with remaining cheese and breadcrumbs. Bake in oven for 15—20 minutes. The top should be golden brown and crisp.

(The celery hearts can be replaced with heads of chicory pre-cooked in boiling salted water with the juice of ½ lemon for 20 minutes. Canned asparagus spears can also be used with no extra cooking.)

Stuffed Ham Rolls

Slices of ham or bacon folded around mushroom stuffing and baked (serves 4, hot)

8 round slices ham
1 oz butter
1 large onion
1 clove garlic
1½—2 oz chopped mushrooms
1—2 oz white breadcrumbs
½ pound minced fat bacon
2 tablespoons parsley and thyme
1 egg
2 tablespoons cranberry or redcurrant
    jelly
½ pint stock

Pre-heat oven to 400°F Mark 6

1. Heat butter and cook finely chopped onion with lid on pan until soft but not brown. Add garlic and chopped mushrooms and cook for a few more minutes.

2. Mix breadcrumbs, minced bacon, and herbs in a bowl. Add onion mixture. Mix well. Beat egg and add to stuffing with the cranberry or redcurrant jelly and seasoning. Add about 2—3 liquid oz stock, to make a fairly moist stuffing.

3. Divide the stuffing into equal portions. Wrap one slice of ham or bacon round each portion, fixing with a cocktail stick. Put the ham rolls in a buttered baking pan. Pour a little stock around the rolls and cook in oven for about 20 minutes.

4. Serve on risotto rice (see lamb kebabs p. 82) leaving out the saffron (or with saute potatoes).

Pork Marseillaise

Fried pork chops, with a delicious puree of onions (serves 4, hot)

4 pork loin chops ¾—1 inch thick
4 onions
8 liquid oz chicken or veal stock
1 large or 2 small egg yolks
a dash of oil
2 oz fresh white breadcrumbs
2—3 oz butter

Pre-heat oven to 450°F Mark 8

1. Peel and slice onions and cook until tender in stock. Puree in liquidizer or put through sieve. Season and keep warm.

2. Coat chops with egg yolks mixed with salt and a dash of oil. Then roll in breadcrumbs. Melt the butter and when foaming fry the chops for about 7—10 minutes until golden brown on each side. Drain on kitchen paper and put into the oven for a further 10 minutes.

3. To serve, pile onion puree in centre of a dish and arrange fried chops around the edge.

Bacon, Egg and Corn Flan

Delicious, light bacon, egg and sweetcorn flan, suitable for supper or picnic (serves 4, hot or cold)

6 oz shortcrust pastry or
    1 packet shortcrust pastry mix
4—6 rashers bacon
3 eggs
large pinch dry mustard
3 tablespoons grated cheddar cheese
3—5 tablespoons canned sweetcorn
2½ liquid oz milk

Pre-heat oven to 375°F Mark 5

1. Roll out pastry and line flan dish or ring. Prick the bottom and bake filled with crumpled greaseproof paper filled with rice or beans. Cook for 15 minutes. Take out paper and beans and let flan case cool.

2. Fry bacon for 2—3 minutes on each side, cool and cut into small pieces and sprinkle over bottom of flan case.

3. Beat eggs together with seasoning and mustard. Add cheese, corn and milk. Pour into flan case. Bake in oven for about 25—30 minutes until mixture is set.

Bacon with Parsley Sauce

*Quick, simple dish of bacon with a delicious parsley sauce
(serves 4, hot)*

12 or 16 rashers lean bacon

SAUCE
1½ oz butter
1 tablespoon finely chopped onion
¾ oz flour
8 liquid oz milk
4—5 tablespoons chopped parsley
a pinch of nutmeg
1 tablespoon cream (optional)

1. Make sauce: Melt butter and cook onion for a few minutes with lid on pan. Add flour and mix well. Add warmed milk and mix until smooth before returning to stove. Bring to the boil stirring constantly, boil for 2 minutes, adding parsley, salt, pepper and a pinch of powdered nutmeg. (If you have a tablespoon of cream this can be added now.)

2. Remove rind from bacon and grill or fry until crisp.

3. Serve the bacon hot with mashed or boiled potatoes and a good helping of parsley sauce for each serving.

Toad in the Hole

Traditional popular dish of sausages in batter (serves 4, hot)

12 sausages
4 oz plain flour
½ level teaspoon salt
1 egg
½ pint milk and water mixed

Pre-heat oven to 425°F Mark 7

1. Sift flour and salt into a bowl. Make a well in centre and put in egg and half liquid. Mix together and gradually draw in flour and beat until it is a smooth batter, about 4—5 minutes. Add remaining liquid. Set aside for at least 30 minutes.

2. Grease a baking tin or shallow ovenproof dish. Put in sausages. Pour batter over. Bake for 40—45 minutes until batter is well risen and brown and sausages are cooked.

3. Serve with brown gravy.

Mock Goose

A filling dish of sausage meat flavoured with onions and sage to resemble goose and served with a sharp apple sauce (serves 4, hot)

1 pound sausage meat
1½—2 tablespoons dripping or lard
2—3 medium onions
1 egg
1—1½ oz breadcrumbs
¼ pint cider
1½—2 level teaspoons of chopped
    dried sage
5—6 cooking apples
a strip of lemon rind
1 level tablespoon sugar

Pre-heat oven to 375°F Mark 5

1. Melt the dripping or lard, slice and cook onions until a medium brown. Add the sausage meat and cook for a few minutes. Beat the egg, and add it and breadcrumbs, cider and sage. Mix well and season. Pack into ovenproof dish and bake in oven for 40—45 minutes.

2. For apple sauce: Put the apples, lemon rind and 2—3 tablespoons of water into a saucepan and cook until apples are soft. Put through a fine strainer or liquidize and add sugar. (The sauce should not be too sweet.) Allow to cool and serve with Mock Goose.

Sausages with Braised Red Cabbage

Red cabbage, cooked with apple and vinegar, makes a delicious accompaniment for sausages (serves 4, hot)

16—20 pork sausages
1 red cabbage about 2 pounds
1 oz bacon fat or butter
1 large onion
2 tablespoons vinegar
2 cooking apples
1 level tablespoon sugar

1. Remove and discard outer leaves from cabbage. Shred the rest finely. Heat the bacon fat or butter in casserole. Chop onion and cook for a few minutes without burning. Add cabbage. Mix well. Add ½ pint of water, vinegar, salt and pepper.

2. Cover and cook for about one hour. Add peeled chopped apple and sugar and cook for another hour stirring from time to time. Remove lid, boil if necessary to evaporate any extra liquid.

3. Grill or bake sausages until brown. Serve with mashed potato and cabbage.

Stuffed Sausageburgers

Hot dogs with a difference. Quick to prepare, tasty to eat.
(serves 4, hot)

1 pound skinless pork sausages
8 hamburger rolls
2 oz butter
1 teaspoon mustard
1—2 oz grated cheddar cheese
1 tablespoon chutney

Pre-heat oven to 350°F Mark 4

1. Brush sausages with a little melted fat and then grill for about 7—10 minutes until cooked all over. Keep warm.

2. Split buns or rolls, spread with half the butter and mustard.

3. Mix the cheese with rest of butter and chutney. Split sausages lengthwise, fill with cheese and chutney mixture. Put one sausage in each bun. Put in oven to warm through.

Ham with Orange and Raisin Sauce

Slices of cooked ham reheated in a clear orange raisin sauce
(serves 4, hot)

4 large or 8 small slices lean cooked
    ham (cut thick)
2—3 oz raisins
1 orange
1 level tablespoon cornflour
a dash of lemon juice
2 oz brown sugar
½ oz butter

Pre-heat oven to 350°F Mark 4

1. Place the slices of ham overlapping in a fireproof dish.

2. Put raisins into pan, cover with water and bring to the boil slowly. Simmer for 4—5 minutes.

3. Remove outer rind from orange. Cut into thin strips and put in a pan of boiling water for 1 minute. Drain and remove. Mix orange and lemon juice with cornflour until smooth. Now add sugar. Pour mixture into the pan with raisins and water, and stir over heat until this thickens and is clear. Stir in orange rind and butter and pour over ham slices.

4. Bake in oven for about 10—15 minutes.

VEAL

Veal Escalopes Parmesan

Tender slices of veal coated in egg, flour and cheese, fried in butter and garnished with lemon, butter and parsley (serves 4, hot)

4 thin veal escalopes (or slices cut from
    leg of veal)
1 large egg
½ tablespoon oil
3 tablespoons flour
a large pinch powdered garlic
2 oz grated parmesan cheese
1½—2 oz butter
juice of ½ lemon
1 tablespoon finely chopped parsley

1. Beat out escalopes between greaseproof paper. Mix egg with oil and beat. Add seasoning and garlic to flour, and mix with cheese. Brush escalopes with egg mixture, then press into cheese and flour until completely coated.

2. Melt butter and fry escalopes until golden brown, about 5—6 minutes on each side. Place on a warm serving dish and keep hot.

3. Add lemon juice to butter in pan. Reheat and pour over escalopes just before serving. Decorate with parsley.

Blanquette de Veau

*Classic French white stew
of tender veal with
button mushrooms, carrots,
and baby onions (serves 4—6, hot)*

2 pounds veal from shoulder or breast
2 oz butter
1 onion
3—4 medium carrots
1 oz flour
1—1¼ pints chicken or veal stock
parsley stems
1 bay leaf
a sprig of thyme (or 1/8 teaspoon)
    dried thyme)
12 button mushrooms
12 baby or pickling onions
½ pint cream
1 large or 2 small egg yolks
a squeeze of lemon

Pre-heat oven to 350°F Mark 4

1. Cut veal into cubes about 1¼ inches square. Put into pan with enough cold water to cover and a little salt. Bring to the boil and cook for 5 minutes. Skim off the scum which rises to the surface. Drain meat and wash well with cold water. Dry.

2. Melt 1½ oz of butter and cook veal cubes slowly together with quartered onion and carrots, shaking frequently and not allowing them to brown at all. Stir in flour, and then add stock, parsley, bay leaf and thyme. Bring to the boil and place in oven or simmer on stove for 1—1½ hours until veal is tender.

3. Meanwhile peel baby onions and cook in salted water for 10—15 minutes. Drain. Melt remaining ½ oz butter and cook mushrooms for a few minutes. Add to onions.

4. Remove veal from stove and place meat in dish, adding carrots, baby onions and mushrooms. Strain cooking liquid and boil to reduce quantity slightly. Remove from heat and cool slightly. Beat egg yolks with cream, add a little hot sauce to this and strain into sauce. Add lemon juice. Do not boil under any circumstances after this point. Pour over meat and vegetables and serve at once.

5. Serve with mashed or riced potatoes, or plain boiled rice.

Osso Bucco

A favourite Italian veal dish (serves 4, hot)

4 meaty slices of shin of veal, 2—3
    inches thick
2—3 oz flour
2—3 tablespoons olive oil
¾ oz butter
1 medium onion
3 stalks celery
1—2 cloves garlic
1½ tablespoons tomato puree
2—3 liquid oz veal or chicken stock
2—3 liquid oz dry white wine
1 teaspoon chopped basil and lemon
    thyme
1 tablespoon chopped parsley
½ lemon

Pre-heat oven to 350°F Mark 4

1. Add salt and pepper to flour, and coat pieces of meat with it. Heat oil, and add butter. When foaming, put in meat and lightly brown all over. Remove and keep warm in a casserole.

2. Slice onions and celery finely, crush garlic, and brown lightly. Add tomato puree, stock and wine to vegetables, and season to taste.

3. Pour this mixture over meat and put casserole with tightly fitting lid into oven for 1½—2 hours. After about 1 hour add the herbs, half the parsley and a few fine strips of lemon rind. Continue cooking for another hour or so, test meat and if not completely done, cook until tender.

4. Drain meat and vegetables onto serving platter. Boil up sauce to reduce slightly, add lemon juice to taste and pour over meat. Sprinkle top with remaining chopped parsley and serve with boiled pasta or a plain risotto.

Veal Cutlets in Tarragon Cream Sauce

Thin slices of veal finished in a rich sauce (serves 4, hot)

4 thin veal cutlets
2—3 oz butter
2½ liquid oz Madeira (or sherry)
¼ pint cream
1 teaspoon fresh tarragon leaves (or
    teaspoon dried tarragon soaked in
    water)

Pre-heat oven to 300°F Mark 2

1. Beat cutlets between oiled greaseproof paper until very thin. Heat half the butter in a frying pan. When foaming, cook half the cutlets for about 3 minutes on each side until golden brown. Remove and keep warm. Repeat with remaining cutlets.

2. Add Madeira or sherry to liquid in frying pan and cook for a few minutes to reduce. Add cream and lightly bruised tarragon leaves. Bring to the boil and season to taste.

3. Pour sauce over cutlets and cook in oven for about 6—8 minutes. Serve immediately.

Wiener Schnitzel

*Tender wafers of veal fried in butter until crisp and garnished with
lemon, capers, paprika, olives and white of hard boiled egg (serves 4, hot)*

1. Beat out escalopes between pieces of waxed paper until wafer thin. Toss
in seasoned flour until completely coated. Shake to remove excess. Beat
the raw egg with a few drips of oil and some salt. Brush each escalope with
this then toss in the dried white crumbs. (A paper bag is a good container
for this process.)

2. Melt butter in frying pan. When foaming, cook escalopes for 3—4
minutes on each side until they are golden brown and crisp.

3. Place on a hot dish and garnish the top of each escalope with 1 slice of
lemon. In the centre of this place an olive, and curl an anchovy fillet
around the olive. Surround this with a portion of chopped egg white,
chopped capers and paprika. Sprinkle all over with chopped parsley.
Decorate with sieved egg yolk, if desired.

4. Serve at once, with the remaining butter from the frying pan as a sauce.
(Extra butter can be added.)

4 large thin veal escalopes
1—2 oz flour
1 egg
**5—6 tablespoons of dried white bread-
    crumbs**
1—1½ oz butter
1 hard-boiled egg
4 slices of lemon
4 anchovies
2 teaspoons capers
2 level teaspoons paprika
4 olives
2 tablespoons chopped parsley

Jellied Veal Loaf

A delicious light concoction of veal and hard-boiled eggs (serves 4–6, cold)

1 pound lean veal
¼ pound bacon
2 hard-boiled eggs
1 tablespoon chopped parsley
1 pint well-flavoured chicken or veal stock
½—¾ oz gelatine

Pre-heat oven to 325°F Mark 3

1. Cut veal into small strips, dice bacon and bring to boil; drain and rinse with cold water.

2. Cut hard-boiled eggs into slices. Arrange meat and eggs in layers in a loaf tin or ring mould. Sprinkle each layer with parsley, salt and pepper. Pour 12 liquid oz stock over meat. Cover with foil, cook in oven for about 1½ hours, and remove to cool.

3. Soak gelatine in remaining stock and melt over gentle heat. Pour this over the meat and put in a cool place to set. When cold put in refrigerator for a short time or until needed.

4. Turn out the jellied veal and decorate dish with green salad, raw cauliflower, watercress and cucumber.

Veal Cutlets Cordon Bleu

Veal cutlets with a delicious stuffing of ham and cheese in a wine sauce (serves 4, hot)

4 thick veal cutlets
4 oz minced cooked ham
4 oz grated gruyere cheese
garlic salt
1 oz butter
1—1½ oz flour
2—3 tablespoons oil
8 liquid oz white wine
4 liquid oz chicken stock
2 level tablespoons chopped parsley and tarragon

Pre-heat oven to 350°F Mark 4

1. Cut a pocket in each cutlet from boneless side, being careful not to pierce the outer surface. Mix ham and cheese together, adding garlic salt and pepper. Melt ½ oz butter and stir in. Stuff cutlets carefully. Do not overfill. Seal openings with toothpicks, and roll cutlets in seasoned flour.

2. Heat oil. Add remaining butter and when foaming fry cutlets taking about 3 minutes to brown each side. Place in ovenproof dish. Add stock and wine to liquid in pan and bring to boil. Stir in chopped herbs. Pour sauce over cutlets and cook in oven until veal is tender, about 20—30 minutes. Remove before serving.

Veal Cutlets in Papillotes

A highly unusual way of cooking veal which keeps all the flavour inside the parcels (serves 4, hot)

4 veal cutlets or slices
1 oz butter
2 oz mushrooms
2 shallots or 1 small onion
a little lemon juice
2½ liquid oz white wine
1 tablespoon thick cream
2—3 tablespoons oil

Pre-heat oven to 375°F Mark 5

1. Cut out 4 large heart shaped pieces of greaseproof paper or foil, at least twice the size of the pieces of veal. (These are the papillotes.) Beat out cutlets on a wet board and season. Brush paper or foil hearts all over with oil and then lay cutlets on one half of the heart near the centre line.

2. Melt butter and cook chopped mushrooms and onion or shallot for 5 minutes. Add lemon juice and white wine and seasoning, cook for a few more minutes to reduce liquid and then add thick cream. Put ¼ of this mixture on each slice of veal. Fold the empty half of the paper over the top and seal the edges together by folding and pinching to make a tight seal.

3. Put in a well buttered baking dish and cook in oven for 25—30 minutes, when the paper should have puffed up. Serve in the papillotes to conserve the flavour.

Saltimbocca

Tender rolls of veal and ham, flavoured with sage and wine (serves 4, hot)

8 thin slices tender veal from leg
8 thin slices ham
8 small fresh sage leaves (or pinches of dried sage)
1—1½ oz butter
6 liquid oz Marsala or white wine
8 slices bread
¼ pint oil
1 oz butter

Pre-heat oven to 350°F Mark 4

1. Beat out veal slices between greaseproof paper. Place a thin slice of ham on each veal slice and then a sage leaf (or a small pinch of dried sage). Season with salt and pepper. Roll each slice up tightly and use cocktail sticks to fasten rolls securely.

2. Heat butter and brown the rolls all over for about 5—7 minutes. Add Marsala or other wine and a little salt and pepper. Cover pan and cook gently in oven (or on top of the cooker) for about 15 minutes, when meat should be tender.

3. Cut bread into rounds, fry in oil and butter until golden brown and crisp.

4. Place each roll on a fried bread crouton and serve around a dish of spinach cooked with butter.

Hungarian Veal Chops

Veal chops in a paprika and white wine flavoured sauce finished with cream (serves 4, hot)

4 veal chops
1—1½ oz butter
1 small onion or shallot
1 tablespoon paprika
¼ pint white wine
¼ pint cream
chopped parsley

Pre-heat oven to 350°F Mark 4

1. Mix 2 teaspoons paprika with 1 level teaspoon salt and black pepper. Sprinkle on both sides of chops and rub in gently.

2. Melt 1 oz butter in frying pan and cook chops for about 2 minutes on each side until well browned. Remove and keep warm. Now add finely chopped onion. Cook gently until tender. Then add remaining paprika, put on lid and cook for another minute or two. Return chops to pan and add a few drops of wine. Bake for about 20 minutes in oven, then place on serving dish to keep warm.

3. Pour white wine into pan and reduce by cooking for a few minutes, stir in cream, simmer again; then stir in remaining butter. Pour over chops, sprinkle top with chopped parsley and serve with plain boiled noodles.

Veal in Soured Cream Sauce

A simple veal stew flavoured with soured cream and caraway seeds (serves 4, hot)

1½ pounds shoulder of veal without
    bone
2—3 oz flour
1 level teaspoon salt
¼ teaspoon black pepper
1 level teaspoon paprika
2—3 tablespoons oil
1 onion
1 clove garlic
¼ pint soured cream
1 teaspoon caraway seeds
1 tablespoon chopped parsley

Pre-heat oven to 350°F Mark 4

1. Cut veal into squares. Roll in flour mixed with salt, pepper and paprika. Heat the oil and fry the veal until golden brown all over. Remove to a casserole and keep warm.

2. Cook finely chopped onion and crushed garlic in remaining oil for a couple of minutes then add ½—¾ pint of hot water and bring to boil. Add meat and stir in. Return to casserole and cover with lid and cook in oven for 35—40 minutes (or simmer on top of cooker) until veal is tender.

3. Stir in soured cream and heat gently without boiling. Sprinkle over the caraway seeds and parsley, and serve with buttered noodles.

Scallopini of Minced Veal

Delicately flavoured light fried cakes of minced veal with a white wine sauce (serves 4, hot)

1 pound minced raw veal
1 tablespoon finely chopped onion
grated rind of ½ a lemon
1 tablespoon chopped parsley
a pinch of mace or nutmeg
a squeeze of lemon juice
1 beaten egg
flour
3 tablespoons oil
1½ oz butter
2½ liquid oz chicken stock
2½ liquid oz white wine

1. Mix veal with onion, lemon rind and parsley. Mix well, adding seasoning and a squeeze of lemon juice. Then mix in beaten egg.

2. Flour a board with seasoned flour and divide meat into 8 equal portions. Roll each portion into a ball. Roll out with a floured rolling pin to the size of small slice not more than ½ inch thick. Dust each side with seasoned flour.

3. Heat half the oil and butter in frying pan, cook 4 slices for about 5—7 minutes on each side or until a good brown. Turn onto a serving dish. Repeat process with remaining slices.

4. Reheat remaining oil and butter. Add stock and white wine, bring to the boil, season and cook for a minute or two. Pour over the scallopini and serve with potatoes and lemon quarters.

Veal and Pork Roulette

A substantial meat loaf served with an unusual mushroom sauce when hot or with salad and pickles when cold (serves 4, hot or cold)

½ pound raw minced pork
½ pound raw minced veal
2 rashers bacon
2 tablespoons chopped onion
2 slices stale white bread
1 large egg
2—3 tablespoons dry white
    breadcrumbs
oil
10—12 medium-sized mushrooms
1 onion
1—1½ oz butter
1 teaspoon Worcestershire sauce
½ oz flour
8—10 liquid oz fresh or soured cream

Pre-heat oven to 450°F Mark 8

1. Mix minced meat, bacon and chopped onion together. Remove bread crusts and soak bread for a few minutes in cold water. Squeeze dry with the hands and add to meat, mixing thoroughly. Now add beaten egg and seasoning.

2. Shape into loaf or put into a buttered loaf tin. Coat or sprinkle with breadcrumbs and bake in the oven for 1—1¼ hours having sprinkled a little hot oil over the top to prevent the breadcrumbs becoming too dry and brown.

3. Make sauce: Chop mushrooms and onion and cook in butter for 10—15 minutes without burning. Add the Worcestershire sauce and then flour. Mix in well. Just before serving, mix in cream, reheat without boiling and serve.

Danish Veal Frikadeller

Fluffy meat balls fried lightly and cooked in a spicy tomato sauce, with the interesting addition of black olives and lemon quarters (serves 4, hot)

1. Put veal with minced fat and finely chopped onion in a bowl. Put bread into a dish and cover with milk or water and leave to soak for 10—15 minutes, then squeeze dry and add bread to meat. Reserve 8—10 liquid oz of liquid. Add chopped herbs and grated lemon rind. Put mixture through the fine mincer once again.

2. Beat the meat mixture well by hand adding the reserved liquid gradually. This beating is important as it affects the final lightness of the Frikadeller. Add salt, pepper, paprika and cayenne pepper, and mix in well. Spoon mixture onto a damp board and roll to marble-sized Frikadeller. Roll these in seasoned flour.

3. Heat butter in frying pan. Cook Frikadeller until brown all over, and place in a shallow casserole. Pour over tomato sauce (see p. 85 — *Spaghetti with Meat Balls*). There should be enough to cover the Frikadeller completely. Then bake for about 20 minutes in oven.

4. Just before serving spoon the yoghurt or soured cream over the top of the dish. Add the black olives, and serve with plain boiled rice, noodles or potatoes, and lemon quarters.

1 pound finely minced veal (or veal and pork mixed)
3 tablespoons veal (or pork) fat
1 onion
4 oz crustless bread
2—3 tablespoons chopped parsley and thyme
grated rind of ½ lemon
¼ teaspoon paprika
a dash of cayenne pepper
4—5 tablespoons flour
2—3 oz butter
tomato sauce (see p. 85)
3—4 tablespoons yoghurt or soured cream
3 oz black olives

Pre-heat oven to 350°F Mark 4

Family Terrine Maison

Delicious cold meat loaf covered with a coating of bacon and jellied stock (serves 4—6, cold)

1. Mince pork or veal coarsely, add sausage meat and finely minced liver. Chop onion very finely. Hard boil egg and chop coarsely. Add to mixture with breadcrumbs and chopped herbs. Season well with salt, black pepper, powdered mace and garlic powder if desired.

2. Line an ovenproof lidded casserole with bacon rashers (or a long loaf tin using foil to cover). Put half the mixture into casserole and lay any remaining slices of bacon over this layer. Fill dish with rest of mixture and flatten, leaving a slight depression in the centre. Put bay leaf in this. Cover with lid or foil and seal with flour and water paste made with 6—7 tablespoons of flour mixed with 5—6 tablespoons water. It should be stiff.

3. Cook for about 1—1½ hours. When cooked remove bay leaf. Cover with a piece of greaseproof paper and a heavy weight. Leave overnight. Then turn out onto a serving dish and spoon setting stock over the top to make jelly coating.

4. Decorate with lettuce leaves, quartered tomatoes, slices of cucumber and watercress around the dish, and cut in thick slices to serve.

¾ pound lean veal (or pork)
¼ pound pork sausage meat
½ pound liver (lamb or pork)
1 onion
1 egg
3—4 tablespoons fresh white breadcrumbs
1 tablespoon chopped parsley
½ teaspoon chopped thyme
a pinch of mace
a little garlic powder (optional)
12 rashers thinly cut bacon
1 bay leaf
6—7 tablespoons flour
¼ pint jellied stock

Pre-heat oven to 325°F Mark 3

Hungarian Veal Goulash

Traditional Hungarian dish of veal in a smooth onion sauce flavoured with paprika, tomatoes and finished with soured cream (serves 4, hot)

1½ pounds tender boneless leg or
    shoulder of veal
2 oz butter
1 pound onions
1 clove garlic
1 level tablespoon paprika
1½ tablespoons tomato puree
1 red pepper
½–¾ pint chicken or veal stock
½ teaspoon chopped thyme
½ teaspoon chopped marjoram
1 bay leaf
½ pint soured cream
1 tablespoon chopped parsley

Pre-heat oven to 325°F Mark 3

1. Heat half the butter and cook finely sliced onion and crushed garlic in a covered pan until they are soft and transparent but not brown. Make into a puree by using liquidizer or putting through a fine sieve. Then put into the bottom of a casserole, mixing in the paprika, tomato puree and herbs.

2. Cut veal into 2 inch squares and cook quickly in the remaining butter without allowing it to colour too deeply. Put on top of the onion puree and add the seeded and diced pepper. Add enough stock to cover meat, adding salt and pepper. Cook in covered casserole in oven (or simmer on a gentle heat) for about 1 hour until meat is tender.

3. Just before serving spoon over soured cream and sprinkle with chopped parsley. Serve with noodles, macaroni or riced potatoes.

LIVER, KIDNEYS & OTHER OFFAL

Saute of Liver with Orange

Liver cooked in delicious sauce, topped with orange, and served with rice pilaff (serves 4–6, hot)

8 slices veal or lamb liver
3–4 oz butter
2 onions
6 oz rice
2 pints beef stock
2 level tablespoons mixed herbs
2 level tablespoons flour
cayenne pepper
1 clove garlic
6 liquid oz red wine
2 small oranges cut in slices
1–2 tablespoons sugar

Pre-heat oven to 350°F Mark 4

1. To make pilaff: Melt 1 oz butter and cook 1 onion gently for 2–3 minutes. Add rice and cook again for a few minutes. Pour on ½–¾ pint stock, add 1 tablespoon herbs, seasoning and cover with foil or a tightly fitting lid, and bake in oven for 20–25 minutes.

2. Remove outer skin from liver. Mix flour with a little salt, pepper and cayenne pepper, and roll the liver in this mixture until it is covered. Heat 1½ oz butter, cook liver slices quickly until both sides are brown. Put in a dish and keep warm.

3. Add finely chopped onion and crushed garlic to pan and cook for 5–6 minutes until golden brown. Sprinkle in remaining flour. Add wine and remaining stock and bring to the boil. Add herbs and seasoning. Pour sauce over liver and cook in oven for five minutes.

4. Melt 1–1½ oz butter in clean frying pan. Sprinkle the orange slices with sugar and put sugar side down in pan. Fry until brown, then sprinkle top of slices with remaining sugar and brown second side. Arrange orange slices over liver. Serve hot with rice pilaff.

Liver and Bacon Burgers

A delicious mixture of liver, bacon and onions, formed into light, small burgers and served with tomato or Provencale sauce (serves 4, hot)

½ pound lamb liver
¼ pound bacon
2 onions
2–3 oz lard or bacon fat
2 oz fresh white breadcrumbs
3 teaspoons tomato puree
Worcestershire sauce
1 egg
2–3 oz flour
2 cloves garlic
1½–2 oz chopped mushroom stems
   and peelings
4 tablespoons oil
¼ pint strong beef stock (or water
   and beef cube)
¼ pint wine or cider
parsley, thyme and a bay leaf

1. Prepare liver and bacon by removing any skin, rind, gristle or bone, and cut into small pieces. Chop 1 onion coarsely. Melt 1 oz of lard or bacon fat in a pan. Cook liver, bacon and onion together in this for several minutes, not long enough to cook completely, but to stiffen liver. Remove from heat and cool slightly.

2. Put breadcrumbs into a large bowl. Mince liver, bacon and onion in mincer. Do not make too fine. Add mixture to the breadcrumbs. Mix well. Add seasoning, 1 teaspoon tomato puree, a dash of Worcestershire sauce, and half the beaten egg, reserving the second half which may not be required. (The mixture should not be too soft to hold its shape when divided into small burgers.)

3. Divide mixture on a floured board and shape with floured hands into small burgers. Coat these with flour, and fry the burgers for about 5–6 minutes on each side in lard or bacon fat. Drain on paper towel and serve with a strong tomato sauce, or piles of fried onions and a Provencale sauce.

4. Make Provencale sauce: Chop 1 onion finely. Cook onion, crushed garlic, and mushrooms for a few minutes in oil to soften. Stir in ¾ oz flour, add stock and wine or cider. Bring to boil. Add herbs and seasoning. Simmer for 15 minutes. Remove bay leaf and add 2 teaspoons tomato puree. Season to taste and serve.

Risotto alla Bolognese

Tasty dish of liver cooked with rice, easy to prepare (serves 4, hot)

½—¾ pound lamb or calf liver
1 onion
1 clove garlic
1—1½ oz butter
3 oz quartered mushrooms
8 oz long grain rice
1 dessertspoon tomato puree
1—1¼ pints stock
1 tablespoon mixed herbs
3—4 oz grated parmesan cheese

1. Cut liver into chunks. Chop onion finely and crush garlic. Quarter the mushrooms. Melt butter and cook onion and garlic for a few minutes with the lid on the pan. Add liver and cook quickly until it changes colour.

2. Remove from heat and add mushrooms, rice, tomato puree, 1 pint of the stock and salt and pepper. Bring to the boil stirring all the time. Reduce the heat and simmer gently for 25—30 minutes, stirring occasionally and adding extra stock if the rice seems to be getting dry.

3. When cooked the rice should have absorbed all the moisture. Sprinkle the top with chopped herbs and serve with grated cheese.

Stuffed Liver and Bacon

*Tender slices of liver baked in cider with bacon and stuffing
(serves 4, hot)*

8 large slices lamb or calf liver
1—2 oz flour
1 oz butter
1 onion
4 mushrooms
2 level tablespoons chopped parsley
2—3 oz fresh white breadcrumbs
1 level teaspoon lemon rind
1 teaspoon lemon juice
8 rashers of bacon
½ pint cider or water

Pre-heat oven to 350°F Mark 4

1. Skin liver and remove gristle. Dip in flour. Heat butter in a frying pan and brown liver quickly for 2 minutes. Place in ovenproof dish.

2. Chop onion and cook for a few minutes to soften. Chop mushrooms and add, cook for 2 minutes. Add this mixture to breadcrumbs with lemon rind and juice, parsley and seasoning.

3. Put this stuffing on top of the slices of liver and place bacon rashers on top. Pour cider around the side of the dish, reserving some if there seems to be too much liquid.

4. Bake in oven until the liver is tender, about 30—40 minutes.

French Grilled Oxtail

An unusual way of cooking oxtail, with a crisp coating of fried crumbs and a piquant sauce (serves 4, hot)

1 large lean oxtail or 2 small cut into sections
several parsley stalks
1 bay leaf
1 sprig of thyme
6—7 peppercorns
3 onions
2 carrots
3—3½ oz butter
2 oz dried white breadcrumbs
2 tablespoons wine vinegar
½ oz flour
½ pint brown stock
1 tablespoon chopped gherkins
1 large teaspoon French mustard

Pre-heat grill

1. Soak pieces of oxtail for at least 3 hours in cold salted water (overnight if possible). Drain and put into a pan of boiling water in which have been put herbs, peppercorns, 2 onions and carrots. Cook slowly for 2—3 hours or until meat is tender.

2. Drain and reserve liquid to use as gravy with vegetables if desired. Dry oxtail. Melt 1½—2 oz butter and roll each piece in this and then in breadcrumbs. Press crumbs on well. Heat grill until red hot. Grill the pieces of oxtail until brown and crisp, turning frequently.

3. Serve with *Sauce Robert:* Melt 1½ oz butter, and cook 1 chopped onion slowly for 6—8 minutes. Add vinegar and simmer for a few minutes. Add flour, then stock, bring to the boil and cook for 10 minutes. Add gherkins and mustard, and salt and pepper. Reheat and serve.

Lamb Kidneys en Chemise

Tender kidneys wrapped in bacon with onion and mushroom, and baked in large jacket potatoes (serves 4, hot)

4 lamb kidneys
4 large potatoes
4 rashers of streaky bacon
½ onion
3—4 mushrooms
2 oz butter
prepared mustard

Pre-heat oven to 350°F Mark 4

1. Wash and scrub the potatoes and bake in their skins for just over 1 hour. Remove from oven and cut a good slice from the top of each one. Take out enough of the potato to make room for a kidney.

2. Skin and core kidneys. Season with salt and pepper. Roll in mixture of finely chopped mushroom and onion, and wrap in half a slice of bacon smeared with mustard. Place wrapped kidneys into potatoes, add ¼ oz butter to each potato, replace potato top, and wrap the whole in foil. Return to oven for another hour to cook kidneys.

Calves, Kidney in Mustard Sauce

Tender pieces of calves' kidney cooked in a delicious brandy and cream sauce with French mustard (serves 4, hot)

1 pound calves' kidney
2—3 oz butter
3—4 oz mushrooms
2—3 tablespoons brandy
¼ oz flour
2 teaspoons French mustard
¼ pint thick cream
½ teaspoon paprika
2 tablespoons chopped parsley

1. Remove core from kidneys and cut into small pieces. Melt butter and cook kidney pieces for 5 minutes. Add sliced mushrooms and cook quickly for 2 minutes.

2. Add brandy. Mix flour and mustard into cream. Pour over kidneys and bring to the boil. Do not boil for more than half a minute. Stir in seasoning and paprika, and sprinkle parsley over the top.

3. Serve at once with plain boiled rice or riced potatoes.

Saute of Lamb Kidneys

A simple, classic dish of kidneys, bacon, onion and mushroom, cooked in sherry or brandy, with cream (serves 4, hot)

8 lamb kidneys
1 oz butter
4 rashers bacon
1 onion
3—4 oz chopped mushrooms
¾ oz flour
½ pint consomme
3 tablespoons sherry or brandy
1 tablespoon chopped mixed herbs
3—4 tablespoons thick cream

Pre-heat oven to 350°F Mark 4

1. Remove skin and cores from kidneys and cut each in half. Melt butter and brown kidneys quickly all over for about 2—3 minutes, then keep warm. Cut bacon into small pieces and brown these quickly and add to kidneys.

2. Add chopped onion to pan and cook until just turning brown. Add chopped mushrooms and cook for 1 minute. Stir in flour. Add consomme. Bring to the boil and cook for 2—3 minutes. Then add sherry or brandy. Pour over kidneys. Add seasoning and herbs. Cover dish and cook in oven for 15 minutes. Do not allow to boil as this hardens kidneys.

3. Remove from oven, stir in cream, and serve with mashed potatoes or rice.

Brochettes of Lamb Kidneys

Tender lamb kidneys cooked on skewers and served with a rich Italian sauce (serves 4, hot)

8 lamb kidneys
8 rashers bacon
16—20 button mushrooms
8 baby onions
1—1½ oz butter
1 tablespoon oil
1 slice lean ham
½ small onion
2—3 liquid oz white wine
8 liquid oz brown stock (or consomme)
1 tablespoon tomato puree
a little chopped parsley

Pre-heat grill

1. Skin and remove core from kidneys and cut each in half. Cut bacon slices in half and curl each up into a small roll. Remove stems from mushrooms and reserve. Peel baby onions and cook for 5—6 minutes in a covered pan in ½ oz of butter. Arrange kidneys, bacon rolls, mushroom caps, baby onions on skewers to make 4 brochettes.

2. Make sauce: Cook chopped mushroom stems for a minute in hot oil. Then add chopped ham and onion. Cook again for a few minutes. Pour in wine and cook for 3—4 minutes without lid. Then add stock and tomato puree, herbs, seasoning and cook together for a few minutes.

4. Brush brochettes with melted butter, and sprinkle with salt and pepper. Grill under hot grill for 6—10 minutes, turning every two minutes. Arrange on a bed of rice and serve with Italian sauce.

Fried Tripe and Onions

Traditional dish of deep fried tripe and onions fried with garlic, cayenne, parsley and lemon juice (serves 4, hot)

1½ pounds already partly cooked and
   blanched tripe or canned tripe
½ pint milk
1½ oz flour
2 tablespoons oil
1 oz butter
3 onions
1 clove garlic
a little cayenne pepper
2 tablespoons chopped parsley
2 lemons
fat for deep frying

1. Put tripe into pan, cover with milk and ½ pint water and cook gently for 1½ hours. Drain and rinse with cold water. Drain and dry. Then cut tripe into strips and toss in seasoned flour.

2. While tripe is cooking, heat oil, add butter and fry sliced onions and crushed garlic until golden. Add cayenne pepper, salt, parsley and juice of 1 lemon, and cook for a few moments more.

3. Heat fat and fry floured tripe until crisp and golden brown. Drain on paper towel. Put fried tripe on top of onion mixture, and serve with quartered lemon and crisp French bread.

Sweetbreads with Garlic

Sweetbreads lightly cooked in butter and garlic and garnished with parsley (serves 4, hot)

1½—2 pounds sweetbreads
juice of ½ lemon
¼ pound butter
2 cloves garlic (more or less according to taste)
1 tablespoon chopped parsley

1. Soak sweetbreads for 3—4 hours in several changes of cold salted water until the water no longer has a pinkish tinge.

2. Put in pan and cover with water and juice of ½ lemon. Bring to the boil and cook for 2—3 minutes. Drain and soak again in cold water. When cool remove all skin and membranes.

3. Melt butter and add finely crushed garlic. Cook gently for 10—12 minutes. Add sliced sweetbreads. Season and turn in hot butter until golden brown. Sprinkle with chopped parsley and serve with boiled rice.

Grilled Sweetbread, Bacon and Prune Kebabs

Sweetbreads wrapped in bacon, stuffed prunes and onions grilled on skewers and served on a pilaff of rice (serves 4—6 hot)

2 pairs calf sweetbreads
2 tablespoons vinegar
1 oz butter
2 onions, chopped
8 oz rice
1½ pint chicken stock
2½ oz raisins
2 oz peeled almonds
1 tablespoon chopped mixed herbs
8 rashers bacon
12 baby onions
12 large cooked prunes
2—3 tablespoons chutney
1 oz butter, melted

Pre-heat grill

1. Soak sweetbreads as described in *Sweetbreads with Garlic*. Then put them in a pan with 4 pints cold water, vinegar and some salt. Bring to boil slowly and simmer for 10—15 minutes. Drain and plunge into cold water. When cool drain and dry them, and remove skin and any tough membranes or tubes. Put into the refrigerator between two plates for 30 minutes.

2. Make pilaff of rice: Melt butter and cook onions for 5 minutes. Add rice and cook for 2—3 minutes. Add stock and bring to the boil. Add raisins, browned sliced almonds and herbs. Cook rice in oven for about 30 minutes until all stock has been absorbed. Then put into a buttered mould and turn onto a serving dish.

3. Divide each sweetbread into 4 or 6. Wrap each piece in ½ rasher of bacon. Cook onions in a little stock for about 10 minutes. Remove stones from prunes and stuff with chutney. Put sweetbread pieces, onions and prunes alternately onto the skewers. Brush with melted butter and season. Grill (or cook over charcoal grill) for 5—7 minutes until bacon is crisp. Put cooked kebabs on the pilaff and serve.

Brains with Black Butter

Brains finished in butter and served with a piquant sauce of butter and wine vinegar (serves 4, hot)

1 pound calf or lamb brains
1 tablespoon vinegar
¼ teaspoon salt
3 oz butter
1 tablespoon wine vinegar
black pepper
chopped parsley

1. Wash brains and soak for 2—3 hours in cold water. Remove skin and then soak again in lukewarm water to remove any blood.

2. Put into a pan of cold water with vinegar and salt. Bring slowly to just below boiling point. Cook for 15 minutes. Do not boil. Drain. Put in cold water until firm. Then dry carefully.

3. Melt half the butter and when hot add brains. Cook until brown all over. Then put onto hot dish and keep warm.

4. Heat rest of butter until it turns brown. Add wine vinegar and pour at once over brains and sprinkle with salt, pepper and chopped parsley.

TASTY LEFTOVERS

Ham, Chicken and Mushroom Patties

Crisp, light pastry patties filled with creamy, savoury ham, chicken and mushroom filling (serves 4, hot)

1. Roll out pastry until ¼ inch thick. Using a 2½ inch diameter cutter, cut out 8 patties. Now using smaller cutter, about 1½ inch diameter, make a central cut in each patty, being careful not to cut through to the bottom. Brush surface of each patty with beaten egg. Do not allow egg to run over sides or this will keep the pastry from rising.

2. Put on a dampened baking sheet and cook for about 10—15 minutes until patties are well risen and golden brown. Remove from oven. Carefully take off the centre lid and scoop out soft pastry inside. Keep warm.

3. Melt butter and cook quartered mushrooms for a few minutes. Mix in flour. Then add milk. Bring to the boil, stirring all the time. Add chopped ham, chicken and parsley. Season with onion salt, pepper and a pinch of mace. When heated through, spoon mixture into patty shells. Place lids on top and serve at once or keep warm for a short time.

3—4 slices cooked ham
3—4 oz cooked chicken
1 package frozen puff pastry, about ½ pound
1 egg
1¼ oz butter
6—8 mushrooms
1 oz flour
½ pint milk (or milk and cream)
1 tablespoon chopped parsley
onion salt
a pinch of mace

Pre-heat oven to 450°F Mark 8

Scandinavian Style Cabbage

Cabbage stuffed with a savoury mixture of ham or meat and breadcrumbs or rice, served with a strong cheese sauce (serves 4, hot)

1. Trim cabbage and cook whole in boiling salted water for about 10—12 minutes. Drain. Plunge in cold water. Remove 3—4 outside leaves and reserve these.

2. Melt butter or margarine and cook onion until soft. Mix with ham, breadcrumbs or rice, herbs, tomato puree, seasoning, tabasco and enough stock (or tomato juice) to make a moist but firm mixture.

3. Cut stalk out of cabbage and enough from centre to fill with stuffing mixture. Cover hole with reserved leaves and tie on with string. Wrap in foil and boil for 1—2 hours until cabbage is tender. Remove string and serve with a cheese sauce.

4. Make sauce: Heat butter. Mix in flour and blend over heat. Add milk gradually. When sauce is smooth, bring to the boil. Add cheese, mustard and seasoning to taste and pour over cabbage.

8 oz chopped ham (or other cold cooked meat)
1 medium sized firm head of cabbage
1 oz butter or margarine
1 onion chopped
4—6 oz breadcrumbs or cooked rice
2 tablespoons mixed herbs
1 tablespoon tomato puree
a dash of tabasco
a little strong stock (or tomato juice)
1 oz butter
¾ oz flour
½—¾ pint milk
3 oz strongly flavoured grated cheese
½ teaspoon dry mustard

Stuffed Marrow

Halves or rings of marrow stuffed with a tasty meat mixture and baked until tender (serves 4–6, hot)

¾ pound chopped cooked meat
1 tender marrow about 2 pounds
2 tablespoons oil
1 onion
3–4 oz chopped mushrooms
½ oz flour
½ pint gravy (or tomato sauce)
1 tablespoon soy or Worcestershire
   sauce
1 tablespoon mixed herbs
2–3 oz leftover peas, beans, carrots,
   corn or rice
3 tablespoons dried white breadcrumbs
a little melted butter
2 tablespoons chopped parsley

Pre-heat oven to 375°F Mark 5

1. Heat oil and cook chopped onion until golden brown. Then add chopped meat and mushrooms, cook for 2 minutes. Sprinkle with flour and mix in. Add enough gravy (or tomato sauce) to moisten, but do not make too soft. Add soy or Worcestershire sauce, mixed herbs and vegetables or rice.

2. Cut marrow in half lengthwise and remove seeds, or cut into 1½ inch thick rings and remove seeds. Boil marrow for 5 minutes and drain. Put in a buttered ovenproof dish and fill with meat mixture.

3. Sprinkle with dried white breadcrumbs. Pour over a little melted butter. Pour remaining gravy round marrow. Cook in oven for about 35–50 minutes, according to the thickness of the marrow. Test with skewer. When tender sprinkle with chopped parsley.

Danish Hash

A delicious hash of meat, potatoes and onions topped with a fried egg per person (serves 4, hot)

½–¾ pound cold meat, preferably beef
   with ham or bacon
2 large potatoes
1 large or 2 medium onions
2–2½ oz bacon fat or butter
1–2 teaspoons Worcestershire sauce
1 teaspoon tomato sauce
1 tablespoon chopped parsley
4 eggs

1. Peel and boil potatoes until just tender but not soft. Dice into pieces about ¼–½ inch square. Cut meat into pieces about the same size. Chop onions coarsely.

2. Cook chopped onions in 1½ oz of melted bacon fat or butter until tender, about 7 minutes. Remove from pan. Brown meat for a few minutes. Add potatoes and cook 2–3 minutes. Return onions and cook whole mixture 3–4 minutes. Add Worcestershire and tomato sauce and seasoning. Sprinkle with parsley and put in ovenproof dish to keep warm.

3. Fry eggs in remaining bacon fat or butter and serve hash at once with 1 fried egg placed carefully to avoid breaking on top of each serving.

Croquettes

Any pieces of cooked meat can easily be made into a delicious main dish with these deep fried croquettes (serves 4, hot)

½–¾ pound cooked minced meat
1 pound potatoes
1 small onion
¾ oz butter
1 tablespoon chutney
1 tablespoon chopped herbs
tomato puree (optional)
1–1½ oz flour
2 eggs
dry white crumbs
fat for deep frying
a bunch of parsley

1. Boil and mash potatoes, finely chop onion, cook in butter for 2 minutes and mix with meat, chutney, herbs and seasoning, adding a little tomato puree if mixture is too dry.

2. Put mixture on a floured board. Make into long roll, and cut into sections about 1 inch thick and 3 inches long. Roll these in seasoned flour. Then brush with beaten egg all over and roll in breadcrumbs.

3. Deep fry in smoking hot fat until well browned. Drain and serve with parsley fried in deep fat for a few seconds and a well-flavoured sauce.

Ham Gougere

A decorative and filling dish of chopped ham, mushrooms, tomato puree and flavouring in a circle of choux pastry (serves 4, hot)

4–5 oz cooked ham (or other meat)
¾ oz butter
1 onion
2–3 oz mushrooms
½ oz flour
1 tablespoon tomato puree
¼ pint stock
1 tablespoon sherry
1 tablespoon chopped herbs
2 oz butter
2½ oz plain flour
2 eggs
1½–2 oz grated cheddar cheese
½ teaspoon dried mustard
2 tablespoons grated parmesan cheese
2 tablespoons cornflake crumbs
2 teaspoons chopped parsley

Pre-heat oven to 375°F Mark 5

1. Melt ¾ oz butter. Cook sliced onion until soft. Add mushrooms and cook for 1 minute. Add flour and when well mixed add tomato puree and stock. Stir until it boils and then cook until it has thickened a little. Add sherry, diced ham and herbs. Allow to cool slightly before spooning into dish.

2. Sift warmed flour. In a pan with sloping sides heat ¼ pint of water and 2 oz butter. When butter has melted bring mixture to the boil. As soon as it boils remove from heat and add all the flour at once. Beat hard with wooden spoon until mixture forms a ball in the bottom of pan. Let cool. Beat eggs. When mixture is cool add egg by degrees, beating hard between each addition. The final mixture should be shiny and smooth and hold its shape. A little egg may be left over. Add cheese and mustard.

3. Butter a fireproof dish about 3 inches deep. Arrange the pastry in a ring around outside of the dish. Put mixture in the centre and brush the top with a little beaten egg to give a shine. Sprinkle the top with grated cheese and cornflake crumbs. Bake in oven for 30–45 minutes for large dish or 15–20 minutes for small. Sprinkle top with chopped parsley and serve.

Cottage Pie

A favourite way of using up the ends of a roast (serves 4—6, hot)

1—1½ pounds diced or minced
   cooked beef or lamb
2 medium onions
1—2 tablespoons oil
4—6 liquid oz beef stock
1 tablespoon chopped mixed herbs,
   mainly parsley
nutmeg
Worcestershire sauce
4—6 medium sized potatoes
½—¾ oz butter
milk

Pre-heat oven to 375°F Mark 5

1. Cook chopped onions in oil until golden brown. (Do not overbrown or this will make dish bitter.) Add meat, stock, seasoning, herbs, and a grating of nutmeg, and a dash of Worcestershire sauce.

2 Peel potatoes and boil until tender in salted water. When soft drain and dry off in saucepan. Mash, and beat in butter and then a little milk, making sure not to make the puree too soft. Season to taste.

3. Put meat mixture into an ovenproof dish, smooth down and pile hot potato on top to make a slightly domed cover. Rough surface evenly with a fork, and sprinkle with small pieces of butter. Bake in oven for 30—40 minutes, by which time the top should be crisp and brown. (As a variation chopped mushrooms may be added to the meat mixture, or a little chutney.)

Cornish Pasties

Traditional pasties of short pastry with a mixed filling of beef, liver and vegetables (serves 6—8, hot)

1 pound chopped cooked beef steak
½ pound chopped cooked liver
¾ pound flour
4½ oz beef dripping or shortening
3 medium potatoes
2 onions
1 small turnip
2 carrots
1 egg

Pre-heat oven to 400°F Mark 6

1. Sift flour into a bowl with salt. Mix in dripping or shortening with a knife or pastry blender. Then rub in lightly with the fingers, and mix with 3—3½ liquid oz cold water to make a firm dough. Put into refrigerator in polythene bag for at least 15 minutes. Remove, cut into 6—8 equal pieces and roll into rounds about 1/8 inch thick.

2. Mix chopped beef and liver together, with salt and pepper. Peel and dice vegetables, and mix together. Cook in a little water for 4—5 minutes, drain and allow to cool. Put a heaped spoonful of the vegetable mixture in the middle of each round, top this with a spoonful of meat mixture.

3. Brush the edges of each pastry round with egg white beaten with a pinch of salt. Bring up edges and press together. Crimp with fingers to make a scalloped edge (see picture) and bake the pasties for 30 minutes in oven.

Veal and Mushroom Pancakes

Light pancakes with a creamy filling of cooked veal, mushrooms and corn, topped with grated cheese and browned under the grill (serves 4–6, hot)

10–12 oz chopped cooked veal
4 oz plain flour
1 egg
1 egg yolk
½ pint milk
1½ oz butter
½ oz flour
4 liquid oz milk
3–4 oz mushrooms
2–3 oz sweetcorn
1 tablespoon chopped parsley
a little cream
a pinch of mace or ground nutmeg
a little oil
2–3 tablespoons grated parmesan cheese
¾ oz melted butter

Pre-heat grill

1. Sift ¼ pound flour with salt and pepper into bowl. Make a hollow in centre and drop in beaten eggs and 3–4 tablespoons of milk. Mix eggs and milk together with spoon before gradually drawing in flour. Add ¼ pint milk as mixture thickens and when it is smooth and like thick cream, beat for about 5 minutes. Then stir in 2 teaspoons of melted butter and rest of ½ pint of milk. Leave batter in a covered bowl for about ½ hour before using.

2. Melt about 1 oz butter and cook sliced mushrooms in covered pan for 3–4 minutes. Remove from stove. Stir in a scant ½ oz flour and add 4 liquid oz of milk. Bring slowly to the boil. Add chopped meat and corn, parsley, mace, seasoning and cream. Keep warm while cooking pancakes.

3. Test thickness of batter which should just coat back of spoon. If too thick, add extra milk and stir well. Grease a 5–6 inch pancake or frying pan with a little oil. When hot, pour in enough batter to coat pan thinly. When browned on one side turn and cook on the other side. Pile up and keep warm. Allow 2 to 3 per person.

4. Put a spoonful of filling in centre of each pancake and roll up. Arrange in overlapping rows in ovenproof dish. Sprinkle with grated cheese and spoon over melted butter and grill until golden brown.

Fleming's Meat-and-Tomato Pudding

*A delicious way of making the remaining slices of a roast into
an interesting and filling dish (serves 4—6, hot)*

6—8 slices of roast lamb
4 oz fresh breadcrumbs
1 onion
8 tomatoes
2 teaspoons brown sugar
a little Worcestershire sauce or mush-
    room ketchup
1 oz butter

Pre-heat oven to 375°F Mark 5

1. Butter a baking dish. Sprinkle in a layer of breadcrumbs. Add a layer of diced cold lamb, then a sprinkling of finely chopped onion and some salt and pepper. Add another layer of tomatoes with sugar, a dash of Worcestershire sauce or ketchup and a little of the butter on top.

2. Repeat this layering again but reserve 1 oz crumbs to sprinkle over the top of the dish. Add remaining butter in small pieces and bake for about 40 minutes in oven until crumbs are brown.

Cold Beef or Lamb Curry
with Mayonnaise

*An unusual way of using remains of a curry, with vegetables and
rich mayonnaise (serves 4, cold)*

8—12 oz cold meat curry with sauce
4 eggs
4 tomatoes
1—1½ pounds cooked cold rice
2 boiled cold potatoes
any leftover peas, beans, carrots, or
    other vegetables
1 lemon

QUICK MAYONNAISE
¼ teaspoon salt
a large pinch of pepper
1 level teaspoon dry mustard
1 teaspoon sugar
1 egg
½ pint salad oil
2 teaspoons lemon juice
2 teaspoons wine vinegar

1. Put rice into a deep dish. Hard boil eggs, cut into quarters and arrange on the rice. Spoon over half of the curry. Make a layer on top with sliced tomatoes and potatoes and left-over vegetables, and spoon over remaining curry.

2. Make mayonnaise: Put salt, pepper, mustard and sugar in liquidizer. Add egg and mix thoroughly at a low speed. Add a few drops of oil and mix in well. Then add the rest of the oil in a steady stream until it has been absorbed and the mayonnaise is very thick. Add lemon juice, vinegar, and lastly 1—2 tablespoons of boiling water which thins it and helps to make it keep, if not to be used immediately. Allow to cool.

3. Pour mayonnaise over cold curry and serve with slices of halved lemon.

Russian Salad

A delicious mixed salad which is a meal in itself (serves 4—6, cold)

½—¾ pound cooked veal or ham
½ small cucumber
2 cooked beetroots
2 cooked medium potatoes
2 cooked carrots
1 apple
2—3 oz cooked peas (or beans)
12 spring onions (optional)
a large pinch of salt
1 large pinch of pepper
¼ teaspoon French mustard
a pinch of sugar
6 tablespoons olive oil
2 tablespoons vinegar (or lemon
    juice)
1 clove garlic
1 crisp lettuce
½ pint thick mayonnaise
4 tomatoes

1. Shred meat and dice lightly salted cucumber. Put in bowl with diced beetroots, potatoes, carrots, apple, peas (or beans) and, if desired, chop spring onions, and add to meat mixture.

2. Make French dressing: Mix salt, pepper, mustard and sugar together with 1 tablespoon oil. Then beat in oil and vinegar alternately. Adjust seasoning. Put in whole clove of garlic, leave until ready to use, then remove. Moisten meat and vegetables with French dressing. Leave for an hour or so.

3. Just before serving arrange washed lettuce leaves around outside of salad bowl. Spoon the Russian Salad into centre. Work the pips from peeled and quartered tomatoes through sieve and add juice to mayonnaise. Spoon mayonnaise over the salad and decorate with tomato quarters. For mayonnaise recipe, see *Cold Curry with Mayonnaise.*

Pork Chop Suey

Simple variation of the popular Chinese dish (serves 4—6, hot)

12 oz cooked pork
3—4 stalks celery
2 oz spring onions
3—4 oz mushrooms
1 green pepper
1 pound can bean sprouts
2 tablespoons oil
½ pint chicken bouillon
1 level tablespoon cornflour
1 tablespoon soy sauce

1. Cut pork into thick strips. Cut celery into slices and spring onions into lengths. Slice mushrooms. Seed and chop the green pepper and cook for 5 minutes in boiling water. Drain. Rinse bean sprouts in cold water and drain.

2. Heat oil and cook celery and onions for 2—3 minutes. Add mushrooms and pork, and cook for 2 minutes. Add chopped pepper and bean sprouts, and cook for 2 minutes, stirring all the time.

3. Add stock with cornflour dissolved in it. Bring to boil and simmer for 5 minutes. Add soy sauce, season and serve with plain boiled rice or fried noodles.

Spanish Omelette

A particularly delicious way of using up small quantities of meat and vegetables (serves 4, hot)

4—6 oz diced ham (or any cold cooked meat or garlic sausage)
1½ tablespoons oil
1 large potato
1 onion
3—4 tomatoes
1 small green or red pepper
6 eggs
3 teaspoons chopped mixed herbs
1½—2 oz butter
1 clove garlic (optional)

1. Heat oil and cook diced potato and finely chopped onion in a covered pan until tender. (Add crushed garlic if liked.) Shake pan to prevent sticking. Dice ham (or meat) and peel, seed and chop tomatoes and pepper. Add to potato mixture and heat through. (Any leftover cooked vegetables can be substituted or added to mixture at this stage.)

2. Mix eggs well with 3 tablespoons water and chopped herbs and seasoning. Heat 1 oz of butter in a large omelette or frying pan. When foaming pour egg mixture into pan and stir in ham and vegetable mixture. Stir gently for 1 minute to mix egg and mixture well. Then leave over moderate heat for 2—3 minutes, until fairly well set. Place a large plate over a frying pan and turn omelette onto it. Heat remaining butter in pan and return omelette with cooked side uppermost. Cook for 2 minutes to brown other side, and serve at once.

Ham and Cheese Souffle

A delicious light concoction of ham and cheese which must be eaten as soon as it is ready (serves 4—6, hot)

6—8 oz chopped or minced ham
12 liquid oz milk
1 onion
1 bay leaf
3 parsley stalks
a pinch of mace
1 oz butter
1 oz flour
2—3 oz grated parmesan or strong cheddar cheese
½ teaspoon French mustard
3 large eggs
a little cayenne pepper (optional)

Pre-heat oven to 375°F Mark 5

1. Heat milk with onion, bay leaf, parsley and mace. Melt butter, remove from heat and stir in flour. Strain milk into pan and stir over gentle heat until smooth. Then bring to the boil stirring all the time. Remove from heat, and add ham, cheese, mustard and seasoning.

2. Separate eggs carefully and mix in yolks one at a time. (At this point the mixture can be left covered, the whites beaten and added just before souffle is due to be cooked.) Beat whites with a pinch of salt, until they stand up in peaks. Add one tablespoon of whites to mixture and mix in well. Then carefully fold in remainder with a spoon without over mixing.

3. Pour mixture into souffle dish and bake in oven until well risen and brown on top, 20—25 minutes. Sprinkle top with a little grated cheese or a dusting of red pepper and serve at once.

Poultry & Game

Poultry is one of the most versatile of foods. A perfectly roasted chicken with a good stuffing makes a memorable meal, but there are dozens of other ways in which poultry and game can be served. I have given recipes in this section for hot and cold dishes pates, casseroles and rice dishes as well as traditional and less usual roasting recipes.
When you have roasted a large chicken or turkey, there are always leftovers from which a great number of delicious and unusual dishes can be made. I have given lots of suggestions in this chapter for using up leftovers, and you will be tempted to keep back some meat specially for them.
When you are using frozen poultry and game, longer, slower cooking methods give the most tender and succulent results. Do be careful over defrosting and make sure the bird is completely unfrozen before you cook it; it is best to defrost poultry in the refrigerator but you can safely speed up the process by leaving the bird under cold running water — never hot water — if necessary.

TURKEY: FOR FESTIVE OCCASIONS

Turkeys are usually roasted for Christmas or other special celebration meals with a variety of stuffings, of which four interesting and delicious examples are given below.

When selecting turkey it is advisable to allow 1 pound of turkey per person (cleaned weight). This will leave enough turkey after the feast to eat cold or to make up on the second day.

The quantities given in the stuffing recipes are worked out for a bird weighing 8–9 pounds which will feed 8–10 people. If a smaller or larger bird is to be cooked, a general rule is to allow approximately 1 teacup of stuffing per pound of bird.

If using a frozen bird give ample time to defrost; otherwise the breast will be dry and over-cooked before the legs are done. It is advisable to use either the slow method or the French roasting method for cooking a frozen bird as this helps to make it more tender and succulent. The French method is also advisable if a turkey is being cooked for eating cold rather than hot.

If roasting a turkey without stuffing the cooking time can be reduced by about 5 minutes per pound.

QUICK METHOD

Pre-heat oven to 450°F Mark 8

Turkey weighing 6–12 pounds, allow 15 minutes per pound and 15 minutes over.

Turkey weighing 12 pounds and over, allow 10–12 minutes per pound and 10 minutes over.

SLOW METHOD

Pre-heat oven to 325°F Mark 3

Turkey weighing 6–12 pounds, allow 20 minutes per pound and 20 minutes over.

Turkey weighing 12 pounds and over, allow 16 minutes per pound and 20–30 minutes over.

FRENCH ROAST METHOD

Pre-heat oven to 350°F Mark 4

Turkey weighing 6–12 pounds, allow 20 minutes per pound and 20 minutes over.

Turkey weighing 12 pounds and over, allow 15 minutes per pound.

Traditional Quick Roast Turkey

For use with a fresh tender turkey which is not too large and has not been frozen (Serves 8–10)

1. Wash turkey inside and out with cold water. Dry thoroughly with paper towel. Rub surface all over with a cut lemon to keep flesh white. Fill the body cavity with sausage meat stuffing and the neck with chestnut stuffing, or if using other stuffings fill the neck first, not too tightly, and put remaining stuffing inside the body. *(cont.)*

**1 fresh turkey unfrozen, weight 8—9
  pounds when plucked and cleaned**
6—8 teacups stuffing
1 onion
3—4 oz butter
**salt, ground pepper and poultry
  seasoning**
8—10 strips fat bacon
6 tablespoons oil
10—20 potatoes according to size
½—¾ pints stock

Pre-heat oven to 450°F Mark 8

2. Use wing tips to help hold neck skin in place under bird and sew down the neck skin to keep stuffing in place. Close the cavity as tightly as possible and put an onion at entrance and tie or sew the leg bones together to keep it closed as much as possible. Rub breast and legs thickly with butter and seasoning, cover with strips of fat bacon and tie these in place. Weigh bird and calculate roasting time using table provided on page 130.

3. Heat 6 tablespoons oil in roasting pan. When hot, put in bird and baste thoroughly. Place a large piece of foil over top and roast for 2½—2¾ hours, basting every 20 minutes and turning bird from one side to the other every 20 minutes to allow legs to cook without overcooking breast. For last 30 minutes place bird breast up and remove foil covering to brown breast.

4. Test if bird is done by running skewer into thickest part of leg. If juice is pink, cook longer; if clear, bird is done. Another indication is when the meat on the legs shrinks back on bones.

5. Par-boiled potatoes can be roasted around turkey during last hour of cooking or in a separate pan in same oven.

6. Remove from roasting pan and put on large serving dish. Keep warm. Pour off fat from pan. Add 1—2 teaspoons flour to juices in pan. Pour on stock. Bring to the boil, stirring constantly. When well-flavoured, skim off any fat that has risen to surface and pour gravy into sauce boat to serve with turkey.

Roast Turkey: Slow Method

1. Prepare and stuff bird as for quick roasting. Weigh and calculate time using table on page 2. Do not cover bird with foil as this will make it soggy. Baste and turn turkey every 20–30 minutes, removing bacon for last 30 minutes and increasing heat to 375°F Mark 5 to brown.

Pre-heat oven to 325°F Mark 3

2. Make gravy using drippings from roasting meat and giblet stock.

Oyster Stuffing

1 pint oysters in own liquid
12–15 oz fresh breadcrumbs
8 oz butter
2 chopped mild onions
3–4 stalks sliced celery
3 tablespoons parsley chopped
juice of ½ lemon
a little white wine or stock

1. Prepare (or buy ready prepared) oysters in their own salty juice. Prepare breadcrumbs made with two-day old loaf. Melt butter and cook onions and celery until soft and light golden brown.

2. Add to breadcrumbs, with chopped herbs and seasoning, lemon juice and the oysters cut in half if large. If too dry, a little white wine or stock may be added, but it must not be too soft. Fill turkey cavity and sew up carefully.

Cornbread, Corn and Mushroom Stuffing

6—7 oz cornbread
6—7 oz fresh white breadcrumbs
4—5 oz whole kernel sweetcorn
4 oz mushrooms
6 oz butter
salt, pepper and a pinch of cayenne pepper
2 tablespoons mixed herbs chopped
2 beaten eggs
5—6 tablespoons stock

1. Crumble cornbread, add breadcrumbs, corn and mushrooms, cooked for few minutes in butter. Cornbread is not readily available in the U.K., so the amount of plain crumbs can be altered and more sweetcorn used 10—12 oz white breadcrumbs with 6 oz whole kernel sweetcorn.

2. Add plenty of seasoning, chopped herbs, beaten eggs and enough stock to make a moist but not runny mixture. Fill this mixture into cavity of bird and sew up opening.

Sausage Meat Stuffing

1 pound pork sausage meat
4—6 stalks celery chopped
1 large or two medium onions
2 oz butter
1 turkey liver
6 oz breadcrumbs
2—3 tablespoons parsley and thyme chopped
1 egg
juice of ½ lemon

1. Put sausage meat in a bowl with chopped celery. Melt butter and fry finely chopped onion and turkey liver for 2—3 minutes. Remove, allow to cool slightly.

2. Then cut into small pieces and mix into sausage meat. Add chopped herbs and breadcrumbs. Add a beaten egg to moisten, and a little lemon juice, and stuff inside turkey. Sew up opening carefully.

Hunter's Turkey (see p. 136)

French Roast Turkey

Turkey stuffed with any of suggested stuffings or with butter, onion or parsley, roasted with stock to produce tender, moist result. Particularly suited for cooking frozen turkey or turkey to be eaten cold (Serves 8–10)

1 turkey 8–9 pounds
½ lemon
3 onions
6–8 oz butter
**salt, ground pepper and poultry
    seasoning**
a few sprigs parsley
giblets
a little mixed herbs
1–1½ teaspoons flour
turkey liver

Pre-heat oven to 350°F Mark 4

1. Wash and dry turkey thoroughly. Rub surface with cut lemon to keep flesh white. Put half the butter inside with 2 peeled onions and several sprigs of parsley and some seasoning, or stuff turkey with one of chosen stuffings and sew in carefully. Weigh turkey and calculate cooking time using chart provided (see above).

2. Rub remaining butter all over breast and legs, season and cover with foil. Put in roasting pan and pour around ½ pint stock made with giblets, 1 onion and herbs.

3. Put into oven and roast for calculated time removing foil every 20 minutes and turning bird from side to side to cook legs. Baste each time with stock, adding more if it seems to be evaporating too quickly. During last half hour place bird breast up and allow to brown. It may be necessary to put oven up to 400°F Mark 6 for last 10 minutes. Test to see if bird is cooked thoroughly by sticking skewer into thickest part of leg. If juice runs pink, further cooking is required; if clear, it is done.

4. Remove turkey to serving dish and make gravy. Skim some of butter from roasting pan and put into a small pan. Fry turkey liver until tender. Sprinkle in flour; then add skimmed pan drippings, plus remaining stock. Bring to the boil and simmer. Add seasoning to taste, and serve.

Chestnut Stuffing

Stuffing to go in neck cavity of turkey

1½ pounds raw chestnuts in shells,
1 pound when peeled (or large tin
of unsweetened chestnut puree)
½—¾ pint milk or well flavoured stock
1—2 oz butter
1 large onion
2—3 rashers streaky bacon

1. If using raw chestnuts cut a slit in each nut and bake in oven in dish of salt until skins come off cleanly, about 20 minutes, or bring to the boil and cook for 5 minutes until skins are loose. Then remove all outer and inner skins, and cook chestnuts in milk or stock until tender. Drain and mash or crush in liquidizer, reserving a few to chop roughly.

2. Melt butter and cook onion until tender. After a few minutes, add chopped bacon and cook. Stir into chestnut puree, add salt and pepper and as much milk or stock as is needed to make an easily moulded stuffing. Do not make too wet. Add roughly chopped chestnuts last. Put this mixture into neck of bird and sew up skin under back of bird or skewer securely using wing tips to help hold in stuffing.

(Tinned fresh pureed chestnuts can be used for this stuffing but will need more onion and seasoning if the stuffing is not to be rather dull in flavour. Moisten with strongly flavoured stock.)

Italian Roast Turkey

1 turkey weighing 8—9 pounds (if
frozen allow ample time to defrost)
STUFFING

2—3 oz raw prunes
1 pound peeled chestnuts (or 1 large
tin unsweetened chestnuts)
8—10 oz sausage meat
1 large onion
1—2 oz butter
1 turkey liver
2 liquid oz white wine (or Italian
vermouth)

FOR BRAISING
1½—2 oz butter
2 onions
2 carrots
4—6 stalks celery
3 rashers bacon
2 cloves garlic
1 spray fresh rosemary (or 2 teaspoons
dried)
8 peppercorns
parsley, thyme and 2 bay leaves
½ bottle red wine
½—¾ pint stock

FOR ROASTING
3—4 tablespoons oil
½ oz butter

Pre-heat oven to 325°F Mark 3

Turkey stuffed with unusual mixture of prunes, chestnuts, sausage meat, pears, white wine and liver, braised in a garlic and herb flavoured sauce, and then roasted (Serves 8—10, hot)

1. Prepare stuffing: Soak and cook prunes in tea. Remove stones when tender, chop roughly. If using fresh chestnuts, cook in boiling water for 5 minutes, then remove outer and inner skins. Cook for 30 minutes in stock, drain and chop roughly. Mix these ingredients with sausage meat. Melt butter and fry turkey liver and onion for 3—4 minutes. Allow to cool, then chop and add to other ingredients. Add seasoning and wine. Stir whole mixture over heat for few minutes until thoroughly blended and hot. Let cool before stuffing turkey.

2. When turkey is stuffed and sewn up, melt butter in flameproof casserole and cook sliced onion, sliced carrot, chopped celery and diced bacon for few minutes. Add garlic, rosemary, peppercorns, and other seasoning and herbs. Place turkey on top of this, pour over ½ bottle red wine and enough stock to come half way up bird. Cover casserole with lid and braise turkey for 3½ hours turning from side to side every half hour to allow all sides to cook equally.

3. Remove from casserole and drain from sauce. Heat some oil and ½ oz butter in a roasting pan, put in turkey and baste. Roast in oven for ½ hour, until the bird has browned and is well done, basting every 10 minutes.

4. Remove garlic cloves. Boil up pan drippings and vegetables to reduce slightly. Strain and serve as sauce.

TURKEY: FOR OTHER OCCASIONS

2 turkey legs cut into 4 joints or 8
   slices turkey
2–3 tablespoons oil
1 onion
1 clove garlic
¾–1 oz flour
2–3 tablespoons tomato puree
2 liquid oz white wine
½ pint brown stock
6–8 mushrooms
1 oz butter
1 tablespoon parsley chopped
¼ teaspoon oregano
1–2 oz grated cheddar cheese
2 tablespoons breadcrumbs

Pre-heat oven to 350°F Mark 4
Pre-heat grill

Hunter's Turkey

Cooked turkey meat in a rich garlic, herb and tomato flavoured wine sauce, finished with cheese (Serves 4–6, hot—see picture, p. 5)

1. Make hunter's sauce: Heat oil and cook chopped onion and crushed garlic until golden brown. Sprinkle in flour, cook for 1 minute to brown lightly. Add tomato puree, wine and stock. Bring to the boil, stirring frequently. Add sliced mushrooms, cooked for few minutes in butter. Add herbs and seasoning, and simmer for few minutes.

2. Joint turkey legs or cut breast into slices, and place in a fireproof dish. Spoon over the sauce.

3. Put in oven for 15 minutes. Then sprinkle top with cheese and breadcrumbs, and put under grill to brown.

1 small turkey weighing 6 pounds
6–8 oz lean minced veal
3–4 oz lean minced ham
2½–3 oz butter
1½–2 oz mushrooms
1½ oz white breadcrumbs
a little milk
2 tablespoons chopped parsley and
   thyme
½ onion chopped or 1 teaspoon onion
   powder
1 egg
4–5 onions
3–4 carrots sliced
3–4 stalks celery
8–9 peppercorns
2–3 bouillon cubes
1½ oz flour
4 liquid oz wine
¾ oz gelatine (if serving cold)

English Boiled Turkey

Turkey stuffed with veal, ham and bread forcemeat, flavoured with mushrooms and herbs, boiled in stock and served in a white sauce; also excellent cold when white sauce has gelatine added (Serves 6–8, hot or cold)

1. First prepare forcemeat or stuffing: Mince lean veal and ham finely. Melt 1 oz butter and cook mushrooms for 5–6 minutes. Allow to cool before adding to the meat. Soak breadcrumbs in milk for 15 minutes; then squeeze out as much milk as possible. Add this to meats with chopped mushrooms, herbs and seasoning and chopped onion or onion powder. Beat together until very smooth. Add egg to bind stuffing.

2. Stuff cleaned turkey with mixture. Sew up opening carefully to prevent forcemeat escaping during boiling. If a large piece of muslin is available wrap bird in this and tie securely.

3. Put into a pan of cold water which just covers bird, with onions, sliced carrots, sliced celery, peppercorns, and bouillon cubes. Bring water slowly to the boil. Then cook slowly, allowing 30 minutes per pound.

4. Remove from cooking liquid and test for tenderness. Strain stock and boil to reduce quantity. Melt 1½ oz butter and add 1½ oz flour. Pour on 1 pint of the stock and white wine. Blend carefully. Bring to the boil, and when smooth and cooked, spoon over turkey and serve hot.

5. If serving cold, add ½–¾ oz gelatine to sauce and dissolve before allowing to cool. When cool, spoon over turkey and leave to set.

Devilled Turkey Legs

2 large cooked turkey legs cut in half
3—4 tablespoons oil or 2 oz butter
juice of ½ onion
juice of 1 crushed clove garlic
1 tablespoon tomato ketchup
1 tablespoon mushroom ketchup
2 tablespoons Worcestershire sauce
1 level teaspoon English mustard
1 rounded teaspoon French mustard
1 teaspoon sugar
a small pinch cayenne pepper
salt, pepper
4 tomatoes
12 oz rice
½ small tin tomatoes
¼ pint turkey stock

Pre-heat grill

Cooked turkey legs marinated in a devil mixture, then fried and served with rice and tomato devil sauce (Serves 4, hot)

1. Make devil mixture: Mix oil or melted butter with onion and crushed garlic juices, tomato and mushroom ketchup, Worcestershire sauce, mustards, sugar, cayenne pepper, salt and black pepper.

2. Disjoint each turkey leg. With a sharp knife cut shallow gashes into meat. Put joints into dish with devil mixture and spoon devil sauce all over them. Marinate for at least 1 hour, longer if possible, turning frequently.

3. Grill joints until brown all over, turning frequently. Grill 4 tomatoes at the same time. Serve with plain boiled rice and sauce made by adding ½ tin tomatoes and ¼ pint stock to remaining devil sauce. Heat sauce and strain. Serve with a green salad.

Smoked Turkey Salad

1 pound smoked turkey breast
½ pound noodles
2—3 tablespoons cream
2—3 lettuce hearts
3—4 tomatoes
3—4 oz cooked sweetcorn and green
   pepper

MAYONNAISE
½ teaspoon salt
¼ teaspoon pepper
½ level teaspoon dried mustard
½—¾ teaspoon sugar
1 egg (or 2 egg yolks)
¼—½ pint salad oil
1 tablespoon lemon juice
1—2 tablespoons wine vinegar

Thinly sliced smoked turkey on a layer of cooked noodles in mayonnaise, with tomatoes, lettuce and corn. This makes a filling first course, or part of an hors d'oeuvre (Serves 4—6, cold)

1. Make mayonnaise: Put pepper, mustard and sugar into liquidizer. Add egg. Mix thoroughly at low speed. Add a few drops of oil. Mix well. Then add remaining oil in steady stream until it has been absorbed and mayonnaise is very thick. Add lemon juice, vinegar, salt and 1—2 tablespoons boiling water, which thins it and helps to make it keep.

2. Boil noodles until tender in salted water, drain and let cool. Add beaten cream to mayonnaise, mix 2/3 with the cold noodles and season to taste.

3. Cut smoked turkey into very thin slices and place on top of noodle mayonnaise in a neat row. Garnish dish with lettuce hearts, peeled tomato quarters, and sweetcorn and green pepper mixed with a little of remaining mayonnaise.

Turkey Stuffed Tomatoes

4—6 oz cooked turkey chopped
4 large red tomatoes
½ cucumber
2 stalks celery
3—4 tablespoons cooked sweetcorn
¼ pint mayonnaise (approx.)
4 slices lemon or chopped parsley

A first course made with cold turkey, cucumber, celery and sweetcorn in mayonnaise, filled into large hollowed tomatoes and served with brown bread and butter (Serves 4, cold)

1. Chop cold turkey. Cut off the tops of the tomatoes, remove seeds, and reserve juice. Peel cucumber, dice, salt and leave for 20 minutes. Then wash and drain. Chop celery and mix with sweetcorn.

2. Make mayonnaise as in *Smoked Turkey Salad* (see above). Add juice from tomatoes.

3. Mix vegetables and turkey with enough mayonnaise to make creamy mixture. Fill into tomatoes, and garnish with sliced lemon or chopped parsley. Serve with brown bread and butter.

Turkey, Celery, Grape and Nut Salad

Chopped turkey, peeled grapes, sliced celery and almonds in orange flavoured mayonnaise, a delicious summer dish (Serves 4, cold)

mayonnaise (see p. 137)
8—10 oz turkey chopped
2—3 oz grapes
3—4 stalks celery
1½—2 oz almonds
juice of ½ lemon
grated rind of ½ orange
lettuce or endive leaves
¼ teaspoon paprika

1. Make mayonnaise as in *Smoked Turkey Salad* (see p. 137).

2. Chop turkey into medium size pieces. Peel grapes after dipping into boiling, then cold, water. Slice celery. Dip almonds in boiling water, remove skins, and brown halved nuts in moderate oven for 2 minutes.

3. Add extra lemon juice and grated orange rind to mayonnaise, to flavour. Mix turkey and other ingredients into mayonnaise. Arrange on lettuce or endive leaves and sprinkle with a little paprika.

Turkey with Lemon Mayonnaise

*Sliced cooked turkey served with a refreshing lemon flavoured mayonnaise on a rice and vegetable salad
(Serves 6—8, cold)*

1½—2 pounds cooked turkey meat
1 pound rice
2—3 oz peas
2—3 oz green beans, chopped
2—3 oz sweetcorn
4 tomatoes
1 medium cucumber
1—1¼ pints mayonnaise (approx.)
grated rind of 2 lemons
1 tablespoon parsley chopped
6—8 thin slices lemon

FRENCH DRESSING
½ teaspoon French mustard
½—¾ pint oil
4—5 liquid oz wine vinegar
1—2 tablespoons fresh mixed herbs
   chopped

1. Boil rice in plenty of salt water for 10—12 minutes or according to instructions on package. Drain and wash well with cold water. Drain and dry. Boil peas, beans and sweetcorn in salt water. Drain and let cool. Peel and slice tomatoes, reserving juice. Peel cucumber, dice and sprinkle with salt. Leave for 20 minutes; then wash well and drain.

2. Make French dressing: Mix salt, pepper and sugar to taste with French mustard and oil. Add vinegar. Beat well. Add chopped herbs.

3. Make mayonnaise as in *Smoked Turkey Salad* (see p. 137) using double quantities and lemon instead of vinegar. Add 2—3 teaspoons grated lemon rind for flavour. Cut turkey into cubes or strips, mix with half the mayonnaise. Thin remaining mayonnaise slightly with the strained juice of the tomatoes.

4. Add all vegetables to cold cooked rice and moisten with French dressing. Arrange this mixture down sides of a dish. Spoon turkey mayonnaise down centre. Spoon little extra mayonnaise over the top. Sprinkle with chopped parsley mixed with remaining lemon rind, and garnish with slices of lemon made into twists.

Turkey Fricassee

Cold turkey re-heated in a cream sauce enriched with egg yolks and served with bacon rolls and fried mushrooms (Serves 4, hot)

1 pound cold turkey meat
3 oz butter (approx.)
1½ oz flour
½—¾ pint mixed stock and milk
½ teaspoon onion powder
1 tablespoon chopped parsley, thyme
   and powdered bay leaf
¼ teaspoon mace
2 egg yolks
3—4 tablespoons cream
4 rashers streaky bacon cut in half
8 mushrooms

Pre-heat oven to 325°F Mark 3
Pre-heat grill

1. Make white sauce: Melt 1½ oz butter, add flour, and pour on mixed chicken stock and milk. Blend well. Then bring to boil, stirring constantly. Simmer for few minutes. Then add onion powder, herbs and seasoning. Beat egg yolks with a little cream. Add a little sauce. Then strain egg yolk into sauce. Do not allow to boil.

2. Cut cold turkey into slices. Place in a buttered ovenproof dish. Cover with buttered paper. Heat in oven for 10—15 minutes. Spoon the sauce over turkey and return to oven for 10 minutes, being careful not to boil sauce.

3. Meanwhile, roll up bacon rashers and put on skewers. Grill until crisp. Put mushrooms into buttered dish with seasoning and a pat of butter on each. Cook in oven for 15 minutes at same time as turkey.

4. Arrange mushrooms around sides of dish and bacon rolls down centre and serve hot, with rice or mashed potatoes.

Turkey, Celery, Grape and Nut Salad

Turkey Timbale

Finely minced cooked turkey mixed with white sauce and eggs, baked in a ring mould and filled with mushrooms cooked in a Madeira sauce (Serves 4, hot)

1. First make a thick cream sauce: Melt 1 oz butter, stir in 1 oz flour until blended. Pour in hot milk and bring to a boil stirring constantly. Cook for few minutes, add seasoning and allow to cool.

2. Mince turkey finely in liquidizer and mix with eggs beaten in cream. Add cooled sauce. Mix everything well together and turn into a thoroughly buttered ring mould allowing a little space at the top for expansion while cooking. Cover with a buttered paper. Put in roasting pan of hot water and bake for 25—35 minutes or until a skewer can be inserted into the centre and come out clean. Run a knife around the outside and inner ring of mould, and turn out on to a large round plate. Pour mushroom sauce into centre and serve at once.

3. While the timbale cooks, make mushroom sauce: Melt 1½ oz butter and cook quartered mushrooms for 2—3 minutes. Then sprinkle in 1 oz flour. Cook for 1 minute, remove from heat and add brown, well flavoured stock and blend thoroughly. Bring to a boil and simmer for a few minutes. Add seasoning, herbs and Worcestershire sauce and Madeira or sherry. Allow flavours to blend well before pouring into centre of mould.

8—12 oz turkey meat chopped
3 oz butter
2 oz flour
8 liquid oz milk flavoured with onion and herbs
2 eggs
3—4 tablespoons double cream
16—20 mushrooms
½—¾ pint well flavoured brown stock
1 tablespoon herbs chopped
2 teaspoons Worcestershire sauce
2—3 tablespoons Madeira or sherry

Pre-heat oven to 350°F Mark 4

Quickly made and tasty filling for French style pancakes, made with minced cold turkey and tinned condensed tomato soup or sauce, and finished with crispy cheesy topping (Serves 6, hot)

PANCAKES

8 oz flour
2 eggs
2 egg yolks
1 pint milk
½ oz butter
oil for frying

FILLING
10—12 oz turkey minced
1 tin condensed tomato soup (or equivalent sauce)
4—6 oz cooked vegetables (as available)
1—2 teaspoons tomato puree (if necessary)
¼ teaspoon onion powder
a pinch of garlic powder
1 oz butter
1 oz grated cheddar cheese

Pre-heat grill

Turkey and Tomato Pancakes

1. Sift flour with salt and pepper into bowl. Make a hollow in centre, and add beaten eggs and ¼ pint milk. Mix eggs and milk together with spoon before gradually drawing in flour. Add quarter pint of milk as mixture thickens. When it is smooth and like thick cream, beat for 5 minutes by hand or in mixer. Stir in melted butter and ½ pint of the milk. Leave batter in covered bowl for 30 minutes before cooking.

2. Test thickness of batter, which should just coat back of spoon. If too thick, add extra milk and stir well. Grease a 5—6 inch griddle or frying pan with little oil. When hot, pour in enough batter to coat pan thinly. Cook until golden brown on one side, turn and cook other side. Pile up and keep warm. Allow 2—3 per person. (After frying, pancakes can be frozen. If using frozen pancakes, allow to defrost before filling.)

3. Mince turkey and mix with tin of condensed tomato soup. Add any cooked vegetables such as peas or sweetcorn, and herbs if available. Heat mixture and add a little tomato puree to taste, if desired. Sprinkle in a little onion and garlic powder, salt and pepper to taste.

4. Put filling into pancakes, roll up and place down centre of fireproof dish. Sprinkle with butter and cheese. Grill until cheese is golden brown and crisp. Serve at once.

Turkey and Mushroom Croquettes

Chopped cooked turkey and fresh mushrooms in a thick cream sauce enriched with egg yolk, shaped into small rolls, coated in egg and breadcrumbs, and fried in deep fat (Serves 4–6, hot)

8–10 oz cooked turkey chopped
2½–3 oz butter
2 oz flour for sauce
4 liquid oz strong turkey or chicken stock
4 liquid oz milk
salt, pepper
a pinch of mace
a small pinch of cayenne pepper
1 tablespoon parsley chopped
1½–2 oz mushrooms chopped
a little lemon juice
1 egg yolk
¼ pound seasoned flour
2 eggs beaten with 1 teaspoon oil
6 oz dried white breadcrumbs
fat for deep frying

1. Make thick sauce: Melt 2 oz butter and add flour. Add stock and milk, and bring to the boil. Cook until thick and smooth. Add seasonings and parsley and allow to cool.

2. Meanwhile, chop turkey into small pieces. Chop mushrooms and cook in ½ oz butter. Sprinkle with lemon juice. Add chopped turkey; then add sauce. Stir well. When almost cold add beaten egg yolk; put mixture into refrigerator to chill and set.

3. Divide mixture into 12 equal portions. Shape each into small roll with floured fingers. Roll in seasoned flour, coating ends carefully. Brush all over with beaten egg and then cover thickly with dried white breadcrumbs.

4. Heat fat to 390°F or smoking hot. Fry 4 croquettes at a time until well browned. Then drain well and serve at once with a piquant brown or tomato sauce.

Turkey and Grape Aspic

Slices of cooked turkey and white grapes in layers of aspic, set in a round mould and turned out on watercress and lettuce (Serves 4–6, cold)

1. Make aspic: Melt gelatine in ½ pint clear hot turkey stock. When melted, add 4 tablespoons white wine, and 1 pint more of stock. Let cool thoroughly.

2. Meanwhile, dip white grapes into boiling water for 10 seconds, then into cold. Remove skins and pips and put in bowl with a little lemon juice to prevent browning. Cut turkey meat into neat small slices and cubes.

(cont.)

(cont.)

1—1½ pounds turkey meat
¾—1 oz gelatine
1—1½ pints clear, well flavoured turkey
    stock
4 tablespoons white wine
1 pound white grapes (or ½ pound,
    and 1 tin of mandarin oranges)
juice of ½ lemon
a few tarragon leaves
lettuce and watercress

3. Pour a layer of aspic into a round mould. Arrange a decorative pattern of grapes with tarragon leaves and leave in refrigerator to set. Pour over another layer of aspic. Now put in a layer of turkey and repeat. Continue making layers of grapes, meat and aspic until all is used, allowing enough aspic to cover top completely.

4. Put in refrigerator and leave until set. Then dip in bowl of hot water to loosen jelly and turn out on to a salad-lined plate. This makes a good buffet dish or ladies' summer luncheon dish. Tinned mandarin oranges can be added or used in place of grapes.

Turkey Noodle Ring (See p. 143)

Turkey and Ham Patties

Crisp pastry patties with creamy filling of turkey and ham (Serves 4, hot)

4—5 oz turkey chopped
3—4 oz ham chopped
1 packet of frozen puff pastry, about
    ½ pound
1 egg
1½ oz butter
1 onion
1¼ oz flour
½ pint milk
1 tablespoon parsley
salt, pepper, a pinch of mace

Pre-heat oven to 450°F Mark 8

1. Roll out pastry until ¼ inch thick. Using 2½ inch diameter pastry cutter, cut out 8 patties. Now using a smaller cutter, 1½ inch in diameter, make a central cut in each patty being careful not to cut through to the bottom. Brush surface of each patty with beaten egg. Do not allow egg to run over sides or this will prevent pastry rising.

2. Put on a dampened baking sheet and bake for about 12—15 minutes until patties have risen and are golden brown. Remove from oven, take off centre lids carefully and reserve. Scoop out the soft pastry inside and throw away. Keep warm.

(cont.)

3. Meanwhile make filling: Melt butter and cook finely chopped onion for 5—6 minutes to soften. Mix in flour. Add milk. Blend well before bringing to boil, stirring all the time. Add chopped turkey and ham, parsley and seasoning. Heat together and spoon into patty shells. Place lids on top and serve at once, or keep warm for a short time.

TURKEY: TASTY LEFTOVERS
Turkey Noodle Ring

A tasty way of using remains of cold turkey to make a filling family meal (Serves 4, hot)

8—10 oz cooked turkey
½ pound noodles
2½—3½ oz butter
3 onions
1 clove garlic
½ pint double cream (fresh or soured)
1 egg
2—3 tablespoons grated cheddar cheese
1 tablespoon herbs chopped
3 oz mushrooms
1 oz flour
¼ pint stock
¼ pint milk
4 oz cooked peas and sweetcorn
2 tablespoons cooked green pepper
　chopped
2 hard boiled eggs
a pinch of paprika

Pre-heat oven to 350°F Mark 4

1. Boil noodles in plenty of salted water until they are almost cooked. Drain. Heat 1½—2 oz butter in pan and cook 1 chopped onion and garlic for few minutes to soften. Stir noodles into this. Then add ½ pint cream (fresh or soured) beaten with egg, grated cheese and chopped herbs. Sprinkle liberally with salt and pepper, and mix thoroughly. Turn into a buttered ring mould and press in well. Cover with buttered paper and put in oven for 45 minutes to set and to finish cooking noodles. Remove when done, and turn out on a hot dish. Fill with turkey filling.

2. Melt 1—1½ oz butter and cook 2 finely sliced onions to soften for 5—6 minutes. Add mushrooms, stir well, then sprinkle in flour. Blend well. Add stock and milk. Bring to the boil and simmer for 4—5 minutes. Then remove from heat. Add chopped turkey meat, cooked peas, sweetcorn, green pepper and 2 hard boiled eggs quartered. Season well and allow to stand in a warm place until noodle ring is ready. Spoon into centre, and sprinkle with paprika.

Sliced Turkey in Chestnut Sauce

Delicious and unusual way of using cold sliced turkey in a chestnut flavoured sauce (Serves 4, hot)

8 large slices cooked turkey
1½ oz butter
2 onions
1 carrot
¾ oz flour
2 teaspoons tomato puree
1¼ pints brown stock
2 liquid oz sherry or wine (optional)
1 bay leaf
a few sprigs of parsley
1 sprig thyme
4—5 tablespoons chestnut puree or
　stuffing
3—4 roughly chopped cooked chestnuts
2 tomatoes (optional)

Pre-heat oven to 350°F Mark 4

1. Make sauce: Chop onions and carrot. Cook in melted butter until tender, about 10 minutes. Then brown gently. Add flour. When blended, add tomato puree and stock. A little sherry or wine can be added in place of some of the stock.) Bring to the boil, cook for 10—15 minutes adding herbs and seasoning. Strain through sieve, and add chestnut puree or stuffing. Re-heat and stir until smooth. Add a few pieces of cooked whole chestnuts to the sauce if available.

2. Cut turkey into thin slices and place in an ovenproof dish. Garnish with sliced tomatoes, if desired. Then spoon over sauce and reheat in oven for few minutes. Serve with crisp fried potatoes and green vegetables.

Turkey Cottage Pie

Chopped cooked turkey mixed with mushrooms, bacon and onions in white sauce, topped with a layer of creamy mashed potato and browned in oven (Serves 4, hot)

¾—1 pound chopped or diced cooked
    turkey
1 pound potatoes
3 onions
3 oz butter
¼ pint milk
2—3 rashers bacon
2 oz mushrooms chopped
1 tablespoon chopped parsley and
    tarragon
½ oz flour
a pinch of mace, salt, pepper
½—¾ pint turkey or chicken stock
2—3 tablespoons milk

Pre-heat oven to 400°F Mark 6

1. Peel potatoes and boil in salted water with 1 peeled onion to flavour. When tender, in 15—20 minutes, remove onion, drain potatoes. Mash thoroughly, beat in 1 oz butter and some warmed milk, enough to make a soft mixture without being at all runny. Heat carefully, adding salt, pepper and mace.

2. While potatoes boil, cook chopped onions gently to soften in 1—1½ oz butter. After 3 minutes add chopped bacon and after another 3 minutes add sliced mushrooms. Cook for 1 minute. Sprinkle in flour and when blended stir in stock, add herbs and seasoning. Bring mixture to the boil, simmer for a few minutes, and add diced or chopped turkey meat. Add a little milk. Then turn into an ovenproof dish.

3. Spread mashed potato carefully all over top of dish and smooth. Score potato with a fork and dot with tiny flakes of butter. Bake in oven for 20—30 minutes, or until surface of potato is golden brown and crisp.

Quick Turkey Hash

Chopped turkey heated gently with a tin of mushroom or asparagus soup, with added mushrooms and vegetables as available (Serves 4, hot)

10—15 oz cooked turkey meat chopped
1 tin condensed mushroom or
    asparagus soup
1 tin evaporated milk
3—4 sliced mushrooms if available
3—4 oz cooked peas, beans, sweetcorn,
    tomato etc.
1 tablespoon chopped herbs or 2—3
    tablespoons grated cheese

1. Empty tin of condensed soup into pan and heat with enough added milk to make consistency of sauce. Add sliced mushrooms if available and cook gently for 4—5 minutes. Then add chopped turkey meat and any available cooked vegetables.

2. Heat the hash gently until completely hot; then add herbs or grated cheese. Serve hot with rice or mashed potatoes.

Fried Turkey Crisps

Chopped turkey in sauce with bacon, mushroom and cheese, made into round balls, coated in egg and breadcrumbs, and fried in deep fat until crisp (Serves 4—6, hot)

4—6 oz cold turkey chopped
1½ oz butter
1 tablespoon chopped onion
4 rashers bacon
2 oz chopped mushrooms
1½ oz flour
8 liquid oz stock
3 egg yolks
2 tablespoons grated Italian cheese
2 tablespoons breadcrumbs
2—4 oz flour seasoned with salt, pepper
    and paprika
2 eggs
4—6 oz dry white breadcrumbs
fat for deep frying

1. Melt butter, cook chopped onion and diced streaky bacon for 3—4 minutes. Then add finely chopped mushrooms, cook again for 2 minutes, sprinkle in flour and blend smoothly. Add stock. When thoroughly mixed, bring to the boil, stirring constantly. Cook for 2 minutes and allow to cool slightly. Add finely chopped turkey. Add beaten egg yolks and seasoning, cheese and breadcrumbs. Cool completely in refrigerator.

2. Form tablespoonsful of the mixture into balls. Roll in seasoned flour. Brush thoroughly with beaten egg all over. Then shake in a bag of dry white breadcrumbs until completely coated.

3. Heat fat to 380°F (until a cube of bread turns brown in 1 minute). Cook crisps until brown all over, remove and drain on paper towel. Serve at once, very hot, with a sharp tomato sauce.

Turkey Salad in Curried Mayonnaise

Shreds of turkey on a salad of cold cooked vegetables coated with curry flavoured mayonnaise, suitable as a first course or part of hors d'oeuvre or summer salad (Serves 4–6, cold)

¾–1 pound turkey meat
12–15 oz mixed cooked vegetables, peas, beans, sweetcorn, celery and green pepper
4 tomatoes
1 bunch watercress
½ oz butter
1 shallot (or 1 tablespoon chopped onion)
2 teaspoons curry powder
1 teaspoon flour
¼ pint stock
2 teaspoons coconut
2 teaspoons chutney
3 teaspoons lemon juice
½–¾ pint mayonnaise
a pinch of paprika
1–2 lemons

1. Cook vegetables separately, and allow to cool. Shred cold turkey. Quarter tomatoes, remove seeds, strain and reserve juice for thinning mayonnaise. Wash watercress and dry thoroughly.

2. Make curry flavouring: Melt butter, cook chopped shallot or onion until tender. Add curry powder or paste and cook for a minute or two. Sprinkle in flour and cook for 1 minute. Add stock and blend well. Then bring to boil, stirring all the time. Sprinkle on coconut, add chutney and lemon juice, and cook for 10–15 minutes. Then strain and allow to cool. Add lemon juice, salt and pepper. When cold, add to mayonnaise.

3. Make mayonnaise as in *Smoked Turkey Salad* (see p. 137). Add cooled curry mixture to taste. Add as much of strained tomato juice as will make spooning consistency.

4. Mix all vegetables together and season with salt and pepper, sprinkle with lemon juice. Put into dish or salad bowl. Arrange turkey shreds in centre, spoon mayonnaise carefully over the top allowing the vegetable salad to show around edges. Sprinkle top with paprika. Arrange tomato quarters and small sprigs of watercress alternately around the edge of dish and serve with lemon quarters separately.

Smothered Turkey

Slices of cooked turkey on a bed of cooked rice, covered with a soured cream sauce and topped with chopped chives

8 large slices of cold turkey
¾ pound rice
1½ oz butter
1 onion
½ pint soured cream
a pinch of nutmeg
2 tablespoons chives chopped

Pre-heat oven to 350°F Mark 4

1. Cook rice in boiling salt water. Drain and rinse with hot water. Dry and put in the bottom of a serving dish.

2. Cut cold turkey into slices and place over rice. Cover with buttered paper and heat through in oven for 15–20 minutes.

3. Melt butter and cook finely chopped onion until tender but not brown, 6–8 minutes. Add soured cream. Blend well. Add salt, pepper and a little nutmeg.

4. Spoon soured cream sauce over turkey and rice and sprinkle with chopped chives. Serve at once.

Turkey Gratin

¾–1 pound chopped cooked turkey (or other poultry or game)
1½ oz butter
1 onion
2–3 large mushrooms
1¼ oz flour
½–¾ pint stock
3–6 oz cooked vegetables (peas, beans, sweetcorn, chopped carrots, green pepper, etc) or 4 oz cooked noodles
3–4 tablespoons double cream
1 tablespoon chopped parsley and thyme
3–4 tablespoons grated cheddar cheese
a little paprika

Pre-heat grill

Useful way of using leftover turkey and cooked vegetables, in a tasty sauce topped with browned grated cheese (Serves 4–6, hot)

1. Melt butter and cook chopped onion until tender. Add chopped mushrooms and cook for 1 minute. Sprinkle in flour and blend well. Pour on stock and bring to boil, stirring constantly. Add chopped turkey and any available cooked vegetables or cooked noodles. Stir well into sauce. Add herbs and cream.

2. Turn into buttered baking dish and sprinkle thickly with grated cheese and a little paprika. Grill until crisp and brown all over. Serve with cooked noodles, rice or potatoes.

CHICKEN: PARTY DISHES

6 pieces frying chicken
4 tablespoons flour mixed with salt,
    pepper and a pinch of cayenne
    pepper
1 egg
1 teaspoon oil
4—5 oz fresh white breadcrumbs
2 tablespoons oil
3—3½ oz butter
3 bananas
6 rashers bacon

FRITTERS
3—4 oz sweetcorn
1 egg
4 oz self raising flour
¼—½ teaspoon curry powder
fat for deep frying

SAUCE
1½ oz butter
1 onion
1 clove garlic
1 small tin tomatoes
1 level tablespoon mixed herbs
½ teaspoon sugar
½ teaspoon paprika
¼ pint cider or stock

Pre-heat grill

Chicken Maryland

Particularly delicious dish of fried chicken served with fried bananas, sweetcorn fritters, bacon rolls, and a savoury tomato sauce (Serves 6, hot)

1. Roll chicken pieces in seasoned flour, then brush all over with egg beaten with oil and coat well with fresh white breadcrumbs. Heat oil and add 2—2½ oz butter. When foaming, put in chicken pieces and fry gently for 20—25 minutes, turning frequently until brown and crisp all over.

2. Meanwhile, prepare sweetcorn fritters: Drain tinned sweetcorn and mix with 1 egg yolk and seasoning. Sift flour and curry powder, stir into sweetcorn mixture. Just before frying, beat egg white and fold into sweetcorn mixture. Heat fat until very hot but not smoking, 370°F. Drop fritter mixture into fat by tablespoonsful and fry until light brown. Drain on paper towel. Keep warm.

3. Fry halved bananas in 1 oz butter until golden brown. Keep warm. Cut bacon rashers in half, roll up carefully. Thread on to skewers, grill until crisp all over. Keep warm.

4. Prepare tomato sauce: Melt butter, cook sliced onion and crushed garlic for 5—6 minutes. Add tomatoes, herbs, seasoning, sugar, paprika and cider or stock. Bring to the boil, then strain or blend in liquidizer and serve hot with chicken.

1 capon or chicken 3—4 pounds
4 rashers unsmoked bacon
12—16 small onions
12—16 button mushrooms
1 clove garlic
2 oz butter
½ pint burgundy or red wine
½—¾ pint strong brown stock
2—3 sprigs parsley or 1 teaspoon dried
    parsley
1 sprig thyme or a pinch of dried
    thyme
1 bay leaf

Pre-heat oven to 325°F Mark 3

Chicken Burgundy

Rich burgundy flavoured casserole of chicken, bacon, onions and mushrooms (Serves 4—6, hot)

1. Thaw the capon or chicken if frozen. Cut it into suitably sized pieces and dry. Chop bacon into small pieces. Peel onions and mushrooms. Crush garlic.

2. Melt 1—1½ oz butter and fry bacon, onions and garlic until golden brown. Remove to casserole and keep warm. Fry chicken pieces in same butter until golden brown all over. Remove to casserole.

3. Pour the red wine into pan and bring to a boil to reduce quantity to half. Meanwhile, flambé wine to burn off the alcohol. Add the stock and boil for 5 minutes. Season with salt and black pepper. Pour this sauce over chicken and vegetables in casserole. Add herbs. Bring to the boil. Then reduce heat and cook for 45—60 minutes over low heat or in oven.

4. While chicken is cooking melt remaining butter and cook the mushrooms. Add to casserole for last 20 minutes of cooking time.

French Roast Chicken

Chicken roasted with butter, herbs and well flavoured stock. Best method of cooking chicken to be eaten cold (Serves 4–6, hot or cold)

1. If frozen, be sure chicken is completely thawed out before cooking. Make stock with giblets, onion, seasoning and water. Cook slowly for 15 minutes. Put ½ the butter inside bird with herbs, salt and pepper. Spread remaining butter over chicken, cover with fat bacon, put into roasting pan and pour half the stock over the chicken.

2. Cook in oven, basting with stock every 15 minutes and turning the bird from side to side. Allow 20 minutes per pound weight. For last 20 minutes remove bacon and place bird breast up to brown.

3. Remove bird on to hot dish and keep hot in oven. Meanwhile skim the butter from top of pan drippings. Add remaining stock to roasting pan and boil until well flavoured. Serve as gravy.

4. Serve chicken either hot or cold with a green salad and garnished with watercress.

1 chicken, 3—4 pounds
chicken giblets and 1 onion (or 1
   chicken cube)
½—¾ pint water
3—3½ oz butter
3—4 sprigs of fresh parsley
2—3 slices fat bacon
1 bunch watercress

Pre-heat oven to 375°F Mark 5

Circassian Chicken

Unusual Middle Eastern dish of chicken in walnut sauce, flavoured with paprika and cayenne
(Serves 4–6, hot)

1. Put chicken in deep pan and just cover with cold water. Add 3 onions each stuck with a clove, chopped celery, herbs, peppercorns and a little salt. Bring to the boil and simmer until tender, about 1 hour. Skim as necessary. Drain and keep warm, reserving stock for sauce.
2. Grind walnuts finely in liquidizer and mix with breadcrumbs. Melt butter and cook 2 chopped onions and crushed garlic until golden brown and soft. Then add to walnut mixture with ¾ pint of the reserved stock, blending carefully. When quite smooth, cook until it reaches boiling point, adding more stock if sauce becomes too thick. Season with salt and a little pepper.
3. Mix oil, paprika and cayenne pepper together, and when oil is red, strain. Add enough of this oil to walnut sauce to make it a delicate pink.
4. Cut chicken into pieces. Put a layer of sauce in the bottom of a fireproof dish, lay chicken pieces on top. Spoon remaining sauce over the top of the chicken. Reheat thoroughly. Decorate top with remaining red oil, sprinkling over surface of dish. Serve with plain boiled rice.

1 chicken, 3–4 pounds
5 onions
3 cloves
3 stalks celery
a few sprigs parsley
1 bay leaf
8 peppercorns
8 oz shelled walnuts
2 oz dry breadcrumbs
1 oz butter
1 clove garlic
1 tablespoon paprika
a pinch of cayenne pepper
3 tablespoons oil

Chicken Curry

4 large chicken pieces
2½ oz butter
2 medium onions
1 tablespoon curry powder (or more
   according to taste)
1 teaspoon curry paste
½ oz flour
1½ cups strong chicken stock
1 apple
1 oz raisins
2 tablespoons chutney
1 bay leaf
2 tablespoons finely shredded coconut
juice of ½ lemon
2 teaspoons redcurrant or other sharp
   jelly
¾—1¼ pounds cooked long grain rice
2—3 teaspoons turmeric powder
1 lemon
½ teaspoon paprika

Pre-heat oven to 350°F Mark 4

Tender chicken pieces browned in butter and cooked in a mild curry sauce, served with plain boiled rice and numerous accompaniments (Serves 4, hot)

1. Heat 1½ oz butter, and brown chicken pieces until golden. Remove and put in a fireproof dish to keep warm.

2. Slice onions finely and cook until golden brown. Then add curry powder and paste, and cook for few minutes. Add flour and allow to brown slightly. Add stock, bring to boil and simmer for 4—5 minutes. Then add chopped apple, raisins, chutney, bay leaf and salt. Cook together for 1 minute. Pour over chicken pieces, and cook in oven for 35—40 minutes, by which time chicken pieces should be nearly tender.

3. Meanwhile, pour 2—3 liquid oz of boiling water over shredded coconut; let stand for 30 minutes. Strain liquid on to chicken, adding lemon juice and jelly. Cook for 15 minutes.

4. When cooked, remove chicken pieces and put in centre of a ring of boiled rice finished with turmeric cooked in remaining butter. Boil up sauce, sieve or liquidize it, season to taste, and spoon over chicken. Garnish with thin slices of lemon and sprinkle with paprika.

Brunswick Stew (see p. 160)

Chicken Suprême with Mushrooms

Tender breasts of chicken cooked in butter, served on sliced cooked mushrooms and covered with a delicately flavoured cream sauce (Serves 4, hot)

4 chicken breasts
3½—4 oz butter
10—12 large mushrooms
2 teaspoons lemon juice
1 tablespoon parsley chopped
1½ oz flour
½ pint chicken stock
salt, white pepper
a large pinch of mace
¼ pint cream
2 egg yolks
**1—2 tablespoons white wine (or a little
    lemon juice)**

Pre-heat oven to 375°F Mark 5

1. Remove 4 complete chicken breasts or "supremes" from 2 chickens, (use remaining chicken parts for another meal). Melt 2—2½ oz butter in a pan large enough to hold all 4 chicken breasts. Cook them in butter very gently, without browning, for 4—5 minutes on each side. Remove from pan and put into a buttered dish, cover with foil and bake in oven for about 10—15 minutes, or until tender and cooked through.

2. Meanwhile, cook sliced mushrooms in butter left from chicken and 1 teaspoon lemon juice for 5—6 minutes. Season; add chopped parsley. Place in bottom of serving dish and when chicken is cooked place "supremes" on top. Reduce oven to 250°F Mark ½ and keep warm while making sauce.

3. Melt 1½ oz butter and stir in flour. When smooth, add stock and bring slowly to the boil, stirring constantly. Cook for 2 minutes. Add salt, white pepper and mace. Mix cream with egg yolks. Mix 3—4 tablespoons hot sauce with cream and eggs; strain carefully into sauce, stirring constantly. Re-heat very gently over a pan of hot water. Do not allow sauce to reach boiling point or eggs will curdle and sauce be ruined. Season to taste and add a little white wine or lemon juice, if desired. Spoon over chicken "supremes" and serve with boiled rice.

Chicken Veronique

Tender chicken roasted in the French manner, served with a white wine sauce and garnished with peeled white grapes (Serves 4, hot)

1 roasting chicken, about 3 pounds
3—3½ oz butter
few sprigs tarragon (or dried tarragon)
1¼ pints stock made with chicken
   giblets (or chicken bouillon cube
   and water)
2 slices fat bacon
4—6 oz white grapes
little lemon juice
¾—1¼ pounds plain boiled rice

SAUCE
1½ oz flour
¾ pint strong chicken stock
¼ pint white wine
2—3 tablespoons heavy cream

Pre-heat oven to 375°F Mark 5

1. Roast chicken as in *French Roast Chicken* (see p. 147) using tarragon as flavouring inside the bird.

2. Meanwhile, dip grapes in boiling water for 10 seconds and then in cold. Peel (and remove pips if necessary). Put grapes in small bowl and sprinkle with lemon juice to prevent browning.

3. Remove chicken from roasting pan when cooked, and carve. Place pieces on rice, cover and keep warm.

4. Skim off 3 oz butter into a saucepan. Heat gently, sprinkle in flour, blend carefully, pour on stock and wine and bring to the boil, stirring constantly. Boil for few minutes, remove from heat and allow to cool slightly. Add cream and grapes. Allow grapes to warm through. Then spoon sauce over chicken, and serve at once.

Chicken à la King

An especially delicious way of using cold chicken to make a party filling for pastry cases, or served on fried croutons, with mushrooms and sweet pimentos in a creamy sauce (Serves 4, hot)

8—10 oz cooked chicken
1 sweet red or green pepper
8 mushrooms
1½ oz butter
a squeeze of lemon juice
1 oz flour
½ pint chicken stock
2 tablespoons sherry
a pinch of mace
2 egg yolks
3—4 tablespoons double cream
4 pastry patty shells or 4 fried rounds
   of bread
1 teaspoon chopped parsley or ¼
   teaspoon paprika

1. Chop the pepper and boil for 5 minutes. Rinse in cold water; drain. Cook sliced mushrooms in ½ oz butter and a little lemon juice until tender, 5—6 minutes. Dice cooked chicken into small pieces.

2. Make sauce: Melt butter and blend in flour smoothly. Add chicken stock, bring to the boil, stirring constantly, simmer for few minutes, then add sherry, mace and seasoning.

3. Mix chicken, mushrooms and peppers into sauce, put in top of double boiler. Mix egg yolks and cream together. Add a little of the hot sauce, stir, strain and add to chicken. Heat carefully; do not boil.

4. Spoon mixture into hot pastry patty shells or on to fried rounds of bread. Sprinkle the top with chopped parsley or paprika, serve at once.

Paella

A delicious Spanish dish of chicken, prawns, clams or mussels, in saffron, onion and garlic flavoured rice (Serves 4—6, hot)

4—6 large chicken pieces seasoned
   with salt and pepper
4—5 tablespoons olive or corn oil
2 onions
1—2 cloves garlic
¾—1 pound long grain rice
2—2½ pints chicken stock (or chicken
   bouillon cube and water)
large pinch of saffron
1—1½ oz butter
3 tomatoes
pinch of mace
1—2 tablespoons chopped parsley and
   thyme
2 oz peas (or green beans)
4—6 oz unshelled prawns or 12 mussels
   or 4—6 clams

Pre-heat oven to 350°F Mark 4

1. Heat oil in a large flat frying pan and when hot cook chicken pieces for 12—15 minutes until golden brown all over. Remove and keep warm.

2. Add sliced onions and crushed garlic to pan, and cook for 5—6 minutes, until golden brown. Add rice and fry for 1 minute, stirring constantly to prevent sticking.

3. Add stock, saffron soaked in 2 tablespoons of hot stock, butter, and peeled and chopped tomatoes. Bring to the boil; then add chicken pieces. Add seasoning, herbs, peas (or beans) and simmer for 10 minutes. If rice appears dry add extra stock.

4. Add prawns, mussels or clams to pan and heat in oven for 15 minutes, when the shells of the mussels or clams should have opened. Serve very hot.

Barbecued Chicken

Tender chicken pieces grilled in a spicy sauce over a charcoal grill (Serves 4, hot)

4 large chicken quarters or halves
BARBECUE SAUCE
4—5 tablespoons oil
1 onion
1 clove garlic
1 medium tin tomatoes (or 3—4
    tablespoons tomato puree)
1 tablespoon tomato ketchup
1 tablespoon chutney
1 tablespoon vinegar
¼ pint stock (or water)
1 tablespoon Worcestershire sauce
1 teaspoon French mustard
1 teaspoon paprika
juice and grated rind of ½ lemon
2 level teaspoons brown sugar
1 tablespoon parsley finely chopped
1 teaspoon mixed powdered thyme,
    nutmeg and bay leaf

1. Prepare barbecue sauce: Heat oil and cook finely chopped onion and crushed garlic for 5 minutes, add sieved tomatoes or puree and all other ingredients. Cook for 20—30 minutes, season to taste, strain and allow to cool.

2. With a sharp knife make small cuts into the chicken pieces. Spoon the cold barbecue sauce over them and let stand for at least ½ hour.

3. Heat charcoal, electric or gas grill. Place chicken pieces on hot grill and turn every 5—6 minutes, basting frequently with barbecue sauce. Allow 30—45 minutes to barbecue quarters depending on heat of grill and thickness of chicken pieces. Test with skewer: if juice from chicken runs clear the chicken is cooked through.

4. Heat remaining sauce, and serve chicken with salad and baked potatoes.

Chicken Cordon Bleu

Chicken breasts stuffed with a mixture of chopped ham and Swiss cheese with garlic, coated in egg and breadcrumbs, and fried in butter (Serves 4, hot)

4 chicken breasts
4 level tablespoons chopped cooked ham
4 level tablespoons grated Swiss cheese
1 small clove garlic
1—2 tablespoons white wine
3—4 tablespoons seasoned flour
1 large egg
2 liquid oz oil
2—3 oz dried white breadcrumbs
2—2½ oz butter

1. Place 4 chicken breasts skin side downwards, and with a sharp knife cut a shallow slit down centre of each without cutting through to skin. Then cut shallow pockets on either side of these slits.

2. Mix ham and cheese with crushed garlic and a little white wine to moisten. Season well. Fill into pockets in chicken breasts and seal slit with the small finger-shaped fillet which is attached to each breast. Put in fridge to chill for thirty minutes.

3. Coat well in seasoned flour, brush carefully with egg beaten with 1 teaspoon of oil, and roll in breadcrumbs. Heat oil, and add butter. When foaming, fry chicken breasts until tender, golden brown and crisp all over. Drain on paper towel.

4. Serve with asparagus spears or broccoli, and a party salad.

Paprika Chicken

A spicy paprika flavoured chicken dish, garnished with soured cream (Serves 4, hot)

1 chicken 2½—3 pounds
2 tablespoons flour seasoned with salt
    and pepper
2 tablespoons oil
2 oz butter
4 onions
1 clove garlic
2 teaspoons paprika
2 tablespoons tomato puree
½ pint white wine
½ pint strong chicken stock
1 tablespoon chopped parsley
1 teaspoon thyme
1 carton or 5 liquid oz soured cream

1. Cut chicken into pieces and roll in seasoned flour. Heat oil. Add 1 oz butter. When foaming, add chicken pieces and fry until golden brown. Remove and put into casserole.

2. Add remaining butter and sliced onions to frying pan. Cover and cook until tender but not brown, about 5—6 minutes. Add crushed garlic; cook for 1 minute. Add paprika and remaining seasoned flour, then the tomato puree. Stir until smooth. Then add wine and stock. Bring to the boil, stirring constantly.

3. Pour sauce over chicken pieces. Add herbs, salt and pepper to taste. Cook slowly until tender, for about 1 hour.

4. Spoon soured cream over top of casserole, and serve with buttered noodles or rice.

Chicken Kiev

A luxurious dish of fried chicken breasts, stuffed with garlic and herb flavoured butter (Serves 4, hot)

4 whole breasts of chicken
3 oz butter
1 clove garlic
1 tablespoon mixed parsley, tarragon and lemon thyme
1 tablespoon lemon juice
2 oz flour
2 eggs
1 teaspoon oil
4—6 oz dried white breadcrumbs
fat (or oil) for deep frying
boiled rice
1 lemon

1. Mix butter with finely crushed garlic, chopped herbs, lemon juice and seasoning, shape into a roll about 3—4 inches long. Wrap in foil and put into refrigerator to freeze.

2. Each chicken breast consists of one large heart shaped piece and a long thin finger shaped piece. The smaller pieces flatten out slightly. Place the large pieces skin side down and make a shallow slit down centre of each. Then make a shallow pocket to each side with a sharp knife. Remove skin. Cut butter roll into 4 long pieces, place one piece on each chicken breast so that it is in the pocket. Place flattened smaller pieces of chicken over butter and then close the slits over them. Turn ends of chicken and shape each breast neatly. Wrap each in foil and put into the refrigerator for at least 30 minutes to firm.

3. Just before cooking, roll each breast in seasoned flour, then brush with egg beaten with oil and cover thickly with dried white breadcrumbs.

4. Heat fat (or oil) to 370° F or until a cube of fresh bread takes 60 seconds to brown. Fry chicken breasts for 5—7 minutes, until golden brown and crisp. Serve at once with boiled rice and lemon quarters. (Warn guests to cut chicken carefully or hot butter will spurt out.)

Chicken in Lemon Sauce

Lemon flavoured chicken casserole garnished with mushrooms and parsley (Serves 4, hot)

4 chicken quarters seasoned with salt and pepper
3 oz butter
2 small onions or shallots
2 carrots
2 stalks celery
1 large lemon
½—¾ pint chicken stock
¼ pint white wine
3—4 parsley sprigs
1 bay leaf
a sprig of lemon thyme
4 oz baby mushrooms
1 tablespoon parsley finely chopped

Pre-heat oven to 350°F Mark 4

1. Lightly brown seasoned chicken pieces in 2 oz butter in fireproof dish or casserole. Remove and keep warm.

2. Chop onions, quarter carrots, slice celery and cook for 5—10 minutes in the butter to soften, without browning. Put chicken pieces back into casserole on top of vegetables, sprinkle with grated rind of ½ lemon and all the juice; pour in stock and wine. Add parsley sprigs, bay leaf and lemon thyme if available. Season and cook in oven for 35—40 minutes, or until chicken pieces are tender.

3. Remove chicken to a serving dish and keep warm. Remove carrots, the bay leaf and herb stalks. Then sieve or liquidize remaining vegetables. Re-heat the lemon and vegetable sauce, and if too thick add enough chicken stock to thin. Check for lemon flavour and add more lemon juice if necessary, to taste.

4. Melt remaining butter and cook the baby mushrooms for 3—4 minutes until tender and place on top of chicken. Spoon sauce over chicken and mushrooms. Cut remaining lemon rind into match-like strips, boil for 2 minutes, drain and dip in cold water to revive colour. Sprinkle over dish with finely chopped parsley.

Traditional Roast Chicken

Chicken stuffed and roasted, served with crisp bacon rolls, grilled chippolata sausages and bread sauce (Serves 4—6, hot)

1 chicken or capon, 3—4 pounds (if frozen thaw completely)
6 oz of butter
1 large onion
4—6 oz fresh breadcrumbs
2 tablespoons chopped cooked ham
1 tablespoon chopped parsley
½ teaspoon chopped thyme
a little grated lemon rind
1 beaten egg or 2—3 tablespoons milk
2—3 tablespoons bacon fat or oil
¾ pint chicken stock made from giblets (or a chicken bouillon cube)
4—6 rashers bacon
8—12 chippolata sausages
BREAD SAUCE
½ pint milk
1 onion
2—3 cloves
½ bay leaf
3 parsley sprigs or 1 teaspoon dried parsley
a pinch of mace or nutmeg
6 peppercorns
2—2½ oz fresh breadcrumbs
½ oz butter
2 tablespoons cream

Pre-heat oven to 400°F Mark 6

1. First prepare stuffing: Melt 2—3 oz butter, cook ½ onion, chopped, for 3—4 minutes to soften. Mix with breadcrumbs, chopped ham, herbs and grated lemon rind. Add seasoning, beaten egg or milk to make fairly moist mixture. Fill into neck end of chicken. Fold skin flap under wings and skewer or sew to hold in place. Put ½ onion and some seasoning inside cavity of bird with a little butter. Rub remaining butter over chicken and sprinkle with seasoning.

2. Melt bacon fat or oil in roasting pan. When hot, add chicken, baste thoroughly, then cover with foil and put into oven. Roast, basting every 15 minutes, turning chicken from side to side, allowing 20 minutes per pound and a little extra time. During the last 15 minutes, remove foil to allow breast to brown. Remove to hot dish and keep warm while making gravy. Pour off fat, pour in remaining chicken stock, bring to the boil. To obtain flavour, reduce liquid by boiling.

3. Meanwhile, prepare bread sauce. Stick cloves into onion, put in pan with milk, herbs, peppercorns. Cook gently for 20—30 minutes without boiling. Strain on to fresh breadcrumbs; heat together until creamy, then at the last minute stir in butter and cream. Add seasoning and serve hot.

4. Divide bacon rashers in half, make into rolls; put on skewers and grill until crisp at the same time as grilling chippolata sausages. Serve chicken surrounded by bacon rolls and sausages, the gravy and bread sauce separately.

Chicken Stuffed with Mushrooms

Spring chickens stuffed with mushrooms, roasted and finished with a cream sauce (Serves 4, hot)

2 small spring chickens or petits poussins
3—4 oz mushrooms
4 oz butter
1 small onion
2—3 liquid oz single cream
1 level teaspoon cornflour (optional)
a little chopped parsley or paprika

Pre-heat oven to 350°F Mark 4

1. Cook finely chopped onion for about 5 minutes in half the butter with lid on pan. Slice or quarter mushrooms, add to onions and cook for 3—4 minutes. Season and allow to cool.

2. Wipe the prepared spring chickens; stuff them with the cooled mushroom mixture. Melt remaining butter in fireproof dish or iron casserole. Fry chickens gently until brown all over. Season and pour over 2 liquid oz water. Cook in oven for about 20 minutes. When tender remove from casserole and split each bird in half. Arrange on warm serving dish and put into low oven while making sauce.

3. Make sauce: Mix cream with gravy in casserole, bring slowly to a boil and season to taste. The sauce will be fairly thin: to thicken, if preferred, mix cornflour with 2—3 tablespoons of cold water until smooth. Add to hot sauce and boil for ½ minute.

4. Spoon a little of this sauce over each bird and serve the rest separately. Decorate with a little chopped parsley or a sprinkling of paprika.

Chicken and Cheesy Rice Ring (see p. 163)

CHICKEN: COLD BUFFETS

Chicken Liver Pate

A rich smooth liver pate decorated with chilled consomme and mushrooms, suitable as first course or cold buffet (Serves 8–10, cold)

1 pound chicken livers (fresh or frozen)
8 oz butter
2 onions
1 large clove garlic (optional)
1 small glass sherry or brandy
1 tablespoonful fresh mixed herbs:
    parsley, lemon thyme, basil,
    marjoram, and summer savory (or
    2 level teaspoons dried herbs)
a pinch of dried mace (optional)
GARNISH
1 tin consomme
3–4 oz button mushrooms
1 bunch watercress

1. Fry finely chopped onions and crushed garlic gently in 3 oz butter for a few minutes. Do not allow to brown as this will ruin the flavour. Add chicken livers and cook for 3–4 minutes. Then add mixed herbs, mace and seasoning. Cook for 1 minute. Remove from stove and let cool.

2. Mash livers to a soft pulp in liquidizer, stirring in 3–4 oz melted butter. Add sherry or brandy. Put the pate into a serving dish, or a lightly oiled mould so that it can be turned out after chilling. It can be made several days before a party if kept in the refrigerator and should be a delicate pink inside when cut.

3. Make garnish: Chop chilled consomme and place around pate. Cook mushrooms gently for a few minutes in remaining melted butter until completely absorbed. Drain on paper towel. Let cool. Decorate the top of the pate with mushrooms and surround with watercress.

Chicken Jelly

*Pretty and delicious jellied chicken
and vegetable dish suitable for
summer buffet party or luncheon
(Serves 4—6, cold)*

**8—12 oz cold chicken meat
2 tins consomme
½—¾ oz gelatine
2 tablespoons sherry
2 eggs
3 tomatoes
4—5 oz mixed peas, carrots, sweetcorn
1 lettuce
1 bunch watercress**

1. Dissolve gelatine in the hot consomme, add sherry and allow to cool. Hard boil eggs for 10—12 minutes and put into cold water to cool thoroughly. Cut up cold chicken meat into long strips, peel and quarter tomatoes. Set aside. Cook vegetables until tender, drain and cool .

2. Pour a layer of consomme into a mould; put in refrigerator to set. Cut hard-boiled eggs into slices and arrange a layer on the chilled consomme in mould with tomato quarters in between. Spoon some more consomme over them and again allow to set. Arrange chicken and vegetables and remaining egg in layers with the consomme, letting each layer set.

3. Chill thoroughly in refrigerator and when set, dip outside of mould for a few seconds into hot water to loosen. Turn out on to serving dish. Garnish with lettuce and watercress.

Chicken Tetrazzini (see p. 161)

Chicken Galantine

*Boned chicken stuffed with sausage meat and tongue forcemeat, boiled
until tender; when cold coated with a chaudfroid white sauce and set with
jelly coating, a buffet or party dish (Serves 6—8, cold)*

1. If possible, buy chicken ready boned, otherwise remove bones with a very sharp knife, first cutting down back and loosening skin and flesh from carcass without piercing skin. Remove bones from legs and wings in same manner. Then place bird skin side downwards and season.

2. Put carcass and giblets into large pan with onions, carrots, celery, peppercorns and herbs. Cover with water, cook for as long as possible to make a well flavoured stock.   *(cont.)*

1 stewing or roasting chicken, 3½—4
    pounds
2 onions
2 carrots
2 stalks celery
8 peppercorns
parsley, thyme and a bay leaf
8—12 oz sausage meat
½ level teaspoon onion powder
2 tablespoons parsley chopped
½ teaspoon chopped thyme
1 teaspoon grated lemon rind and little
    juice
2 hard boiled eggs
2 oz chopped tongue
3—4 closed button mushrooms
a squeeze of lemon juice

CHAUDFROID SAUCE
1½ oz butter
1½ oz flour
¾ pint milk, flavoured with onion and
    herbs
½ oz gelatine
3—4 tablespoons double cream

ASPIC JELLY
½ oz gelatine
¾ pint strong chicken stock
2 tablespoons sherry

3. Mix sausage meat with seasoning, onion powder, chopped parsley, thyme, lemon rind and juice. Place half this mixture down centre of chicken and a layer of sliced hard boiled egg and chopped tongue on top. Place half remaining sausage meat on top, using other half to stuff legs and wings.

4. Re-shape bird as well as possible, tidily folding in loose ends of skin at neck and opening. Allow the skin which was cut down back to overlap slightly. Sew up tightly with clean white string. Wrap chicken in clean cloth or muslin, put in suitably sized pan, cover with stock and cook very gently for 2—3 hours according to size and age of bird. Check from time to time to make sure that there is enough liquid to cover bird which should be turned once after 1—1½ hours.

Chicken Chop Suey (see p. 161)

5. When cooked, remove from pot and when slightly cool improve shape if necessary. Allow to get cold, preferably overnight. Remove string.

6. Make white or cream sauce with butter, flour and milk, add gelatine dissolved in hot stock and when cool add cream. When it begins to set and has consistency of thick cream, put chicken on cake rack and spoon mixture over entire surface. Allow to set. Cook sliced mushrooms in a little stock and lemon juice until tender. Cool, then place carefully down centre of bird to decorate.

7. Dissolve gelatine in hot stock with sherry and let it cool. When it begins to set spoon carefully all over the chaudfroid sauce on chicken. Let it cool completely in refrigerator, and serve on dish decorated with lettuce, sliced cucumber, tomatoes and radish flowers.

Dessert apples stuffed with diced chicken suitable for buffet party or summer lunch (Serves 4, cold)

8 oz white cooked chicken meat
½ pint mayonnaise
2—3 tablespoons double cream
2 oz pineapple chunks
3—4 oz grapes
2 stalks celery
4 large apples
1 level teaspoon grated lemon rind
2 tablespoons slivered almonds

1 roasting chicken
½—¾ pints chicken stock made from giblets (or chicken bouillon cube and water)
3 oz butter
2 slices fat bacon
3—4 sprigs parsley
1 bunch tender asparagus (or 1 tin green asparagus spears)
½ pint mayonnaise
2 liquid oz double cream
2—3 oz cooked peas, chopped beans or sweetcorn (optional)
lettuce or endive
¼ teaspoon paprika

Chicken Stuffed Apples

1. Make mayonnaise as in *Smoked Turkey Salad* (see p. 137). Add lightly beaten cream and season to taste.

2. Dice chicken finely and mix with drained pineapple chunks, peeled seeded grapes and chopped celery. Mix with mayonnaise.

3. Polish apples and cut off tops. Scoop out flesh with a grapefruit knife or spoon. Remove core and dice remaining apple; add to mayonnaise.

4. Fill the apples with chicken mayonnaise. Sprinkle top with grated lemon rind and lightly browned almonds.

Chicken and Asparagus Mayonnaise

Cold chicken and asparagus with delicately flavoured mayonnaise, arranged on endive salad, suitable for buffet or summer lunch (Serves 4—6, cold)

1. Cook chicken as in *French Roast Chicken* (see p. 147) or buy ready cooked chicken. Remove meat from bones and cut into cubes.

2. Trim asparagus and cook in boiling salted water until tender and drain, or open tin of green asparagus spears and drain carefully.

3. Make mayonnaise as in *Smoked Turkey Salad* (see p. 137)

4. Mix chicken and mayonnaise. Add a little cream and peas, beans or sweetcorn, if available. Arrange in centre of a lettuce or endive-lined dish and place asparagus around edge in little bundles. Sprinkle top of chicken mound with paprika, and serve with crusty French bread and butter.

CHICKEN: EVERYDAY DISHES

Chicken and Ham Pie

Tasty pie of chicken, ham, mushrooms and onions, in a well flavoured sauce under a light pastry crust (Serves 4—6, hot or cold)

1 chicken weighing 3 pounds
4 onions
2 carrots
3 stalks celery
several parsley sprigs
1 bay leaf
6 peppercorns
2½ oz butter
3 oz mushrooms
1 oz flour
½—¾ pint strong chicken stock
2 level tablespoons mixed chopped
   parsley, thyme, tarragon
a pinch of mace
6 medium thick slices ham
1 package frozen puff pastry
1 egg

Pre-heat oven to 425°F Mark 7

1. Cut meat off chicken bones in large chunks. Put carcass and giblets in pan with 2 onions, carrots, celery, herbs and peppercorns. Cover with water and cook until well flavoured; strain and add salt.

2. Melt 1 oz butter, cook 2 thickly sliced onions for 3—4 minutes. Then add mushrooms; cook for 1 minute, remove and keep warm. Heat another 1 oz butter and fry chicken pieces in pan for 4—5 minutes to seal meat. Sprinkle in flour, then pour on stock and bring to boil, stirring constantly. Simmer for 1 minute. Then add onions and mushrooms. Sprinkle in herbs and seasoning.

3. Chop ham and make a layer at bottom of pie dish. Spoon in half chicken mixture, another layer of ham, remaining chicken mixture, and top with ham. Allow to cool.

4. Roll out pastry, place thin strip around moistened edge of pie dish. Brush this strip with water and place the large piece of pastry on top. Crimp edges together; then cut off excess with sharp knife. Make 3—4 holes to allow steam to escape, decorate with pastry leaves and flowers. Brush pastry with beaten egg.

5. Bake in hot oven for 25 minutes to cook pastry. Cover pastry with damp greaseproof paper or foil. Reduce heat to 375°F or Mark 5 for another 20 minutes to cook chicken.

Oven Fried Chicken

Chicken pieces coated with egg and breadcrumb mixture, baked in the oven and served with piquant tomato sauce (Serves 4, hot)

4 chicken parts or quarters
1—1½ oz flour
a little paprika
1—2 eggs
4—6 tablespoons breadcrumbs
4 tablespoons butter

TOMATO SAUCE
1 oz butter
1 onion
1 clove garlic
½ oz flour
2 level tablespoons tomato puree
1 small tin tomatoes
½ pint stock
1 tablespoon chopped mixed herbs
6 peppercorns
strip of lemon rind
pinch of cayenne pepper
1 teaspoon sugar

Pre-heat oven to 350°F Mark 4

1. Roll chicken pieces in flour seasoned with salt, pepper and paprika, brush thoroughly with beaten egg and roll in dried breadcrumbs. Put chicken in a well buttered ovenproof dish.

2. Pour melted butter over chicken, put into oven and cook for 30—35 minutes, or until pieces are crisp and brown.

3. Meanwhile, make tomato sauce: Melt butter, cook finely chopped onion and crushed garlic until golden. Sprinkle in flour and add tomato puree, tinned tomatoes and stock. Bring to the boil; simmer for 20 minutes adding herbs, peppercorns, lemon rind and a pinch of cayenne pepper. Strain sauce and add sugar. Season to taste.

4. Serve the chicken very hot with sauce and rice or mashed potatoes.

Persian Chicken Pilau

Chicken pieces fried in butter and cooked in an aromatic apricot cinnamon yoghurt sauce layered with rice and finished with almonds (Serves 4—6, hot)

4—6 chicken pieces about 2 pounds or more
2 tablespoons oil
3½—4 oz butter
1 large onion
4 oz dried apricots
½ level teaspoon cinnamon
grated rind of 1 lemon
1 carton natural yoghurt
12 oz long grain rice
2 tablespoons almonds

Pre-heat oven to 350°F Mark 4

1. Heat oil and add 1 oz butter. When foaming, fry chicken pieces until golden brown. Remove and allow to cool. Cook sliced onion until golden in the same oil and butter. Add chopped apricots; sprinkle with cinnamon, lemon rind, salt and ground black pepper. Remove bones from chicken pieces and shred meat. Mix yoghurt and onion mixture and soak chicken in this while rice is cooking.

2. Cook rice in boiling salted water for 10—12 minutes. Drain and rinse with boiling water. Dry for a few minutes. Heat 1½ oz butter in thick pan or casserole, put half rice into pan and mix well with butter and seasoning. Spoon chicken mixture over rice, and put remaining rice on top. Sprinkle with salt and pepper.

3. Melt remaining butter and spoon over rice. Cover pan with cloth and lid, and cook gently for 15—20 minutes until all the flavours are blended; the cloth absorbs extra moisture. (This process can be done in the oven but cloth should not be used.)

4. Brown slivers of almonds, sprinkle on top of rice, and serve at once.

Brunswick Stew

Chicken stewed with potatoes, broad beans, tomatoes, onions and sweetcorn using a method originally devised for cooking squirrels (Serves 4—6, hot—see picture, p. 150)

1 stewing or roasting chicken, about 3—4 pounds
½ teaspoon salt
3 potatoes
1 large onion
1 small tin broad beans
1 small tin tomatoes (or 5—6 sliced fresh tomatoes)
1 level tablespoon sugar
2—3 oz sweetcorn
1 tablespoon ketchup or Worcestershire sauce
2 oz butter

1. Cut chicken into pieces and put in casserole with enough boiling water to cover; add a little salt. Simmer for about 45 minutes.

2. Add sliced potatoes, sliced onion, broad beans, tomatoes and sugar to casserole. Cook for 45 minutes, when beans and potatoes should be tender.

3. Remove as many bones as possible from chicken, add sweetcorn. Cook for 10 minutes. Then season to taste, and add ketchup or Worcestershire sauce if desired. Add butter and stir well.

Chicken Marengo

Chicken pieces cooked in wine, tomato and vegetable sauce, with a fried egg on fried bread (Serves 4, hot)

4 pieces frying chicken
6 liquid oz oil
2½ oz butter
1 rasher bacon
1 onion
1 clove garlic
3 carrots
2 stalks celery
1 oz flour
2 tablespoons tomato puree
4 liquid oz white wine or sherry
½ pint stock
1 bay leaf
several parsley sprigs
3—4 oz mushrooms
4 slices bread
4 eggs
1 tablespoon parsley chopped

Pre-heat oven to 350°F Mark 4

1. Heat 2 tablespoons oil and add ½ oz butter. When foaming, cook chicken pieces until golden brown. Place in casserole.

2. Fry bacon, finely chopped onion, crushed garlic, sliced carrots and celery for about 5 minutes. Sprinkle in flour and cook for 1 minute. Add tomato puree, wine or sherry and stock. Bring to a boil, add seasoning and pour over chicken pieces. Add herbs and sliced mushrooms. Cover casserole and cook in oven for about 1 hour.

3. After about 50 minutes, fry bread cut in rounds in remaining oil and ½ oz butter, and drain on paper towel. Fry eggs in 1½ oz butter and when cooked place on fried bread.

4. Serve chicken pieces on a hot dish. Boil up sauce and strain over chicken, reserving excess. Sprinkle top with chopped parsley. Place the fried eggs around the dish at the last moment, and serve.

Chicken Tetrazzini

Shredded boiled chicken served on a bed of spaghetti with a delicately flavoured wine sauce, topped with cheese and crisp browned almonds (Serves 4—6 hot—see picture, p. 156)

1 stewing chicken weighing about 3—4
    pounds
2 onions
2 carrots
parsley, thyme and a bay leaf
½ pound spaghetti
3 oz butter
dash of garlic powder
2 oz flour
¼ pint white wine
6—8 mushrooms
3—4 tablespoons double cream
1½—2 oz grated Parmesan cheese
2 tablespoons dried breadcrumbs
2 tablespoons sliced almonds

Pre-heat oven to 400°F Mark 6

1. Cook chicken slowly in water with onions, carrots and herbs until tender. Let cool in stock, if possible, overnight. Then remove skin and bones, and cook these in stock until it is well flavoured and reduced to 2—3 cups.

2. Boil spaghetti in usual way and finish off in ½ oz butter flavoured with a little garlic powder. Place in fireproof dish and keep warm.

3. Make velouté sauce. Melt 2 oz butter, add flour and when blended add ½ pint chicken stock, bring to boil and cook for 2 minutes. Then add wine and simmer for few minutes.

4. Meanwhile, cut cold chicken into long strips, place in a mound on top of spaghetti, and sprinkle with salt and pepper. Cook sliced mushrooms in ½ oz butter for 2—3 minutes; then put on top of chicken.

5. Add cream to sauce; check seasoning. Spoon sauce over dish; then sprinkle the top with cheese and crumbs. Bake in oven for 10—15 minutes, until the dish is well heated, and the top brown and crisp. Lastly, sprinkle browned almonds over the top and serve at once.

Chicken Chop Suey

Chinese dish of chicken in a clear sauce with mushrooms, onions, celery, and bean sprouts, served with rice (Serves 4, hot—see picture p. 157)

1 chicken weighing 3 pounds
4 onions
2 carrots
1 bunch herbs
6—8 peppercorns
1 chicken bouillon cube
8 oz rice
3—4 stalks celery
6—8 mushrooms
squeeze of lemon juice
1 tin bean sprouts
2 tablespoons soy sauce
1 tablespoon cornflour

1. Boil chicken with 2 onions, carrots, herbs and peppercorns until tender. Let it cool in water. When cool, remove skin and bones, and boil up stock with these and a chicken bouillon cube to make a well flavoured stock.

2. Boil rice in usual way, drain well and keep warm in oven.

3. Cut chicken into large chunks and reserve. Slice 2 onions and celery, and put these to cook in a little of the stock until just tender, 8—10 minutes. Cook sliced mushrooms in a little stock and lemon juice for 3—4 minutes; add to chicken. Mix chicken with drained vegetables, add drained bean sprouts, soy sauce, seasoning and ½ pint of chicken stock.

4. Heat gently. Meanwhile, mix cornflour with ½ pint of stock, add this to chicken mixture. Heat until sauce thickens and serve with boiled rice.

Chicken Florentine

Pieces of fried chicken on creamy spinach with a cheesy topping (Serves 4, hot)

4 pieces frying chicken
2—3 tablespoons seasoned flour
3 oz butter
1 pound spinach
½ oz plain flour
3—4 tablespoons cream
pinch of mace and paprika
2—3 tablespoons grated Italian cheese
2 tablespoons breadcrumbs

Pre-heat oven to 400°F Mark 6

1. Roll chicken pieces in seasoned flour; then fry in 1½ oz hot butter until golden brown, about 10 minutes.

2. Cook spinach. Drain and chop. Add 1 oz butter. When melted, sprinkle in flour. Bring to a boil; then add cream and seasoning, with a dash of paprika. Pour this into buttered fireproof dish. Place chicken pieces on top.

3. Mix cheese and breadcrumbs together, and sprinkle thickly over top of chicken. Dribble remaining butter over the top. Cook in oven for about 25—30 minutes, or until the topping is crisp and brown.

4 large chicken pieces
1½–2 oz flour
½ teaspoon salt
a large pinch of garlic powder
¼ teaspoon pepper
2 medium onions
2½ oz butter
2 tomatoes
2 liquid oz white wine
6–7 liquid oz chicken stock
2–3 oz raisins
2 oz pimento-stuffed olives
pinch oregano, parsley and thyme
¼ teaspoon cinnamon
3 tablespoons slivered almonds

Pre-heat oven to 400°F Mark 6

1 chicken 2½–3 pounds in weight
2–3 slices onion
3–4 parsley sprigs or 1 teaspoon dried
  parsley
a pinch of mace or nutmeg
6 white peppercorns
1 bay leaf
¾ pint white wine
¼ pint chicken stock
2 oz butter
1½ oz flour
2 teaspoons tarragon leaves
2 liquid oz double cream

Pre-heat oven to 350°F Mark 4

*Creamy chicken and mushroom
mixture on crispy fried bread
squares making a delicious
quick supper dish (Serves 4, hot)*

8 oz cooked chicken chopped or
  diced
1 oz butter
¾ oz flour
½ pint milk
8 mushrooms sliced
4 tablespoons stock
3 oz cooked peas or sweetcorn
5 thick slices of white bread
8 liquid oz oil
½ oz butter
1 tablespoon parsley chopped

Mexican Chicken

*Chicken pieces cooked in an exotic flavoured sauce with onion, tomatoes,
raisins, olives and cinnamon, and served with rice (Serves 4, hot)*

1. Roll chicken pieces in flour seasoned with salt, garlic powder and
pepper. Remove and toss onion slices in the same flour.

2. Melt butter; when foaming, fry chicken pieces until golden brown,
about 7–10 minutes. Remove; keep warm in an ovenproof casserole. Add
sliced onions and chopped tomatoes to butter. Cook for 4–5 minutes.
Then add wine, stock, raisins, olives, herbs and seasoning. Bring to the boil,
and pour over chicken pieces. Put into oven for 35 minutes or until
chicken is tender.

3. Sprinkle with cinnamon and stir in. Lastly, sprinkle over browned
almonds and serve at once with plain boiled rice.

Chicken in White Wine Sauce

*Tender chicken cooked in white wine and served in a creamy sauce,
flavoured with wine and tarragon (Serves 4, hot)*

1. Cut chicken into pieces and put into casserole with onion, parsley
sprigs, mace, peppercorns and bay leaf. Add wine and stock and cook in
oven for 35–45 minutes, until tender. Remove chicken pieces, put into
serving dish and keep warm.

2. Boil liquid left in casserole for a few minutes to strengthen flavour, and
reduce quantity. Melt butter, stir in flour and when smooth strain in ¾ pint
of the liquid. Season, and add 1 teaspoon tarragon leaves and cream.

3. Spoon sauce over chicken and sprinkle top with remaining tarragon
leaves. Serve at once, with rice or mashed potatoes.

CHICKEN: TASTY LEFTOVERS

Chicken Crisps

1. Make cream sauce: Melt butter and blend in flour. Gradually add milk;
when smooth, bring to the boil, stirring constantly. Boil for 3 minutes, then
cool slightly.

2. Slice mushrooms and cook in stock for 3–4 minutes. Chop or dice
chicken, and mix with mushrooms and cooked vegetables. Add mixture to
cream sauce, season well, heat thoroughly, and keep warm.

3. Remove crusts from slices of bread, and with a small cutter cut 4
crescent shaped pieces from the fifth slice. Heat oil and add butter. When
foaming, fry bread slices until golden brown on both sides. Also fry the 4
small crescents. Drain on paper towel.

4. Arrange the fried squares on a serving dish, spoon the hot chicken
mixture on to the squares, and decorate with the crescents and chopped
parsley.

Chicken and Cheesy Rice Ring

Cheese flavoured rice, baked in a ring mould and filled with creamy chicken and mushroom sauce with crisp topping (Serves 4—6, hot—see picture, p. 155)

12—15 oz cooked chicken (or chicken and ham)
3 oz butter
2 onions
12—14 oz cooked rice
1 egg
½ pint milk
5 oz grated cheddar cheese
2 level tablespoons mixed herbs chopped
½ teaspoon dry mustard
½ teaspoon paprika
4—6 large mushrooms
1 oz flour
½ pint stock (or tin condensed chicken or mushroom soup)
a pinch of nutmeg
1 green or red pepper
2—3 tablespoons breadcrumbs
Pre-heat oven to 350°F Mark 4

1. Melt 2½ oz butter and cook finely chopped onions for 4—5 minutes to soften, without browning. Remove half and put into bowl. Add rice to onion in bowl. Add beaten egg mixed with milk, 3—4 oz grated cheese and 1 level tablespoon herbs. Season with salt, pepper, dry mustard and half the paprika.

2. Butter a 7 inch ring mould and fill with rice mixture, packing it in well. Bake for about twenty minutes. When firm and cooked, remove from oven and turn out on a platter.

3. Meanwhile, prepare chicken sauce: Add sliced mushrooms to onion in pan and cook for two minutes. Remove from heat, add flour, mix well; then add stock (or condensed soup). Blend well, bring to the boil, cook for few minutes and add diced chicken, remaining herbs and seasoning. Flavour with nutmeg.

4. Boil coarsely chopped pepper for five minutes, drain and add to sauce. Keep sauce warm to allow flavours to blend. Spoon hot sauce into centre of rice ring. Any excess can be re-heated and served separately.

5. Sprinkle top with remaining cheese and crumbs mixed, dot over the last spoon of butter and brown under grill for a few minutes or in hot oven. Sprinkle with paprika and serve hot.

Duck Pate (see p. 167)

Fried Goose with Apple Rings (see p. 176)

Chicken and Corn Croquettes

Creamy chicken and sweetcorn mixture cooked in crispy coating of egg and breadcrumbs (Serves 4, hot)

1. Make a thick cream sauce. Melt 2 oz butter and stir in 2 oz flour. Add milk and blend smoothly. Bring to boil and cook for several minutes to reduce quantity slightly.

2. Melt ½ oz butter, and cook onion and sweetcorn for 3–4 minutes. Add chicken meat, chopped parsley, lemon juice, mace and mix well. Add 6 liquid oz of sauce, season well. Let cool; then add 1 egg yolk. Spread mixture out on plate to cool and thicken.

3. Divide into 8 equal portions and form into rolls. Turn in 3 oz flour seasoned with salt and pepper until completely covered. Brush all over with egg beaten with oil. Then coat completely with breadcrumbs. (They can be left for up to 1 hour at this stage before cooking.)

4. Heat oil or fat until gently smoking, then lower 3–4 croquettes at a time into hot fat and cook until golden brown and crisp. Drain on paper towel, and serve at once with lemon quarters and a salad or green vegetables.

8–10 oz finely chopped chicken
2½ oz butter
5 oz flour
½ pint milk
1 teaspoon onion finely chopped
2–3 oz tinned sweetcorn
2 teaspoons parsley
1 teaspoon lemon juice
a pinch of mace
3 eggs
1 teaspoon oil
5–6 oz dried white breadcrumbs
fat for deep frying

Chicken Liver Risotto

Tender chicken livers cooked with savoury rice, garnished with grated cheese for extra flavour (Serves 4, hot)

1½ oz butter
1 small onion
1 clove garlic
6—8 chicken livers
4—6 mushrooms
8 oz rice
1¼ pints well-flavoured stock or water and chicken stock cube
2 tablespoons parsley chopped
4—5 oz grated cheddar cheese

1. Melt butter, and cook chopped onions and crushed garlic for a few minutes. Then add halved chicken livers and quartered mushrooms. Cook until the livers change colour and stiffen slightly.

2. Add rice, stir well into other ingredients. Pour on half of the stock, and add seasoning and parsley. Bring to boil; then add most of remaining stock. Simmer gently for about 20—30 minutes, stirring from time to time and adding remaining stock to moisten, if necessary.

3. Serve with grated cheese in a separate bowl.

Duck Stuffed with Apricots (see p. 170)

Fried chicken with unusual peanut butter sauce (Serves 4, hot)

1 chicken, 2½—3 pounds
2 tablespoons oil
2 onions
1 level teaspoon curry powder
2 tablespoons tomato puree
½ pint chicken stock
1 tablespoon mixed parsley and thyme
1 bay leaf

PEANUT SAUCE
6—7 tablespoons peanut butter
¾ pint chicken stock

Chicken with Peanut Sauce

1. Cut chicken into pieces, season with salt and pepper. Heat oil and brown chicken pieces all over. Remove and keep warm.

2. Cook sliced onion until tender. Add curry powder and tomato puree. Stir until smooth, add stock and bring to boil. Add herbs and seasonings. Pour over chicken pieces. Simmer until tender, about 1 hour.

3. Make peanut sauce: Mix peanut butter with stock and season. When smooth, pour over chicken, heat for 10—15 minutes, and serve with boiled rice.

Chicken Koulibiaca

Diced chicken and mushrooms in a delicious light pastry roll (Serves 4, hot)

6—8 oz diced chicken
1—1½ oz butter
1 small onion
3—4 oz mushrooms chopped
¼ oz flour
2—3 liquid oz chicken stock
3—4 tablespoons cooked peas,
   sweetcorn or beans
1 tablespoon parsley chopped
1 level teaspoon tarragon chopped
1 medium package frozen puff pastry
1 egg

Pre-heat oven to 450°F Mark 8

1. Melt butter and cook chopped onion until tender, 3—4 minutes. Add chopped mushrooms and cook for 1 minute. Stir in flour, then add stock and bring to boil. Mix diced chicken into sauce, with herbs, seasoning and cooked peas, sweetcorn or chopped beans. Allow to cool completely.

2. Roll out completely thawed puff pastry into a rectangle and place on a baking sheet. Spoon cooled chicken mixture down the centre of one side of pastry rectangle. Brush edges of pastry with water, fold flap of pastry over top, seal edges and crimp to make a pretty edge. With a sharp knife cut 3—4 slashes diagonally across pastry to allow steam to escape. Brush the whole surface with beaten egg.

3. Bake in oven for about 30 minutes, until pastry is brown and done. Remove to serving dish and serve hot.

Kitty's Chicken Cream

Delicious light and economical chicken dish suitable for both old and young (Serves 4—6 hot)

1 pound cooked chicken
6—8 oz fresh breadcrumbs
2 oz butter
1 oz flour
½ pint milk
a large pinch of ground mace or nutmeg
1 tablespoon parsley chopped
1 egg

Pre-heat oven to 375°F Mark 5

1. Mince chicken and mix with fresh breadcrumbs.

2. Make cream sauce: Melt 1 oz butter and blend in flour. Add milk gradually. When smooth, bring to a boil, stirring constantly. Boil 2—3 minutes; add mace or nutmeg and herbs. Let cool slightly.

3. Add sauce to chicken mixture. Stir well, adding remaining butter and beaten egg. Season well. Put in buttered fireproof dish, allowing room for chicken cream to rise slightly, and cook in oven for 30—35 minutes.

DUCK

Duck Pate

Delicious pate made from duck, liver, pork, bacon and herbs mixed with brandy and egg, baked in slow oven and then pressed; suitable for buffet (Serves 6–8, cold–see picture, p. 35)

1 pound cooked duck
½ pound duck and lamb liver chopped
¼ pound lean raw pork or veal chopped
4–6 oz fat bacon chopped
1 onion
½ clove garlic
4 tablespoons breadcrumbs
1 small egg
2 tablespoons milk
1 tablespoon parsley and thyme chopped
2 teaspoon grated orange rind
2–4 liquid oz brandy
a pinch of mace
10–12 rashers streaky bacon
4 slices orange
½ tin consomme
¼ oz gelatine
1–2 tablespoons brandy (or sherry)

Pre-heat oven to 325°F Mark 3

1. Mince livers, pork or veal, fat bacon, finely chopped onion and crushed garlic together. Mix in breadcrumbs, egg beaten with milk, chopped herbs, orange rind and brandy (or sherry). Add seasoning and mace.

2. With a knife stretch bacon rashers by scraping, and line a loaf or pate pan completely with them. Cut cooked duck into strips and sprinkle half into the loaf pan, season, then cover with half the meat mixture. Put in rest of duck, then remaining mixture. Fold over any overlapping pieces of bacon. Cover the whole pan carefully with foil. Put in a baking pan of water and bake in oven for 2–3 hours.

3. Half an hour before the pate is done, remove foil and place 4 slices of orange down the centre, re-cover, continue cooking. When done, remove from oven and allow to cool. Put a double layer of greaseproof paper on top and weights to press pate and make it firm.

4. Dissolve gelatine in half a tin of consomme, let cool and add 1–2 tablespoons brandy (or sherry). When nearly set, turn pate out on to wire rack and spoon jelly consomme over it. Leave to set. Serve on a salad lined plate with orange segments for flavour and colour.

Cold Duck Souffle

Delicious light souffle of minced duck mixed with cream sauce, sherry, whipped cream and egg whites topped with a layer of orange slices set in jellied consomme (Serves 4–6, cold–see picture, p. 166)

12 oz cold duck minced
½ pint milk
1 onion
1 carrot
6 peppercorns
a pinch of mace
4 stalks parsley (or 2 teaspoons dried parsley)
1 sprig of thyme (or ¼ teaspoon thyme)
1 bay leaf
3 cloves
1 oz butter
1 oz flour
1 tin beef consomme
¾ oz gelatine
3 tablespoons sherry
4 liquid oz double cream
2 eggs
2 oranges

1. Make cream sauce: Put milk into small pan with sliced onion and carrot, peppercorns, mace, herbs and cloves. Heat slowly for 20 minutes. Melt butter, stir in flour, strain on milk and bring to the boil, stirring constantly. Simmer for 3–4 minutes. Allow to cool.

2. Meanwhile dissolve ½ oz gelatine in ½ tin consomme. Add 1 tablespoon sherry and the finely minced duck. Mix well.

3. When sauce is cool beat and mix into duck and jelly mixture. Season well, as the flavour dulls when cold. Put bowl into large bowl containing iced water and ice. Stir from time to time. When on the point of setting stir in whipped cream and whipped egg whites. Put into souffle dish large enough to leave a little space for orange garnish and jelly. Put in refrigerator to set.

4. Meanwhile prepare garnish: With a sharp serrated knife, remove peel, pith and skin from oranges; cut into wafer thin slices. In remaining consomme dissolve ¼ oz gelatine. When cool add 2 tablespoons sherry.

5. When souffle has set, arrange orange slices in overlapping layers on top and spoon over the setting consomme. Return to refrigerator to set jelly and serve with green salad and potato with mayonnaise.

Duck

Duck stuffed with apples and prunes, roasted and served with a creamy gravy as traditionally eaten at Christmas in some Danish households (Serves 6, hot)

1 large duck, 5 pounds or more
½ oz butter
1 pound apples
4—6 oz stoned prunes
grated rind of ½ orange
salt, pepper, sugar
2 tablespoons oil
¾ pint brown stock
2 liquid oz port or red wine (optional)
1 level tablespoon cornflour
2 liquid oz double cream

Pre-heat oven to 350°F Mark 4

Danish Christmas Duck

1. Rinse duck out with cold water and dry thoroughly. Prick breast with a fork and rub over with butter and seasoning.

2. For stuffing, peel and thickly slice apples. Remove stones from soaked prunes. Mix both with some grated orange rind and a little salt and sugar. Stuff inside duck and sew up opening.

3. Heat oil in oven. When hot, add duck and baste thoroughly. Roast for 1¼—1½ hours, basting frequently, adding a little stock half way through cooking. Just before duck is done, pour off pan drippings and brown bird in slightly hotter oven.

4. Put duck on to serving dish and keep hot while making sauce. Skim fat off roasting juices and add remaining stock. Cook for a few minutes; add port or red wine (if available). Mix cornflour with a little cold water. Spoon a little hot sauce into cornflour, then return to pan and bring to the boil. Lastly, add cream and seasoning. Serve with red cabbage and browned potatoes.

1 tender roasting duck, 3—4 pounds
4 tablespoons honey
2 teaspoons wine vinegar
1½ tablespoons soy sauce
2 teaspoons sherry
1 orange
1 onion

Pre-heat grill or barbecue charcoal grill

Peking Duck

An exotic way of roasting duck on a spit while basting with a special sauce which gives crisp rich texture to skin of duck (Serves 4, hot)

1. Prepare special basting sauce: In a pan put honey, vinegar, soy sauce, sherry, juice of ½ orange and 1 tablespoon water. Heat all these ingredients together and bring to boil. Allow to cool.

2. Prick skin of duck lightly with a sharp fork, pour over several pints of boiling water to soften skin. Dry. Put onion and ½ orange inside duck and season. Put bird on spit and when grill or barbecue is very hot cook bird, basting frequently with special sauce. Allow 20 minutes per pound and lower heat after first half hour. Test if duck is done by sticking skewer deeply into leg meat. If juice is clear, duck is done.

3. Remove from heat and serve with rice and bean sprouts.

2 wild ducks, about 1½ pounds each
2 onions
4 stalks celery
2 tablespoons lemon juice
3 oz butter
1½ tablespoons oil
4 small oranges or mandarins
3 teaspoons sugar
¼ pint clear stock

Pre-heat oven to 400°F Mark 6

Roast Wild Duck with Baked Oranges

Wild ducks roasted simply with butter, and served with oranges baked whole as a garnish (Serves 4, hot)

1. Put a quartered onion and some celery into each duck with a little lemon juice and seasoning. Rub breasts over with 1 oz butter; sprinkle with salt. Heat oil and 1 oz butter in roasting pan. When hot, put in birds, basting well. Roast in oven for 25—30 minutes, depending on size of birds, basting every 15 minutes.

2. Wipe small oranges or mandarins, rub skins with butter. Put them around ducks for the last 20 minutes of cooking time.

3. Remove ducks, put on serving dish and keep warm. Make a hole in each orange, fill with a little sugar and arrange around the ducks. Skim fat from pan drippings and add stock. Boil for several minutes to reduce quantity and season to taste. Serve with a salad and crisp potatoes.

Wild Duck with Red Cabbage

Wild duck cooked on top of a dish of braised red cabbage, with onion apple and caraway seeds (serves 4, hot)

1 wild duck, 2—3 pounds
1 small red cabbage, 1—1½ pounds
3 onions
2 tablespoons vinegar
2 tablespoons water
4 cooking apples
1 level teaspoon sugar
2 tablespoons oil
1 teaspoon caraway seeds
¼ pint stock
1 tablespoon parsley chopped

Pre-heat oven to 350°F Mark 4

1. First braise red cabbage: Shred cabbage very finely, discarding any hard stem. Chop 1 onion and mix with cabbage. Put in well-buttered casserole. Add vinegar, water and seasoning. Cover and cook in oven for 1 hour. Add sliced apples and a little sugar. Cook for 15 minutes more.

2. Cut duck into 4 pieces. Heat 2 tablespoons oil and when hot brown pieces of duck all over. Remove and place on top of cabbage in casserole. Cook 2 sliced onions in remaining oil until soft without browning. Sprinkle in caraway seeds and add a little stock. Add seasoning and pour over pieces of duck. Return to oven for 30—40 minutes, until tender.

3. Scrape onion mixture off duck and mix it well into red cabbage. Arrange duck pieces on top of cabbage and sprinkle with chopped parsley. Serve hot, with mashed potatoes and redcurrant jelly.

Barbecued Duck

Duck basted with a barbecue sauce, roasted or grilled over a barbecue grill or on a rotary spit (Serves 4—6, hot)

1 duck, 3—4 pounds
4—5 tablespoons oil
¼ teaspoon dry mustard powder
1 clove garlic
a large pinch of seasoning salt
1 level teaspoon sugar
a pinch of cayenne pepper
black pepper
1 onion
1 tablespoon Worcestershire sauce
3 tablespoons bitter marmalade
1—2 tablespoons ketchup
1 tablespoon honey
1 tablespoon vinegar
1 orange
3—4 tablespoons stock
1 oz butter

Pre-heat rotary grill (or charcoal grill)

1. Mix 2 tablespoons oil with mustard, crushed garlic, seasoning salt, sugar, cayenne and black pepper. Prick breast of duck and rub this paste all over. Fix duck on rotary spit or barbecue spit. Put an onion and lump of butter and some seasoning inside.

2. Prepare the charcoal grill or heat the rotary spit element to red hot. Start grilling duck, turning frequently if over charcoal. Allow 20 minutes per pound, basting with oil for first 45 minutes then frequently with sauce.

3. Mix 2 tablespoons oil with Worcestershire sauce, bitter marmalade (sieved), ketchup, honey, vinegar, grated rind and juice of orange, ground pepper and 3—4 tablespoons stock. Heat thoroughly and baste duck.

4. When duck is tender and brown all over, remove from spit. Serve hot with watercress and orange salad.

Duck and Green Pea Pancakes

PANCAKES
4 oz flour
1 egg
1 egg yolk
8 liquid oz milk
½ oz butter
oil for frying

FILLING
5—7 oz diced cooked duck
2 oz butter
1 onion
6—8 mushrooms
¾ oz flour
¼ pint strong stock
2—3 oz peas
1 tablespoon chopped parsley and thyme
3—4 tablespoons cream
2 tablespoons browned breadcrumbs
grated rind of 1 orange

Pre-heat oven to 350°F Mark 4

Remains of roast duck mixed with cooked peas in a thick, tasty sauce, rolled in light French style pancakes, topped with orange crumbs (Serves 4—6, hot)

1. Make pancakes as in *Turkey and Tomato Pancakes* (see p. 140).

2. Melt 1 oz butter, and cook chopped onion and mushrooms in covered pan for 3—5 minutes to soften. Stir in flour, blend well. Then add stock. When smooth bring slowly to boil and cook for a few minutes. Add diced duck meat, peas and herbs. Heat for few minutes. Add cream last. Keep warm while cooking pancakes.

3. Put a spoonful of filling in centre of each pancake and roll up. Arrange in overlapping row in ovenproof dish. Spoon over remaining melted butter and some breadcrumbs, mixed with a little grated orange rind. Heat for few minutes in oven and serve.

Duck

Roast duck stuffed with apricots, basted with honey and orange juice, and served with a sauce laced with apricot brandy (Serves 4–6, hot, see picture, p. 165)

**1 roasting duck weighing 4–5 pounds
1 pound fresh apricots (or 1 large tin, drained)
1 orange
1 onion
2 tablespoons oil
2–3 tablespoons honey
½ pint stock made with duck giblets (or a chicken stock cube)
2–3 tablespoons apricot brandy**

Pre-heat oven to 400°F Mark 6

Duck Stuffed with Apricots

1. Stuff duck with half the stoned apricots and 3 strips of orange zest (the thin outer skin of orange), finely chopped onion and seasoning. Prick skin of duck with fork to allow the fat to run out while cooking and season with pepper and salt.

2. Heat oil in baking pan. When very hot add duck and baste all over with oil. Roast in oven, allowing 20 minutes per pound. Half an hour before cooking is completed, spoon over the melted honey and juice of orange which will give the skin a shiny crispness. 10 minutes before end of cooking, add rest of apricots to pan to heat through and brown slightly. Remove duck to a warm dish, and remove stuffing to a bowl. Arrange roasted apricots around duck.

3. Pour off fat from roasting pan, add stuffing to pan with stock and bring to boil, stirring all the time. When the sauce has a pleasant flavour, strain or blend in liquidizer. Return to heat and add apricot brandy. Serve at once with duck and apricots.

**1 duck, 3½–4 pounds
2 tablespoons oil
1 oz butter
3 onions
12 small or 6 medium white turnips
½–¾ pint stock
salt, pepper and a pinch of mace
3–4 stalks parsley
1 sprig thyme
1 bay leaf
1 tablespoon parsley chopped**

Pre-heat oven to 350°F Mark 4

Duck with Turnips

Duck cooked in stock and vegetable sauce garnished with small white turnips (Serves 4–6, hot)

1. Prick breast of duck with a fork; then rub with salt and pepper. Heat oil and butter, and when foaming brown duck all over. Keep warm while cooking sliced onions to a golden brown and peeled turnips to colour outsides slightly. Pour in stock, add seasoning and herbs and bring to a boil. Then return duck to casserole and spoon sauce over it. Cook in oven for 1–1½ hours.

2. When tender remove duck and turnips to serving dish, skim off fat from sauce. Boil this for a minute or two and season to taste. Add chopped parsley and spoon around bird. Serve at once.

**1 duck over 1 year old
3 onions
thinly pared zest or rind of 1 orange
thinly pared zest or rind of 1 lemon
2–3 tablespoons oil
3–4 carrots
3–4 stalks celery
1 small white turnip
1½ oz flour
1 teaspoon tomato puree
¾ pint brown stock
¼–½ pint cider or red wine
several stalks parsley
1 sprig thyme
1 small sage leaf
1 bay leaf**

Pre-heat oven to 350°F Mark 4

Braised Duck

An excellent way of cooking an older duck, braised in oven in a a rich brown vegetable sauce (Serves 4, hot)

1. Prick breast of bird all over with fork. Rub skin with salt and pepper. Put an onion inside bird with a few pieces of orange and lemon zest (thin outer skin of fruit). Heat oil and brown duck all over for 6–8 minutes. Remove and keep warm.

2. Now add 2 sliced onions, carrots, celery, and turnip to pan and brown slowly but thoroughly. Cool slightly, add flour and cook for 2–3 minutes. Add tomato puree, stock and cider or wine. Boil for 1 minute. Add parsley, thyme, sage leaf, bay leaf, and remaining orange and lemon zest.

3. Place duck in casserole, cover with sauce and braise slowly in oven for 2 hours, until duck is tender.

4. Remove duck and carve. Place pieces on a hot dish. Strain sauce and boil to reduce slightly, skimming off fat which rises to top. Season to taste, spoon a little sauce over duck, and serve the rest separately.

Braised Quails with Risotto (see p. 191)

Duck with Cherries

Duck roasted with stock and wine or Madeira, served with a rich brown sauce and red cherries, party fare (Serves 4–6, hot)

1 duck, 4–5 pounds
2 onions
4 stalks celery
1½ oz butter
2 tablespoons oil
2 small carrots
4–5 mushrooms
¾ oz flour
2 teaspoons tomato puree
¾ pint stock made with giblets (or chicken stock cube)
a few stalks parsley
1 bay leaf
¼–½ pint red wine (or Madeira or port)
1 pound fresh red cherries (or 1 tin)
1 orange
¼ teaspoon sugar

Pre-heat oven to 400°F Mark 6

1. Put 1 onion and 2 stalks celery inside the duck. Rub breast with ½ oz butter and sprinkle with salt and pepper. Heat 1 oz butter (or use oil); when hot put duck into roasting pan and baste well. Put into oven and roast for 15 minutes per pound, basting every 15 minutes. This will not cook bird completely, allowing 20 minutes for it to be cooked in the sauce.

2. Meanwhile prepare sauce: Melt 2 tablespoons oil, add one finely chopped onion, 2 carrots, 2 stalks celery and mushrooms. Cook for 7–10 minutes, allowing vegetables to brown lightly, stir in flour, brown for 1 minute. Add tomato puree, stock made from duck giblets and herbs. Bring to boil; then simmer for 30 minutes. Strain, add seasoning, bring to boil again and skim off any impurities which rise to surface. Add half the wine (or Madeira or port) and heat again.

3. Carve duck and arrange pieces in covered casserole. Pour sauce over and cook in oven for 20 minutes.

4. Meanwhile, prepare cherries. If fresh, remove stones, if tinned, drain off juice and remove stones. Put into small pan with juice and grated rind of orange, ¼ pint red wine and a little sugar. Heat gently for 6–7 minutes.

5. When duck is cooked, arrange pieces on serving dish, spoon sauce over top and arrange cherries around edge of dish. Serve hot.

Pigeons stuffed with Orange Rice (see p. 180)

Roast Duck with Orange Salad

Succulent duck roasted with a coating of honey, stuffed with celery, onions and herbs, and served with an orange salad (Serves 4, hot)

1 duck, 3—4 pounds
2 onions
4 stalks celery
1 oz butter
1 tablespoon chopped parsley and
    thyme
1 orange
2—3 tablespoons oil
2—3 tablespoons melted honey
4 oranges
¼ teaspoon salt
¼ teaspoon sugar
½ teaspoon freshly ground black
    pepper
3 tablespoons salad oil
2 tablespoons lemon juice
½ pint red wine
½ pint chicken stock

Pre-heat oven to 400°F Mark 6

1. Slice onions and celery, cook for a few minutes in a little butter, and mix in herbs and seasoning, including grated rind of half an orange and the juice of a whole orange. Cool slightly before stuffing into duck. Rub skin of duck with butter and season.

2. Heat oil in roasting pan. When hot, add duck and baste with hot oil. Roast for 20 minutes per pound, basting every 15 minutes. During the last half hour, baste with melted honey. The honey produces a marvellous shiny brown skin.

3. Meanwhile, prepare the orange salad: Remove thin orange skin from one orange with a peeler, cut into match like shreds. Boil for 3 minutes in water, drain, refresh under cold tap to restore colour, leave to dry. With a sharp serrated knife, remove pith and skin from oranges and cut in thin slices, place in overlapping circles in glass dish. Mix salt, sugar and pepper with oil, then add lemon juice. Spoon dressing over oranges and sprinkle orange shreds over top. Chill in refrigerator.

4. When duck is cooked, remove from oven and keep warm on serving dish. Pour off excess fat, and pour red wine and stock into roasting pan. Bring to the boil, and cook until well flavoured. Add seasoning. The gravy may be too sweet because of the honey, so a little lemon juice may be added.

Salmi of Duck

Duck partly roasted, then cooked in rich wine sauce, and garnished with heart shaped bread croutons spread with cooked duck liver (Serves 6, hot)

1 duck, 4—5 pounds
½ pint oil
2½ oz butter
1 onion chopped
¾ oz flour
1 level tablespoon tomato puree
¾ pint stock
a few stalks parsley, a sprig of thyme
    and a bay leaf
¼ pint port or red wine
12 button mushrooms
6 slices white bread
1 tablespoon parsley chopped

Pre-heat oven to 400°F Mark 6

1. Heat 2 tablespoons oil and roast duck for 35 minutes with giblets, but not liver. Let it cool enough to handle. Then carve the breast off in two pieces. Remove legs and any other meat carefully, reserving any blood that runs out while carving. Break up the carcass bones and remove skin from carved joints. Put bones and skin in pan with giblets and any blood or juice from duck. Place meat in a covered dish and keep warm.

2. Make sauce: Heat 1 oz butter and cook onion until tender. Then brown slightly, add flour, stir well and allow to brown a little. Cool slightly, add tomato puree and stock, bring to the boil and add duck bones, skin etc., herbs and seasoning. Cover pan and cook for 30 minutes. Then strain and add ¼ pint port or red wine. Cook again for few minutes, season to taste.

3. Cook mushrooms in ½ oz butter, then add to sauce. Melt another ½ oz butter in same pan and sauté duck liver until tender, season and chop or pound as fine as possible.

4. Carve duck's legs into two pieces and breast into slices and arrange these on an ovenproof serving dish. Spoon sauce over meat and cover dish with lid or foil and bake in oven until legs are tender, 20—30 minutes.

5. Meanwhile, cut bread slices into heart shaped croutons. Heat oil and add ½ oz butter. When foaming, fry croutons until golden brown all over. Drain and spread with duck liver paste.

6. When salmi is cooked, remove lid and sprinkle with chopped parsley and arrange croutons around the edge of the dish.

Goose stuffed with onion, apple and chesnut stuffing, roasted in hot oven (Serves 6—8, hot)

1 goose, 8—10 pounds
2 pounds chestnuts
¾ pint stock
6 apples
2 onions
1 goose liver
½ oz butter
4—6 oz breadcrumbs
2 tablespoons parsley chopped
1 tablespoon mixed thyme and marjoram
grated rind of ½ lemon
1 oz flour
4—6 tablespoons oil
1½ tablespoons redcurrant jelly
juice of ½ lemon
½—¾ pint cider or stock

Pre-heat oven to 400°F Mark 6

GOOSE & PIGEON

Continental Roast Goose with Chestnut and Liver Stuffing

1. Prepare stuffing: Put chestnuts in boiling water for 5—6 minutes or until skins will remove completely. Then cover peeled nuts with stock and simmer until tender. Drain and allow to cool. Reserve stock for moistening stuffing. Peel and chop apples, chop onions and cook for 3—4 minutes, then mix in chestnuts. Cook goose liver in butter and when firm, chop and add to stuffing with 4—6 oz breadcrumbs. Add chopped parsley, thyme, marjoram, lemon rind, salt and pepper. Mix together adding enough stock to make a moist but firm mixture.

2. Stuff goose and sew up opening. Prick goose all over lightly with sharp fork, sprinkle with ½ oz flour and seasoning. Heat oil or fat in roasting pan. Put goose into pan, on a rack if possible to allow the fat to drain, and cook for 20—25 minutes per pound, basting every 20 minutes, turning from side to side. Reduce heat slightly after first 20 minutes. For last 30 minutes pour off most of fat, place bird breast up and allow to brown, raising heat again if breast is not becoming crisp and brown. Test with skewer in thick part of leg to see whether cooked. When cooked, remove to serving dish and keep warm while making gravy. *(cont.)*

3. Skim off any remaining fat from roasting pan, sprinkle in ½ oz flour and blend with roasting juices in pan. Add redcurrant jelly and lemon juice; stir in well. Add cider or stock and bring to boil. Cook for 2—3 minutes, strain, season to taste and serve hot with goose.

Roast Goose with Sage and Onion Stuffing

Goose stuffed with sage flavoured onion, apple and crumb stuffing, roasted in hot oven and served with gravy and apple sauce; a Christmas dish (Serves 6—8, hot)

1 young goose weighing 8—10 pounds
3—4 oz butter
2 pounds onions
8—9 fresh sage leaves (or 2 teaspoons powdered dried sage)
2 large cooking apples
10—12 oz fresh white breadcrumbs
grated rind of 1 lemon
1 egg
¾ pint strong stock made from giblets of goose (or chicken stock cube)
3—4 tablespoons oil
1 teaspoon flour
a little cider
1 large tin apple sauce

Pre-heat oven to 400°F Mark 6

1. Prepare stuffing: Melt butter and cook sliced onions slowly for 10—15 minutes without browning, stirring frequently. If using fresh sage leaves, dip these into boiling water for 1—2 minutes, drain and chop. Peel and chop 1 apple and mix with breadcrumbs, add chopped (or dried) sage, and lemon rind. Mix in softened onions, beaten egg and a few spoons stock. Season well with salt and pepper.

2. Wipe goose thoroughly inside and out. Weigh and calculate cooking time, allowing 20—25 minutes per pound. Fill cavity inside with stuffing allowing roughly 1 teacup per pound weight of bird. Sew up opening. Prick breast over lightly with a sharp fork to allow fat to run while cooking. Heat oil in oven, and when hot, put goose into roasting pan on a rack if possible. Baste well with hot oil. Season with salt and pepper. Put into oven and cook for 20—25 minutes per pound basting every 20 minutes. Reduce heat to 350°F Mark 4. During the last half hour put a sour cooking apple into roasting pan, as this gives the gravy a pleasant tang. If goose does not have a nice brown crisp skin at last basting, increase heat to 400°F for last 20 minutes. Remove bird when cooked and keep hot while making gravy.

3. Pour off all fat from roasting pan and sprinkle in flour. Add stock and bring to the boil, mashing roasted apple into sauce; a little cider may be added in place of some stock. Strain gravy into sauce boat, and serve apple sauce separately.

Potted Goose

A rich and delicious paté of goose liver and remains of roast goose pounded with butter and herbs; suitable as a first course or for a buffet party (Serves 6—8, cold)

1 goose liver
1—1½ pounds cold goose chopped
¾—1½ pounds butter
1 onion
1 clove garlic
2—3 tablespoons brandy or sherry
1 tablespoon chopped parsley and thyme
a large pinch of powdered mace (or slightly less nutmeg)

Pre-heat oven to 300°F Mark 2

1. Melt 1 oz butter and cook chopped goose liver until it has changed colour and stiffened. Remove and cool. Add 1 more oz butter and soften chopped onion and crushed garlic for 6—8 minutes without browning. Mix in herbs; add to liver.

2. Chop cold goose meat finely and mix with liver mixture. Pound together until smooth or put into liquidizer to mince finely, adding a little brandy or sherry if mixture seems to stick.

3. Weigh the resulting paté and for each pound add 8 oz softened butter. Season with powdered mace or nutmeg, salt and pepper. Beat together to mix thoroughly. Pack into a thick ovenproof mould. Cover with lid, heat through in oven for 15—20 minutes. Remove and cover with layer of unsalted butter. This helps the potted goose to keep longer.

4. Serve with lots of toast or hot French bread and butter.

Goose en Daube

Classic French method of cooking wild or domestic goose with wine, brandy, bacon, shallots or onions, garlic and herbs in slow oven; served cold in jellied sauce (Serves 6—8, cold)

1 goose, wild or domestic
3—4 oz bacon diced
4 oz shallots or mild onions chopped
2 cloves garlic
several stalks parsley
a sprig of thyme
2 sprigs basil (or ½ teaspoon dried basil)
1 large or 2 small bay leaves
2 cleaned and washed pig's trotters
   if available (or ½ oz gelatine added
   after cooking)
2 liquid oz brandy
½—1¼ pints red wine
¾ pint water or more if necessary to
   cover bird
3—4 tablespoons flour mixed to a
   thick paste for sealing casserole

Pre-heat oven to 300°F Mark 2

1. Put goose into a thick fireproof casserole with lid, on top of a layer of mixed bacon, onion and other dry ingredients, sprinkling the rest over the top. Pour in all liquids, which should cover bird. Cover with lid and seal this with a paste made from flour and water. Cook in oven for about 4½—5 hours.

2. When dish has cooled, break seal and remove goose. Carve all meat and put slices in a large dish. Strain cooking liquid off all pieces of vegetables etc; skim off any fat, and check seasoning. If no pig's trotters were included, dissolve ½ oz gelatine in hot liquid. Pour this liquid over goose and put in refrigerator to set.

3. Serve cold with endive and orange salad, and hot potatoes.
(This method can also be used to cook duck or chicken but cooking time is shorter.)

Fried Goose with Apple Rings

Slices of cooked goose fried in egg and breadcrumbs, garnished with fried apple rings, served with a piquant sauce (Serves 4, hot—see picture, p. 164)

8 slices cooked breast of goose
2—3½ oz flour
1—2 eggs
¼ pint oil
4—6 oz fresh white breadcrumbs
2—2½ oz butter
2 cooking apples
1 level tablespoon sugar
½ pint brown gravy or sauce
1 tablespoon white vinegar
2 teaspoons Worcestershire sauce

1. Cut 8 thin slices of goose from breast of cooked bird. Season well. Cover well with flour, then dip in egg beaten with a little oil until completely coated. Then cover with dried white breadcrumbs.

2. Heat remaining oil and when hot add butter. When foaming, cook slices of goose until golden brown and crisp all over. Remove, drain and keep warm.

3. Peel, core and slice apples into 8 rings. Reheat fat in which goose was fried having removed any loose crumbs which may burn. Fry apple rings until golden brown, sprinkling each side with sugar to brown.

4. Make sauce by adding 1 tablespoon wine vinegar and 2 teaspoons Worcestershire sauce to brown gravy. Heat and season to taste.

Roast pigeons with savoury rice, almond and raisin stuffing (Serves 4, hot)

4 tender pigeons
4—6 oz cooked rice
2 onions
1½ oz butter
2—3 tablespoons peeled flaked
   almonds
1 tablespoon chopped herbs
3 tablespoons raisins
2—3 tablespoons sherry
4 slices fat bacon
2—3 tablespoons oil
1 teaspoon flour
¼ pint red wine
¼ pint stock

Pre-heat oven to 400°F Mark 6

Pigeons Stuffed with Almonds and Raisins

1. Prepare stuffing: Boil rice until tender. Drain and let it cool. Chop 2 onions and cook until soft in 1½ oz butter. Add peeled flaked almonds and cook until all are golden brown. Add 8 tablespoons rice to pan, cook for 1 minute. Add chopped herbs, raisins which have been soaking in sherry and seasoning. Stuff mixture into pigeons.

2. Tie a slice of fat bacon around breast of each bird. Heat oil in oven, add pigeons and baste thoroughly. Roast in oven for about 35—40 minutes, basting and turning every 10 minutes. Remove bacon for last 15 minutes to brown breast. Remove to a serving dish and keep warm.

3. Pour away oil and sprinkle in flour, blend into pan drippings and add wine and stock. Stir until smooth and boiling, add seasoning and pour into sauce boat.

Cassoulet of Goose

A homely dish suitable for a cold winter's night; goose stewed with beans, garlic sausage, onions, tomatoes and stock; excellent way of using leftovers (Serves 4–6, hot)

2–3 pounds cooked goose joints
½–¾ pound dried broad beans (medium sized, or they will need longer cooking)
1¼–1½ pints strong brown meat stock (or water and beef stock cubes)
2½–3 oz goose fat (or butter)
2 medium onions
2–3 cloves garlic
4–5 slices fat smoked bacon
3–4 tablespoons tomato puree
1 tablespoon chopped parsley and thyme
a pinch of sage
1 bay leaf
6–8 slices garlic sausage
4–6 oz dried white breadcrumbs

Pre-heat oven to 300°F Mark 2

1. The day before you cook cassoulet put beans to soak. Next day put them in pan with water and bring slowly to the boil, lower heat and simmer for 2½ hours. Drain.

2. While beans cook, prepare stock: Cut goose into portions, add carcass to cooking stock to add flavour, and simmer until required. Melt 1–1½ oz of fat in which goose was roasted. Add sliced onions, crushed garlic and chopped bacon; cook for 5–6 minutes. Add tomato puree, herbs and seasoning. Add the strained stock. Bring to the boil, and simmer for 30 minutes.

3. Add drained beans to stock ingredients and stir well. Then pour half this mixture into bottom of thick casserole. Put in pieces of goose; then pour remaining bean mixture over top. Add sliced garlic sausage and submerge under liquid. Bring to a boil, add more seasoning if necessary, then sprinkle thick layer of breadcrumbs all over surface. Dot surface with 1 oz butter or goose fat. Put into oven and cook for about 1 hour, until beans have cooked and top is crusty and brown.
(This recipe can also be used for duck or turkey leftovers.)

Pigeon and Bacon Brochettes

Breast meat of pigeons marinated in wine and herbs grilled on skewers with bacon rolls, mushrooms and baby onions, served with a brown sauce (Serves 4, hot)

2–3 pigeons
¼ pint red wine
2 onions
1 level tablespoon chopped herbs
6 rashers bacon
8–12 baby onions
½–¾ pint stock
8–12 baby mushrooms (use stems for sauce)
3 tablespoons oil
1 clove garlic crushed
2 carrots chopped
2 stalks celery
1 oz flour

Pre-heat grill

1. Remove breasts from pigeons and cut each into 2 pieces. Put into bowl and cover with wine, one chopped onion, herbs and pepper. Allow to marinate for a few hours.

2. Cut 4 bacon rashers in half and make each into a roll. Cook peeled baby onions in ¼ pint stock for 5 minutes, drain and reserve stock for sauce. Peel mushrooms, remove stems and reserve for sauce. Remove pieces of pigeon from marinade and dry. Thread these ingredients alternately on to skewers.

3. Make brown sauce: Heat oil and cook 2 chopped rashers bacon, one chopped onion, crushed garlic, chopped carrots, chopped celery stalks and mushroom stems until they are golden brown. Sprinkle in 1 oz flour, blend well and add stock and ¼ pint strained marinade. Bring to boil and simmer for ½ hour. Strain and add seasoning.

4. Heat grill and cook brochettes, brushing with butter or oil, for about 8 minutes depending on heat of grill. The pigeon must not be overcooked as it becomes tough and tasteless if allowed to do so.

5. Serve with boiled rice, brown sauce and a salad.

Pigeons in Parcels

Halved pigeons pre-cooked slightly, then covered with a mushroom and paté mixture, wrapped in parcels of foil and baked in oven (Serves 4, hot)

2 large pigeons
3½—4 oz butter
2 rashers bacon
1 small tin goose or duck liver paté
4 oz mushrooms
1 tablespoon chopped parsley,
   marjoram and tarragon
a pinch of mace
1 tablespoon sherry

Pre-heat oven to 350°F Mark 4

1. Cut each pigeon in half and brown all over in 3 tablespoons butter with bacon. Cover dish and roast in oven for 20 minutes. Remove pigeons and allow to cool.

2. Mix paté with chopped mushrooms, 2 oz butter, chopped mixed herbs, seasoning and a dash of sherry. Cut 4 large squares of foil, butter these, place 1/8 of stuffing in the centre of each square. Place the halved pigeons on top; then spread another 1/8 of mixture over each pigeon. Fold the foil over the birds and seal edges by turning over several times.

3. Turn oven up to 400°F Mark 6 and bake parcels for 35 minutes. Serve a parcel per person, and open them at the table to get the full effect of the aroma.

Braised Pigeons with Red Cabbage

Tender pigeons braised in casserole with red cabbage and apples (Serves 4–6, hot)

2–3 large plump pigeons
4 oz butter
8 rashers bacon
3 onions
1 small or ½ large red cabbage
½–¾ pint strong stock
1 teaspoon sugar
1 tablespoon vinegar
4 cooking apples
2 liquid oz red wine

Pre-heat oven to 350°F Mark 4

1. Melt 3 oz butter in casserole and brown pigeons all over; remove and keep warm. Cook diced bacon, add sliced onions and brown. Then add thinly sliced red cabbage. Cook for 1 minute; then return the pigeons to pan. Pour over stock. Add salt, pepper, 1 teaspoon sugar and vinegar. Cover casserole, and cook in oven for 45 minutes.

2. Then remove casserole from oven, and add 2 sliced apples and wine. Cook again for 30 minutes; then remove pigeons and if cabbage is not quite cooked, simmer again until tender, keeping pigeons warm.

3. Cut pigeons in half, and lay on top of red cabbage. Fry remaining apples cut in rings in 1 oz butter and a sprinkling of sugar, and put one ring on top of each pigeon. Serve with a brown gravy.

Braised Pigeons with Mushroom Stuffing

Pigeons stuffed with mushroom and bread stuffing, braised in bacon flavoured brown sauce (Serves 4, hot)

4 pigeons
3 onions
1–1½ oz butter
2–3 oz mushrooms sliced
2 oz fresh white breadcrumbs
2 tablespoons oil
4 rashers bacon
½ pint stock
¼ pint red wine
1 tablespoon parsley and thyme
1 bay leaf
1 tablespoon parsley chopped

Pre-heat oven to 350°F Mark 4

1. Chop 1 small onion and cook for 3–4 minutes in butter; slice mushrooms and cook until tender. Add breadcrumbs, salt and pepper. Fill pigeons with this mixture.

2. Heat oil in casserole and cook chopped bacon until golden; remove and keep warm. Now brown pigeons all over in the hot oil. Remove and keep warm while cooking remaining chopped onion for a few minutes until golden brown. Add bacon; put back pigeons. Pour over stock and red wine. Add herbs and pepper, cover with lid and cook in oven for about 1 hour, until tender.

3. When cooked, remove birds and keep warm; skim fat from casserole. Boil sauce and season to taste. Serve birds in the sauce, sprinkled with chopped parsley.

Pigeon and Steak Pie

Lean steak and pigeon joints cooked with small onions and mushrooms in a savoury sauce, topped with a puff pastry, or browned mashed potatoes as topping. This dish is best if meat is cooked day before dish is to be eaten (Serves 4–6, hot)

1. Cut lean steak into cubes. Cut pigeons into quarters. Chop onion and peel baby onions. Quarter mushrooms.

2. Heat oil, brown meat cubes and pigeons until brown all over, and remove to pie dish or casserole. Brown chopped onion and baby onions until golden brown, adding mushrooms after a few minutes. Stir in flour away from heat and blend, and add stock (or water) and cider or beer. Bring to boil; then add herbs, bay leaf, meat and pigeons. Cover with lid or foil, and cook in oven for 1–1½ hours, until meat is tender.

3. Allow to cool, if possible overnight. Skim off any surplus fat. Add more seasoning if needed and a little mushroom ketchup or Worcestershire sauce to give a lively flavour.

4. Roll out pastry thinly and cut a strip to go around edge of dish. Stick this to dish with water. Moisten top of pastry strip with water; then place large sheet of pastry over whole dish. Press edges together and cut off excess with a sharp knife. Crimp edges and cut air vents in pastry crust. Decorate with pastry leaves. Brush whole top with beaten egg. (If not using pastry, mashed potatoes can be used as a topping.)

5. Pre-heat oven to 425°F and bake pie for 20–30 minutes until pastry is crisp and brown. (If using mashed potatoes, heat oven to 400°F and brown for 15–20 minutes.)

1 pound lean steak
2 tender pigeons
1 onion
12 baby onions
4 oz mushrooms
2–3 tablespoons oil
1 oz flour
½ pint stock
¼ pint cider or beer
1 tablespoon mixed chopped parsley
    and thyme
1 bay leaf
1 tablespoon mushroom ketchup or
    Worcestershire sauce
1 package of frozen puff pastry (or 2
    cups of potato mashed with butter
    and milk)
1 egg

Pre-heat oven to 325°F Mark 3 for
    cooking meat
Pre-heat oven to 425°F Mark 7
    for pastry
Pre-heat oven to 400°F Mark 6 for
    potato topping

Pigeons Stuffed with Orange Rice

Pigeons roasted with stuffing of rice, orange rind and segments and peeled grapes (Serves 4, hot—see picture, p. 172)

4 tender pigeons
6—8 oz rice
3 oranges
2—3 oz seedless grapes
a little powdered onion
4 slices fat bacon
2—3 tablespoons oil
1—2 teaspoons flour
¼ pint white wine
¼ pint chicken stock

Pre-heat oven to 400°F Mark 6

1. Prepare stuffing: Cook rice and let cool. Grate rind of 1 large orange, mix with 8—9 tablespoons cooked rice. Remove pith and skin from 2 oranges with a serrated knife and cut out segments; add these to rice. Dip grapes into boiling water for few seconds, then into cold, peel and add to stuffing with salt, pepper and little powdered onion. Stuff mixture into pigeons.

2. Roast birds as in *Pigeons Stuffed with Almonds and Raisins* (see p. 176)

3. Pour away oil and sprinkle in flour, blend with pan drippings and add wine and a little stock. Bring to a boil and simmer for 1 minute. Add juice of 1 orange and a few strips of rind, and serve with the pigeons.

5 PHEASANT & GUINEA FOWL

Hot Pheasant Souffle

Delicious light concoction of eggs and minced pheasant (Serves 4, hot)

1. Melt butter, sift in flour and blend smoothly; heat for a minute or two, then add seasoned milk. Blend thoroughly and bring to the boil, stirring constantly. When boiling cook for 1 minute, then remove from heat and allow to cool.

(cont.)

4–6 oz cooked pheasant
1¼ oz butter
1 oz flour
½ pint milk seasoned with onion,
peppercorns, mace, parsley and bay
leaf
a large pinch of onion powder
1 level tablespoon mixed herbs
a pinch of mace (or nutmeg)
3 eggs

Pre-heat oven to 375°F Mark 5

2. Chop or mince pheasant meat. Add to sauce, with onion powder and mixed herbs. Season highly, adding mace or nutmeg. Stir in beaten egg yolks. Allow mixture to get quite cool.

3. 25–30 minutes before you expect to eat souffle beat up egg whites with a pinch of salt. When very stiff fold in 1 tablespoon thoroughly, and then fold in remainder quickly, and lightly. Put into a 7 inch souffle dish and bake for 25–30 minutes until well risen. Serve at once.

---

1 guinea fowl large enough to feed 4
or two smaller birds
4–5 oz mixed chopped onion, carrot
and celery
3 stalks parsley
1 bay leaf
6 peppercorns
2 chicken stock cubes
4 oz mushrooms
1½–2 oz butter
1 teaspoon lemon juice
1½ oz flour
¼ pint white wine
4 liquid oz stock
4–5 tablespoons single cream
a pinch of mace

Guinea Fowl in White Wine Sauce

Guinea fowl cooked in stock until tender, then carved, covered with a white wine and mushroom sauce (Serves 4, hot)

1. Put cleaned guinea fowl in large pan with 4–5 oz mixed chopped vegetables, parsley stalks, bay leaf, peppercorns and 2 chicken stock cubes. Bring to the boil and cook gently until tender. Drain and carve, placing pieces in serving dish.

2. Cook quartered mushrooms in butter and lemon juice. Add flour and, when blended, the white wine and stock. Bring to boil slowly. Simmer for 2–3 minutes. Add cream and seasoning. Spoon over guinea fowl, and serve hot with rice or fried potatoes and a green vegetable.

PANCAKES
4 oz flour
1 egg
1 egg yolk
8 liquid oz milk
½ oz butter
oil for frying

FILLING
6—8 oz cold cooked pheasant meat
3—3½ oz butter
2 medium onions
8 mushrooms
1 oz flour
1 teaspoon tomato puree
a dash of Worcestershire sauce
6 liquid oz strong stock
2 tablespoons sherry
1 level tablespoon chopped parsley,
**   thyme and marjoram**
a pinch of nutmeg
2—3 tablespoons dry white
**   breadcrumbs**
2 tablespoons grated parmesan cheese
1 tablespoon parsley finely chopped
**   or ½ teaspoon paprika**

Pre-heat grill

Pheasant and Mushroom Pancakes

Delicious method of using up remains of cold pheasant with mushrooms heated in a tasty sauce and rolled in wafer thin pancakes (Serves 4—6, hot)

1. Make pancakes as in *Turkey and Tomato Pancakes* (see p. 140)

2. Melt 2—2½ oz butter and cook finely chopped onions until tender without browning. Add chopped mushrooms and cook for a few minutes. Sprinkle in flour, stir well and add tomato puree, Worcestershire sauce and stock. Bring to boil and simmer for 3—4 minutes. Add sherry and herbs, seasoning and nutmeg. Lastly, add pheasant meat, cut into shreds. Allow to heat thoroughly without boiling. Keep warm while making pancakes.

3. Put large spoonful of filling on each pancake and fold into triangle shape over filling or roll up. Place in an overlapping row down centre of ovenproof dish. Sprinkle with 2 tablespoons melted butter, then with breadcrumbs mixed with cheese. Grill until golden brown. Garnish with chopped parsley, or a sprinkling of paprika.

Pheasant Chasseur

Jointed pheasant browned in butter, then cooked in chasseur sauce (Serves 4, hot)

1 pheasant
2½ oz butter
2 oz mushrooms chopped
3 shallots or 1 mild onion
¼ pint white wine
2 teaspoons tomato puree
½ pint brown sauce (or strong stock)
1 level teaspoon tarragon chopped
1 tablespoon parsley chopped

Pre-heat oven to 350°F Mark 4

1. Make sauce: Heat 1 oz butter or 2 tablespoons oil, and brown chopped mushrooms for a few minutes, add chopped shallots or onion, cook for another minute. Add white wine and reduce liquid by half. Add tomato puree and brown sauce. Cook together for a minute or two, then add chopped tarragon and 1 tablespoon chopped parsley.

2. Joint pheasant and brown each piece in 1–1½ oz butter. Put into casserole and pour the sauce over. Cook in oven for 40–50 minutes until tender. Just before serving add a lump of butter to sauce. Sprinkle top with remaining parsley and serve hot.

Roast Pheasant

Tender young pheasant roasted in butter, served with a red wine gravy, fried breadcrumbs, bread sauce and game chips (Serves 4, hot)

1 young pheasant cleaned and drained
2–3 slices fat bacon
1 onion
3 oz butter
2–3 stalks parsley
½ pint chicken stock
½ pint red wine
1 pound potatoes
fat for deep frying

1. Tie slices of fat bacon over breast of pheasant; put onion and 1 oz butter with some seasoning and parsley stalks inside it.

2. Melt 1½–2 oz butter in roasting pan without burning. Place pheasant in roasting pan on rack and baste well. Pour on ¼ pint stock and ¼ pint red wine. Put bird in oven and cook for 40–60 minutes depending on size, basting every 15 minutes, and turning bird from side to side. For last 15 minutes, remove bacon and string, and allow breast to brown.

3. Remove bird and keep warm while making gravy. Pour off butter from roasting juices and add ¼ pint stock and ¼ pint red wine. Bring to boil, stirring constantly. Season to taste and after 3–4 minutes strain into a sauce boat.

4. Game chips are made from very thinly sliced potatoes, washed and dried carefully and fried in very hot, deep fat, a few at a time, until brown and crisp.

Roast Pheasant with Cream and Redcurrant Sauce

Pheasant or other game birds roasted with red wine and butter, served with a sauce enriched with cream and sharpened with redcurrant jelly; a Scandinavian speciality (Serves 8, hot)

2 young pheasants
3½ oz butter
1 onion
4–6 slices fat bacon
½ pint red wine
½ pint single cream
2 tablespoons redcurrant jelly

Pre-heat oven to 400°F Mark 6

1. Put ½ oz butter and half an onion inside each bird and rub ½ oz butter over skin of each. Sprinkle with pepper and salt and cover with slices of bacon. Tie these on securely. Melt 1½ oz butter in roasting pan. When hot, put in birds and baste well with hot fat. Put into oven and roast for 45–60 minutes depending on size, basting every 15 minutes. After first half hour, pour wine over and baste. For last 15 minutes remove bacon and brown breasts well. When cooked, remove birds and make sauce.

2. Pour off all fat. Pour cream into the sauce left in pan and stir well. Then bring slowly almost to the boil, add softened redcurrant jelly and seasoning to sauce, strain into sauce boat and serve with pheasant.

3. Serve with game chips as in *Roast Pheasant* (see above) and watercress and orange salad.

Pheasant part roasted, part braised, on a layer of apples with a cream and apple brandy sauce (Serves 4, hot)

1 pheasant
3—5 medium sized cooking apples
1 oz butter
½ pint double whipping cream
½ lemon
3—4 tablespoons Calvados (optional)

Pre-heat oven to 425°F Mark 7

Normandy Pheasant

1. Put pheasant on to rotary spit if available or into a hot oven in a little butter and brown all over for 10—15 minutes. Remove and put into casserole which is lined with half the peeled, sliced cooking apples. Pour over any fat or juice from spit pan or roasting pan, and put remaining apples on top.

2. Put into oven at 350°F Mark 4 and cook for about 30—35 minutes. Then add cream and lemon juice, and Calvados if available. Return to oven and cook for 10—15 minutes, until pheasant is tender.

3. Serve with the apple cream mixture as a thick sauce.

Sautéed pheasant served on slices of toast, spread with cooked liver and covered with a cream sauce (Serves 4—6, hot)

1 large pheasant
4 oz butter
1 onion
1 level tablespoon chopped parsley
½ pint double cream
1 pheasant liver
1 large slice toast
1 teaspoon brandy (optional)
1 level teaspoon cornflour (optional)

Pheasant a la Creme

1. Heat 3 oz butter. When foaming, brown pheasant on all sides. Add the finely chopped onion and parsley. Cover casserole with lid or foil, and simmer for 40 minutes, until pheasant is nearly cooked. Pour over cream and cook for 5—10 minutes.

2. Meanwhile, melt 1 oz butter and sauté pheasant liver until it has changed colour and stiffened. Remove from cooker and mash with seasoning and a teaspoon of brandy, if available. Spread on toast. When pheasant is done place on toast and keep warm.

3. If sauce seems rather thin and buttery, mix cornflour with 1 tablespoon cold water and add to sauce; heat gently until it thickens, season to taste, and pour over pheasant. Serve at once.

Braised Pheasant with Chestnut Puree and Orange

Pheasant braised in a well flavoured sauce, served on a puree of chestnuts garnished with segments of orange and orange rind; a good way of using an older bird (Serves 4—6, hot)

1 large pheasant
2—2½ oz butter
2 onions
2 small carrots
2—3 stalks celery
1 oz flour
½—¾ pint stock
¼ pint cider (or white wine)
3 oranges
1 tablespoon mixed herbs
1 large tin chestnut puree

Pre-heat oven to 350°F Mark 4

1. Melt 1—1½ oz butter in casserole. Brown bird slowly, all over. Remove bird and keep warm. Now add sliced onions, carrots and celery. Cook until they are beginning to brown slightly; add flour and cook for a few minutes. Add stock and cider or wine. Stir well and bring to boil. Simmer for a few minutes. Add 3 strips of orange rind, herbs and seasoning. Put the pheasant back into casserole and spoon sauce over it. Cover casserole and put into oven for about 50 minutes, until pheasant is tender. When pheasant is removed from casserole, boil up cooking juices and put into liquidizer. When smooth, return to pan and if too thick add a little extra stock. Season to taste and re-heat.

2. Meanwhile, melt 1 oz butter in pan and add chestnut puree. Heat, to soften puree, adding 2—3 tablespoons strong stock and seasoning. Keep warm until pheasant is tender; then place it down centre of serving dish. Place carved slices and joints on top. Spoon sauce over all.

3. Remove rinds of oranges carefully and cut into thin shreds. Cook in boiling water for a few minutes, drain and put in cold water to restore colour. Remove white pith and skin from oranges with sharp knife and divide into segments. Arrange orange segments around edge of dish and the orange strips down centre. Serve hot with fried or croquette potatoes, and a green vegetable.

Pheasant, Celery and Apple Casserole

Whole pheasant braised on a bed of onion, celery and apples with a white wine sauce, garnished with fried apple rings (Serves 4, hot)

1 pheasant
2—2½ oz butter
2 onions
3—4 stalks celery
2 medium sized apples
1—1½ pints chicken stock
¼ pint white wine
1 tablespoon mixed herbs
1 bay leaf
1 teaspoon sugar
1 tablespoon parsley chopped

Pre-heat oven to 350°F Mark 4

1. Melt 1—1½ oz butter in a casserole, add pheasant and brown slowly all over. Remove bird and keep warm. Slice onions, add to butter and soften for 5 minutes. Then add sliced celery, cook again for 2—3 minutes and add 1 sliced apple. Return pheasant and pour over stock and white wine. Sprinkle with salt and pepper; add herbs and bay leaf. Cover the casserole and cook in oven for 50 minutes, until bird is tender.

2. Remove pheasant to serving dish or carve into portions. Remove bay leaf, then put pan drippings and vegetables into liquidizer and blend until smooth. Re-heat, skim off any surplus butter that rises to surface. Season to taste, and pour over the pheasant.

3. Cut remaining peeled and cored apple into rings, sprinkle with sugar. Melt 1 oz butter and fry rings until golden brown. Place on top of dish, and sprinkle with chopped parsley.

American Pheasant

Pheasant split and flattened, sautéed in butter, covered with crumbs and grilled; served with grilled bacon, mushrooms and tomatoes (Serves 4, hot)

1 pheasant
4—6 oz butter
6—8 oz fresh white breadcrumbs
salt, pepper and a pinch of cayenne pepper
4 tomatoes
4 rashers bacon
8 flat mushrooms

Pre-heat grill to moderate temperature

1. Cut pheasant open along back with sharp knife. Open it out and flatten with a heavy rolling pin. Season with salt and pepper. Melt butter in large pan and when hot sauté pheasant on both sides. Remove from heat.

2. Make plenty of fresh white breadcrumbs and cover surface of pheasant with these; sprinkle with a little cayenne pepper. Heat grill and grill slowly so that the crumbs do not become too brown before bird is cooked. Test with skewer in thickest part of leg.

3. At the same time, grill halved and seasoned tomatoes. Also grill bacon, and mushrooms filled with butter and seasoned.

4. When pheasant is cooked, serve on a platter surrounded by grilled accompaniments and some butter balls rolled in parsley. Serve a salad with French dressing, separately.

Pheasant with Grapes and White Wine Sauce

Pheasant fried in butter then cooked in a white wine sauce, and garnished with white grapes (Serves 4, hot)

1 pheasant
2 oz butter
1 oz flour
¼ pint clear stock
¼ pint white wine
4—6 oz white grapes, seedless if available
2 tablespoons lemon juice

Pre-heat oven to 350°F Mark 4

1. Melt butter in casserole; when hot fry pheasant gently all over until golden brown. Remove bird. Add flour, stock and wine. Blend smoothly; then bring to the boil. Add seasoning. Return bird to casserole. Cover and cook in oven for 35—45 minutes, until pheasant is tender, turning over during cooking.

2. Peel grapes by dipping in boiling water for a few seconds and then in cold. Strip skins and if not seedless remove seeds. Cover with a little lemon juice to prevent browning.

3. When bird is tender, remove and carve. Place meat on a serving dish and keep warm. Add grapes to sauce and cook for couple of minutes. Season to taste and then spoon over the pheasant. Serve with mashed potatoes and peas or spinach.

American Braised Guinea Fowl

Guinea fowl or pheasant cut in quarters and braised in a piquant sauce (Serves 4, hot)

1 guinea fowl (or pheasant)
1½ oz butter
1 onion
1 clove garlic
¼ teaspoon dry mustard
2 teaspoons wine vinegar
6 liquid oz chicken stock
1 tablespoon chopped parsley and tarragon
¾–1 pound cooked rice
1 teaspoon paprika

Pre-heat oven to 350°F Mark 4

1. Cut guinea fowl or pheasant into quarters and brown all over in butter. Add sliced onion, crushed garlic, mustard, vinegar, stock, chopped herbs and seasoning. Cover casserole and simmer on top of cooker or in oven for 30–35 minutes when bird should be almost tender. Remove lid and allow to simmer until liquid is much reduced, and bird is cooked through.

2. Boil rice and arrange in a ring around dish, spoon the guinea fowl into centre and sprinkle with paprika as garnish.

Roast Guinea Fowl

Young guinea hens stuffed with bread, mushroom and onion stuffing roasted to perfection in butter and stock (Serves 4, hot)

2 guinea hens
4–6 oz dry white breadcrumbs
8 oz butter
1 onion
2–3 oz mushrooms chopped
1 oz parsley chopped
2 tablespoons thyme and basil chopped
a pinch of mace
1 egg
a little milk
½ pint stock
a little white wine (optional)

Pre-heat oven to 350°F Mark 4

1. Prepare mushroom and herb stuffing: Put breadcrumbs in bowl. Melt 4 oz butter and cook finely chopped onion gently for 5 minutes without browning. Add mushrooms and cook for 2 minutes. Stir into breadcrumbs. Add parsley, thyme and basil. Season with salt, pepper and mace. Add beaten egg and enough milk to moisten without becoming runny. Allow to stand for a few minutes before stuffing into guinea hens. Sew up openings.

2. Rub breast and legs of guinea hens over with 1 oz butter. Sprinkle with seasoning. Melt 2–2½ oz butter (or 4 tablespoons oil) in roasting pan. When hot, put bird into pan and baste. Pour in ¼ pint stock. Roast slowly in oven, allowing 25 minutes per pound unstuffed weight, basting frequently and turning birds from side to side; but stand breast side up for last 30 minutes and turn up heat slightly to brown. When cooked, remove from pan and place on hot dish; keep warm. Pour off fat from roasting pan, add ¼ pint of stock and stir into pan drippings to make delicious gravy. (A little white wine can be added to gravy, if desired.)

Guinea Fowl Chasseur

1 large or 2 small guinea fowl (or 1 pheasant)
2½ oz butter
2–3 oz mushrooms chopped
3 shallots or 1 mild onion
¼ pint white wine
2 teaspoons tomato puree
½ pint brown sauce (or strong stock)
1 teaspoon tarragon chopped
GARNISH
4 rashers streaky bacon
2 large slices white bread
4–6 tablespoons oil
1–1½ oz butter
1 guinea fowl liver
1 teaspoon onion chopped (or a little onion powder)
1 teaspoon sherry
1 tablespoon parsley chopped

Pre-heat oven to 350°F Mark 4

Guinea fowl or pheasant cut into pieces, browned in butter and cooked in chasseur sauce, garnished with bacon rolls and croutons spread with guinea fowl liver (Serves 4, hot)

1. Cook bird as in *Pheasant Chasseur* (see p. 183) except for garnish.

2. Make garnish: Cut bacon rashers in half, roll up and put on skewer. Grill or bake in oven until crisp. Cut bread into triangles. Fry these until golden brown in oil and butter. Drain; keep hot. Cook liver in 1 oz butter with a little onion and a teaspoon sherry. When cooked spread the mashed liver on to the croutons and arrange around dish alternately with the bacon rolls. Sprinkle with chopped parsley.

Turkish Guinea Fowl

1 guinea fowl
2—3 tablespoons oil
3 onions
several stalks parsley
1 bay leaf
8 peppercorns
1½—2 oz butter
1 clove garlic
8 oz rice
1—1¼ pints stock
2 oz raisins
½ teaspoon ground cinnamon
1 tablespoon herbs chopped
3 tablespoons almonds halved
1 tablespoon parsley chopped

Pre-heat oven to 325°F Mark 3

Guinea fowl simmered in stock until tender, then cooked with rice, almonds, herbs and raisins (Serves 4—6, hot)

1. Brown guinea fowl all over in oil. Then put into a large pan or casserole and barely cover with water. Add 2 sliced onions, parsley stalks, bay leaf, peppercorns and salt. Cook gently until tender, about 1½ hours. Drain and allow to cool, reserving stock for cooking rice.

2. Heat 1½—2 oz butter in pan, cook one chopped onion and crushed garlic until golden. Add rice and cook for a few minutes. Pour in 1—1¼ pints stock and bring to boil, add raisins and herbs, cinnamon and seasoning. Cut guinea fowl meat into good sized chunks and add to rice mixture. Cover dish and cook in oven for 20—30 minutes until all liquid has been absorbed and guinea fowl is tender. Sprinkle top with browned almonds and chopped parsley, and serve hot.

OTHER GAME

Grouse, Partridge or Pheasant Paté

Game mixed with liver, bacon and herbs to make a rich paté (Serves 6–8, cold)

1. Cut meat off birds and cut in slices, chop liver and bacon. Melt 1 oz butter (or bacon fat) and cook chopped onion and crushed garlic until tender. Add chopped bacon and liver, cook for a few minutes. Allow to cool slightly; then mince in liquidizer or pound in bowl. Add seasoning and chopped herbs.

2. Cook game pieces in 1 oz butter for 2–3 minutes. Then allow to cool. Arrange game and liver paste in layers in a thick casserole with a lid, making sure top layer is liver. Put a bay leaf on top. Cover, and seal with flour and water paste.

3. Put into deep baking pan of hot water, and cook in oven for 2½ hours. When cooked, remove lid and put several layers of greaseproof paper on top. Press down with weight and leave overnight. Either turn out and eat at once or pour layer of clarified butter over the top and keep in refrigerator.

2 grouse or partridges or 1 pheasant
½–¾ pound calf or chicken livers
6 rashers streaky bacon
2–3 oz butter (or bacon fat)
1 onion
1 clove garlic
2 level tablespoons chopped parsley,
    thyme and savory
1 bay leaf
2 oz flour
6 oz clarified butter

Pre-heat oven to 325°F Mark 3

A deliciously filling dish for using up cold, cooked game, in a rich sauce and served in a ring of savoury choux pastry (Serves 4, hot)

5 oz flour
4 oz butter
½ pint water
3 large eggs
4 tablespoons grated cheddar cheese
¼ teaspoon dried mustard

FILLING
6—8 oz cold cooked grouse and partridge (or other game)
1 oz butter
1 onion chopped
6—8 mushrooms sliced
½ oz flour
1 teaspoon tomato puree
¼ pint stock
2 tablespoons sherry
1 tablespoon chopped herbs
2—3 oz cooked vegetables, as available
1 teaspoon Worcestershire sauce
2 tablespoons grated Parmesan cheese
2 tablespoons breadcrumbs
1 tablespoon parsley chopped

Pre-heat oven to 375°F Mark 5

Gougere of Grouse, Partridge and Mushrooms

1. Sift flour with a large pinch of salt and put in oven to warm. In a sloping sided pan heat ½ pint water and 4 oz butter. When butter has melted, bring to the boil. As soon as it boils, remove from heat and add flour all at once. Beat hard with a wooden spoon until mixture forms a ball in bottom of pan. Spread out on a plate to cool. Beat eggs. When mixture is cool, add egg by degrees, beating hard between each addition. Final mixture should be shiny and smooth, and will hold its shape. A little egg may be left over. Add cheese with mustard and seasoning.

2. Make filling: Melt butter and cook chopped onion for 5—6 minutes until soft. Add mushrooms, cook for 1 minute. Sprinkle in flour. When mixed in, add tomato puree and stock. Bring to the boil; cook for few minutes to thicken. Add sherry, diced game, herbs and any cooked vegetables such as peas, beans, sweetcorn or pepper, which are available. Add Worcestershire sauce. Allow to cool slightly.

3. Butter a fireproof dish about 3 inches deep. Arrange pastry in a ring around the outside of dish. Brush over with any remaining egg to give a shiny finish. Spoon filling into centre of pastry ring. Sprinkle the top with grated cheese and breadcrumbs. Bake in oven for 30—45 minutes. Sprinkle top with chopped parsley and serve.
(This recipe can be used for any other game.)

Hot Game Cutlets

Remains of game or turkey chopped and added to mashed potato, mixed with chutney, egg and herbs, fried in egg and crumbs (Serves 4, hot)

4—6 oz game
1 oz butter
1 onion
4—6 oz mashed potato
1 tablespoon herbs chopped
2 tablespoons chutney
1 egg
1½—2 oz flour
1—2 beaten eggs with 1 teaspoon oil
4—6 oz dry white breadcrumbs
fat for deep frying
tomato sauce

1. Chop 4—6 oz cold game. Heat butter and cook chopped onion until tender. Add to game with enough mashed potato to make a firm mixture. Add herbs, chutney, beaten egg and seasoning.

2. Mould into cutlet shapes, and when firm, roll in seasoned flour. Then brush with eggs beaten with oil and cover completely with dry white breadcrumbs.

3. Heat fat and fry cutlets for a few minutes, until golden brown, drain and serve with tomato sauce.

Cold Game Souffle

Minced game mixed with stock, gelatine, eggs and sherry to make a light cold souffle; suitable for cold buffet (Serves 4, cold)

8 oz minced cold game or turkey
¾ pint stock
¾ oz gelatine
2—3 tablespoons dry sherry or port
2 eggs
3—4 tablespoons double cream
cucumber and watercress for garnish
seasoning

1. Mince game. Dissolve gelatine in hot stock. Add to game with sherry or port. Beat egg yolks thoroughly and stir into mixture. Add seasoning.

2. When cold and almost set, add whipped cream and fold in beaten egg whites. Turn into souffle dish and allow to set. Keep cold in refrigerator.

3. Decorate with cucumber and watercress, and serve with a salad.

Braised Quails with Risotto

Quails wrapped in vine leaves, cooked on a bed of vegetables, and served on a rich risotto with almonds, raisins, green peppers and olives (Serves 4, hot—see picture, p. 171)

4 quails
4 vine leaves
1½ oz butter
2 onions
1 carrot
2 stalks celery
2—3 oz mushrooms
¼ pint stock
2—3 tablespoons sherry
1 tablespoon herbs chopped

RISOTTO
1 oz butter
1 onion
8 oz rice
1¼ pints stock
2 tablespoons raisins
1 green pepper
1 tablespoon herbs chopped
8—10 olives
2 tablespoons almonds

Pre-heat oven to 350°F Mark 4

1. Wrap quails in vine leaves and put a small piece of butter inside each one. Melt 1 oz butter, and cook sliced onions, carrot and celery, and chopped mushrooms until golden brown. Place quails on top of vegetables in an ovenproof dish and add a little sherry, 3—4 tablespoons stock, a sprinkling of herbs and seasoning. Put into oven and braise for 25 minutes, or until tender.

2. Make risotto: Heat butter and cook chopped onion until golden brown. Add rice and cook for 1 minute. Pour on stock and add raisins, chopped pepper and herbs. Put in moderate oven for 20—30 minutes or until rice has absorbed all liquid. Mix in olives and browned almonds, and serve on dish with the quails on top, and with a sauce made from the pan gravy and remaining stock and sherry.

Braised Partridges with Cabbage

Partridges cooked on a bed of bacon and cabbage with braising vegetables (Serves 4, hot)

2 partridges
1—1½ oz butter or bacon fat
2 onions
1 carrot
½ oz flour
½ pint stock
2 tablespoons parsley chopped
1 firm cabbage
8—10 rashers bacon
1 bay leaf

Pre-heat oven to 325°F Mark 3

1. Cut each partridge in half, and brown all over in 1—1½ oz butter or bacon fat. Remove and keep warm. Add sliced onions, carrot and cook until golden brown. Stir in flour, brown slightly, and add stock and chopped parsley.

2. Cut cabbage into quarters and remove hard core. Boil in salted water for 5—7 minutes, drain and allow to dry slightly.

3. Line casserole with bacon rashers and place half the cabbage on top with half the sauce. Then put partridges on top. Place remaining cabbage on top, and pour over rest of sauce. Put a bay leaf on top. Put on lid, and cook in oven for 1—1½ hours, until partridges and cabbage are tender.

4. Remove from oven and place partridges on top of cabbage to serve. Remove bay leaf.

Game Pie

Old game birds cooked with bacon and steak and mushrooms in wine, finished with a crust of pastry (Serves 4—6, hot or cold)

2 grouse (or other game)
½ pound steak
½ pound streaky bacon
1 large onion
4—6 mushrooms
2 tablespoons chopped herbs
salt, pepper and a pinch of nutmeg
½ pint red wine
½ pint stock
1 package frozen puff pastry
1 egg

Pre-heat oven to 325°F Mark 3 for meat
Pre-heat oven to 425°F Mark 7 for pastry

1. Cut meat off two grouse (or other game birds), cut steak into small pieces and dice bacon. Arrange in pie dish in layers with finely chopped onion, mushrooms, herbs and seasoning between each layer. Pour over ½ pint red wine and enough stock to barely cover meat. Cover with foil and bake very slowly for 1—1½ hours until all meat is tender. Allow to cool completely.

2. Roll out pastry and place strip around edge of dish, moistened with water. Moisten pastry strip and place a large piece of pastry on top. Press edges together. Cut off surplus and crimp edges. Make slashes in top to release steam and decorate with pastry leaves.

3. Put into hot oven to bake pastry for about 30 minutes. Serve hot or cold.

Other Game

1 blackcock or capercaillie 4–6 pounds
4 tablespoons oil
1 oz butter
3 onions
¼ pound mushrooms
2 oz bacon diced
¾ pint red wine
¾–1 pint stock (or more if necessary)
2 tablespoons mixed herbs chopped
1 bay leaf

Pre-heat oven to 350°F Mark 4

Braised Blackcock or Capercaillie

1. Heat oil and butter, and brown blackcock or capercaillie all over. Remove to casserole and keep warm. Cook sliced onions, mushrooms and chopped bacon until brown, add red wine and bring to a boil. Set light to wine; when flames die, pour on stock. Add herbs and seasoning. Pour over the bird and cover with lid.

2. Place in oven and cook for 1½ hours, or until tender. Remove from casserole and carve. Place pieces on serving dish. Bring cooking sauce to boil and strain, skim off fat, and serve as gravy.

3. Serve with potatoes or noodles and redcurrant or cranberry jelly.

Quails stuffed with butter and wrapped in vine leaves and bacon, roasted in butter and served on slices of buttered toast (Serves 4, hot)

4 quails
2½ oz butter
a squeeze of lemon juice
4 tender vine leaves
4 slices fat bacon
4 slices white bread
fried breadcrumbs

Pre-heat oven to 450°F Mark 8

Roast Quail in Vine Leaves

1. Clean and truss quails neatly. Put ¼ oz butter inside each with lemon juice and salt and pepper. Wrap each one in a vine leaf; then tie a slice of fat bacon around each bird.

2. Heat butter, put quails into roasting pan and baste. Roast in oven for 15 minutes or grill on a spit.

3. Make 4 slices of toast and butter lightly. When birds are cooked, spread toast with pan drippings and serve.

Tender young grouse stuffed with bacon and roasted; served with bread sauce, gravy, and game chips (Serves 4, hot)

2 young grouse
2 oz butter
4 slices fat bacon
¼–½ pint red wine
2 slices bread
¼ pint stock

Pre-heat oven to 425°F Mark 7

Roast Grouse

1. Put 1 oz butter with seasoning inside each bird. Wrap them in bacon, and roast in oven for 30–35 minutes, until tender. Pour 2 glasses of red wine into pan after about 15 minutes and baste.

2. Make two slices of toast and when birds are done put one on each. Carve each bird in half for serving.

3. Meanwhile, make bread sauce as in *Roast Chicken* (see p. 154) and game chips as in *Roast Pheasant* (see p. 183).

4. Make gravy from pan drippings, adding stock and a little more wine. boil up and serve.

Half cooked game, jointed and simmered in stock and served with thickened sauce (Serves 4–6, hot)

2 grouse or partridges or small guinea
   fowl
3 tablespoons oil
3–4 rashers streaky bacon
pinch thyme and parsley
¾ pint strong stock
¼ pint red wine (or port)
½ oz flour
½ oz butter
1 tablespoon parsley chopped

Pre-heat oven to 400°F Mark 6

Salmi of Grouse or Partridge

1. Heat oil in roasting pan, cover birds with bacon and roast in hot fat for 20 minutes. Remove from oven and allow to cool slightly. Carve birds into pieces and put into a casserole. Cover with strong stock, add herbs and seasoning, and cook gently in oven for 15 minutes, or until tender.

2. Remove birds to serving dish and keep warm in oven. Bring pan drippings to the boil and reduce quantity slightly. Add wine (or port) and cook for a few minutes. Thicken sauce with small pieces of butter and flour paste, and continue heating until sauce thickens. Spoon over pieces of game, sprinkle with chopped parsley, and serve.

Pies & Casseroles

In this chapter are recipes for hot and cold pies and tarts of meat, game, fish, eggs, cheese and vegetables. Some have pastry top and bottom, in others the filling is put into a pastry case or into a pie dish or plate and then covered with pastry.

You will also find some pies covered with potato crust instead of pastry. If a recipe calls for 8 oz pastry, it means pastry made with 8 oz flour and the correct proportion of fat, etc. — not 8 oz finished pastry.

It is best to use plain flour for all pastry except suet crust. If baking powder is required in any other pastry it will be indicated in the recipe, e.g. in the recipe on p. 197.

When making pastry it should be kept cool and handled as little as possible. If time permits, leave the pastry to chill for at least 1 hour before using it. Hot water pastry is the only exception to this rule.

When a light custard mixture is used as a filling — e.g. Smoked Salmon Quiche on p. 217, or a baked custard — the bottom of the case can be brushed with a little lightly beaten egg white and this will prevent the pastry rising through the filling.

The casserole section begins on p. 226.

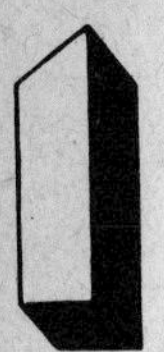

MAKING PASTRY

Basic Short Crust Pastry

1. Sift flour and salt into a bowl. Rub in the fat with the tips of the fingers until the mixture resembles fine breadcrumbs. Add enough water to bind. Chill until required.

Note

If a pastry case is baked without a filling it is referred to as being baked 'blind'. Line the pie plate with the pastry, prick the bottom with a fork or put a piece of greased paper (greased side downwards) in the bottom and fill with rice or beans, or crusts of bread. This can then be stored for future use. Remove paper and beans a few minutes before the end of the cooking.

8 oz plain flour
1/8 teaspoon salt
4 oz fat*
cold water, approximately
    2 tablespoons

***Fat may be butter or margarine**
    lard or any other cooking fat

Suet Crust

This pastry can be used for both savoury and sweet dishes and can be boiled, steamed or baked. It is always used for Steak and Kidney Pudding

1. Mix the flour, baking powder, salt and finely chopped suet together.

2. Stir in enough cold water to make a light elastic dough, which will leave the basin clean.

3. Turn on to a lightly floured board, knead very lightly, roll out and use as required.

1 lb plain flour or 12 oz plain flour
    and 4 oz fine breadcrumbs
1 tablespoon baking powder
2 teaspoons salt
6—8 oz suet
cold water to mix

Flaky Pastry

This is sometimes used for meat and fish pies, and for sweet dishes

1. Sift flour and salt into a bowl. Divide the fat into 3 portions. Rub one portion into the flour and mix with cold water.

2. Turn on to a lightly floured surface, knead until cracks have disappeared then roll into an oblong shape.

3. Place the second portion of fat in dabs 2/3 down the strip. Fold in three, give half a turn round and seal the open edges with the rolling pin.

4. Repeat with the remaining portion of fat, and then fold and roll a fourth time.

5. Cover and leave in a cold place to chill. If the pastry becomes sticky — chill in between the rollings.

8 oz plain flour
1/8 teaspoon salt
6 oz fat*
cold water, approximately 5—6
    tablespoons

***See note as above**

Lamb and Potato Pies (see p. 201)

Hot Water Pastry

This is used for cold meat and game pies

1. Sift flour and salt into a bowl and make a well in the centre. Drop in the egg yolk and cover with some of the flour.

2. Put lard and water into a small pan, heat slowly until lard melts, then increase the heat and bring to boiling point.

3. Pour all the liquid into the flour and mix with a wooden spoon until pastry is cool enough to handle, then use the hand and knead until the dough is smooth.

4. Leave to rest in a warm place for 20—30 minutes and use warm.

10 oz plain flour
½ teaspoon salt
1 egg yolk
3 oz fat—lard for preference
¼ pint water

Pate Brisee

This is a French pastry used for both savoury and sweet pies and tarts. It will stand a moist filling and is particularly suitable for such dishes as Quiche Lorraine (see p. 224). It can be made well in advance.

8 oz plain flour
1/8 teaspoon salt
3 tablespoons cold water
4 oz butter or margarine
1 egg

If a sweet pastry is required sift 2 oz sugar with the flour and salt.

1. Sift flour and salt on to a pastry board or slab, make a well in the centre, add water.

2. Work in the butter and egg, then gradually draw in the flour. Knead until smooth. Cover and chill for 1—2 hours before using.

MEAT PIES

![Mexican Beef Pie photograph]

Mexican Beef Pie

This pie should be well-seasoned and spicy, but reduce the quantity of chili powder if you do not like it too hot (serves 5—6, hot)

8 oz short crust pastry (see p. 194)
2 tablespoons vegetable oil
1 small onion, chopped
½ green pepper, chopped
1 lb minced raw beef
1 teaspoon salt
¼ teaspoon freshly-ground
    black pepper
1 dessertspoon chili powder
1 can (about 8 oz) tomato sauce
6—8 stuffed olives, sliced

Pre-heat oven to 400°F Mark 6

1. Line a 9 inch pie plate with half the pastry.

2. Heat the oil in a pan, sauté onion and green pepper for 5 minutes. Add beef and cook until browned, stirring frequently.

3. Add seasonings and tomato sauce and cook over low heat for 15 minutes. Leave to cool. Add olives, then turn the mixture into the pastry case.

4. Roll out remaining pastry and cut into thin strips. Arrange over the meat in a lattice pattern.

5. Bake for 35—40 minutes or until pastry is well browned.

Beef Roll

This roll should be cut into slices for serving, and if left to get cold and served with salad, makes a good buffet supper dish (serves 6, hot or cold)

FILLING
1 tablespoon vegetable oil
1 lb minced raw beef
1 onion, peeled and chopped
2 oz mushrooms, chopped
1 teaspoon salt
¼ teaspoon freshly-ground black
    pepper
¼ teaspoon dry mustard
6—8 stuffed olives, chopped
2 tablespoons finely-chopped parsley
about ½ pint gravy or stock

PASTRY
8 oz plain flour
1 teaspoon salt
1 teaspoon baking powder
3 tablespoons finely-chopped parsley
3 oz fat
milk to mix

Pre-heat oven to 400°F Mark 6

1. Heat the oil in a pan, add meat, onion and mushrooms and cook, stirring frequently, until the meat and onion are brown. Stir in all the dry ingredients, olives, parsley and enough gravy or stock to moisten. Stir all together over low heat for 5 minutes, then leave to cool while making the pastry.

2. Sift flour, salt and baking powder into a bowl, add parsley. Rub in the fat until the mixture looks like breadcrumbs. Add enough milk to make a fairly soft dough. Turn on to a floured surface and knead lightly.

3. Roll into an oblong shape about 10 by 14 inches. Spread the meat mixture over the dough to within ½ inch of the edges. Dampen the edges of the pastry and roll up like a swiss roll, pressing the edges well together.

4. Place on a greased baking sheet and bake for about 30 minutes. Serve hot, cut into slices, with the remaining gravy, or cold with salad.

1½ lb pie veal
½ lb cooked ham
2 tablespoons very finely-chopped
   parsley
¼ teaspoon thyme
¼ teaspoon marjoram
½ teaspoon grated lemon rind
1 teaspoon salt
1/8 teaspoon pepper
3 hard-boiled eggs
about ¼ pint stock
4 oz short crust pastry (see p. 194)
1 egg

Pre-heat oven to 325°F Mark 3

Veal and Ham Pie

Serve this pie cold with salad of your choice (serves 6)

1. Trim any excess fat from the veal and ham, and cut into cubes.

2. Mix all the herbs together, add salt and pepper. Arrange the veal, ham, herbs, flavourings and slices of egg alternately in a deep 8 inch pie plate. Add stock. Dampen the edge of the pie plate, put on the pastry, press the edge down well and decorate as desired.

3. Make a hole in the top and decorate with leaves made from the pastry trimmings. Brush with beaten egg and bake for 1—1¼ hours. Chill in the refrigerator for at least 3—4 hours or leave overnight.

Beef and Mushroom Pie

8 oz short crust pastry (see p. 194)
1 oz butter or margarine
1 tablespoon corn oil
2 small onions, peeled and finely
    chopped
4 oz mushrooms, sliced
2 tablespoons flour
1 beef stock cube
¾ lb minced cooked beef
2 teaspoons finely chopped parsley
1 teaspoon prepared horseradish
milk

Pre-heat oven to 425°F Mark 7

The meat in this pie is already cooked so it only needs a short cooking time. It is a very good way of using up a small quantity of cooked beef (serves 4–5, hot)

1. Line an 8 inch pie plate with half the pastry.

2. Heat the butter and corn oil in a sauté pan, add onion and mushrooms, and cook until lightly browned.

3. Stir in flour and crumbled stock cube, add 3/8 pint water and stir until boiling. Remove from the heat, stir in meat, parsley and horseradish and check the seasoning.

4. Put into the pastry case and cover with the rest of the pastry, pressing the edges well together. Decorate the edge, brush with milk and bake for 20–30 minutes.

Beef in Batter

BATTER
4 oz plain flour
½ teaspoon salt
1/8 teaspoon nutmeg
a pinch of cayenne pepper
2 eggs
½ pint milk

FILLING
1½ lb minced beef
1½ teaspoons salt
½ teaspoon black pepper
3 tablespoons grated or finely-chopped
    onion
1 tablespoon finely-chopped parsley
2 tablespoons corn oil

Pre-heat oven to 425°F Mark 7

This is not exactly a pie, but it is included here because it is an unusual recipe and makes an excellent alternative (serves 5–6, hot)

1. Sift the flour, salt, nutmeg and cayenne into a bowl. Gradually add the beaten eggs and milk and beat until the mixture is smooth. Chill for at least ½ hour then beat again until frothy.

2. Mix the beef with seasonings, onion and parsley.

3. Put the oil into a shallow baking pan about 8 by 12 inches and heat in the oven. Pour in half the batter, put in the meat and pour remaining batter on top.

4. Bake for 15 minutes. Then reduce heat to 350°F Mark 4 and cook for 20 more minutes, when the batter should be well puffed up and brown. Serve with tomato or mushroom sauce.

Beef Pie with Potato Crust

4 tablespoons olive oil
2–3 onions, peeled and chopped
1½ lb minced beef
1 teaspoon salt
a few drops of tabasco
2 tablespoons finely-chopped parsley
3 oz seedless raisins
12 green olives, sliced
¼ pint beef stock
3 hard-boiled eggs, sliced
¾–1 lb hot mashed potatoes
1 oz butter or margarine
1 egg
milk

Pre-heat oven to 400°F Mark 6

With potatoes as a topping, this pie can be made and cooked quickly. It has an interesting filling of beef with olives and raisins (serves 5–6, hot)

1. Heat the oil in a pan, sauté the onion until transparent; then add beef and cook until browned. Add salt, tabasco, parsley, raisins and olives. Stir in the stock and mix well.

2. Put half the meat mixture into a buttered baking dish, arrange slices of egg on top and cover with the rest of the meat.

3. Beat the potatoes, butter and egg until light and fluffy, spread over the meat. Ridge the top with a fork, brush with milk and bake 15–20 minutes until crust is well browned.

Steak and Kidney Pie

To ensure that the meat is well cooked and the pastry not overcooked it is advisable to cook the meat for the pie before covering with pastry (serves 4–5, hot)

1. Cut the steak into strips and pound lightly. Put a piece of kidney on each strip and roll up.

2. Mix some salt and pepper with the flour, and dredge the meat rolls.

3. Put the meat into a pie dish with the onion and sprinkle any remaining flour on top. Add enough stock or water to half fill the dish, cover with foil and cook about 1½ hours. Set aside to get quite cold.

4. Reset oven to 425°F Mark 7. Roll out the pastry thinly and cover the pie, pressing the edges of the pastry well down. Make a hole in the centre and decorate as desired with leaves cut from the pastry trimmings. Brush with beaten egg or milk and bake for about 30 minutes.

1½ lb stewing steak
6 oz beef kidney
1 oz plain flour
2 onions, peeled and finely chopped
beef stock or water
6 oz flaky pastry (see p. 194)
egg or milk for glazing

Pre-heat oven to 300°F Mark 2

Pork and Cauliflower Pie

This is a good way of using up cooked pork. This pie is covered with short crust pastry, but home-made or frozen flaky pastry can be used instead (serves 6, hot)

1. Cook the cauliflower until just tender in boiling salted water. Drain, and divide into small flowerets.

2. Heat the oil in a sauté pan, add onion and garlic and sauté for a few minutes. Add tomatoes, thyme, salt, pepper and paprika. Simmer for 10 minutes, then press through a sieve.

3. Blend the flour with a little cold water, add to the sauce and stir until boiling.

4. Put the pork and cauliflower into a pie dish and pour the sauce over.

5. Cover with the pastry and bake for about 25 minutes or until the crust is well browned.

1 medium-sized head of cauliflower
1 tablespoon oil
2 small onions, peeled and very finely
    chopped
1 clove garlic, crushed
1 can tomatoes
a pinch of thyme
¼ teaspoon paprika
2 tablespoons flour
1¼ lb diced cooked pork
6 oz short crust pastry (see p. 194)

Pre-heat oven to 450°F Mark 7

Veal and Pork Pie

For this pie, the filling of meat and vegetables is cooked and allowed to get cold before covering with pastry. If it is more convenient, this can be done in advance (serves 4, hot or cold)

1. Heat the oil in a pan, add the veal and pork cut into 1 inch pieces and stir until lightly browned.

2. Add 1 pint boiling water, salt, paprika, bay leaf and cloves. Cover, and simmer for 15 minutes.

3. Remove bay leaf and cloves, add vegetables, cover and cook over low heat for 20 minutes.

4. Mix the flour to a smooth paste with a little cold water, stir into the meat and season to taste. Transfer all into a pie dish and leave to get cold.

5. Cover with pastry and bake for 25–30 minutes.

2 tablespoons oil
½ lb veal
½ lb lean pork
1 teaspoon salt
½ teaspoon paprika
1 small bay leaf
2 cloves
1 small carrot, peeled and sliced
    lengthways
3 stalks celery, cut into diagonal
    pieces
2–3 potatoes, diced
8 small white onions
1 tablespoon flour
6 oz short crust pastry (see p. 194)

Pre-heat oven to 425°F Mark 7

Lamb and Potato Pies

*These are individual pies, and fresh uncooked meat should be used
(serves 4—5, hot—see picture, p. 195)*

12 oz short crust pastry (see p. 194)

FILLING
¾ lb lean lamb, shoulder cut
¾ lb potatoes, peeled and diced
1/8 teaspoon dried rosemary
a pinch of dried thyme
1 tablespoon finely-chopped onion
egg or milk to glaze

Pre-heat oven to 425°F Mark 7

1. Make the pastry, roll out thinly and cut into rounds the size of a saucer.

2. Cut the meat into very small pieces, mix with potato, seasoning, herbs and onion and add 2—3 tablespoons water.

3. Divide equally among the rounds of pastry, moisten the edge, fold over and press the edges well together. Flute with the fingers.

4. Stand the pies upright on a baking sheet, glaze with egg or milk and bake about 20 minutes or until the pastry begins to brown. Reduce the heat to 325°F Mark 3 and cook for another 40—45 minutes.

Cold Pork Pies

*Hot water pastry is used for these pies. They are very good for outdoor
meals or for the lunch box (makes about 5 pies)*

hot water pastry (see p. 195)
1 lb lean pork
½ teaspoon salt
¼ teaspoon pepper
a pinch of mixed herbs
2 hard-boiled eggs, sliced
egg or milk for glazing
2 teaspoons gelatine
¼ pint stock or water

Pre-heat oven to 400°F Mark 6

1. Divide pastry into 4—5 portions and cut about 1/3 from each portion for the lid of the pie. Keep these pieces warm.

2. Mould the 5 pieces of dough into a pie shape with the hands or mould the dough around a glass jar. Fix a double band of waxed paper around each and secure with string.

3. Cut the pork into small cubes, sprinkle with salt, pepper and herbs. Put into the pie cases with slices of egg and add 1—2 tablespoons water.

4. Roll out the small portions of dough for the lids. Moisten the edges of the pastry and put on the lids. Make a hole in the top and flute around the edges. Decorate as liked.

5. Bake for 30 minutes, then remove the paper and brush the top and sides of the pies with beaten egg or milk. Return to the oven and cook for 20—25 minutes.

6. Dissolve the gelatine in the stock. If water is used add a little meat extract. When just beginning to set, pour into the cooled pies through the hole in the top. Allow to get quite cold before using.

Ham and Egg Patties

*These little patties are useful for packed meals and a good way of using up
a small amount of cooked ham*

6 oz short crust pastry (see p. 194)

FILLING
1 lb chopped cooked ham
2 hard-boiled eggs, chopped
1/8 teaspoon prepared mustard
2—3 tablespoons white sauce
egg or milk to glaze

Pre-heat oven to 425°F Mark 7

1. Roll out the pastry to 1/8—1/4 inch in thickness and cut into rounds about 4½—5 inches across.

2. Mix the ham with the eggs; add salt, pepper, mustard and enough sauce to bind.

3. Divide the mixture evenly between the pastry rounds, moisten the edges and fold over. Press and crimp the edge, glaze with egg or milk and bake for about 25 minutes.

Sausage Pie

If you keep a supply of baked pastry cases in your deep freeze, this pie can be made up quickly for an emergency meal. Otherwise, it is best to partly cook the pie case before putting in the filling (serves 4—5, hot)

6 oz short crust pastry (see p. 194)
6 oz butter or margarine
1 small onion, peeled and chopped
4 tablespoons chopped cooked ham
3 oz mushrooms, sliced
1 tablespoon flour
3/8 pint milk
1/8 teaspoon grated nutmeg
1 egg yolk
2 tablespoons double cream
8 small sausages
2—3 tablespoons grated cheese

Pre-heat oven to 400°F Mark 6

1. Line an 8 inch pie plate with the pastry, prick the bottom and bake for 10—15 minutes. Remove from the oven.

2. Heat 2 oz of the butter in a small pan, sauté onion, ham and mushrooms until onion is transparent, then set aside.

3. Make a sauce with another 2 oz of the butter, flour and milk. When smooth and thickened, add salt, pepper and nutmeg. Remove from the heat, stir in egg yolk and cream.

4. Sauté sausages in the remaining butter until lightly brown.

5. Put the onion and ham mixture into the pie case. Arrange sausages in spoke fashion on top. Pour the sauce over, sprinkle with cheese, and bake for about 20 minutes.

Sweetbread Pie

This pie—very good for a special occasion—has an unusual pastry. If possible, let it stand overnight before using. The filling is a savoury custard mixture holding the sweetbread and tongue (serves 4—5, hot)

PASTRY
6 oz plain flour
½ teaspoon salt
6 oz butter or margarine
3—4 tablespoons sour cream

FILLING
½ lb cooked or canned spaghetti or other pasta
1 pair blanched and parboiled sweetbreads
½ lb cooked diced tongue
2 egg yolks
¼ pint double cream
2—3 tablespoons dry sherry

Pre-heat oven to 400°F Mark 6

1. Sift flour and salt into a bowl, cut in butter until mixture looks like breadcrumbs. Mix lightly with the sour cream, tossing the mixture together until it forms a ball. Wrap in foil and chill overnight if possible.

2. When ready to use, roll out pastry and line an 8 inch pie plate. Reserve the pastry trimmings for decoration.

3. Arrange layers of spaghetti, sweetbread and tongue in the pastry case. Beat the egg yolks, cream and sherry together, season carefully and pour over the contents of the pie case.

4. Use the trimmings of pastry to make a lattice design on top or use leaves of pastry.

5. Bake for 15 minutes; then reduce the heat to 350°F Mark 4 and cook for 20 minutes, or until the pastry is browned and the custard set.

Ham and Apricot Pie

This is an unusual pie and very good to eat (serves 4, hot)

1 gammon rasher (about 1—1¼ lb)
   cut 1 inch thick
prepared mustard
4 oz dried apricots, soaked overnight
3 tablespoons seedless raisins
3—4 tablespoons stock or water
6 medium potatoes, peeled and sliced
½ oz butter or margarine

Pre-heat oven to 350°F Mark 4

1. Heat a sauté pan, put in the ham and brown lightly on both sides.

2. Put into a deep baking dish, spread very lightly with mustard and sprinkle with pepper.

3. Arrange apricots and raisins on top.

4. Add stock or water and cover with slices of potato. Sprinkle very sparingly with salt and dot with butter. Cover with waxed paper and bake for ¾ hour. Remove the paper and bake for 15—20 minutes more.

Pigs in Blankets

This intriguing name is used for a simple snack composed of sausages cooked in pastry (serves 6, hot or cold)

6 sausages
prepared mustard
6 thin fingers cheese
flaky pastry (see p. 194)
egg or milk to glaze

Pre-heat oven to 425°F Mark 7

1. Split the sausages, spread very lightly with mustard and insert a finger of cheese in each.

2. Roll the pastry thinly and cut into 6 inch squares. Place 1 sausage diagonally on each square, and bring together the other two diagonal corners of the pastry, so that the ends of the sausages are exposed.

3. Put on to a baking sheet, glaze with egg or milk and bake for 20 minutes.

4. Serve hot with grilled tomatoes or cold with salad.

CHICKEN & GAME PIES

Chicken with Scone Topping

This elegant looking pie is topped with scones instead of pastry. The recipe is given below (serves 4, hot)

FILLING
2 tablespoons oil
1 small onion, peeled and chopped
½ green pepper, finely chopped
2 oz mushrooms, sliced
1 tablespoon cornflour
½ pint milk
¾–1 lb cooked chicken, cut
    into cubes

SCONES
½ lb plain flour
1 teaspoon salt
2 teaspoons baking powder
2 oz fat
milk to mix

Pre-heat oven to 425°F Mark 7

1. Heat the oil in a saucepan, add onion, green pepper and mushrooms and sauté for a few minutes. Add cornflour and cook for 1 minute, stirring all the time.

2. Add milk, gradually, stir until boiling, add chicken and seasoning. Turn into a deep 8–9 inch pie plate.

3. To make the scones: Sift flour, salt and baking powder, rub in the fat until mixture looks like coarse breadcrumbs. Using a fork, stir in enough milk to make a soft but not sticky dough. Knead lightly on a floured board, roll out about ½ inch thick and cut into 1½ inch rounds.

4. Place the rounds on top of the chicken mixture, brush with milk and bake for 10–15 minutes.

Chicken and Ham Pie

This pie is served cold and is made with hot water pastry. Special raised pie moulds are sometimes used, but a loaf or cake tin is quite suitable. An equal quantity of veal can be substituted for the chicken (serves 4—5)

1. Make pastry and keep warm until required.

2. Cut ham and chicken into 1 inch cubes and sprinkle with salt, pepper, lemon rind and rosemary.

3. Use about two-thirds of the pastry to line sides and bottom of a loaf tin, about 9 by 5 by 2¾ inches or a 6 inch cake tin. Place half the ham and chicken into the tin. Cut the eggs in halves and arrange on top, then cover with the rest of the meat and add 3—4 tablespoons chicken stock. Turn the top edges of the pastry lining in over the meat and dampen all around. Roll out remaining pastry to make a lid and press down well, making as secure as possible. Make a hole in the centre, decorate the top with pastry leaves and brush all over with beaten egg.

4. Bake for 2—2¼ hours, then leave to get cold.

5. Melt gelatine in remaining stock and when beginning to set, pour into the pie through the hole in the top. Leave to get quite cold and set before serving.

hot water pastry (see p. 195)
½ lb ham
1½ lb boned uncooked chicken
1 teaspoon grated lemon rind
½ teaspoon dried rosemary
2 hard boiled eggs
¼ pint chicken stock
1 egg
1 teaspoon gelatine

Pre-heat oven to 350°F Mark 4

Chicken and Bacon Pie

Use a frying chicken for this pie, as the chicken and pastry are cooked together and an older bird would take too long to cook (serves 4, hot or cold)

1 frying chicken (2—2½ lb)
6 slices bacon, chopped
2 small onions, peeled and chopped
3 tomatoes
¼ teaspoon dried rosemary
a pinch of thyme
chicken stock
flaky pastry (see p. 194)
egg or milk to glaze

Pre-heat oven to 450°F Mark 6

1. Skin the chicken and cut all the meat from the bones.

2. Arrange layers of chicken, bacon, onions and tomatoes in a baking dish. Sprinkle with herbs and a little seasoning and moisten with the stock.

3. Cover with pastry, crimp and flute the edge, and decorate as desired. Glaze with egg or milk.

4. Bake for 25—30 minutes, then reduce heat to 350°F Mark 4 and cook for 1—1¼ hours. Cover the pastry with a piece of waxed paper towards the end of the cooking if it seems to be getting too brown.

Chicken and Celery Pie

Cooked chicken is used in this pie and the crisp texture of the celery and almonds is very pleasant in the creamy sauce (serves 4—5, hot)

8 oz short crust pastry (see p. 194)
¾ lb diced cooked chicken
3 oz mushrooms, sliced
4 stalks celery, sliced diagonally
1 oz blanched slivered almonds
½ pint fairly thick white sauce
egg or milk to glaze

Pre-heat oven to 425°F Mark 7

1. Line an 8 inch pie plate with half the pastry.

2. Mix all the ingredients for the filling and season carefully.

3. Turn into the pastry case, moisten the edges of the pastry and put on the top crust. Press the edges with the back of a knife and decorate the top of the pie with the pastry trimmings.

4. Glaze with egg or milk and bake for 10 minutes. Then reduce the heat to 350°F Mark 4 and bake for 20—30 minutes, until the pastry is crisp and brown.

Cold Game Pie

This pie can be baked in a 7 inch cake tin with a loose bottom or moulded with the hand. Special game pie moulds are available, but instructions here are for using a cake tin. As for the hot pie (see p. 210) the choice of game used depends on what is available (serves 4—5)

hot water pastry (see p. 195)
¾ lb sausage meat
4 oz diced lean ham
6 oz cubed lean steak
meat from 1 cooked pheasant or
**   2 pigeons or partridge**
1 egg
½ oz gelatine
½ pint chicken stock

Pre-heat oven to 375°F Mark 5

1. Make the pastry and keep it warm while preparing the ingredients for the filling. Cut off a quarter of the dough, and keep it warm for the top.

2. Butter a 7 inch loose-bottomed cake tin and line it with the dough rolled about ¼ inch thick.

3. Line the base and sides of the pie with sausage meat. Mix the ham, steak and game, season well and fill the pie with the mixture.

4. Dampen the edge of the pie, roll out the dough for the lid and press it on tightly, fluting the edge. Make a small hole in the centre and decorate the top of the pie with pastry leaves made from the pastry trimmings.

5. Bake for 1½ hours. Then remove the pie from the cake tin and put it onto a baking sheet. Brush the top and sides with beaten egg, return to the oven and bake for ½ hour.

6. Dissolve the gelatine in the stock and pour into the pie through the hole in the top. Leave to get quite cold—preferably overnight—before cutting. Serve with salad.

Chicken and Mushroom Pie

2 oz butter or margarine
2 oz flour
¾ pint milk
1 lb diced cooked chicken
3 oz mushrooms sliced
2 tablespoons chopped green olives
2 tablespoons blanched slivered
    almonds
6 oz flaky or short crust pastry
    (see p. 194)
1 egg
milk

Pre-heat oven to 425°F Mark 7

This is a good way of using up cooked chicken or turkey. It can be made with flaky pastry or short crust (serves 4—5, hot or cold)

1. Make a sauce with the butter, flour and milk and season carefully. Add chicken, mushrooms, olives and almonds and mix well. Turn into an 8 inch pie plate.

2. Cover with the pastry, use trimmings to make pastry leaves to decorate the top.

3. Glaze with beaten egg and milk and bake for 15 minutes, then reduce the heat to 350°F Mark 4 and bake for 20 minutes, until pastry is well browned.

4. Serve hot with vegetables or cold with salad.

Chicken and Oyster Pie

Canned or bottled oysters are very good for this pie. One jar of oysters generally contains about 12 (serves 4—5)

2 oz butter
½—¾ lb cooked chicken, cut into strips
2 oz mushrooms, sliced
½ oz cornflour
¼ pint milk
¼ pint single cream
salt, cayenne pepper
1 egg yolk
1 can or jar of oysters
1 eight-inch baked pastry case
chopped parsley
1 canned pimento

1. Heat 1 oz butter in a sauté pan, add the strips of chicken and mushrooms and sauté for 4—5 minutes.

2. Make a sauce with the remaining butter, cornflour and milk, stir in the cream, except 1 tablespoon, and add salt and pepper to taste.

3. Mix the egg yolk with the remaining cream, stir a little of the hot sauce into it then return all to the pan.

4. Add the chicken, mushrooms and oysters, check the seasoning and heat through without boiling.

5. Pour into the warm pastry case, sprinkle with parsley and decorate with strips of pimento.

Chicken and Pineapple Pie

The fresh, tangy flavour of pineapple blends very well with chicken in this pie (serves 4—5, hot)

1 oz butter or margarine
1 oz plain flour
3/8 pint milk
¼ pint single cream
4 rashers streaky bacon
1 can (about 8 oz) pineapple cubes
4 oz cooked peas (or 1 package
    frozen)
½ lb diced cooked chicken
1 baked 8—9 inch pastry case

Pre-heat oven to 350°F Mark 4

1. Make a sauce with the butter, flour and milk. Add cream and seasoning.

2. Chop the bacon and fry until crisp. Add to the sauce.

3. Drain the pineapple, reserve some cubes for decoration, and add the rest to the sauce. Add the peas and chicken and mix all well. Check the seasoning and pour into the pastry case.

4. Decorate with remaining pineapple, and put into the oven just long enough for the pie to heat through.

Chicken in Potato Nest

Mashed potato is used as a base for this pie. It is a good way of using up leftover chicken or turkey and potatoes (serves 4, hot)

1 lb cooked mashed potatoes
1 oz butter or margarine
1 oz plain flour
½ teaspoon pepper and salt
½ pint chicken stock
4 tablespoons double cream
2 oz mushrooms, sliced
1 lb cooked chicken, diced
2 tablespoons grated Parmesan
   cheese

Pre-heat oven to 400°F Mark 6

1. Line a buttered 8–9 inch pie plate with the potatoes.

2. Melt the butter in a pan, stir in the flour. Add the stock gradually, stir until boiling. Add cream and mushrooms and cook for a few minutes. Add seasoning to taste.

3. Put the chicken into the prepared pie plate, pour over the sauce and sprinkle with the cheese.

4. Bake for 25–30 minutes.

Giblet Pie

Giblets of chicken or turkey, consisting of neck, liver, heart and kidney, are used for this pie, but you may like to add extra chicken livers (serves 4–5, hot)

giblets, as available
flour
8 oz short crust pastry (see p. 194)
2 hard-boiled eggs
2 oz mushrooms, sliced
6 rashers streaky bacon
egg and milk to glaze

Pre-heat oven to 425°F Mark 7

1. Wash the giblets and simmer in salted water until tender. Drain, and retain some of the stock.

2. Remove meat from the neck of the chicken and chop the liver, heart and kidney. Coat with flour to which salt and pepper has been added.

3. Line an 8 inch pie plate with half the pastry. Put in half the giblet meat, sliced eggs, mushrooms and bacon. Add 2–3 tablespoons giblet stock and cover with the rest of the meat.

4. Cover with the remaining pastry, press the edges well together, and use the trimmings to make a decoration for the top of the pie. Glaze with egg and milk, and bake for 20 minutes. Reduce the heat to 350°F, Mark 4 and bake for 20–25 minutes.

South African Chicken Pie

1 chicken, 2½–3 lb
1 teaspoon salt
1 teaspoon white peppercorns
2 bay leaves
3 carrots, peeled and sliced
2 onions, peeled and quartered
2–3 sticks celery, diced
3–4 sprigs parsley
2–3 slices cooked ham
2 hard-boiled eggs, sliced
1 oz butter or margarine
1 oz flour
2–3 tablespoons sherry
1 tablespoon lemon juice
1 teaspoon sugar
a pinch of ground mace
1 egg yolk
6 oz short crust pastry (see p. 194)
egg or milk to glaze

Pre-heat oven to 400°F Mark 6

This pie can be prepared in advance and baked just before it is to be served (serves 4–5, hot)

1. Cut the chicken into quarters and put into a large saucepan with the seasoning, vegetables and enough water to just cover. Put on a lid and simmer for about ½ hour. Strain off the stock and set aside.

2. Cut the meat from the chicken in fairly large chunks, cut up the cooked vegetables. Arrange alternate layers of chicken, vegetables, ham and eggs in a fireproof baking dish.

3. Make a sauce with the butter, flour and ½ pint of the chicken stock. Add sherry, lemon juice, sugar and mace. Cook until well mixed and thickened. Stir in egg yolk, re-heat without boiling, check seasoning.

4. Pour the sauce over the chicken and vegetables and cover with the pastry. Cut a line from the centre of the pie towards each of the four corners and fold each pastry triangle back, leaving an open square. Glaze the pastry with beaten egg or milk and bake about ½ hour.

Chicken Cream Pie

For this pie, cooked chicken is blended with a little cream and flavouring and cooked in a square of pastry (serves 4, hot or cold)

¾—1 lb diced cooked chicken
1 hard boiled egg, chopped
½ teaspoon grated lemon rind
1 teaspoon finely chopped parsley
3—4 tablespoons double cream
flaky pastry (see p. 194)
egg or milk to glaze

Pre-heat oven to 425°F Mark 7

1. Mix the chicken and egg with flavourings and seasoning, and blend with the cream.

2. Roll the pastry into a square shape and put the chicken mixture in the centre. Moisten the edges of the pastry and fold the four corners up to the centre, pressing them well together. Decorate with a rose and leaves cut from the trimmings of the pastry. Glaze with egg or milk.

3. Bake for 15 minutes. Then reduce the heat to 350°F Mark 4 and bake for 25 minutes.

Swiss Cheese and Chicken Pie

Gruyère cheese is used with cooked chicken for this pie, which makes a very good light luncheon dish. Serve it with a tossed green salad (serves 4, hot)

6 oz short crust pastry (see p. 194)
¾ lb chopped cooked chicken
6 oz grated Gruyère cheese
1 tablespoon plain flour
3 eggs
3/8 pint single cream or milk

Pre-heat oven to 375°F Mark 5

1. Line an 8 inch pie plate with the pastry and decorate the edge.

2. Mix the chicken and cheese together, sprinkle with the flour, then put into the pastry case.

3. Beat the eggs, add cream and seasoning, pour over the chicken and cheese.

4. Bake for 10 minutes then reduce heat to 300°F Mark 2 and bake for 35—40 minutes, or until the pastry is brown and the custard set.

Hot Game Pie

A game pie can be served hot or cold but generally hot water crust is used for a cold game pie (see p. 207). This one is made with flaky pastry and is served hot. The filling depends very much on the game available. This is a basic recipe which can be varied to suit yourself (serves 5—6)

6 oz flaky pastry (see p. 194)
2 partridge, pigeons or pheasant as
   available
6 tablespoons red wine
6 tablespoons cognac
1 tablespoon finely-chopped parsley
2 tablespoons finely-chopped onion
3 tablespoons oil
2 oz butter or margarine
¾ lb veal, cut into strips
½ lb cooked ham, cut into strips
2 oz mushrooms, sliced
¼ teaspoon oregano
¼ teaspoon marjoram
1 bay leaf
about ¼ pint game or chicken
   stock
egg for glazing

Pre-heat oven to 400°F Mark 6

1. Cut the game into serving pieces, removing as much bone as possible.

2. Put the wine, cognac, parsley, onion and seasoning into a bowl, put in the pieces of game and marinate for 3—4 hours; then remove and drain well.

3. Heat the oil and most of the butter in a sauté pan. Sauté the game until golden brown.

4. Put the veal and ham into a deep oval baking dish, arrange the pieces of game on top, add mushrooms and herbs. Pour over the marinade and stock, and dot with the remaining butter.

5. Roll out the pastry into an oval shape. Dampen the edge of the dish and line with a strip of pastry, dampen the strip, put on the pastry and press the edges well together. Press and flute the edge of the pastry. Make a hole in the centre and decorate with pastry leaves made from the trimmings. Glaze with beaten egg and bake for 20 minutes. Reduce the heat to 325°F Mark 3 and bake for 1½—2 hours.

Souffle Pie

The filling for this light and fluffy pie consists of cooked chicken flavoured with bacon and mushrooms (serves 4, hot)

1½ oz butter or margarine
2 oz mushrooms, sliced
1 tablespoon cornflour
1 chicken stock cube
3/8 pint milk
1 egg
½ lb finely chopped cooked chicken
4 rashers bacon, cooked and chopped
1 eight-inch baked pastry case

Pre-heat oven to 375°F Mark 5

1. Heat the butter in a sauté pan, add mushrooms and sauté until tender. Add cornflour and crumbled stock cube, and cook for 1 minute. Gradually add milk and stir until boiling.

2. Remove from the heat; add egg yolk, chicken and bacon.

3. Beat egg white stiffly and fold into the mixture. Turn into the baked pastry case and cook for 25—30 minutes.

Garnish if liked with a little chopped cooked ham.

Australian Pie

This pie has a filling of chicken and raisins combined in a creamy cheese sauce (serves 4—5, hot)

8 oz short crust pastry (see p. 194)
1 oz butter or margarine
1 oz plain flour
3/8 pint milk
4 tablespoons double cream
4 oz grated cheese
1 egg
¾ lb chopped cooked chicken
3 oz seedless raisins
egg or milk to glaze

Pre-heat oven to 400°F Mark 6

1. Line an 8 inch pie plate with half the pastry.

2. Make a sauce with the butter, flour and milk, add cream, cheese and seasoning. Remove from the heat, stir in beaten egg.

3. Put alternate layers of chicken and raisins into the pastry case and pour the sauce over.

4. Cover the pie with remaining pastry, pressing the edges well together. Decorate the edge as liked, make 2—3 cuts in the top and bake for about 30 minutes.

FISH PIES

Russian Fish Pie

Flaky pastry is best to use for this pie. The filling is traditionally haddock, but any other white fish could be used (serves 4, hot)

1½ lb fillets of haddock, or
 other fish
1 teaspoon grated lemon rind
2 hard-boiled eggs, chopped
3—4 tablespoons white sauce
flaky pastry (see p. 194)
egg to glaze

Pre-heat oven to 400°F Mark 6

1. Remove any skin from the fish and cut into small pieces.

2. Add seasoning, lemon rind and chopped eggs and bind with the sauce.

3. Roll the pastry into a square and put the fish mixture in the centre.

4. Dampen the edges of the pastry and fold each corner to the centre keeping the square shape.

5. Decorate the centre with pastry leaves, brush with beaten egg and bake for 30—40 minutes.

Salmon Supper Ring

This is a 'pie' with a difference. The savoury fish mixture is cooked in scone dough and shaped into a horseshoe. Follow the recipe on page 205 for Chicken with Scone Topping (serves 4, hot or cold)

1. Make a sauce with the butter, cornflour, milk and seasoning. Add the salmon, capers and lemon juice and mix all well.

2. Roll the dough thinly into an oblong shape, spread with the filling, moisten the edges of the dough and roll up. Then move carefully onto a greased baking sheet and twist into a horseshoe shape.

3. Using kitchen scissors or a sharp knife, make some cuts about two-thirds of the way into the roll. Turn each section onto its side so that the filling is exposed a little.

4. Glaze with egg or milk, bake for 15—20 minutes, and serve with salad.

1 oz butter
½ oz cornflour
¼ pint milk
1 small can salmon, drained and
    flaked
1 teaspoon chopped capers
1 teaspoon lemon juice
scone dough (see p. 205)
egg or milk to glaze

Pre-heat oven to 425°F Mark 7

Seafood Pie

A mixture of seafood can be used for this pie, which makes a good buffet party dish (serves 6—8, hot)

6 oz short crust pastry (see p. 194)
1½ oz butter or margarine
4—5 spring onions or chives, finely chopped
prawns, lobster, scallops as available
1 tablespoon tomato purée
cayenne pepper
3 tablespoons sherry
4 eggs
½ pint single cream
grated Gruyère cheese

Pre-heat oven to 425°F Mark 7

1. Line a 9 inch pie plate with the pastry, prick the bottom and bake for 15 minutes. Remove from the heat and leave to cool.

2. Melt the butter in a sauté pan, add the onion, and sauté for about 2 minutes. Add fish, cut into small pieces, and stir over low heat for 2 minutes. Add tomato purée, seasoning and sherry.

3. Beat the eggs, add cream and stir in the cooled seafood mixture. Season to taste and pour into the pastry case. Sprinkle with cheese, and bake for 25—30 minutes at 350°F Mark 4.

4. Serve cut into wedges.

Eel Pie

Eels are not to everyone's taste, but the ancient Egyptians worshipped the eel as a god. This pie is generally served hot but is equally good cold. Ask your fishmonger to skin the eels (serves 5—6)

2—2½ lb eels
salt
½ oz butter or margarine
1—2 cloves
small piece of mace
few peppercorns
¼ pint cider
3 hard boiled eggs
2 onions, peeled and chopped
2 tomatoes, peeled and chopped
black pepper, paprika pepper
6 oz flaky pastry (see p. 194)
milk to glaze

Pre-heat oven to 425°F Mark 7

1. Cut the skinned and washed eels into 2 inch pieces and put into a saucepan with ½ teaspoon salt, butter, cloves, mace and peppercorns. Add cider and ¼ pint water, bring to boiling point and simmer for 10—15 minutes.

2. Remove the eels from the stock and arrange in a buttered pie dish alternately with the slices of egg, onion and tomatoes.

3. Reduce the stock to half, then strain over the contents of the pie dish. Sprinkle lightly with pepper and salt if required.

4. Cover with the pastry, glaze with milk and cook for 20 minutes, then reduce the heat to 350°F Mark 4 and cook a further 15—20 minutes.

Salmon Pie

Canned salmon is used for this pie, but tuna or smoked haddock could be used in the same way (serves 4, hot)

1 oz butter or margarine
1 oz plain flour
¼ pint milk
4 tablespoons single cream
1 egg
4 oz cottage cheese
2—3 chives, chopped
1 small can salmon
1 eight-inch baked pastry case
2—3 tomatoes, peeled and sliced

Pre-heat oven to 350°F Mark 4

1. Make a thick sauce with the butter, flour and milk. Remove from the heat, stir in cream, egg yolk, cheese, chives and salmon, drained and flaked. Season to taste.

2. Beat egg white stiffly and fold into the mixture.

3. Turn into the baked pastry case, and bake for 20 minutes. Arrange slices of tomato around the edge, and bake for 10 minutes.

Sea Fish Pie

This pie can be made to look very decorative. Any kind of white fish can be used (serves 4—5, hot or cold)

8 oz short crust pastry (see p. 194)
1 oz butter or margarine
1 oz cornflour
¼ pint milk
¼ pint single cream
1 egg
½ teaspoon anchovy paste
1 teaspoon lemon juice
1 teaspoon chopped capers
½ small onion, very finely chopped
1 teaspoon chopped parsley
1¼lb cooked flaked fish
egg or milk to glaze
cucumber, tomato, radishes to garnish

Pre-heat oven to 375°F Mark 5

1. Line an 8 inch pie plate with half the pastry.

2. Make a sauce with the butter, cornflour, milk and cream. Remove from the heat, add the lightly beaten egg and all the other ingredients. Season to taste.

3. Turn into the pastry case, dampen the edges of the pastry, cover with the pastry lid, pressing the edges well together, and decorate the edge.

4. Mark a small circle in the centre of the pastry (a 2—3 inch cutter is best to do this). Cut the circle across in four and turn the pointed ends back to expose the filling.

5. Glaze the pie with beaten egg or milk and bake for ¾—1 hour. Garnish with radish roses and thin overlapping slices of tomato and cucumber.

Fish and Macaroni Pie

This pie has a topping of cheese made crisp and brown under the grill (serves 4–5)

1. Put the fish into a pan, sprinkle with salt and pepper and barely cover with milk. Simmer for 10 minutes.

2. Cook the macaroni according to package instructions and drain well.

3. When the fish is cooked, pour off the stock and retain. Remove any skin from the fish and flake with a fork.

4. Make the stock up to ½ pint with milk and use to make a sauce with 1 oz of the butter and the flour. Add half the cheese and season carefully.

5. Stir the fish and macaroni into the sauce and pour into a buttered fire-proof dish. Mix the remaining cheese with the breadcrumbs and sprinkle on top. Dot with the remaining butter and brown under the grill.

1 lb hake, fresh haddock or cod
milk—about ½ pint
½ lb quick cooking macaroni
1½ oz butter or margarine
½ oz flour
3 oz grated cheese
1 tablespoon breadcrumbs

Haddock and Tomato Pie

Fresh haddock, flavoured with onion and tomato, makes this an appetizing luncheon or supper dish. The pastry for the base is fairly rich, but short crust may be used if preferred (serves 4, hot)

1. Sift the flour and salt, rub in the butter and margarine and mix with beaten egg yolk and water if required. Set aside to chill as long as possible, then line a deep 7 inch pie plate. Bake 'blind' (see p. 194).

2. Heat the butter in a saucepan, add onion and sauté until soft. Stir in the flour, add milk and stir until boiling. Remove from the heat, add seasoning and beaten eggs.

3. Arrange fish and tomatoes, cut side down, in the pastry case, season, pour over the sauce and sprinkle with cheese.

4. Bake for 20–25 minutes, and serve with a plain tossed green salad.

PASTRY
6 oz flour
a pinch of salt
3 oz butter
1 oz margarine
1 egg yolk
1–2 tablespoons water

FILLING
1 oz butter or margarine
1 small finely-sliced onion
½ oz plain flour
¼ pint milk
nutmeg
2 eggs
3 tomatoes, peeled, halved and
    seeded
1 lb cooked flaked haddock
grated cheese

Pre-heat oven to 350°F Mark 4

Cabillaud au Gratin

This is a simple version of a famous French dish, but it is very good to eat and much less trouble to make. The fish is covered with a potato crust instead of pastry (serves 4–5, hot)

1. Cook the potatoes in boiling salted water, drain thoroughly and dry over low heat. Add 1 oz butter, cream and beaten egg and whip until fluffy.

2. Put the fish into a pan with the wine, lemon juice and enough salted water to barely cover. Poach for 15 minutes. Drain carefully and retain the stock. Flake the fish coarsely, removing any skin.

3. Make a sauce with the remaining 1 oz butter, flour and ½ pint of the fish stock. Add the prawns and cheese and season to taste.

4. Put the fish into an oven dish, add enough sauce to moisten and cover with the potatoes. Brush with a little milk and bake for about 30 minutes, or until the potato crust is brown.

5. Serve any remaining sauce separately, thinning it down if necessary with a little of the fish stock.

1 lb potatoes
2 oz butter or margarine
2 tablespoons cream or milk
1 egg
1½ lb cod fillets
2 tablespoons dry white wine
2 teaspoons lemon juice
1 oz plain flour
1 small packet frozen prawns or
    shrimps
2 oz grated Gruyère cheese
milk

Pre-heat oven to 425°F Mark 7

Smoked Salmon Quiche

For a very special occasion, this pie is quite delicious. Pate Brisee should be used for the pastry shell (serves 5–6, hot or cold)

Pate Brisee (see p. 195)
4 whole eggs
2 egg yolks
¾ pint double cream
¼ lb smoked salmon
freshly ground pepper
1 oz butter

Pre-heat oven to 350°F Mark 4

1. Line a 9 inch pie plate with the pastry, prick the bottom and bake for 10 minutes. Leave to cool.

2. Beat the eggs, egg yolks and cream together and season carefully.

3. Pour about two-thirds of the mixture into the cooled pastry case. Cut the salmon into pieces and arrange on top, then pour the rest slowly on top.

4. Dot with butter, and bake for about 25 minutes.

Spanish Fish Pie

Fillets of sole are used in this recipe but other white fish could be substituted. The fish is lightly cooked with onion and tomato before putting into the pastry case (serves 5–6, hot)

10 oz short crust pastry (see p. 194)
4 tablespoons olive oil
2–3 onions, peeled and chopped
1½ lb fillets of sole
2–3 tomatoes, peeled and chopped
1 clove garlic, crushed
2 tablespoons finely-chopped parsley
salt, black pepper
6 stuffed olives, chopped
2 hard-boiled eggs, chopped

Pre-heat oven to 375°F Mark 5

1. Line a 9 inch pie plate with half the pastry.

2. Heat 3 tablespoons of the oil in a pan. Sauté onion for about 10 minutes. Add fish, cut into strips, tomato, and garlic. Cook over low heat about 10 minutes, stirring frequently. Add parsley, seasoning, olives and chopped eggs.

3. Turn into the pastry case and cover with the rest of the pastry, pressing the edges well together. Make a small hole in the top and brush the top of the pie with the remaining 1 tablespoon oil.

4. Bake for about 35 minutes, or until the pastry is golden brown, and serve cut in wedges.

Tuna Pie

You will probably have most of the ingredients for this pie in your storage cupboard. Served with a salad it is a most useful recipe to have when unexpected guests arrive. It is equally good hot or cold (serves 6)

8–10 oz short crust pastry (see p. 194)
1 small can (about 8 oz) tuna fish
1 small finely-chopped onion
2 oz mushrooms, sliced
1 can cream of mushroom soup
2 tablespoons grated Parmesan cheese
2 teaspoons lemon juice
1 teaspoon finely-chopped parsley
1/8 teaspoon celery seed
1/8 teaspoon thyme
4 hard-boiled eggs, sliced

Pre-heat oven to 425°F Mark 7

1. Line an 8–9 inch pie plate with half the pastry.

2. Drain the oil from the tuna fish and put 1 tablespoon of it into a sauté pan. Add the onion, sauté until transparent, then add mushrooms and continue cooking until onion and mushrooms begin to colour. Add mushroom soup, stir until smooth then remove from the heat. Add cheese, lemon juice and flavourings.

3. Arrange flaked fish and eggs in the pastry case, pour the sauce over and cover with the remaining pastry. Crimp the edges and make one or two slits in the top to allow steam to escape.

4. Bake for 10 minutes. Then reduce heat to 325°F, Mark 3 and bake for 30–35 minutes, or until pastry is well browned.

5. Before serving, garnish with slices of gherkin.

Finnan Haddie Tricornes

Smoked haddock is generally used for these little fish pies but any other cooked fish could be substituted. They are very useful for packed meals (serves 4—6, hot or cold)

PASTRY
make 6 oz short crust pastry (see p. 194) but add 2 oz grated cheese before mixing with water

FILLING
½ lb cooked smoked haddock or other fish
2 oz grated cheese
2 oz butter or margarine
a pinch of cayenne pepper
1 tablespoon milk
1 egg
paprika

Pre-heat oven to 425° F Mark 7

1. Roll the pastry about 1/8 inch thick and cut into rounds about 4 inches across.

2. Flake the fish finely, add cheese, butter, pepper, and salt if white fish is used (it may not be required with smoked fish). Add milk and enough beaten egg to bind.

3. Put a spoonful of the mixture on each round of pastry, moisten the edges and gather up to form a triangle. Press the edges well together, brush with the remaining egg or milk and sprinkle with paprika.

4. Put onto a baking sheet and bake for 10—15 minutes.

VEGETABLE, EGG & CHEESE PIES

Asparagus Pie

For this pie, asparagus is put into a pastry case and a cheese soufflé mixture poured on top. It is generally served hot, but is equally delicious cold. Be prepared, however, for the fluffy mixture to sink a little. If fresh asparagus is used, it should be cooked first (serves 5—6, hot)

PASTRY
8 oz plain flour
½ teaspoon salt
4 oz fat
3—4 tablespoons milk

FILLING
2 cans (about 8 oz each) asparagus spears
1 oz butter or margarine
1½ oz plain flour
3/8 pint milk
a pinch of cayenne pepper
4 oz grated cheese
3—4 tablespoons double cream
2 eggs
tomatoes

Pre-heat oven to 400° F Mark 6

1. Make the pastry in the usual way but use milk instead of water for mixing. Chill as long as possible, then roll out and line a 9 inch pie plate.

2. Drain the asparagus and arrange the spears in a wheel shape in the pastry shell. Set aside in a cool place while making the sauce.

3. Melt the butter in a pan, stir in the flour and cook for 2 minutes stirring constantly. Add the milk gradually, and stir until boiling. Add seasoning, grated cheese, cream and beaten egg yolks. Fold in stiffly-beaten egg whites.

4. Pour over the asparagus, bake for 30—40 minutes, and serve with grilled tomatoes and a green salad.

Cheese Custard Pie

1 eight-inch baked pie case
1 egg white
½ pint milk
¼ pint single cream
4 oz grated cheese
¼ teaspoon paprika
½ teaspoon grated onion
a small pinch of cayenne pepper
3 eggs

Pre-heat oven to 325°F Mark 3

For this pie, the pastry case is baked before the filling is added. Serve it for lunch or as a light supper dish (serves 4, hot)

1. Brush the baked pie case with lightly beaten egg white.

2. Scald the milk and cream, remove from the heat, add cheese, and stir until it has melted. Add salt, paprika, onion and cayenne pepper.

3. Beat in the eggs, one at a time, then pour into the pastry case.

4. Bake for about 45 minutes, or until the custard is firm.

Cheese Pie

PASTRY
6 oz plain flour
¼ teaspoon salt
a pinch of cayenne pepper
3 oz butter
1–2 tablespoons water

FILLING
1 clove garlic
4 oz cottage cheese
2 oz grated Gruyère cheese
2 tablespoons grated Parmesan cheese
3 spring onions, chopped
3 eggs
4–5 tablespoons double cream
a pinch of nutmeg
a pinch of cayenne pepper

Pre-heat oven to 375°F Mark 5

The filling for this pie is fairly rich, but very delicious. A mixture of cheese is blended with a creamy custard and cooked in a short crust which should be made with butter (serves 4, hot)

1. Sift the flour, salt and cayenne. Make a well in the centre. Add softened butter and 1 tablespoon water, and blend with the fingers, adding a little more water if required. Chill for at least 1 hour before using, then roll out and line an 8 inch pie plate.

2. Rub the bottom of the pastry shell very lightly with cut garlic.

3. Sieve the cottage cheese, add the Gruyère, Parmesan and onions. Add beaten eggs, cream and seasoning, and stir the ingredients together until smooth.

4. Pour into the pastry case, and bake for about 30 minutes.

Mushroom and Onion Quiche

For this quickly-made creamy quiche canned mushrooms can be used (serves 4—5, hot)

Pate Brisee (see p. 195)
2 oz butter or margarine
2 onions, peeled and chopped
1 can button mushrooms
2 eggs
½ can evaporated milk
2 oz grated cheese
a pinch of dry mustard

Pre-heat oven to 375°F Mark 5

1. Line a deep 8 inch pie plate with the Pâte Brisée.
2. Heat half the butter in a sauté pan and cook the onion until transparent. Drain well and put into the pastry shell with most of the mushrooms, cut in halves.
3. Beat the eggs, stir in the evaporated milk, grated cheese and seasoning. Pour over the mushrooms. Decorate with the trimmings of the pastry. Bake for about 35 minutes.
4. Sauté the remaining mushrooms for a few minutes in the remaining butter. Drain, and cut into thin slices.
5. When the pie is cooked, decorate with the sliced mushrooms.

Egg and Bacon Pie

Short crust pastry is used for this pie, but the flavour is improved with the addition of a little cheese. It can be added to the flour before rubbing in the fat (serves 6, hot)

6 oz short crust pastry (see p. 194)
   plus 2 oz grated cheese added
   before mixing with water
1 oz butter or margarine
2—3 onions, peeled and chopped
6 rashers bacon, chopped
3 eggs
¾ pint milk
¼ teaspoon dry mustard
2 teaspoons chopped parsley

Pre-heat oven to 350°F Mark 4

1. Line a deep 8 inch pie plate with pastry.

2. Heat butter in a sauté pan, add onion and bacon, and fry for 3—4 minutes.

3. Beat eggs in a bowl, add warmed milk, drained onion and bacon, salt, pepper, mustard and parsley.

4. Pour into the pastry case, and cook for 35—40 minutes. If desired, extra rashers of rolled bacon can be grilled and used as garnish.

Pissaladiere

This delicious pie consists of a pastry shell filled with tomatoes and onions and garnished with anchovies and olives. The picture shows individual pies (serves 6, hot)

1. Line a 9 inch pie plate with the pastry and set aside to chill.

2. When required, brush the bottom with beaten egg yolk and bake just long enough to set the crust—about 15 minutes. Remove from the oven and reduce the heat to 350°F Mark 4.

3. Heat 4 tablespoons of the oil in a sauté pan, add tomatoes and tomato purée and cook over low heat, stirring occasionally, until excess moisture has evaporated. Add pepper, a pinch of salt and a pinch of sugar.

4. In another pan, sauté onions in remaining oil until golden brown.

5. Sprinkle the bottom of the pie case with cheese, add onion and rosemary and cover with the tomato mixture.

6. Arrange anchovies in a lattice pattern on top and place an olive in the centre of each square. Brush lightly with oil and bake for about 30 minutes.

6 oz short crust pastry (see p. 194)
1 egg yolk
6 tablespoons oil
6 large tomatoes, peeled, seeded and chopped
2 tablespoons tomato purée
1/8 teaspoon black pepper
2 tablespoons grated Parmesan cheese
3 large onions, peeled and sliced
2 sprigs fresh rosemary or tarragon, or ¼ teaspoon dried rosemary
1 small can anchovy fillets*
black olives

Pre-heat oven to 425°F Mark 7

*If anchovies are a little salty for your taste, soak them in milk for about 20 minutes and dab dry before using.

Fidget Pie

This comes from a very old Shropshire recipe. The pie was served in the farmhouses as a supper dish for the harvesters. In those days, home-cured ham was used (serves 4—5, hot)

1 lb potatoes, peeled and sliced
1 lb cooking apples, peeled, cored and
    sliced
2—3 onions, peeled and sliced
¾ lb bacon or ham, cut into dice
about ½ pint stock or consomme
4 oz short crust pastry (see p. 2)

Pre-heat oven to 400°F Mark 6

1. Arrange the potatoes, apples, onions and bacon in layers in a fairly deep baking dish, sprinkling each layer with pepper and a very little salt.

2. Add the stock; then cover with the pastry. Make a slit in the top, and decorate as desired.

3. Bake for ½ hour; then reduce the heat to 350°F Mark 4 and bake for 1 hour.

Mushroom Pie

The savoury mushroom filling for this pie is put into a pastry case and then decorated with strips of pastry arranged in a lattice pattern over the top (serves 4, hot or cold)

8 oz short crust pastry (see p. 194)
3/8 pint milk
1 blade mace
1 bay leaf
6 peppercorns
1½ oz butter or margarine
1 small onion, peeled and sliced
    thinly
6 oz mushrooms, sliced
1½ oz plain flour
2 tablespoons double cream
1 egg yolk
1 egg

Pre-heat oven to 375°F Mark 5

1. Line an 8 inch pie plate with about two thirds of the pastry.

2. Put the milk into a pan, add mace, bay leaf and peppercorns, and place over a very low heat to infuse. Strain off the milk and discard the flavourings.

3. Heat half the butter in the pan, add the onion and sauté until soft but not coloured. Add mushrooms, increase the heat a little and cook for 2—3 minutes, stirring occasionally. Add remaining butter, and stir in the flour. Add milk gradually, stir until boiling; then remove from the heat. Add cream, egg yolk and seasoning. Leave to cool a little; then put into the pastry case.

4. Roll out remaining pastry, and cut into thin strips. Arrange in lattice form over the pie, pressing the ends of the strips well down onto the edge of the pastry. Brush with beaten egg, bake for about 30—35 minutes, and serve with a green salad.

Bacon Crust Pie

This pie has an unusual and delicious crust and is very little trouble to prepare (serves 4—5, hot)

BACON CRUST
1 lb minced lean bacon
1 small can tomato purée
3 oz breadcrumbs
1 small onion, very finely chopped
½ small green pepper, chopped

FILLING
5 oz cooked rice
1 small can tomato purée
1/8 teaspoon oregano
6 oz grated Gruyère cheese

Pre-heat oven to 350°F Mark 4

1. Mix all the ingredients for the crust together, knead well and press into the bottom of an 8—9 inch pie plate. Flute round the edge.

2. Mix rice, tomato purée, oregano, salt, pepper and 4 oz of the cheese, and spoon into the pie case. Cover with waxed paper and bake for 15—20 minutes.

3. Remove the paper, sprinkle with the remaining cheese, and brown lightly under a hot grill.

Onion Pie

Served with a tossed green salad this makes a good luncheon dish (serves 6, hot)

6 oz short crust pastry (see p. 194)
1½ oz butter or margarine
2½ lb Spanish onions, peeled and
   sliced
3 eggs
½ pint sour cream
2—3 tablespoons dry sherry
1 teaspoon celery salt
1 egg white
4 rashers bacon

Pre-heat oven to 425°F Mark 7

1. Line a 9 inch pie plate with the pastry, prick the bottom and leave to chill while preparing the filling.

2. Heat the butter in a heavy sauté pan, and sauté the onions until transparent. Remove from the heat.

3. Beat the eggs, add sour cream, sherry, celery salt and seasoning, and heat just long enough to blend ingredients together. Stir into the onions.

4. Brush the bottom of the pastry case with lightly-beaten egg white, and pour in the filling. Arrange strips of bacon on top.

5. Bake for 10 minutes, then reduce the heat to 300°F Mark 2 and bake for ½ hour, or until pastry is cooked.

Quiche Lorraine

There are many variations of this dish. This one has a filling of cheese and bacon. It can be served as the first course of a meal or as a light luncheon or supper dish (serves 6, hot)

6 oz Pate Brisee (see p. 195)
6 oz Gruyère cheese
4 rashers bacon
1 small onion, peeled and finely
   chopped
3 eggs
¼ pint single cream
¼ teaspoon nutmeg

Pre-heat oven to 425°F Mark 7

1. Line an 8 inch pie plate with the pastry, and refrigerate while preparing the filling.

2. Cut cheese into thin slices, or use packaged cheese slices, and cut into 2 inch strips.

3. Cut bacon into small pieces, fry until crisp and then drain.

4. Arrange alternate layers of cheese and bacon in the pie case and sprinkle with chopped onion.

5. Beat eggs lightly, combine with cream, nutmeg and seasoning and pour over bacon and cheese.

6. Bake for 10 minutes, then reduce heat to 300°F Mark 2 and bake for 30 minutes, or until custard is set and pastry is cooked.

Lyonnaise Pie

This pie is made with onion and a seasoned custard and is just as good served either hot or cold (serves 6)

6 oz short crust pastry (see p. 194)
1 onion, peeled and chopped
1 oz butter or margarine
¾ pint milk
3½ oz soft breadcrumbs
3 eggs
½ teaspoon Worcestershire sauce
bacon rolls
watercress

Pre-heat oven to 350°F Mark 4

1. Line an 8—9 inch pie plate with the pastry. Trim and crimp the edge.

2. Sauté the onion in the butter until soft and golden brown; then spread over the bottom of the pastry.

3. Heat the milk, pour on to the breadcrumbs, add the beaten eggs and mix well. Add Worcestershire sauce and seasoning.

4. Pour into the pastry case, and bake for about 45 minutes, or until the pastry is brown and the custard set. Garnish with grilled bacon rolls and watercress.

Cheese, Bacon and Tomato Pie

This pie can be served hot or cold, and is ideal for a packed lunch (serves 4—5, hot or cold)

8 oz short crust pastry (see p. 194)
6 oz rashers of bacon
2—3 tomatoes, peeled and sliced
½ lb Cheddar cheese (cut into thin slices or slices of processed cheese)
cayenne pepper
1 egg or milk to glaze

Pre-heat oven to 450°F Mark 7

1. Line an 8—9 inch pie plate with half the pastry and prick the bottom.

2. Trim the bacon, cut the rashers into two or three pieces, and put half in the bottom of the pastry case.

3. Cover with half the tomatoes, sprinkle sparingly with salt and more generously with cayenne pepper. Cover with half the slices of cheese, and repeat the layers.

4. Dampen the edge of the pastry and cover with the remaining pastry. Press the edges together neatly, make a hole in the centre and decorate the pie with pastry leaves made with the trimmings.

5. Glaze with beaten egg or milk, bake for 30—40 minutes, and serve hot with tomato sauce, or cold with salad.

Spinach and Ricotta Pie

The Italian ricotta cheese is ideal for this recipe, but cottage cheese can be substituted if necessary. It will be almost as good (serves 5—6, hot)

6 oz cheese pastry (see p. 218—Finnan Haddie Tricornes)
1—2 packets frozen spinach (about ¾ lb)
1 oz butter
½ lb ricotta or cottage cheese
3 eggs
2 oz grated Parmesan cheese
4—6 tablespoons double cream
nutmeg

Pre-heat oven to 425°F Mark 7

1. Line a deep 8 inch pie plate with the pastry, flute the edges, prick the bottom and chill.

2. When required, bake for about 15 minutes, just long enough to set the pastry, then leave to cool.

3. Reduce oven heat to 350°F Mark 4.

4. Cook the spinach in the butter, drain well, add salt, pepper, ricotta cheese, beaten eggs, half the grated cheese, cream and a good pinch of nutmeg.

5. Spread in the pastry case, sprinkle with remaining cheese and bake for about 30 minutes, or until mixture is firm and pastry browned.

Swiss Cheese Pie

In Switzerland this is sometimes called Salé. A creamy cheese filling is cooked in a pastry case, preferably made with Pâte Brisée (serves 5—6, hot)

6 oz Pate Brisee (see p. 195)
½ pint white sauce
3—4 tablespoons double cream
4 eggs
6 oz grated Gruyère cheese
nutmeg

Pre-heat oven to 400°F Mark 6

1. Make the pastry and chill for as long as possible, then line a 9 inch pie plate.

2. Make a white sauce, and add all the other ingredients.

3. Season to taste, and pour into the pastry case.

4. Bake for about 25 minutes, and serve with a tossed green salad.

PASTRY
4 oz plain flour
cayenne pepper
1/8 teaspoon dry mustard
3 oz fat
2 oz grated Cheddar cheese
1 egg yolk

FILLING
4—5 tomatoes, peeled and sliced
1 small onion, finely chopped
2 oz butter or margarine
2 eggs
6 tablespoons milk
2 oz grated cheese
chopped parsley

Pre-heat oven to 350°F Mark 4

Tomato Quiche

The pastry for this quiche is very short and crisp, so allow the pie to cool a little before serving (serves 4, hot)

1. Sift the flour and mustard with salt and pepper. Rub in the fat, add cheese and bind with the beaten egg yolk. If required, add a little water but by teaspoons only. Chill if possible, then roll out and line a deep 7 inch pie plate.

2. Arrange the tomatoes in the bottom, leaving one or two slices for decoration. Sauté the onion in butter until soft and place on top of the tomatoes.

3. Beat the eggs, add the milk, half the cheese and seasoning. Pour carefully over the tomatoes, sprinkle with remaining cheese and bake for about 40 minutes or until the custard is firm.

4. Garnish with remaining slices of tomato, return to the oven, just to heat through, and sprinkle with parsley before serving.

CASSEROLES

Introduction

Perhaps the greatest advantage of casserole cookery is that most of the preparation can be done early in the day, and once the dish is in the oven it needs very little attention. You can enjoy a cocktail with your family and friends, and there is no need to rush out to the kitchen, just when the conversation is getting exciting.

Most of the dishes which follow will make a meal in themselves but they can also be the main course of a more elaborate meal.

Many casserole dishes—and what gay ones there are available—can be used on top of the stove as well as in the oven, and it is often an advantage to start the cooking this way; then the casserole can come to the table in the dish in which it is cooked. There is a wide variety of materials from which to choose—earthenware, china, ovenproof glass, cast iron (with or without a porcelain enamel lining) and gleaming copper—and all in a wonderful range of colours and designs.

The casserole should have a tightly fitting lid, but one can always be improvised by using heavy duty foil.

You can be relaxed about quantities too, and use your imagination as far as flavourings are concerned. No casserole would be ruined if you used a little more or little less meat, or a little less or little more vegetable—and if you have a particular aversion to one specific herb or spice, there is always a substitute.

Finally, a casserole can wait on your guests. It will come to no harm even if it is left for an hour or two beyond the scheduled time, as long as the heat is turned very low.

7 BEEF CASSEROLES

Beef Burgundy

There are many ways of making this delicious stew of beef cooked in red wine, some elaborate, but this is fairly simple and equally as good (serves 5—6, hot)

2 lb stewing beef
1 oz plain flour
2 tablespoons oil
6 oz chopped lean bacon
15—18 small white onions
5—6 small carrots
1 clove garlic, crushed
1 tablespoon tomato paste
4 tablespoons red wine
½ pint beef stock
3 oz mushrooms, sliced

Pre-heat oven to 300°F Mark 2

1. Cut the meat into 2 inch cubes and dredge with flour mixed with some salt and pepper. Heat the oil in a pan, sauté the meat until well browned, and remove to casserole. Then sauté the bacon in the pan for a few minutes, add the onions, carrots and garlic, and cook until the onions begin to brown. Put the bacon and vegetables into the casserole with the meat.

2. Stir the remaining flour into the fat left in the pan and cook until it begins to brown. Add tomato paste, wine and stock, and stir until boiling. Taste for seasoning; then pour it over the meat and vegetables.

3. Cover tightly and cook for about 3 hours. Add mushrooms and cook for 15—20 minutes more.

4. Serve with green peas or other green vegetables, a tossed salad and garlic bread.

Nasi Goreng

There are several versions of this famous Indonesian dish. This one contains beef and seafood and makes an excellent dish for a buffet supper (serves 6, hot)

½ lb lean beef, minced
2 tablespoons bread or cereal crumbs
2 onions, peeled and chopped
4—5 tablespoons corn oil
1 egg
4—5 stalks celery, diced
½ lb canned crabmeat
½ lb shelled shrimps or prawns
¾ pint chicken stock
½ lb cooked rice
2 tablespoons curry powder

Pre-heat oven to 325° F Mark 3

1. Mix the meat, breadcrumbs, 2 tablespoons of the onion and salt and pepper and bind with the beaten egg. Shape into small balls the size of a walnut and leave in a cold place for about 40 minutes.

2. Heat 2 tablespoons of the oil in a pan and sauté the rest of the onion and the celery. Put into a large casserole.

3. Heat a little more oil in the pan and sauté the crabmeat and shrimp for 2—3 minutes. Put into the casserole with the onion and celery.

4. Brown the meat balls and add to the other ingredients in the casserole.

5. Put the chicken stock into the pan with the rice, curry powder and any remaining oil. Bring to boiling point. Then pour over the contents of the casserole. Stir to mix the ingredients together, then cover and cook for about ½ hour.

Casserole of Beef with Walnuts

The beef is cooked with some red wine and the casserole looks very attractive with its garnish of walnuts, celery and strips of orange rind (serves 4—5, hot)

1 oz dripping
1½—2 lb stewing beef
12 small white onions, peeled
½ oz flour
4 tablespoons red wine
bouquet garni
1 clove garlic
1½—1¾ pints beef stock
1 small head celery
½ oz butter or margarine
1½—2 oz walnuts
**rind of ½ orange, shredded and
    blanched**

Pre-heat oven to 300°F Mark 2

1. Heat the dripping in a sauté pan and brown the meat. Remove to a casserole. Sauté onions in remaining fat until they just begin to colour, then put with the meat.

2. Pour off any excess fat leaving about 1 tablespoon. Stir in flour, add wine, bouquet garni, garlic (crushed with a little salt) and ½ pint stock. Stir until boiling, and pour over contents of casserole. Add the extra stock, if necessary, just to cover the meat. Add a little seasoning. Cover tightly and cook for about 2 hours.

3. Trim the celery and cut into strips crossways. Heat the butter, add celery, walnuts and a pinch of salt. Toss over heat for a few minutes.

4. When ready to serve, scatter the celery, walnuts and orange rind over the meat.

Bouillabaisse (see p. 252)

Beef and Rice Casserole

The addition of wine gives a delicious flavour to this casserole but it can be replaced with consomme if you prefer. For a complete meal, only a salad is required. Lettuce, grated carrot and slices of cucumber would be a good choice (serves 4–5, hot)

½ lb streaky bacon
2 lb stewing steak
2 onions, peeled and sliced
6 oz rice, uncooked
3/8 pint dry red wine
about ¾ pint beef stock
1 clove garlic, crushed
1 sprig fresh thyme or ½ teaspoon
   dried
1 teaspoon chopped parsley
¼ teaspoon saffron
3–4 tomatoes, chopped
2 oz grated Parmesan cheese

Pre-heat oven to 300°F Mark 2

1. Cut the bacon into strips and fry in a pan until crisp. Then remove the bacon to a large casserole.

2. Cut the meat into cubes and brown in the bacon fat. Remove to the casserole.

3. Add onions and rice to the remaining fat, stir until the rice begins to colour, then set aside.

4. Put the wine, stock, garlic, herbs and saffron into the casserole, cover, and cook for 1 hour.

5. Remove the casserole from the oven, skim off any excess fat and stir in the rice and onion mixture and tomatoes. Cover, and return to the oven for another hour, checking occasionally to see if any extra liquid is required.

6. Before serving, adjust the seasoning, and stir in the cheese.

Spanish Style Kidney

Ox kidney is very suitable for this recipe as the long slow cooking ensures that it will be tender. Served on spaghetti, it makes a good luncheon dish (serves 4, hot)

1–1½ lb ox kidney
2 oz plain flour
2 oz butter or margarine
3 oz mushrooms, sliced
1 clove garlic, crushed
½ teaspoon dried basil
5–6 tomatoes, peeled, seeded and
　chopped
4–5 tablespoons Marsala
bacon rolls
cooked spaghetti

Pre-heat oven to 300°F Mark 2

1. Remove core and any fat from the kidney, cut into slices and leave to stand in cold water for ½ hour. Drain and dry.

2. Coat kidney with flour to which a little salt and pepper has been added, brown in hot fat, and remove to a casserole.

3. Sauté mushrooms and garlic in remaining fat for about 5 minutes. Then add to the kidney. Add basil.

4. Stir any remaining flour into the fat left in the pan, mix well, add tomatoes and Marsala and a little water if required. Stir until boiling, then pour into the casserole. Cover, and cook for 2 hours.

5. Adjust the seasoning, and serve with grilled bacon rolls and spaghetti.

Hearty Beef Casserole

Carrots and potatoes are cooked with the meat to make a complete meal with real family appeal (serves 6, hot)

1½–2 lb beef chuck, cut into 1½ inch
　cubes
1 teaspoon salt
¼ teaspoon pepper
2 oz plain flour
6 tablespoons bacon fat
1 large onion, peeled and sliced
1 beef stock cube
1 teaspoon marjoram
1 teaspoon basil
1 large can whole tomatoes
6 carrots, sliced
6 small potatoes, quartered

Pre-heat oven to 300°F Mark 2

1. Trim any excess fat from the meat. Mix salt and pepper with the flour and coat meat well.

2. Heat fat in a pan and brown meat on all sides. Add onion and cook until golden. Remove meat and onion to a casserole.

3. Stir remaining flour into the fat left in the pan, add about ¾ pint water and stock cube. Stir until boiling and thickened. Add herbs, cook for a few more minutes; then pour over the meat.

4. Add vegetables, cover, and cook for about 2½ hours.

Beef with Dumplings

This makes a substantial meal with very little trouble. Use a casserole heavy enough to start the cooking on top of the stove (serves 4–5, hot)

1 oz plain flour
1½ teaspoons salt
¼ teaspoon pepper
2 lb lean beef chuck
3 tablespoons oil
3 medium onions, peeled
3 cloves
4 carrots, peeled and cut into strips
　lengthways
¾ pint beef stock
1 tablespoon red or white wine
　vinegar

DUMPLINGS
4 oz self raising flour
1/8 teaspoon salt, pepper
2 oz shredded suet
3 tablespoons chopped chives

Pre-heat oven to 325°F Mark 3

1. Sift the flour with salt and pepper. Cut meat into 1 inch cubes and dredge well with the flour.

2. Heat the oil in a casserole, add the meat and onions, each stuck with a clove and stir until the meat is well browned. Add carrots, stock and vinegar. Bring to a boil, then cover and remove to oven. Cook for about 1 hour.

3. Make the dumplings by mixing the dry ingredients and adding enough water to make a firm dough. Shape into balls with floured hands. Drop them into the casserole, replace the lid and continue cooking for 30 minutes. Sprinkle with chives before serving.

4. Spinach, cooked and chopped, with a pinch of nutmeg and a few sautéed mushrooms added, would make a very good accompaniment.

Paprika Goulash

This colourful casserole with tomatoes and sour cream is of Hungarian origin. It should be spicy, and paprika is always the distinguishing seasoning (serves 4, hot)

1½ lb stewing beef
3 tablespoons oil
3 medium onions, peeled and sliced
2 tablespoons paprika
1 oz plain flour
2 teaspoons tomato purée
¾ pint beef stock
bouquet garni
1 clove garlic, crushed
1 red or green pepper
2—3 tomatoes, peeled and sliced
6 tablespoons sour cream

Pre-heat oven to 300°F Mark 2

1. Cut meat into cubes. Heat oil in a pan and brown meat over fairly high heat, then transfer to a casserole.

2. Reduce the heat in the pan, sauté onions in remaining oil, add paprika, flour, tomato purée and stock. Stir until boiling, then pour over the meat in the casserole. Add bouquet garni, seasoning and garlic. Cover, and cook about 1¾ hours.

3. Blanch the pepper, remove seeds and cut into strips. Add to the casserole with tomatoes, and cook for 15 minutes more.

4. Just before serving, stir in sour cream and adjust the seasoning. Serve with noodles.

Daube of Beef

3 lb top side beef
¼ lb carrots, peeled and sliced
  lengthways
1 tablespoon chopped fresh or 1
  teaspoon dried oregano
1 tablespoon chopped fresh or 1
  teaspoon dried basil
a few rashers of bacon
3 tomatoes, peeled and chopped

Pre-heat oven to 275°F Mark 1

MARINADE
½ pint oil
1 onion, peeled and chopped
4 shallots, peeled and chopped
1 stalk celery, cut into pieces
1 carrot, peeled and coarsely chopped
¼ pint dry red wine
6 white peppercorns
2 cloves garlic, crushed
1 bay leaf
1 tablespoon fresh or 1 teaspoon
  dried thyme
1 tablespoon fresh or 1 teaspoon
  dried marjoram
2 sprigs parsley

This does take a little time to prepare but the result is well worth the trouble. The meat is marinated and then cooked in one piece and sliced at the table (serves 6—8, hot)

1. Put all the ingredients for the marinade into a saucepan and simmer gently for 15—20 minutes. Cool, then pour over the meat in a large bowl. Leave for 12—24 hours, piercing the meat and turning it over occasionally.

2. Transfer the meat to a casserole, add the liquid from the marinade. Arrange carrots and herbs around the meat and cover with rashers of bacon.

3. Cover the casserole tightly with foil, then put on the lid and cook for about 2½ hours. Add tomatoes and cook for another ½ hour.

4. Adjust seasoning, and serve with buttered noodles and a green vegetable.

LAMB CASSEROLES

Summer Casserole

2—2½ lb stewing lamb
1 oz dripping or margarine
1 onion, peeled and chopped
½ lb young carrots, sliced lengthways
1 small turnip, peeled and chopped
about 1 pint stock or water
1 sprig mint
1 sprig thyme
¼ lb green peas

Pre-heat oven to 325°F Mark 3

This is a pleasant lamb dish to make when fresh young vegetables are available (serves 4—6, hot)

1. Trim the meat and cut into pieces. Heat the fat in a sauté pan, brown the meat and place in a casserole.

2. Brown the onion in the remaining fat and add to the casserole. Add all other ingredients except peas, cover, and cook for 1¼ hours.

3. Add peas, and continue to cook for another 20—30 minutes. Before serving, remove mint and thyme, and adjust seasoning to taste.

Lamb and Vegetable Casserole

1½ lb shoulder of lamb, cut in 2 inch
   squares
salt, pepper
1 tablespoon oil
1 clove garlic, crushed
white tops of 6 spring onions,
   chopped
2 small turnips, peeled and diced
6 small carrots, peeled and sliced
4 medium potatoes, peeled and sliced
½ pint stock
¼ pint dry white wine
¼ teaspoon thyme
½ teaspoon marjoram
1 small bay leaf
plain flour

Pre-heat oven to 350°F Mark 4

*Serve this with cottage cheese, mixed with chopped chives, parsley and
fresh basil and chilled (serves 4–5, hot)*

1. Sprinkle the lamb with salt and pepper and sauté in the hot oil with the
garlic and onions. Remove to a casserole.

2. Lightly brown the turnips and carrots in the remaining oil then put
into the casserole with the meat and add the potatoes.

3. Pour in the stock and wine and add the herbs. Mix all well, cover tightly
and cook for about 1½ hours or until the meat is tender.

4. If a thicker gravy is required, mix about 1 tablespoon flour to a smooth
paste with water, stir into the casserole and cook a further few minutes.
Check the seasoning before serving.

Holiday Stew

2–2½ lb boned shoulder of lamb
6 rashers of streaky bacon
2 onions, peeled and sliced
3 medium potatoes, peeled and sliced
1 can (about 12 oz) whole kernel corn
2 tomatoes, peeled and sliced
1 tablespoon Worcestershire sauce
3/8 pint dry white wine or cider
1 tablespoon chopped parsley

Pre-heat oven to 300°F Mark 2

*This is a very satisfying dish to make when the children are home from
school (serves 4–5, hot)*

1. Cut the meat into pieces, sprinkle with salt and pepper.

2. Put half the bacon into a deep casserole, cover with half the meat and
half the onions. Add remaining bacon, and cover with potatoes.

3. Add the rest of the meat, corn and tomatoes.

4. Mix the Worcestershire sauce with the wine, and pour over the contents
of the casserole. Cover very tightly and cook for about 3½ hours. Sprinkle
with parsley before serving.

Curried Lamb Casserole

The addition of fruit makes this an unusual and delicious dish (serves 4, hot)

2 oz prunes
2 oz dried apricots
4 thick lamb chops
1 tablespoon oil
2 oz sultanas
1 lemon, thinly sliced
½ lb rice
2 teaspoons curry powder

Pre-heat oven to 350°F Mark 4

1. Soak prunes and apricots in cold water for at least 3 hours, then drain.

2. Trim the chops and sauté them in the hot oil for a few minutes.

3. Put a layer of fruit in a deep, buttered casserole with a tightly-fitting
lid, sprinkle with sultanas and add one or two slices of lemon and some of
the rice. Sprinkle with curry powder, salt and pepper. Continue in alternate layers till all the ingredients are used up.

4. Place chops on top and pour in 1¼ pints water. Cover tightly, and cook
for 1–1¼ hours, or until most of the liquid has been absorbed. Adjust the
seasoning, and serve with a tossed green salad.

Lamb and Potato Casserole

This makes a complete meal. The meat is cooked with onions and tomatoes, and covered with a layer of potatoes (serves 4, hot)

**1 oz plain flour
4 large loin chops or 8 cutlets
2 oz butter or margarine
½ lb onions, peeled and sliced
1 small clove garlic, crushed
4 tomatoes, peeled and sliced
1—2 sprigs fresh or 1/8 teaspoon
    dried rosemary
1 lb potatoes, peeled and sliced
3—4 tablespoons stock or water**

Pre-heat oven to 325°F Mark 3

1. Mix the flour with a little salt and pepper, and dredge chops well.

2. Heat most of the butter in a sauté pan, brown the chops on both sides; then remove from the pan. Add onion and garlic to the remaining fat, and cook until softened.

3. Arrange the meat, onion, tomato, rosemary and potatoes in layers in a casserole, seasoning each layer lightly and finishing with potato. Add the stock or water, and dot with the remaining butter.

4. Cover, and cook for about 2 hours. About 15 minutes before the end of the cooking, remove the lid to allow the potatoes to brown.

Bitter-Sweet Lamb Casserole

The meat for this casserole is cooked with orange juice and herbs, and served with boiled rice or noodles (serves 4—6, hot)

**2—2½ lb best end neck of lamb
2 tablespoons oil
½ pint stock or water
3 tablespoons vinegar
1 can (6—8 oz) orange juice
2 teaspoons Worcestershire sauce
½ teaspoon salt
1/8 teaspoon freshly-ground pepper
a pinch of dry mustard
a pinch of paprika
½ teaspoon each, celery seed, basil,
    oregano
3—4 cloves
2 teaspoons sugar
cooked rice or noodles**

Pre-heat oven to 325°F Mark 3

1. Trim and cut meat into chops, brown in the hot oil and put into a casserole with ½ pint stock or water and vinegar. Cover, and cook for 1 hour.

2. Put orange juice, Worcestershire sauce, seasonings and flavourings into a small pan and simmer, uncovered, for 10 minutes.

3. When the meat has cooked for 1 hour, stir in orange juice mixture and cook for another hour.

4. Serve with rice or noodles.

Devilled Lamb Chops

For variety, the tomato soup used in this recipe can be replaced with a can of mushroom or asparagus soup (serves 4—5, hot)

**1½—2 lb best end neck of lamb
butter or margarine
1 onion, peeled and chopped
3—4 stalks celery, finely chopped
1 clove garlic, crushed
1 can (about 10 oz) tomato soup
1 tablespoon Worcestershire sauce
1 tablespoon lemon juice
2 tablespoons sherry
1 dessertspoon brown sugar
1 teaspoon prepared mustard**

Pre-heat oven to 325°F Mark 3

1. Trim and cut the meat into chops and arrange in a buttered casserole. Sprinkle with salt, pepper, onion, celery and garlic. Cover, and cook for about 20 minutes. Remove any excess fat.

2. Heat the tomato soup, add all the other ingredients and mix well. Adjust seasoning, and pour over the chops.

3. Cover, and cook for about 1 hour, basting occasionally.

4. Serve with some chutney or pickled pears.

Casseroled Lamb with Pears

This may sound an unusual combination, but you will find it is quite delicious (serves 4, hot)

2 lb stewing lamb
2 teaspoons ground ginger
6 medium-sized cooking pears,
    peeled, quartered and cored
1 packet frozen runner beans
white wine

DRESSING

¼ pint sour cream
1 teaspoon lemon juice
½ teaspoon dry mustard
2 teaspoons poppy seeds (optional)

Pre-heat oven to 350°F Mark 4

1. Trim any excess fat from the meat, and cut it into pieces.

2. Put the meat into a lightly-greased sauté pan and brown it in its own fat. Then transfer to a casserole with a tightly fitting lid.

3. Sprinkle the ginger over the meat and add pears, beans and a little salt and pepper. Add 2 tablespoons white wine; the juice from the pears should provide sufficient liquid, but if it begins to look dry, add a little more white wine. Cover tightly, and cook for 1¼ hours.

4. A plain lettuce salad with a sour cream dressing makes a good accompaniment. For the dressing, mix the sour cream with lemon juice, dry mustard and poppy seeds.

Hungarian Lamb Casserole

This is a substantial casserole, flavoured with paprika in the Hungarian style (serves 4—5, hot)

2 lb stewing lamb
3 tablespoons oil
1 large onion, peeled and sliced
1 sweet red pepper, seeded and sliced
1½ oz plain flour
1 tablespoon paprika
1 chicken stock cube
2 oz small haricot beans, soaked
  overnight
3—4 potatoes, peeled and cut into
  slices

Pre-heat oven to 325°F Mark 3

1. Trim the meat, and cut it into small pieces.

2. Heat the oil in a sauté pan, add meat, onion and red pepper, and sauté for a few minutes. Then remove to a casserole.

3. Add flour, paprika, crumbled stock cube and a little salt to the pan drippings, mix well, add 1 pint water, and stir until boiling. Add drained beans and simmer for 5 minutes. Pour all into the casserole. Cover, and cook for 2 hours.

4. Arrange potatoes in overlapping slices on top of the casserole and cook for another 25—30 minutes, or until potatoes are tender.

9 PORK & BACON CASSEROLES

Jagasee

This is one version of the popular Caribbean dish. It is a splendid casserole to leave ready for a party of hungry teenagers to help themselves. Provide plenty of salad and some chutney (serves 6—8, hot)

2 tablespoons bacon fat
2 large onions, peeled and sliced thinly
1 package frozen broad beans
½ lb salt pork
1 large can tomatoes
½ green or red pepper, diced
3—4 stalks celery, diced
¾ lb rice

Pre-heat oven to 325°F Mark 3

1. Heat the fat, sauté the onions until they begin to colour then put into a large casserole with a tightly fitting lid. Add the beans.

2. Dice the pork and scald with boiling water. Put into the casserole with tomatoes, green pepper, celery, rice and seasoning. Add 1¼ pints water.

3. Cover tightly, and cook for 2½—3 hours, adding more water from time to time as necessary. Check seasoning before serving.

Pork Chops in Sour Cream

After browning, the pork chops are casseroled in sour cream and served with sections of grilled fruit (serves 4, hot)

4 thick pork chops
flour
¼ pint sour cream
1 tablespoon lemon juice
½ teaspoon grated lemon rind
1 teaspoon sugar
½ teaspoon powdered thyme
orange or grapefruit sections
honey

Pre-heat oven to 350°F Mark 4

1. Trim excess fat from the chops and dredge lightly with flour. Put the fat trimmings into a sauté pan, and fry to render the fat. Remove the pieces of skin which remain, put the chops in the pan and brown lightly on both sides. Remove to a casserole.

2. Mix the cream with lemon juice, lemon rind, sugar, salt, pepper and thyme. Add ¼ pint water, and pour over the chops. Cover and cook for 45–50 minutes.

3. Brush some sections of orange or grapefruit (or both) with a little honey and grill for a few minutes.

4. Garnish the chops with the fruit, and serve with string beans, or spinach.

Casserole of Pork

The herbs give a very pleasant flavour to this casserole. Served with mashed potatoes and buttered green beans it makes a good main meal (serves 6, hot)

2 lb pork shoulder or fillet
12 small white onions
1 oz plain flour
¼ pint dry white wine
¼ pint chicken stock
2—3 sprigs fresh rosemary or 1 teaspoon dried
1 teaspoon dried oregano
1 teaspoon chopped parsley
1 lb tart cooking apples, peeled, and quartered

Pre-heat oven to 300°F Mark 2

1. Trim the fat from the meat and cut it into slices. Put the fat trimmings into a pan and fry until the fat melts. Then remove the pieces of brown skin, and sauté the meat and onions in the fat. Remove to a casserole.

2. Pour off excess fat from the pan leaving 2 tablespoons. Mix in the flour, add wine and stock, and stir until boiling and the sauce is smooth and thickened. Add seasoning and herbs, and pour over the meat in the casserole. Cover very tightly, and cook for 1½ hours.

3. Add the apple quarters, cover again and cook for another ½ hour.

Honeyed Beans with Bacon

This is generally popular with the young. If time is short, the beans can be cooked in a pressure cooker, or use canned beans (serves 4—5, hot)

½ lb small haricot beans, soaked overnight
6 rashers bacon
1 onion, peeled and chopped
1 teaspoon dry mustard
1 tablespoon chopped crystallised ginger
2 tablespoons chopped chutney
8 oz honey

DRESSING
¼ pint sour cream
a dash of lemon juice
1 teaspoon caraway seeds

Pre-heat oven to 325°F Mark 3

1. Drain the beans from the water in which they were soaked and simmer in boiling salted water until tender.

2. Dice the bacon, put into a sauté pan with the onion, stir until the fat begins to melt, and sauté until the onion is transparent.

3. When the beans are cooked, drain and put into a deep casserole. Add the bacon and onion, seasoning, mustard, ginger and chutney and mix well. Stir in the honey. Cover, and cook for about 1 hour. Then uncover, and cook for another ½ hour.

4. Cole slaw with a sour cream dressing is an excellent accompaniment. For the dressing, mix sour cream with lemon juice and caraway seeds.

Paprika Pork with Sauerkraut

This is based on a popular Hungarian dish, and is delicious served with rice, noodles or mashed potatoes (serves 6, hot)

2½ lb pork shoulder meat
1½ oz plain flour
1½ teaspoons salt
¼ teaspoon pepper
3 tablespoons oil
3—4 onions, peeled and sliced
2 tablespoons paprika
2 cans (about 15 oz each) sauerkraut
1 green pepper, seeded and chopped
¼ pint sour cream

Pre-heat oven to 350°F Mark 4

1. Trim the meat and cut into 1½ inch cubes. Mix flour with 1 teaspoon salt and half the pepper and dredge the meat thoroughly. Heat the oil in a pan and sauté the meat until brown. Remove to a casserole.

2. Brown the onion in the remaining oil, add paprika, ¾ pint water and the rest of the pepper. Simmer until all the brown pieces in the pan are loosened. Add sauerkraut, green pepper and remaining salt. Mix well and pour over the meat in the casserole.

3. Cover, and cook for 1½ hours. Just before serving, adjust the seasoning, and stir in the sour cream.

Pork in Cider Sauce

2 lb pork fillet
2 tablespoons brown sugar
2 teaspoons dry mustard
2 tablespoons corn oil
1 dessertspoon cornflour
1 orange
cider
1 clove garlic, crushed
6 stuffed olives, sliced
4 cloves
pineapple

Pre-heat oven to 350°F Mark 4

In this recipe the pork is coated with a mixture of sugar and mustard and cooked in cider and this gives a very pleasant sweet-sour flavour. Chops could be used, but they should be boned (serves 4, hot)

1. Have the meat cut into slices and pound them flat.

2. Mix sugar and mustard and coat both sides of the meat. Heat oil in a sauté pan, brown meat on both sides, remove to a casserole.

3. Add cornflour to remaining fat, stir and cook for 1 minute. Add orange juice, made up to ½ pint with cider. Stir until boiling, boil for 2 minutes. Add seasoning, garlic, olives and cloves. Pour over the meat, cover and cook for 30—35 minutes.

4. Remove cloves, check seasoning and serve with grilled slices of pineapple.

Spicy Pork Casserole

6 loin pork chops
1 clove garlic
2 teaspoons butter or margarine
2 cooking apples, peeled, cored and cut into ½ inch slices
2 onions, peeled and sliced
1 oz plain flour
1 tablespoon lemon juice
about ¾ pint apple purée
¼ teaspoon ground cinnamon
¼ teaspoon ground nutmeg
1/8 teaspoon ground cloves

Pre-heat oven to 325°F Mark 3

In this recipe, pork chops are cooked in a spicy apple purée (serves 6, hot)

1. Trim the chops, rub both sides with a cut clove of garlic and sprinkle with salt and pepper. Put into a lightly-buttered pan and brown on both sides.

2. Put a layer of apples and onions into a buttered casserole, arrange chops on top and cover with remaining apple and onion slices.

3. Stir flour into the sediment in the pan, add ¾ pint boiling water, and stir until thickened. Add lemon juice, apple purée and spices. Mix all well and pour into the casserole. Cover, and cook for 1½ hours, removing the lid for the last 20 minutes.

VEAL CASSEROLES

Veal and Ham Casserole

1½ lb veal fillet, cut into thin slices
about 3—4 tablespoons breadcrumbs
1 egg
milk
2 tablespoons oil
1½ oz butter
1 lb cooked ham, sliced thinly
½ lb mushrooms, sliced
2 cans (about 8 oz each) tomato sauce
¼ pint chicken stock
1 oz blanched almonds
1 teaspoon oregano
¼ teaspoon powdered mace
¼ teaspoon thyme
¼ teaspoon rosemary

Pre-heat oven to 300°F Mark 2

This is a good main dish for a party. It is unusual, in as much as the veal is first cooked as for escalopes and then finished in a casserole with herbs and almonds. Once it is in the oven it needs no further attention, and you are free to enjoy an aperitif with your guests (serves 7—8, hot)

1. Pound the slices of veal thinly, coat with breadcrumbs, dip in egg and milk, and coat again with breadcrumbs. Heat the oil and butter in a sauté pan, and cook veal until crisp and golden. Remove to a deep casserole.

2. Crisp the ham in the sauté pan and add to the veal.

3. Sauté the mushrooms in the remaining fat for about 5 minutes, adding a little extra butter if necessary. Add tomato sauce, chicken stock and almonds, and stir well. Add seasoning and herbs, simmer for about 10 minutes; then pour into the casserole.

4. Cover, and cook for about 1¼ hours. Adjust the seasoning, and serve with noodles or rice.

Veal Casserole

2 lb stewing veal
1 oz plain flour
4 tablespoons oil
1 large onion, peeled and chopped
2 carrots, peeled and chopped
2 stalks celery, cut diagonally
1 sprig parsley, ¼ teaspoon each of
    oregano, basil and rosemary, all
    tied in a piece of muslin
½ pint chicken stock
4 tablespoons dry white wine
2 tomatoes, peeled and chopped
1 clove garlic, crushed
1 tablespoon chopped parsley
1 teaspoon grated lemon rind
1 tablespoon lemon juice

Pre-heat oven to 350°F Mark 4

The addition of herbs makes this a really savoury dish. Served with rice, and a tossed green salad it would be suitable for a buffet meal (serves 5–6, hot)

1. Cut the veal into 2 inch cubes, and dredge with flour mixed with a little salt and pepper. Heat the oil in a pan and brown the meat, a few pieces at a time and adding extra oil as required. As the meat is browned, remove to a casserole.

2. Sauté onion, carrot and celery in remaining oil. Sprinkle over the meat.

3. Add herbs, chicken stock, wine, tomatoes and garlic to the pan, cook for 2–3 minutes; then pour over the meat. Cover, and cook for about 1½ hours.

4. About 20 minutes before the end of the cooking, uncover, adjust the seasoning, and stir in the parsley, lemon rind and lemon juice. Remove bag of herbs before serving.

Veal Marengo

2 lb boneless veal
2 oz plain flour
1 oz butter or margarine
1 tablespoon oil
1 clove garlic, crushed
¼ pint dry white wine
¾ pint boiling water
2 chicken stock cubes
1 tablespoon tomato purée
10–12 small white onions
2 tomatoes, peeled and coarsely
    chopped
4 oz mushrooms, sliced
chopped parsley

Pre-heat oven to 350°F Mark 4

This is a traditional dish of veal with tomatoes, which add both colour and flavour (serves 6, hot)

1. Trim and cut veal into pieces, toss in flour mixed with a little salt and pepper. Heat butter and oil in a sauté pan, sauté meat until golden brown and remove to a casserole.

2. Add garlic and remaining flour to the fat left in the pan, and stir until flour begins to brown. Gradually add wine and water in which stock cubes have been dissolved. Stir until boiling. Add tomato purée, and simmer until the quantity has been reduced by half.

3. Pour over veal, cover and cook for about 1 hour.

4. Add onions, tomato and mushrooms and cook for 20–30 minutes more. Sprinkle with parsley, and adjust seasoning before serving. New potatoes and green peas go well with this dish.

Veal with Tarragon

2 lb stewing veal
4 tablespoons oil
1½ oz plain flour
¼ pint dry white wine
2 oz mushrooms, sliced
2 tablespoons chopped fresh tarragon
    or 2 teaspoons dried
1 onion, peeled and chopped
2 egg yolks
¼ pint sour cream
2 tablespoons tarragon vinegar
chopped parsley

Pre-heat oven to 275°F Mark 1

The tarragon gives a piquant flavour to this dish. Serve it with fluffy rice, hot garlic bread and a tossed green salad (serves 4–5, hot)

1. Cut the meat into 1 inch cubes and brown in the oil, a few pieces at a time, in a heavy pan. Remove the meat to a plate as it is browned.

2. Stir the flour into the remaining oil and when absorbed, return the meat to the pan, and add wine, ¼ pint water, seasoning, tarragon and onion. Add mushrooms, sautéed in a little butter, and stir until the mixture begins to bubble. Then remove to a casserole.

3. Cover, and cook for 1¾–2 hours.

4. Mix egg yolks and cream, stir into the casserole, add vinegar and cook for 5–10 minutes uncovered. Sprinkle with parsley before serving.

Veal Paprika

This is a simplified version of a popular Hungarian dish. Serve it with noodles and a mixed green salad (serves 4, hot — see picture, opposite)

1½ lb fillet of veal, 1 inch thick
2 tablespoons bacon fat
2–3 onions, very finely chopped
1 tablespoon flour
2 teaspoons prepared mustard
1 can tomatoes (14—15 oz)
1 teaspoon paprika
¼ pint sour cream

Pre-heat oven to 350°F Mark 4

1. Cut the meat into fairly large pieces and brown in the bacon fat. Then put into a shallow casserole with a tightly-fitting lid.

2. Brown the onion in the remaining fat, stir in the flour, add mustard, tomatoes, a little salt and ¼ pint water. Stir until boiling. Then pour over the meat which should be just covered. Add a little extra tomato juice if necessary.

3. Cover, and cook for about 45 minutes, or until the veal is tender.

4. Stir in paprika and cream, and mix well. Re-heat without boiling. Adjust seasoning to taste before serving.

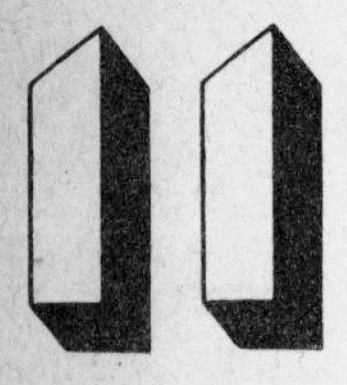

CHICKEN & GAME CASSEROLES

Chicken Cerise

4 chicken joints
paprika
4 oz butter or margarine
1½ oz plain flour
1 teaspoon sugar
¼ teaspoon each, ground cloves and
    ground cinnamon
1/8 teaspoon dry mustard
1 large can cherries
1 chicken stock cube
1 small can crushed pineapple
cooked rice

Pre-heat oven to 375°F Mark 5

Chicken goes well with a wide variety of flavours. Try this with cherries and pineapple. It is very good (serves 4, hot)

1. Sprinkle chicken pieces with salt and paprika. Heat the butter in a pan, brown the chicken on all sides and remove to a casserole.

2. Combine flour, sugar and spices with the remaining fat, add juice from the cherries and crushed stock cube, stir until boiling and thickened, and pour over the chicken. Cover, and cook for 30 minutes.

3. Add cherries and pineapple, and cook for 30 minutes more.

4. Adjust the seasoning, and serve on a bed of rice sprinkled with parsley.

Chicken Casserole

This is a perfect dish for a small dinner party. The chicken is combined with artichoke hearts and garnished with crisp fried bacon and almonds (serves 4, hot)

4 oz butter or margarine
4 chicken breasts
1 can (about 15 oz) artichoke hearts
1 onion, peeled and chopped
2 teaspoons paprika
1½ oz plain flour
¼ pint water
1 chicken stock cube
¼ pint sour cream
½ pint dry white wine
2–3 rashers bacon, fried
slivers of browned almonds

Pre-heat oven to 350°F Mark 4

1. Heat butter in a sauté pan, put in chicken, sprinkle with salt and pepper, and brown on both sides. Put into a casserole with the drained artichokes.

2. Add onion and paprika to remaining fat, and sauté until onion is soft. Remove from the heat, stir in the flour, return to the heat, and cook for 1 minute.

3. Gradually add water in which the stock cube has been dissolved, stir until boiling. Remove from the heat, add sour cream and wine. Re-heat for a few minutes without boiling, then pour over the chicken.

4. Cover and cook for about 1 hour. Before serving, sprinkle with crumbled fried bacon and slivered almonds.

Chicken with Almonds

4 tablespoons oil
1 oz butter or margarine
1 frying chicken (2–2½ lb) jointed
2 onions, peeled and thinly sliced
3 tomatoes, peeled, seeded and
    chopped
a pinch of cinnamon
¾ pint chicken stock
2 oz blanched almonds
2 oz seedless raisins
6 oz rice, cooked
chopped parsley

Pre-heat oven to 350°F Mark 4

In this recipe, a young frying chicken is cooked with almonds and raisins. If you use a larger and older bird, increase the cooking time. The chicken is served in a border of rice, so a crisp green salad would be a good accompaniment (serves 4, hot)

1. Heat oil and butter in a sauté pan, and brown chicken pieces on all sides. Add onions, tomatoes, seasoning and cinnamon. Cook together for a few minutes. Then remove all to a casserole.

2. Add chicken stock, cover and cook for 30 minutes. Add almonds and raisins and cook for 30 minutes more.

3. Line a large oval dish with the hot cooked rice, pile the chicken pieces in the centre, season the sauce to taste, and pour over the chicken.

Pigeons with Water Chestnuts

The crunchy texture of water chestnuts adds extra interest to this casserole (serves 4, hot)

2—4 young pigeons
1½ oz plain flour
1½ oz butter or margarine
1 chicken stock cube
¾ pint water
1 teaspoon sugar
1 tablespoon soy sauce
1 tablespoon sherry
2 spring onions or 1 shallot, chopped
10 water chestnuts, sliced

Pre-heat oven to 350°F Mark 4

1. Split the pigeons in halves, and dredge with flour. Heat butter in a pan, brown pigeons on all sides, and remove to a casserole.

2. Put remaining flour into the pan with the crumbled stock cube and water. Stir until boiling, add sugar, seasoning, soy sauce, sherry, onion and water chestnuts, and pour all over the pigeons.

3. Cover and cook for 1—1¼ hours.

Brunswick Stew

This is an all the year round casserole of chicken, as good use can be made of canned or frozen vegetables. If you like rabbit, it can be prepared in the same way (serves 4, hot)

2 tablespoons oil
1 chicken, jointed
3—4 spring onions, chopped
1 can (about 15 oz) tomatoes
1 packet frozen (or 1 can) whole kernel corn
1 packet frozen (or 1 lb fresh) green beans
¾ pint chicken stock
1 bay leaf
½ teaspoon powdered thyme
1 small can (about 8 oz) new potatoes

Pre-heat oven to 350°F Mark 4

1. Heat the oil in a sauté pan, brown the chicken pieces and onions, and remove to a casserole.

2. Add all the other ingredients except potatoes.

3. Drain potatoes, brown in the oil left in the sauté pan; then add to the casserole.

4. Cover, and cook for 1—1¼ hours. Serve with a tossed salad.

Chicken-Peach Casserole

This is sometimes called Polynesian Chicken. You will enjoy the flavour combination of chicken and peaches (serves 6, hot)

1. Disjoint and skin the chicken. Heat the butter and oil in a pan, brown the chicken pieces on all sides; then cover, reduce the heat and cook for about 10 minutes. Remove the chicken and arrange in a large casserole.

2. Sauté the onion and pepper in the remaining fat until the onion is transparent.

3. Drain the peaches but reserve the syrup. Mix the cornflour smoothly with the soy sauce and vinegar, add ½ pint peach syrup and pour into the pan. Stir until boiling, and boil until clear. Add peaches and tomatoes. Then pour the contents of the pan over the chicken.

4. Cover the casserole, and cook for 30—40 minutes, removing the lid for the last 5 minutes.

5. Adjust the seasoning, and serve with rice to which some cooked green peas and a few strips of red pepper have been added.

1 frying chicken (about 3½ lb) or 6—8 chicken joints
1 oz butter or margarine
1 tablespoon oil
1 large onion, peeled and sliced
1 green pepper, seeded and cut into strips
1 large can sliced peaches
1 tablespoon cornflour
1 tablespoon soy sauce
3 tablespoons white wine vinegar
2 tomatoes peeled and thickly sliced

Pre-heat oven to 375°F Mark 5

1 frying chicken (2½—3 lb)
1 tablespoon flour
2 oz butter or margarine
1 large onion, peeled and sliced
1 can tomatoes (about 14—15 oz)
1 teaspoon brown sugar
1 teaspoon prepared mustard
4 medium potatoes, peeled and sliced
2 apples, peeled, cored and sliced

CREAM SLAW
1 small head firm white cabbage,
   shredded
1 small green pepper, seeded and
   shredded
1 teaspoon prepared mustard
½ teaspoon paprika
2 teaspoons lemon juice
¼ pint sour cream

Pre-heat oven to 350°F Mark 4

Chicken Hot Pot

In this recipe, browned joints of chicken are cooked on a bed of potatoes and apples, and served with cream slaw (serves 4—5, hot)

1. Disjoint the chicken, dredge with flour mixed with a little salt and pepper, and brown on all sides in the butter. Remove from the pan.

2. Lightly brown the onion in the remaining butter. Add tomatoes, sugar and mustard and heat gently. Arrange the potatoes in the bottom of a buttered casserole, season lightly, add apples, and cover with the tomato mixture.

3. Put the chicken pieces on top, cover and cook for about 1½ hours.

4. Mix the cabbage and green pepper. Add the other ingredients to the sour cream, blend well, and toss cabbage and pepper lightly in the dressing.

1 small stewing fowl
1 tablespoon cornflour
2 oz butter or margarine
3 small onions, peeled and halved
4 small carrots, peeled and quartered
1 clove garlic, crushed
4 tablespoons red wine
½ pint chicken stock or water
a few black olives

Pre-heat oven to 300°F Mark 2

Chicken Provencale

Long slow cooking improves the flavour of this dish, so a small stewing fowl is very suitable (serves 4—5, hot)

1. Cut the fowl into neat pieces. Mix salt and pepper with the cornflour and dredge the pieces of chicken well. Heat the butter in a sauté pan, brown the chicken; then remove to a casserole.

2. Add vegetables and garlic to the remaining fat with any remaining cornflour. Cook for a few minutes. Then add wine and stock. Stir until boiling. Then pour over the chicken.

3. Cover tightly and cook for 2½—3 hours. Just before serving, adjust the seasoning and add the olives.

1 pheasant
2 rashers streaky bacon
4 oz butter or margarine
2—3 shallots, peeled and chopped
1 small can button mushrooms
chicken stock
lemon juice

STUFFING
4 oz chopped cooked ham
6 tablespoons cooked rice
3 tablespoons sherry
salt, pepper
pinch marjoram
a pinch of powdered thyme
1 egg

Pre-heat oven to 325°F Mark 3

Pheasant Casserole

This is an excellent way of serving pheasant when you are entertaining as it requires no last minute attention. The pheasant is stuffed with a savoury filling and cooked whole (serves 4, hot)

1. Mix all the ingredients for the stuffing and bind with beaten egg. Stuff the pheasant, truss and wrap bacon slices over the breast.

2. Heat butter in a pan and brown the pheasant all over. Then put into a casserole.

3. Sauté shallots and drained mushrooms in the remaining butter, and add to the casserole. Moisten with a little stock, cover, and cook for about 1½ hours.

4. Just before serving, adjust seasoning and sprinkle with lemon juice.

Pheasant Normandy

You will need a fairly deep casserole for this, as the pheasant is cooked whole. The apples give it a delicious flavour (serves 4, hot)

1. Truss the pheasant as for roasting. Heat the butter in a pan and brown the pheasant on all sides.

2. Put half the apple slices in a deep casserole, pour over a little of the butter and place the pheasant on top. Surround with remaining apple slices.

3. Pour remaining butter and cream on top and sprinkle with salt and pepper. Cover tightly and cook for 1—1¼ hours.

4. When ready to serve, remove trussing string and place pheasant on a serving dish. Add the calvados to the contents of the casserole, adjust the seasoning (a little sugar may also be necessary) and serve the sauce separately.

5. Broccoli spears and a tossed salad would be a suitable accompaniment.

1 pheasant
4 oz butter or margarine
1½ lb cooking apples, peeled, cored and sliced
¼ pint single cream
1 tablespoon calvados (or cider)

Pre-heat oven to 350°F Mark 4

Curried Chicken Casserole

This is another way in which a small stewing fowl can be used. The long slow cooking brings out all the flavour of the ingredients (serves 4—5, hot)

1. Heat the butter and oil in a large pan, add onions and apple, and fry until just soft. Add curry powder and flour, and cook for 3 minutes, stirring. Add turmeric, ginger, seasoning and sugar and mix well. Add stock or water, and stir until boiling.

2. Add chicken, cut into neat pieces, and all the other ingredients. Remove to a casserole, cover tightly and cook for 2½—3 hours.

3. Stir occasionally while cooking to be sure the sauce does not stick, and serve with boiled rice and chutney.

1 small stewing fowl
1 oz butter or margarine
2 tablespoons oil
2 onions, peeled and sliced
1 large apple, peeled, cored and sliced
1 tablespoon curry powder
1 tablespoon flour
½ teaspoon powdered turmeric
¼ teaspoon ground ginger
2 teaspoons sugar
1¾ pints giblet stock or water
1 teaspoon curry paste
2 stalks celery, chopped
2 tablespoons seedless raisins
2 teaspoons chutney
2 teaspoons lemon juice

Pre-heat oven to 300°F Mark 2

Braised Pigeons

This is a splendid party dish. Your guests will be intrigued to find half an orange tucked inside the birds. Choose small ones so that each guest may have one to himself (serves 4, hot)

1. Prepare the pigeons and put half an orange in each one. Tie a slice of bacon over each breast. Heat the butter in a sauté pan, brown the pigeons on all sides and remove to a casserole.

2. Add mushrooms and onion to remaining fat and sauté until onion is transparent. Stir in cornflour, add sherry and chicken stock, and stir until boiling. Then pour over the pigeons.

3. Add the bouquet garni, sprinkle with parsley, cover and cook for about 1½ hours.

4. Put the birds onto a serving dish, adjust the seasoning in the sauce and strain over the birds. Serve with artichoke hearts, marinated in a little French dressing, and a green salad.

4 young pigeons
2 small oranges, peeled and halved
4 rashers streaky bacon
2 oz butter or margarine
3—4 mushrooms, chopped
1 small onion, peeled and sliced
2 teaspoons cornflour
¼ pint sweet sherry (or Marsala)
½ pint chicken stock
bouquet garni
chopped parsley

Pre-heat oven to 325°F Mark 3

Casserole of Pigeons

*Young pigeons are excellent cooked in this way. If small, allow one
for each person or if you have larger birds, one between two (serves 4, hot)*

2–4 young pigeons
3 tablespoons flour
2 oz butter or margarine
1 onion, peeled and chopped
½ lb carrots, peeled and sliced
1 chicken stock cube
½ pint water
3–4 tomatoes, peeled and sliced
1 bay leaf

Pre-heat oven to 325°F Mark 3

1. Split pigeons in halves and dredge with flour mixed with a little salt and pepper. Heat butter in a sauté pan, brown pigeons on all sides, and remove to a casserole. Add onion and carrots sautéed in remaining fat.

2. Put any remaining flour and a crumbled stock cube into the pan, add water, and stir until boiling. Then pour over the contents of the casserole. Add tomatoes and bay leaf, cover, and cook for about 2 hours.

3. Remove bay leaf and adjust seasoning before serving.

FISH CASSEROLES

Casserole of Halibut with Almonds

*The sauce for this dish makes a pleasant contrast in flavour, texture and
colour (serves 4, hot)*

4 oz butter or margarine
3 tablespoons blanched slivered
   almonds
2 teaspoons dry mustard
1 tablespoon tarragon vinegar
3 tablespoons sliced green olives
4 small or 2 large halibut steaks

Pre-heat oven to 350°F Mark 4

1. Heat butter in a sauté pan, and sauté almonds until just beginning to colour. Add mustard, vinegar, 1 tablespoon water and olives. Stir well for a few minutes.

2. Arrange the fish in a shallow buttered casserole, pour the sauce over, cover, and cook for 25–30 minutes.

3. Serve with rice, cooked in chicken stock, a tomato salad and some French bread.

Flounder with Oyster Sauce

*The first five ingredients make a court bouillon. It is well worth poaching
the fish in this to improve the flavour. Fillets of plaice or lemon sole can
be used instead of Flounder. Fresh or canned mussels could be used instead
of oysters (serves 4, hot)*

1 small onion, peeled and chopped
1 carrot, peeled and chopped
¾ pint dry white wine
peppercorns
1 bay leaf
1½ lb fillets of flounder or plaice
1½ oz butter or margarine
1 oz plain flour
¼ pint double cream
paprika
1 can or bottle of oysters
4 oz white seeded grapes

Pre-heat oven to 325°F Mark 3

1. Put the onion and carrot into a pan with the wine, add a little salt, about 6 peppercorns and a bay leaf. Simmer for 15 minutes.

2. Put in the fish, and poach gently for 7–10 minutes. Remove the fish carefully, drain and arrange in a shallow casserole.

3. Strain the court bouillon and if there is less than ½ pint, make up the quantity with a little more wine.

4. Make a sauce with the butter, flour and court bouillon. Add cream and paprika to taste, and stir over low heat until the sauce is smooth and thick. Add the oysters, adjust the seasoning, and pour over the fish.

5. Arrange the grapes on top, cover and cook for about 20 minutes.

6. Serve with baked potatoes and sliced cucumber, dressed with a little tarragon vinegar.

1 oz butter or margarine
4 large potatoes, peeled and sliced
  thinly
1½ lb cod steaks or fillet
4–5 onions, peeled and sliced thinly
1 large can tomatoes
1 tablespoon corn oil
½ pint fish stock or water
1 green pepper, seeded and chopped
breadcrumbs

COLE SLAW
1 small head of white cabbage, finely
  shredded
4–5 tablespoons double cream
3–4 tablespoons white vinegar
2 tablespoons sugar

Pre-heat oven to 350°F Mark 4

Codfish Palermo

Codfish, cooked with tomatoes and onions, is particularly good served with cole slaw and a sweet cream dressing (serves 4–5, hot)

1. Use half the butter to grease a deep casserole. Arrange half the potatoes, fish, onion and tomatoes in alternate layers in the casserole. Sprinkle with oil, salt and pepper. Then repeat the layers in the same order.

2. Pour in the stock, sprinkle with chopped green pepper and breadcrumbs, and dot with the remaining butter.

3. Cook, uncovered, for 35 minutes.

4. For the cole slaw, toss the cabbage with the cream, vinegar and sugar, well mixed.

Salmon and Spaghetti Casserole

When unexpected guests arrive, if you have a can of salmon in the store cupboard, this is a splendid way of making a quick supper dish (serves 5–6, hot)

4 oz butter or margarine
2 oz plain flour
1 pint hot chicken stock
a pinch of nutmeg
4 tablespoons dry sherry
1 can (about 15 oz) salmon
4 tablespoons single cream
4 oz mushrooms, sliced
½ lb spaghetti, cooked
2 oz grated Parmesan cheese
2 tablespoons bread or cereal crumbs

Pre-heat oven to 350°F Mark 4

1. Make a sauce with half the butter, the flour and the chicken stock. Season with salt, pepper and a good pinch of nutmeg.

2. Add sherry and the liquid from the salmon, and simmer over a low heat for 5 minutes. Stir in the cream and adjust the seasoning. Sauté the mushrooms in the remaining butter and add to the sauce.

3. Mix half the sauce with the cooked spaghetti, and put into a shallow casserole. Flake the salmon, mix with the remaining sauce, and pour over the spaghetti.

4. Sprinkle with cheese and breadcrumbs mixed together, and cook for about 20 minutes, or until well browned.

Casserole of Sole Véronique

In this recipe, the sole is very lightly poached in milk before the final cooking in the casserole, and the milk forms the basis for the sauce. The addition of grapes give an unexpected and delightful flavour (serves 6, hot)

1 pint milk
2½ lb fillets of sole
½ lb mushrooms, sliced
4 oz butter or margarine
4–6 oz white seedless or seeded grapes
1½ oz plain flour
lemon juice
4 tablespoons breadcrumbs
2 tablespoons grated cheese

Pre-heat oven to 350°F Mark 4

1. Heat the milk in a pan. When just below boiling point, put in the fish, and poach very gently for 5 minutes.

2. Sauté the mushrooms in half the butter for 3 minutes. Then put into a lightly-buttered casserole with the grapes. Arrange the drained fish on top.

3. Make a sauce with the remaining butter, flour and the milk in which the fish was cooked. Season with salt, pepper and lemon juice, and pour over the fish.

4. Sprinkle with breadcrumbs and cheese, mixed together, and dot with butter. Cook for 25–30 minutes, or until the top is golden brown.

5. Serve with parsley-buttered potatoes, buttered green peas and a tomato salad.

Fish Rolls with Sesame Seeds

Any kind of white fish fillets can be casseroled in this way. The sesame seeds give a contrasting texture. They are available at many super market stores and Delicatessens (serves 5—6, hot)

1½ lb fillets of fish, hake, flounder, cod, fresh haddock etc.
¾ pint milk
1½ oz butter or margarine
1 oz plain flour
2 tablespoons sesame seeds, toasted
4 oz grated cheese
3 tablespoons lemon juice
paprika

Pre-heat oven to 325°F Mark 3

1. Prepare the fillets, roll up and fasten with toothpicks. Arrange in a shallow buttered casserole, sprinkle with salt and pepper, pour the milk over, cover, and cook for about 30 minutes. Then carefully pour off the milk and reserve, and remove toothpicks from the fish.

2. To toast sesame seeds, put them in a pan and toss over medium heat until they begin to colour or spread them out on a baking sheet and toast in the oven.

3. Melt the butter in a pan, stir in flour and sesame seeds, and cook for 2 minutes. Gradually add the milk in which the fish has been cooked, and stir until boiling. Add cheese and lemon juice. Stir until the cheese has melted. Adjust the seasoning, and pour over the fish.

4. Sprinkle with paprika, brown under a hot grill for a few minutes, and serve with riced potatoes, and carrots.

Bouillabaisse

This is based on the authentic Bouillabaisse of the Mediterranean, and is almost the same. The fish is cooked slowly in its own juice and the result is wonderful (serves 6—7, hot—see picture, p. 230)

6 tablespoons olive oil
2 cloves garlic, crushed
2—2½ lb firm fish, halibut, turbot, flounder
12 mussels, well scrubbed
½ lb shelled shrimps
3—4 tablespoons finely chopped parsley

Pre-heat oven to 350°F Mark 4

1. Heat the oil and garlic in a casserole. Put the large fish in first, then the mussels and shrimps. Add salt and pepper, and sprinkle with the parsley.

2. Cover tightly with foil. Then put the lid on the casserole—it should be well fitting—and cook about 30 minutes, or until the fish is tender and the mussels have opened. Baste from time to time with the juices.

3. Serve in hot deep dishes with Spanish rice, tossed green salad and plenty of French bread.

Prawn and Rice Casserole

This simple luncheon dish is very good served with a salad of crisp lettuce, slices of avocado pear and segments of grapefruit, lightly dressed with French dressing (serves 4, hot)

4 rashers bacon
1 small onion, peeled and chopped
½ lb rice
1 large can tomatoes
1 bay leaf
½ lb fresh prawns or scampi, peeled and de-veined

Pre-heat oven to 350°F Mark 4

1. Dice the bacon and fry slowly until crisp. Remove from the pan and drain on a paper towel.

2. Add onion and rice to the bacon fat and stir over low heat for about 5 minutes. Transfer to a casserole.

3. Add tomatoes, ½ pint water, seasoning and bay leaf. Cover and cook for about ½ hour.

4. Add bacon and prawns and cook for another 10 minutes.

13 EGGS, VEGETABLES & CHEESE CASSEROLES

Casserole of Stuffed Peppers

Red or green peppers can be used for this casserole and the stuffing can be varied to suit your taste (serves 4, hot)

1. Cut a slice from the stem end of the peppers and remove all seeds and pith.

2. Heat the butter in a sauté pan, add onion and sauté until soft. Add rice and shrimps, season carefully and add lemon juice to taste.

3. Fill the peppers with this mixture and arrange in a buttered casserole. Add the stock, cover, and cook for about 30 minutes, or until tender.

4 large red or green peppers
1 oz butter or margarine
1 small onion, peeled and chopped
4 oz cooked rice
1 small can (or small package frozen)
    shrimps
lemon juice
½ pint stock

Pre-heat oven to 350° F Mark 4

Lasagne and Cheese Casserole

This is a simple supper dish with an intriguing flavour. Use broad lasagne noodles; the green spinach ones add to the appearance of the dish (serves 4, hot)

1. Soak the raisins in the rum.

2. Cook the noodles in boiling salted water until just tender. Drain, rinse with cold water, drain again and put into a deep buttered casserole. Sprinkle with a little salt and pepper.

3. Mix the sour cream with the cottage cheese and raisins, pour over the noodles and toss together lightly. Sprinkle with the almonds, and cook for about 20 minutes.

4. Serve with a salad of watercress, sliced radishes and cucumber with a little French dressing.

1 packet (½ lb) lasagne
3 oz seedless raisins
1—2 tablespoons rum
½ pint sour cream
8 oz cottage cheese
2—3 tablespoons blanched, slivered
   almonds

Pre-heat oven to 350°F Mark 4

Egg and Mushroom Casserole

Made with fresh mushrooms, this is a delicious light luncheon dish, but for a quick meal a can of condensed mushroom soup can be substituted for the basic sauce and mushrooms (serves 4, hot)

½ lb mushrooms, sliced thinly
4 hard-boiled eggs, sliced
1½ oz butter or margarine
1 oz plain flour
¾ pint milk
a pinch of nutmeg
2 tomatoes, peeled and sliced
breadcrumbs
chopped parsley

Pre-heat oven to 400°F Mark 6

1. Make a sauce with 1 oz of the butter, the flour and milk. Add salt, pepper and a good pinch nutmeg. Add mushrooms and simmer for 10 minutes.

2. Arrange slices of egg and tomato in a casserole, pour over the sauce and sprinkle with bread crumbs. Dot with the remaining butter and cook for about 20—25 minutes, until the top is crisp and brown.

3. Sprinkle with parsley before serving.

Cheese Pilaf

This is a good accompaniment to roast duck or chicken (serves 4, hot)

1 oz butter or margarine
1 tablespoon oil
1 clove garlic
½ lb long-grain uncooked rice
1 pint chicken stock
1 oz grated Parmesan cheese

Pre-heat oven to 350°F Mark 4

1. Heat the butter and oil in a sauté pan. Add the garlic, crushed finely with a little salt, and the rice. Sauté until the rice begins to colour.

2. Pour contents of the sauté pan into a casserole, add stock, cover, and cook for about 25—30 minutes or until the liquid has been absorbed.

3. Remove from the oven, add the cheese, and stir with a fork until it has melted and is well mixed with the rice.

4. For variety, some seedless raisins, seeded black or white grapes or strips of blanched red or green pepper can be stirred into the rice with the cheese.

Leeks au Gratin

In France, leeks have been called the asparagus of the poor. Cooked this way, they make a delicious dish in themselves or they can be served with any roasted meat (serves 4, hot)

8—12 leeks, according to the size
1½ oz butter or margarine
½ oz plain flour
½ pint milk
4 oz grated Cheddar cheese
½ teaspoon prepared mustard
lemon juice
4 tablespoons breadcrumbs

Pre-heat oven to 375°F Mark 5

1. Wash the leeks thoroughly and trim off the coarse green tops. Cook until only just tender in boiling salted water, then drain well and put into a buttered casserole.

2. Make a sauce with 1 oz of the butter, the flour and milk. Add the cheese and stir until it has melted, add salt, pepper, mustard and a squeeze of lemon juice.

3. Pour the sauce over the leeks, sprinkle with breadcrumbs and dot with the remaining butter.

4. Cook for about 25 minutes until the top is crisp and brown.

Breakfast Special

Try this on the days when you can enjoy a late leisurely breakfast. It is best cooked in individual casseroles (serves 4, hot)

8 eggs
1 oz butter or margarine
1 lb chicken livers
¼ pint milk
a pinch of nutmeg
chopped parsley or chives

Pre-heat oven to 325°F Mark 3

1. Heat the butter in a sauté pan and cook the chicken livers for about 7 minutes, then divide into 4 lightly-buttered small casseroles.

2. Beat the eggs, add milk, seasoning and a good pinch of nutmeg. Pour over the livers and bake for 20 minutes, or until the eggs are set.

3. Sprinkle with chopped parsley or chives before serving.

Ratatouille

This vegetable 'medley' can be served as a dish in itself or as an accompaniment to meat. Usually it is served hot, but it is equally good cold (serves 4)

olive oil
2 onions, peeled and finely chopped
2 peppers, seeded and chopped
3—4 courgettes, sliced thinly
1 small aubergine
4 tomatoes, peeled, seeded and
    chopped
3—4 tablespoons chopped parsley
1 clove garlic, crushed
grated Parmesan cheese

Pre-heat oven to 275°F Mark 1

1. Heat some oil in a heavy pan, sauté onions until they begin to colour. Add peppers, sauté a few more minutes.

2. Add courgettes and aubergine—adding a little more oil if necessary—cook for about 5 minutes, then turn all the vegetables into a large casserole and add tomatoes. Cover, and cook in the oven for 1¼ hours.

3. Add parsley, garlic and seasoning, cook a further 20 minutes. Sprinkle generously with cheese before serving.

Curried Rice

This unusual dish makes an excellent luncheon dish if served with a tossed green salad (serves 4, hot)

4 oz rice
1 pint hot water
1 small can tomatoes
½ small onion, finely sliced
½ small red or green pepper,
    thinly-sliced
1 oz butter or margarine, melted
¾ teaspoon curry powder

Pre-heat oven to 350°F Mark 4

1. Put the rice into a casserole, add the water and leave to stand about ¾ hour.

2. Add all the other ingredients and mix well.

3. Cover and cook for about 1½ hours, stirring occasionally.

4. Most of the liquid should now be absorbed, but serve the rice while it is still moist.

Salads & Snacks

The story of salads begins with the ancient Egyptians who served raw greens with oil and vinegar mixed with Oriental spices. The Romans are credited with popularizing salads—in fact one legend has it that Augustus Caesar built an altar to honour the healthful qualities of lettuce.

Salads are the most versatile of foods. In the following recipes you will find salads suitable to serve as hors d'oeuvre, as a regular course, as an accompaniment to other foods and as dessert. No other dish you make offers such possibilities for your imagination—in blending colours, flavours and textures.

Select the best quality salad greens available. Prepare them carefully—pat them dry with a soft towel and refrigerate as soon as possible after purchase to ensure crispness. Whatever the salad, there is always a dressing to improve it, but add the dressing at the last minute unless the recipe suggests otherwise.

In the second section you will find a selection of snacks—for quick lunches, late-night suppers, or just a bite between meals.

MEAT SALADS

Oriental Ham Salad

This salad makes a complete luncheon dish and the ingredients can be varied to suit your own taste (Serves 4–6)

6 oz cooked ham, cut into strips
1/2 lb cooked rice
4 oz sultanas
2 oz peanuts
2–3 spring onions, diced
1 teaspoon curry powder
1 small can pineapple pieces
1 small can (2 oz) tomato purée
4 oz cottage cheese
1 can or 1 packet frozen prawns
lettuce

1. Combine the ham, rice, sultanas, nuts, onions, curry powder and pineapple.

2. Add the tomato purée to the cottage cheese and mix well.

3. Spoon over the ham mixture, then add the prawns and toss lightly.

4. Chill for at least 1 hour.

5. Line a salad bowl with lettuce and pile the salad mixture in the centre.

Ham and Pineapple Salad

This salad of pasta and ham makes a complete luncheon dish (Serves 4)

2 oz shell or other small pasta
3 tablespoons mayonnaise (see p. 24)
1 green pepper, seeded and chopped
4 large slices ham
lettuce
4 rings pineapple
2 tomatoes

1. Cook the pasta in boiling salted water for 10 minutes. Drain well.

2. While still warm, add mayonnaise, green pepper and seasoning, then set aside to get quite cold.

3. Place a spoonful of the mixture on one half of each slice of ham, fold the other half over.

4. Arrange on a bed of lettuce and place a ring of pineapple on each slice of ham. Garnish with wedges of tomato.

Swiss Ham Salad

A simple salad of ham and Gruyère cheese (Serves 4–5)

3/4 lb ham, cut in thick slices and
   diced
3/4 lb Gruyère cheese, diced
6 tablespoons olive oil
2 tablespoons white wine vinegar
salt, freshly ground black pepper
cos lettuce or curly endive
finely chopped parsley or fresh herbs

1. Combine the ham and cheese in a bowl.

2. Make a dressing with the oil, vinegar, salt and pepper, pour over the ham and cheese and toss lightly. Refrigerate and leave about 1 hour to marinate.

3. Arrange the lettuce in a salad bowl, pile the ham and cheese in the centre and sprinkle with parsley or herbs.

Rainbow Salad

A colourful salad of ham, cottage cheese, apple, carrots and hard-boiled eggs (Serves 4)

1/4 lb ham, diced
1/2 lb cottage cheese
a pinch of cayenne pepper
1/4 teaspoon salt
1/2 cucumber
4 sticks celery, chopped
2 red dessert apples, cored and
    chopped but not peeled
2 carrots, grated
2 tablespoons lemon juice
lettuce
2 hard-boiled eggs
parsley or watercress

DRESSING
4 fl. oz yoghurt
1 teaspoon lemon juice
a pinch of garlic salt
1 teaspoon prepared mustard
black pepper, paprika pepper
Combine all ingredients

1. Combine the ham, cottage cheese, pepper and salt.

2. Arrange some thin slices of cucumber around the edge of a large platter and cut the rest into 1/4 inch dice.

3. Put the diced cucumber, celery, apples and carrots into a bowl, add the lemon juice and mix well. Arrange on the platter, put some lettuce leaves in the centre and place the ham and cheese mixture on top.

4. Cut the eggs in halves lengthways and arrange on top. Place a sprig of parsley or watercress in the centre.

5. Serve with the dressing.

Ham Rolls

Slices of ham, filled with a mixture of rice flavoured with curry powder and blended with apple and onion (Serves 4)

3 oz rice
chicken stock or water
1 bay leaf
1 tablespoon oil
1 oz butter
1/2 small onion, peeled and finely
    chopped
1 small apple, peeled, cored and
    chopped
1.1/2 teaspoons curry powder
4 tablespoons single cream
grated rind of 1 lemon
2 tablespoons lemon juice
2 tablespoons chopped ham
2 tablespoons chopped red pepper
8 slices ham

1. Cook the rice in boiling stock or salted water with the bay leaf. Drain, and while still hot stir in the oil, making sure the rice is well coated.

2. Heat the butter in a frying pan, add onion and apple and cook for 5 minutes. Stir in curry powder, cook for a few minutes. Remove from the heat, add cream, grated lemon rind and juice, chopped ham, red pepper, and rice. Set aside for about 1 hour to chill.

3. Roll this mixture in slices of ham and secure with a cocktail stick or toothpick if necessary.

4. Arrange on a serving dish and garnish with watercress.

Chicken Salad with Lychees

The lychees and mandarins add colour and interest to this salad
(Serves 5—6)

1 lb cooked diced chicken
2—3 sticks celery, chopped
1 green pepper, chopped
6 fl. oz French dressing (see p. 282)
lettuce
1 can lychees
1 small can mandarins

DRESSING
6 fl. oz mayonnaise (see p. 280)
2 fl. oz sour cream
2 teaspoons curry powder
2 tablespoons grated onion
2 tablespoons chopped parsley

1. Combine the chicken, celery and green pepper. Add salt, pepper and the French dressing. Toss lightly together and chill for about 1/2 hour.

2. Arrange the lettuce leaves round a large platter and pile the chicken mixture in the centre.

3. Drain the lychees and mandarins. Place a mandarin segment in each lychee and arrange round the edge or down the centre.

4. Blend all the ingredients for the dressing together, chill well and serve the dressing separately.

Luncheon Salad Bowl

1 cut clove of garlic
handful shredded cabbage lettuce
handful shredded cos lettuce
handful shredded chicory
1 small bunch watercress
1/2 green pepper, seeded and cut into rings
1/2 can luncheon meat, shredded
1/4 lb Cheddar cheese, cut into strips
3 hard-boiled eggs, cut into wedges
French dressing, about 4 fl. oz
   (see p. 282)

A variety of salad greens is used for this salad, and the ingredients can be varied to suit your taste. The salad should be served as soon as it is prepared (Serves 5–6)

1. Rub a wooden salad bowl with the cut clove of garlic.

2. Arrange all the ingredients in the bowl. Add the dressing and toss lightly until all the ingredients are coated.

Turkey and Pomegranate Salad

1/2–3/4 lb cooked turkey, cut into cubes
2–3 sticks celery, chopped
seeds from 1 large ripe pomegranate
4 oz blanched chopped almonds
salt, black pepper
mayonnaise (see p. 280)
lettuce
2 slices pineapple, cut into wedges

The shiny red seeds of the pomegranate add colour and interest to this salad. Try not to bruise the seeds while preparing the salad (Serves 5–6)

1. Combine the turkey, celery, pomegranate seeds and almonds. Season carefully with salt and freshly ground black pepper.

2. Add enough mayonnaise to moisten and toss all lightly together.

3. Serve on a bed of lettuce and garnish with wedges of pineapple.

Macaroni Salad (see p. 265)

Chicken Salad

This salad, topped with grapes and crunchy almonds, makes a good party dish (Serves 5—6)

1/4 lb mushrooms
4 fl. oz French dressing (see p. 282)
1 Webbs Wonder or cos lettuce
1/2 lb diced cooked chicken
1 can artichoke hearts, drained and cut in halves
1 small red pepper, seeded and cut into strips
1/2 lb cooked green beans, sliced
6 oz grapes, halved and pipped
1 oz browned flaked almonds

1. Wash and slice the mushrooms and place in a shallow bowl. Pour the French dressing over them and set aside for 1 hour, stirring occasionally.

2. Wash the lettuce, discarding outer leaves, and line a deep salad bowl or large platter.

3. Combine the chicken, artichoke hearts, red pepper and beans. Add the mushrooms and the dressing, season to taste, and toss all lightly together. Refrigerate until ready to serve, then spoon the chicken mixture over the lettuce.

4. Sprinkle with grapes and browned almonds.

Avocado and Chicken Salad

A mixture of chicken and orange arranged in avocado pear halves (Serves 6)

3 ripe avocado pears
2 tablespoons orange juice
about 5 oz diced cooked chicken
1—2 sticks celery, diced
3 oranges
4 tablespoons mayonnaise (see p. 280)
a pinch of paprika pepper
1 tablespoon chopped pimento
lettuce

1. Halve avocados, remove the stones and scoop out some of the flesh. Brush the avocados with orange juice.

2. Cut the scooped out avocado flesh into small pieces and place in a bowl with the chicken and celery.

3. Peel and section 2 of the oranges, removing pips and white pith. Cut into small pieces and add to the chicken and celery mixture.

4. Combine the mayonnaise with the paprika, add salt to taste and blend with the chicken.

5. Fill the avocado halves and sprinkle with chopped pimento. Serve on a bed of lettuce and garnish with sections of the remaining orange.

Potato and Frankfurter Salad

(Serves 4)

1 lb potatoes
6—8 spring onions, chopped
1 teaspoon chopped parsley
cream dressing (see p. 281)
1 lettuce
4 frankfurters
4 slices ham
2 hard-boiled eggs, quartered
3—4 tomatoes

1. Cook, peel and dice the potatoes. Add onion and parsley and while potatoes are still warm add 3—4 tablespoons cream dressing. Toss lightly and set aside to chill.

2. Put the potato in the centre of a platter lined with lettuce leaves.

3. Put a frankfurter on each slice of ham and roll up. Arrange the ham rolls around the dish and garnish with hard-boiled eggs and tomatoes.

VEGETABLE SALADS

Raw Mushroom Salad

(Serves 5—6)

1. Remove the stalks from the mushrooms, wash and dry the caps and cut into slices. Arrange in a shallow salad bowl.

2. Blend the lemon juice and oil, add salt and pepper to taste and pour over the mushrooms. Toss carefully and set aside to chill for at least 1/2 hour.

3. Before serving, sprinkle with the chives and parsley.

VARIATION
Prepare the mushrooms as above and add 3—4 tablespoons mayonnaise to the lemon and oil dressing.

1 lb button mushrooms
juice of 1 lemon
8 tablespoons olive oil
salt, freshly ground black pepper
1 teaspoon finely chopped chives
1 teaspoon finely chopped parsley

Peanut Crunch Slaw

*A coleslaw mixture with a crunchy topping of browned peanuts and cheese
(Serves 6—7)*

1. Combine cabbage and celery. Sprinkle with a little salt and pepper and set aside to chill.

2. Combine all ingredients for the dressing, season and chill.

3. When required for use, brown the peanuts in the butter and stir in the cheese.

4. Toss the vegetables and dressing together and sprinkle the nuts and cheese on top.

1 small white cabbage, shredded
2—3 sticks celery, diced

DRESSING
4 fl. oz sour cream
4 fl. oz mayonnaise (see p. 280)
1 oz chopped spring onions
1/4 green pepper, chopped
1/4 cucumber, chopped

TOPPING
2 oz salted peanuts, coarsely chopped
1/2 oz butter
2 tablespoons grated Parmesan cheese

Coleslaw with Almonds

(Serves 4—5)

1. Wash and drain the cabbage, discard outer leaves and hard stalk.

2. Shred the cabbage finely and mix with the celery, cucumber, green pepper and onion.

3. Mix the mayonnaise and vinegar, add salt and pepper to taste and pour over the vegetables. Toss with two forks until the vegetables are evenly coated.

4. Put into a serving dish and sprinkle with browned almonds.

1/2 medium-size white cabbage
2 sticks celery, chopped
1/2 cucumber, thinly sliced
1/2 green pepper, shredded
1 onion, peeled and finely chopped
5 fl. oz mayonnaise (see p. 280)
1 tablespoon vinegar
1 oz flaked browned almonds

Pasta Slaw

2 tablespoons mayonnaise (see p. 280)
1 tablespoon sour cream
1 tablespoon vinegar
2 teaspoons sugar
4 oz pasta, cooked (any kind)
3 tablespoons grated carrot
3 tablespoons diced green pepper
1/4 small white cabbage, shredded

A good salad to serve with any kind of cold meat or poultry (Serves 4–5)

1. Make a dressing with the mayonnaise, sour cream, vinegar and sugar.

2. Add the pasta and vegetables and toss lightly, but be sure all the ingredients are well coated with the dressing.

Salad Andalouse

4–5 oz boiled rice
4 tomatoes, peeled and cut into
    quarters
2 canned pimentos, cut into thin
    strips
1 clove garlic, crushed
1/2 onion, peeled and finely chopped
French dressing (see page 282)
finely chopped parsley

A simple salad of rice with tomatoes and pimentos. A good way of using left-over rice (Serves 4)

1. Combine the rice, tomatoes, pimento, garlic and onion. Add seasoning if required.

2. Add enough French dressing to coat all ingredients well but avoid adding excess dressing.

3. Sprinkle with parsley before serving.

Macaroni Salad

A salad of macaroni, cheese, gherkins and peas blended with mayonnaise. Excellent as an accompaniment to any grilled meat (Serves 6—see picture, p. 262)

8 oz shell or ring macaroni
1 oz butter
4 oz cubed Cheddar cheese
4 oz sliced gherkins
2 oz very finely chopped onion
12 oz cooked peas
8 tablespoons mayonnaise (see p. 280)
seasoning
lettuce

1. Cook the macaroni in boiling salted water, drain well, add the butter and toss lightly.

2. Add cheese, gherkins, onion and peas.

3. Stir in the mayonnaise and blend carefully, making sure the macaroni is well mixed with the mayonnaise.

4. Check the seasoning and set aside to chill.

5. Serve individually in lettuce leaves or on a bed of shredded lettuce.

Stuffed Tomatoes

A good accompaniment to cold chicken or turkey (Serves 4)

8 firm ripe tomatoes
2 ripe avocado pears
juice of 1 lemon
1 tablespoon onion juice
salt, black pepper
a pinch of chilli powder
4 tablespoons finely chopped celery or
    green pepper
1 tablespoon finely chopped parsley

1. Skin the tomatoes after plunging them into boiling water for 1 minute and then in cold water.

2. Cut in half crossways and remove the seeds and pulp. Cover loosely with foil and chill in the refrigerator until required.

3. Peel the avocados, remove the stone and mash well with a wooden spoon. Add lemon juice, onion juice, salt, pepper, chilli powder and celery or green pepper. Set aside to chill.

4. When ready to use, fill the tomato halves with the avocado mixture and sprinkle with parsley.

Caesar Salad

A plain green salad topped with crispy bacon and bread croûtons (Serves 4–5)

2 small cos lettuces
1 oz butter
1 clove garlic, crushed
2 slices bread, cut into 1/2 inch cubes
2 rashers bacon, chopped
grated Parmesan cheese
chopped parsley

DRESSING
1 coddled egg
5 fl. oz French dressing (see p. 282)
1 teaspoon salt
1 teaspoon prepared mustard

1. To make the dressing, coddle the egg first by putting it into boiling water for 1 minute and then removing the shell. Then mix well with all the other ingredients.

2. Remove any tough outer leaves from the lettuce, wash and dry well. Break up into pieces, put into a salad bowl, add the dressing and toss lightly.

3. Heat the butter in a frying pan, add crushed garlic and cubes of bread and cook until crisp and golden brown. Fry the bacon until crisp, then drain on absorbent paper.

4. Scatter the bacon and croûtons over the salad and sprinkle generously with grated cheese and parsley.

Wilted Lettuce Salad

(Serves 4)

1 large head cabbage lettuce
6 radishes, thinly sliced
1 hard-boiled egg
5–6 rashers bacon
1 teaspoon sugar
4 fl. oz red wine vinegar
1/4 teaspoon grated horseradish
a pinch of black pepper
5–6 spring onions, chopped

1. Wash and drain the lettuce and break it up into a salad bowl. Add sliced radishes.

2. Remove the yolk carefully from the hard-boiled egg and set aside. Chop the white of egg and sprinkle over the lettuce.

3. Cook the bacon in a frying pan until crisp. Remove, and drain on absorbent paper.

4. Add sugar, vinegar, horseradish and pepper to the bacon fat in the frying pan. Mix well, add spring onions and heat until the mixture bubbles, then pour at once over the lettuce. Toss lightly. Add the crumbled bacon and sprinkle with the sieved hard-boiled egg yolk.

Hot Potato Salad

Another hot salad of potato, bacon and eggs. Very good to serve with frankfurters (Serves 4)

3 large potatoes
2 tablespoons vinegar
1 teaspoon salt, pepper
1/2 lb bacon, chopped
3 eggs
1 oz chopped spring onions
lettuce
4 frankfurters

1. Scrub the potatoes, cook in boiling salted water, then drain, peel and cut into dice. Add vinegar, salt and pepper.

2. Fry the bacon until crisp.

3. Hard-boil the eggs.

4. Combine the potatoes, bacon, 2 tablespoons of the bacon fat, chopped eggs and onion and mix well.

5. Serve hot on a bed of lettuce with frankfurters.

Ratatouille Salad

Ratatouille is the well known Provencal dish consisting of a selection of vegetables cooked in oil. Try it this way—served cold as a salad (Serves 4)

2 aubergines
olive oil, about 4 fl. oz
1 onion, peeled and chopped
1 large red pepper, seeded and cut
  into small pieces
4 tomatoes, peeled and chopped
2 cloves garlic, crushed
12 coriander seeds
chopped basil or parsley

1. Wipe the aubergines, cut into 1/2 inch squares and put into a colander. Sprinkle with coarse salt and leave to drain.

2. Heat some of the oil in a frying pan and sauté the onion for about 10 minutes or until it begins to soften. Add a little more oil, put in the aubergines and red pepper, cover and simmer for 30—40 minutes.

3. Add tomatoes, garlic and coriander, and continue to cook until the tomatoes are soft and mushy, adding a little more oil if necessary. Adjust the seasoning, then chill.

4. Drain off any excess oil and sprinkle with basil or parsley.

Hot Macaroni Salad

This is an unusual salad in that it is served hot. It makes a good luncheon dish (Serves 5—6)

about 7 oz macaroni
6 rashers bacon, diced
2 tablespoons vinegar
1 tablespoon finely chopped onion
1/2 teaspoon salt
1/4 teaspoon pepper
5 tablespoons salad cream (see p. 279)
2 oz sliced radishes
1/4 green pepper, chopped
1/2 oz chopped parsley

1. Cook the macaroni in boiling salted water.

2. While the macaroni is cooking, fry the bacon until crisp then remove from the pan and drain off excess fat from the pan, leaving about 1 tablespoon. Add vinegar, onion and seasoning and bring to boiling point.

3. Add drained macaroni and all the other ingredients and toss lightly.

4. Serve hot with a green salad if desired.

SEAFOOD SALADS

Seafood Medley

A quickly prepared salad of seafood, made with celery and cucumber. Canned shrimps can be replaced with fresh if preferred (Serves 5—6)

1 can tuna fish
1 can crab meat
1 can shrimps
2 tablespoons French dressing (see p. 282)
2—3 sticks celery, diced
1/4 cucumber, diced
6—8 radishes, chopped
1 tablespoon capers
2 tablespoons lemon juice
4 fl. oz mayonnaise (see p. 280)
salt, pepper, paprika pepper
lettuce

1. Drain the tuna and break up into flakes. Add flaked crab meat and shrimps. Stir in the French dressing and set aside to chill for about 15 minutes.

2. Add celery, cucumber, radishes and capers.

3. Blend lemon juice with the mayonnaise, add seasoning to taste and toss all ingredients lightly together.

4 tomatoes, peeled and quartered
2 small green peppers, seeded and
   sliced thinly
4 sticks celery, chopped
1 small cooked beetroot
2 hard-boiled eggs, cut into quarters
1 can anchovy fillets
1 can tuna fish, drained and flaked
green and black olives

DRESSING
2 tablespoons white wine vinegar
6 tablespoons olive oil
salt, freshly ground black pepper
1/2 teaspoon prepared mustard
1 teaspoon each finely chopped
   tarragon, chives, chervil and parsley

Anchovy and Tuna Salad

(Serves 4)

1. Arrange the tomatoes, green peppers, celery, beetroot and eggs in a salad bowl or on a large platter.

2. Combine all the ingredients for the dressing together and blend well.

3. Arrange the anchovy fillets, tuna and olives attractively on top and pour the dressing over.

Shrimp and Rice Salad

A main meal salad of shrimps and rice with mushrooms and ham
(Serves 4—5)

1 oz butter
2 small onions, peeled and chopped finely
1/4 lb mushrooms, sliced
4 oz rice, boiled
6 oz cooked peas
1 small red pepper, seeded and cut into strips
2 tablespoons chopped parsley
4 oz ham, cut into strips
1 lb or 1 pint shrimps
French dressing (see p. 282)
lettuce
slices of cucumber for garnish

1. Heat the butter and sauté the onions until lightly browned. Remove from the pan. Add a little more butter if required and fry the mushrooms for 3 minutes.

2. Mix onion, mushroom and any pan juices with the rice. Add peas, red pepper, parsley, ham and shrimps, saving a few for the garnish. Mix lightly and add enough dressing to moisten.

3. Arrange the rice mixture on a serving dish and surround with shredded lettuce.

4. Top with the reserved shrimps and arrange slices of cucumber on the ring of lettuce.

Crab Mayonnaise

A delicious summer luncheon dish. The mayonnaise is flavoured with tomato purée, curry powder and honey. Lobster can be served in the same way (Serves 5–6)

1 lb fresh, canned, or frozen crab
   meat
1 tablespoon oil
1 small onion, peeled and chopped
2 teaspoons curry powder
2 teaspoons tomato purée
1 tablespoon clear honey
6 tablespoons red wine
4 tablespoons water
juice of 1/2 lemon
8 fl. oz mayonnaise (see p. 280)
1/2 red or green pepper, cut into strips
black olives
2–3 tomatoes
lettuce

1. Arrange the crab meat in a shallow oval dish.

2. Heat the oil in a frying pan, fry the onion for 2–3 minutes then add curry powder and fry for another 2 minutes.

3. Add tomato purée, honey, wine and water. Bring to boiling point, add seasoning and lemon juice. Simmer until the mixture becomes thick and syrupy, then strain and leave to cool.

4. Stir this dressing into the mayonnaise and spoon it over the crab.

5. Arrange the strips of pepper in a lattice pattern over the top, put an olive into each square and slices of tomato around the edge. Chill and serve with crisp lettuce.

Salad Nicoise

2 lettuce hearts
4 tomatoes, peeled, seeded and
   quartered
1/2 Spanish onion, peeled and thinly
   sliced
1 green pepper, seeded and cut into
   strips
8 small radishes
4 sticks celery, sliced
1 can tuna fish
8 anchovy fillets
2 hard-boiled eggs
8 black olives

DRESSING
2 tablespoons white wine vinegar or
   lemon juice
6 tablespoons olive oil
few leaves fresh basil, chopped

A favourite luncheon salad of lettuce, vegetables and tuna fish garnished with anchovy fillets and black olives (Serves 4)

1. Line a salad bowl with the lettuce. Combine the vegetables and arrange in the salad bowl.

2. Combine the ingredients for the dressing, pour over the lettuce and vegetables, and toss lightly.

3. Drain the tuna fish, break it up into fairly large pieces and place them on top.

4. Top with the anchovy fillets and wedges of egg, and dot with olives.

Crab Salad

6 oz rice
nutmeg
lemon juice
olive oil
1 can crab claw meat (12 or 16 oz),
   or 1 lb fresh white crab meat
6 black olives, stoned
1 red or green pepper, seeded and cut
   into strips
1/2 clove garlic, crushed
3–4 raw mushrooms, sliced
a few walnuts

Fresh crab is best for this salad, but use canned if fresh is not available (Serves 4)

1. Cook the rice in boiling salted water until just tender (about 12 minutes). Drain well and while still warm add a good pinch of nutmeg, squeeze of lemon juice and enough oil to moisten.

2. Add crab meat cut into squares, olives, red or green pepper, garlic and mushrooms. Mix lightly together.

3. Arrange in a bowl or on a platter and sprinkle chopped walnuts on top.

EGG & CHEESE SALADS

Egg and Shrimp Mayonnaise

For this attractive salad shrimps are combined with mayonnaise, blended with sour cream, flavoured with curry powder and used to coat hard-boiled eggs (Serves 6)

4 fl. oz mayonnaise (see p. 280)
1 small carton (5 fl. oz) sour cream
1 teaspoon curry powder
6 hard-boiled eggs
lettuce
6—8 oz fresh or frozen shrimps
paprika pepper
brown bread or rolls

1. Combine the mayonnaise, sour cream and curry powder and chill for 1 hour.

2. Shell and cut the hard-boiled eggs in halves and arrange rounded side up on crisp lettuce.

3. Fold the shrimps into the mayonnaise and spoon over the eggs. Sprinkle with paprika.

4. Serve with rolls or thinly sliced buttered brown bread.

Cheese and Lettuce Salad

A lettuce stuffed with a mixture of cheese, sour cream and vegetables (Serves 5—6)

1 large firm lettuce
3 oz cream cheese
8 oz cottage cheese
2 tablespoons sour cream
2 tablespoons very finely chopped or
    minced onion
1/4 green pepper, chopped
2 carrots, grated
1 oz chopped nuts
French dressing (see p. 282)

1. Wash, drain and dry the lettuce. Remove the hard central stalk, making a cavity large enough to hold the cheese mixture.

2. Beat the cream cheese, cottage cheese, sour cream and onion together until soft and creamy, add all the other ingredients and blend well.

3. Stuff the lettuce and chill for several hours. Cut into wedges and serve with French dressing.

Cheese and Fruit Salad

A refreshing salad of cream cheese and fruit. Serve as dessert or as an accompaniment to cold poultry or ham (Serves 4)

8 oz cream or cottage cheese
1.1/2 oz chopped walnuts
2 rings canned or fresh pineapple,
    chopped
1 large crisp lettuce
1 large grapefruit
2 bananas
juice of 1/2 lemon
French dressing (see p. 282)

1. Combine the cheese with the nuts and pineapple.

2. Arrange the lettuce on a platter, reserving some of the heart for garnish. Pile the cheese in the centre.

3. Arrange segments of grapefruit and slices of banana brushed with lemon juice around the cheese and tuck pieces of lettuce heart in between.

4. Pour the dressing over the top. If canned pineapple is used, 1 tablespoon pineapple juice can be substituted for 1 tablespoon of the oil in the French dressing.

Salad Provencale

This colourful salad consists of red and green peppers, tomatoes and hard-boiled eggs, garnished with anchovies and black olives (Serves 6)

1. Wash and dry the peppers, then grill them quickly, turning frequently until the skin has charred on all sides. Remove the skin under cold water, then cut the peppers lengthways into 6 or 8 pieces. Wash off the seeds and remove excess fibre, then pat dry.

2. Arrange the slices of tomato in the bottom of a large flat serving dish. Sprinkle with some of the dressing, cover with the pieces of green pepper, sprinkle with more dressing, add the pieces of red pepper and sprinkle again with dressing.

3. Shell and slice the hard-boiled eggs and put on top of the red pepper. Add the rest of the dressing.

4. Arrange anchovy fillets in a lattice pattern on top and place an olive in the centre of each square. Chill before serving.

2 red peppers
2 green peppers
6 firm tomatoes, peeled and thickly
    sliced
6 hard-boiled eggs
anchovy fillets
black olives
herb dressing (see p. 280)

5 MOULDED SALADS

Cheese and Macaroni Salad Ring

An attractive salad suitable to serve alone as a light luncheon dish, or as an accompaniment to cold meat or poultry. Any other pasta can be used in place of macaroni (Serves 6–9)

1. Cook the macaroni in boiling salted water for about 10 minutes. Drain well and while still warm add the French dressing and mix well. Set aside to chill.

2. Add the other ingredients except lettuce, radishes and olives, mix lightly but thoroughly and press into a quart ring mould. Chill for several hours.

3. When ready to serve, arrange some lettuce on a platter. Loosen the mixture from the side of the mould with a knife and turn out on the lettuce.

4. If the salad is to accompany poultry or meat, cut the meat into neat dice, bind with a little mayonnaise, season, and pile in the centre of the macaroni ring.

5. Garnish with radish roses and slices of olive.

4 oz macaroni
2 fl. oz French dressing (see p. 282)
1 lb cottage cheese
2 tablespoons diced pimento
2 tablespoons diced green pepper
2 tablespoons very finely chopped
    onion
2 tablespoons chopped parsley
lettuce
radishes and stuffed green olives for
    garnish

Moulded Tuna Salad

1/2 oz gelatine
2 fl. oz cold water
6 fl. oz hot water
2 tablespoons lemon juice
1 teaspoon prepared mustard
1/4 teaspoon paprika pepper
2 cans (6.1/2—7 oz each) tuna fish
2—3 sticks celery, chopped
4 fl. oz double cream, whipped
lettuce

DRESSING
4 fl. oz mayonnaise (see p. 280)
1 oz finely diced cucumber
1 tablespoon chopped green pepper
1 teaspoon tarragon vinegar
a dash of cayenne pepper

(Serves 5—6)

1. Soften the gelatine in cold water for 5—10 minutes, add hot water and stir until the gelatine has melted. Add lemon juice, mustard, paprika and salt to taste. Set aside to chill until partially set.

2. Add drained and flaked tuna and celery and fold in the whipped cream.

3. Spoon into individual moulds and chill until set.

4. Turn out on a bed of lettuce. Combine all the ingredients for the dressing, and serve separately.

Ham Mousse

1/2 oz gelatine
2 fl. oz cold water
2 fl. oz white wine vinegar
10 oz finely cubed cooked ham
2—3 sticks celery, finely diced
1 tablespoon sugar
1 tablespoon piccalilli
4 fl. oz double cream, whipped
lettuce
stuffed olives

HORSERADISH CREAM
3 teaspoons grated horseradish
1/2 teaspoon salt
6 fl. oz whipped cream

A light moulded mixture of ham, celery and whipped cream. Makes a good party salad (Serves 4—5)

1. Soften the gelatine in the cold water for about 5 minutes. Add the vinegar and heat over hot water until dissolved.

2. Combine ham, celery, sugar and piccalilli. Stir in the melted gelatine and whipped cream. Check the seasoning and pour into a mould rinsed in cold water. Chill until set.

3. Unmould on a bed of lettuce and garnish with slices of stuffed olives.

4. Fold the horseradish and salt into the whipped cream, and serve separately.

Moulded Chicken Salad

*The red and green pepper makes a decorative topping for this salad
(Serves 5—6)*

1/2 oz gelatine
2 fl. oz cold water
8 fl. oz hot chicken stock
2 tablespoons chopped red pepper
2 tablespoons chopped green pepper
10 oz diced cooked chicken
1 tablespoon finely chopped onion
2—3 sticks celery, chopped
2 oz rice, boiled
1/2 teaspoon salt
2 fl. oz French dressing (see p. 282)
a pinch of paprika pepper
4 fl. oz mayonnaise (see p. 280)
lettuce

1. Combine the gelatine and cold water and leave for about 10 minutes to soften. Add hot chicken stock and stir until the gelatine has melted.

2. Rinse a mould with cold water, put in the red and green peppers. Cover with 4 tablespoons of the melted gelatine and refrigerate until set.

3. Mix all ingredients except lettuce and add the remaining gelatine.

4. When the gelatine in the mould is quite firm, spoon the chicken mixture on top and leave until set.

5. Unmould and serve on a bed of lettuce.

Tomato Jelly Ring

A ring of well flavoured tomato jelly and noodles. The centre can be filled with any meat, poultry or fish mixture (Serves 4–6)

1 pt. 12 fl. oz tomato juice
2 teaspoons salt
1/4 teaspoon freshly ground black pepper
1/4 teaspoon finely chopped basil
1 onion, peeled and finely chopped
1 oz gelatine
2 fl. oz cold water
2 teaspoons grated horseradish
2 tablespoons sugar
2 tablespoons lemon juice
1/4 lb noodles, cooked

1. Put the tomato juice, seasoning, basil and onion into a frying pan, heat to boiling point, and simmer for 10 minutes. Then strain.

2. Soak the gelatine in the cold water for 5 minutes, add to the hot tomato juice, and stir until dissolved.

3. Add horseradish, sugar and lemon juice, adjust the seasoning to taste, and set aside to chill until the mixture begins to thicken.

4. Stir in the cooked macaroni, and pour into a lightly oiled 9 inch ring mould. Chill until set.

5. Unmould and fill the centre if desired.

Moulded Apricot Ring

An attractive ring of apricot jelly sandwiched with cream cheese and green pepper (Serves 4)

1. Drain the apricots, finely chop enough to make 2 fl. oz and reserve the rest.

2. Mix 8 fl. oz apricot syrup with the pineapple juice and heat to boiling point.

3. Soften the gelatine for 5 minutes in the water. Then dissolve it in the hot fruit juice.

4. Add the chopped apricots to half the gelatine and pour into a small ring mould. Refrigerate until set.

5. Chill the remaining gelatine until it begins to thicken.

6. Blend the cream cheese with the cream, add green pepper, paprika and salt, and spread on top of the firm gelatine.

7. Cover with the remaining thickened gelatine and set aside until firm.

8. Unmould and fill the centre with watercress or lettuce sand the remaining apricots.

about 1 lb 4 oz canned apricots
8 fl. oz pineapple juice
1/2 oz gelatine
2 tablespoons water
3 oz cream cheese
1 tablespoon double cream, whipped
1/2 small green pepper, blanched and
    finely chopped
a pinch of paprika pepper
a pinch of salt
watercress or lettuce

Moulded Grapefruit Salad

To serve with chicken, ham or veal (Serves 4)

1 can (about 16 oz) grapefruit
1 oz gelatine
2 tablespoons lemon juice
1 dessert apple, peeled, cored and
    chopped
2—3 stalks celery, chopped
lettuce

1. Drain the syrup from the grapefruit, and add sufficient water to make 12 fl. oz.

2. Soften the gelatine in a little of the syrup for 5—10 minutes. Then stir over hot water until melted. Add the rest of the syrup and lemon juice, and leave in a cold place until it begins to thicken.

3. Stir in the grapefruit, apple and celery. Pour into a prepared mould or into individual moulds, and refrigerate until set.

4. Serve on a bed of lettuce.

Tomato and Apple Jelly

A colourful accompaniment to any cold meat or poultry (Serves 4)

1/2 oz gelatine
4 fl. oz water
12 fl. oz tomato juice
1 tablespoon Worcestershire sauce
seasoning
1 large apple, peeled, cored and chopped
1–2 oz chopped ham
lettuce

1. Soften the gelatine in the water for 5–10 minutes.

2. Put it into a saucepan with the tomato juice and melt over low heat.

3. Remove from the heat, add Worcestershire sauce and seasoning and set aside until it begins to thicken.

4. Add apple and ham, correct the seasoning and pour into 4 prepared individual moulds.

5. Refrigerate until set, then serve on a bed of lettuce.

Jellied Tongue and Potato Salad

When this salad is unmoulded, the meat is on the top and the vegetables form the base (Serves 6)

3/4 oz gelatine
2 fl. oz cold water
12 fl. oz stock
1/4 teaspoon dry mustard
a pinch of cayenne pepper
1 teaspoon Worcestershire sauce
8 oz diced cooked tongue
8 oz diced cooked potato
1–2 sticks celery, diced
1/4 green pepper, diced
2 fl. oz mayonnaise (see p. 280)
2 tablespoons vinegar
1/2 teaspoon salt
a pinch of pepper

1. Soften the gelatine in the cold water for about 10 minutes. Add boiling stock, stir until the gelatine has melted, then divide in half and leave to cool.

2. Mix the mustard and cayenne smoothly with the Worcestershire sauce and add to one half of the melted gelatine.

3. Put the tongue into the bottom of a plain mould or loaf tin rinsed out with cold water and pour the seasoned gelatine on top. Refrigerate until set.

4. Combine all the other ingredients with the rest of the gelatine and when the meat layer is set, pour it on top.

5. Leave until set. Then unmould and garnish as desired.

DRESSINGS

Salad Cream

This salad cream will keep well in the refrigerator (Makes about 12 fl. oz)

2 eggs
2 teaspoons sugar
1/2 oz butter
8 fl. oz milk
6 fl. oz vinegar
1 teaspoon salt
a small pinch of cayenne pepper
1 teaspoon dry mustard
2 teaspoons cornflour

1. Separate the eggs and put the yolks, sugar, butter, 2/3 of the milk, vinegar and seasonings into the top of a double saucepan. Stir over boiling water until the ingredients are well blended.

2. Blend the cornflour with the remaining milk, add to the other ingredients and stir until the mixture thickens.

3. When cold, fold in the stiffly beaten egg whites.

Green Sauce

For seafood or green salads (Makes about 8 fl. oz)

1 slice white bread
4 fl. oz water
2–3 oz parsley
3 tablespoons drained capers
4 anchovy fillets
2 cloves garlic
2 tablespoons chopped onion
1 small gherkin
4 fl. oz olive oil
1/2 teaspoon salt
1/4 teaspoon freshly ground black
    pepper
1 tablespoon white wine vinegar

1. Soak the bread in the water, drain, and mash smooth.

2. Put all except the last four ingredients into a blender and blend into a paste. If a blender is not available, chop the ingredients very finely, or put through a mincer, and work into a paste.

3. Turn the mixture into a bowl and work in 2 teaspoons of the oil, salt and pepper. Then add the remaining oil gradually, stirring all the time until the mixture is smooth.

4. Stir in the vinegar and adjust the seasoning to taste.

Herb Dressing

1 clove garlic, crushed
1 tablespoon each finely chopped
    parsley, tarragon, chervil and chives
8 tablespoons olive oil
3 tablespoons white wine vinegar
salt, freshly ground black pepper

Combine garlic and herbs with oil and vinegar. Add salt and pepper to taste.

Mayonnaise

(Makes about 8 fl. oz)

1. Rinse a bowl with hot water and dry well.

2. Put in the egg yolks, salt and mustard and 1 teaspoon of the vinegar. Beat vigorously or at low speed with an electric mixer.

3. Add half the oil, drop by drop, and then the remaining vinegar.

4. Beat in the rest of the oil in a steady stream.

5. Add lemon juice.

2 egg yolks
1/2 teaspoon salt
1/4 teaspoon dry mustard
1.1/2 teaspoons wine vinegar
8 fl. oz olive oil
1/2 teaspoon lemon juice

Note

If the mayonnaise curdles, break an egg yolk into a clean basin and gradually beat the curdled mixture into it.

Cooked Mayonnaise

2 tablespoons wine vinegar
2 tablespoons water
2 tablespoons sugar
1/2 oz butter
1/2 teaspoon salt
1 teaspoon dry mustard
1 beaten egg

1. Combine all the ingredients in a saucepan. Stir over a low heat until the butter melts and the mixture thickens slightly.

2. Remove from the heat and chill.

Chiffonade Dressing

8 fl. oz French dressing (see p. 282)
1 hard-boiled egg, chopped
1 teaspoon finely chopped parsley
1 tablespoon finely chopped pimento
1 teaspoon finely chopped chives
a pinch of paprika

For vegetable salads

Combine all ingredients.

Cottage Cheese Dressing

8 fl. oz French dressing (see p. 282)
3 tablespoons cottage cheese
2 tablespoons chopped parsley
1 tablespoon finely chopped mango
   chutney

For fruit, vegetable or green salads

Combine all ingredients and chill before serving.

Cucumber Cream Dressing

2 tablespoons vinegar
2 tablespoons sugar
1/2 cucumber, peeled and diced
1/4 pint carton double cream, whipped

For meat or chicken salads

Mix the vinegar, sugar and cucumber and fold into the whipped cream.

Aïoli

This garlic sauce is very popular in France. Serve with fish, potato salad or boiled beef (Makes about 12 fl. oz)

1 slice French bread
milk
3 cloves garlic, crushed very finely
2 egg yolks
a pinch of salt
8 fl. oz olive oil
1/2 teaspoon cold water
1 teaspoon lemon juice

1. Remove crust from the bread, and discard it. Soak bread in a little milk, then squeeze it out.

2. Add garlic, egg yolks and salt, and beat well.

3. Add oil very slowly as for mayonnaise and, as the dressing thickens, beat in the water and lemon juice.

Cream Dressing

To serve with lettuce (Makes about 8 fl. oz)

1/2 teaspoon prepared mustard
1 teaspoon sugar
2 teaspoons tarragon vinegar
1/2 clove garlic, crushed
1 hard-boiled egg
1 teaspoon chopped tarragon or chives
4 fl. oz single cream

1. Mix the mustard, sugar and vinegar together, add the garlic and yolk of the hard-boiled egg. Mix well, then stir in cream and chopped tarragon or chives. If the vinegar makes the cream too thick for pouring, add a few drops of water or milk.

2. Chill thoroughly, then pour over crisp lettuce hearts and sprinkle with the chopped egg white.

French Dressing

Mix vinegar with salt and pepper to taste. Add oil and beat with a fork until the mixture thickens.

2 tablespoons white wine vinegar
salt
freshly ground black pepper
6—8 tablespoons olive oil

Note
For a slightly thicker dressing, add a cube of ice and stir for 1—2 minutes longer, then remove the ice cube.

VARIATIONS

TARRAGON DRESSING
Add 1 teaspoon chopped fresh tarragon leaves.

CURRY DRESSING
Add 1/2 teaspoon curry powder and 1 teaspoon finely chopped shallots.

CAPER DRESSING
Add 1 teaspoon chopped capers, 1/2 clove garlic, finely crushed, and a little anchovy paste.

ROQUEFORT DRESSING
Add 3 tablespoons crumbled Roquefort cheese and blend well. Chill before serving.

Russian Dressing

For egg or vegetable salads or with fish (Makes about 8 fl. oz)

Combine all ingredients.

8 fl. oz mayonnaise (see p. 280)
1 tablespoon chilli sauce
1—2 teaspoons chopped chives
2 teaspoons chopped red pepper or canned pimento

Note
Chilli sauce varies considerably in strength. It is advisable to add about 1/2 teaspoon, then taste and increase the quantity as necessary. The quantity given is for a mild chilli sauce.

Green Goddess Dressing

8 fl. oz mayonnaise (see p. 280)
1 clove garlic, crushed
2 tablespoons finely chopped parsley
2 tablespoons chopped chives
1 tablespoon lemon juice
1 tablespoon tarragon vinegar
1/2 teaspoon salt, black pepper
2 teaspoons anchovy paste
2 tablespoons cream

For all seafood salads (Makes about 12 fl. oz)

Combine all ingredients and stir until dressing is smooth.

Thousand Island Dressing

8 fl. oz mayonnaise (see p. 280)
1 tablespoon chilli sauce (see note above)
1 tablespoon chopped green olives
2 teaspoons finely chopped chives

For meat or fish salads (Makes about 8 fl. oz)

Combine all ingredients.

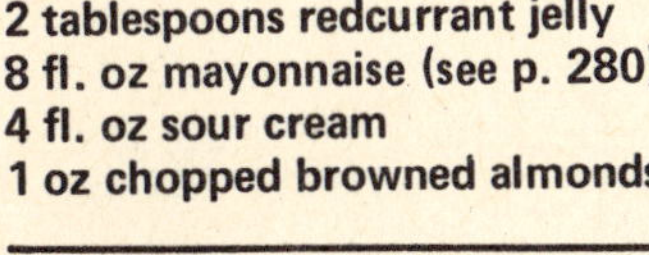

Dressings (see p. 282)

Fruit Salad Dressing

(Makes about 12 fl. oz)

2 tablespoons redcurrant jelly
8 fl. oz mayonnaise (see p. 280)
4 fl. oz sour cream
1 oz chopped browned almonds

1. Melt the jelly and leave to get cold.

2. Combine with the other ingredients and chill before using.

FRUIT SALADS

Stuffed Pears

Fresh pears stuffed with crab meat, apple and celery. Very good served with cold pork or poultry or as an hors d'oeuvre (Serves 6)

3 large ripe pears
lemon juice
2 red skinned dessert apples, cored
    and diced but not peeled
2–3 sticks celery, diced
1 can crab meat
1 tablespoon finely chopped onion
1 tablespoon chopped parsley
French dressing (see p. 282)
lettuce

1. Wipe the pears but do not peel them. Cut in halves, remove the cores and scoop out some of the flesh. Brush the pear halves with lemon juice.

2. Put the scooped-out flesh into a bowl and add apple, celery, crab meat, onion and parsley. Add enough French dressing to moisten, mix well and check the seasoning.

3. Spoon into the pear halves, arrange on a bed of lettuce and garnish with thin slices of unpeeled apple brushed with lemon juice.

Honeyed Salad

To serve with cold turkey or galantines (Serves 4—5)

4 dessert apples
3 oz seeded or seedless raisins
1.1/2 oz chopped walnuts
1/2 lb carrots, cooked and diced
a pinch of salt

DRESSING
1 tablespoon clear honey
3 tablespoons lemon juice

1. Peel, core and dice three of the apples and combine with the raisins, nuts and carrots. Add a pinch of salt.

2. Add the honey and lemon juice blended together, toss lightly and set aside in a cool place for about 1 hour.

3. Arrange in a salad bowl or on a platter and garnish with the remaining apple—unpeeled, cut into slices and brushed with lemon juice.

Frozen Fruit Salad

3 oz cream cheese
3 tablespoons mayonnaise (see p. 280)
a pinch of salt
8 fl. oz double cream, whipped
2 tablespoons chopped dates (seeded)
2 tablespoons maraschino cherries
2 tablespoons crushed pineapple
2 tablespoons chopped kumquats
   (seeded)
1 tablespoon finely chopped preserved
   ginger
2 oz chopped blanched almonds
lettuce

A delicious mixture of fruit and cream cheese, folded into whipped cream and frozen (Serves 6—8)

1. Blend the cheese and mayonnaise, add a pinch of salt and fold in the whipped cream, fruits and ginger.

2. Pour into refrigerator trays, sprinkle with almonds and freeze until firm.

3. Cut into squares and serve on lettuce.

Pear and Grape Salad

This exciting looking salad is delicious served with cold ham or pork
(Serves 4)

4 ripe dessert pears
8 oz cream cheese
1—2 tablespoons French dressing
**   (see p. 282)**
1/2 lb black grapes

1. Peel the pears, cut in half and scoop out the core with a teaspoon.

2. Blend the cream cheese with enough French dressing to make it spreadable and coat the rounded side of each pear half.

3. Halve and pip the grapes and press them into the cheese, close together so that each pear half resembles a small bunch of grapes.

Brandied Fruit Salad

A simple but delicious fruit salad for a special occasion dessert
(Serves 5—6)

3 apples, peeled, cored and thinly
**   sliced**
3 pears, peeled, cored and sliced
2 oranges, peeled, all white pith
**   removed, then sliced**
1 melon, cut into balls
1/2 lb cherries, stoned
4 oz sugar
2 fl. oz brandy
10 fl. oz white wine
sugar

1. Combine all the fruit, sprinkle with sugar. Mix the brandy and wine and pour over the fruit.

2. Mix lightly but thoroughly and chill for at least 3 hours to blend the flavours.

Pear and Cheese Salad

A very good flavour combination is obtained by stuffing pears with Gorgonzola cheese (Serves 3)

3 large ripe pears
4 oz Gorgonzola cheese
2—3 tablespoons double cream, whipped
seasoning
curly endive or lettuce
paprika pepper

1. Peel, halve and core the pears.

2. Combine the cheese, whipped cream and a little seasoning and beat until smooth and creamy.

3. Put into a piping bag with a rose nozzle and pipe some cheese mixture into the centre of the pears. Press the two halves together, and pipe the remaining cheese where the pears join.

4. Arrange on a bed of endive or lettuce and sprinkle lightly with paprika.

Waldorf Salad

A good winter salad of fruit and nuts combined with mayonnaise and sour cream (Serves 3—4)

4 fl. oz mayonnaise (see p. 280)
4 fl. oz sour cream
1 tablespoon honey
2—3 sharp apples, peeled, cored and diced
2—3 sticks celery, diced
3 oz walnuts, coarsely chopped
6 oz halved grapes, pipped

1. Combine mayonnaise, sour cream and honey.

2. Add apple and mix well to prevent the apple discolouring.

3. Add celery, walnuts and grapes. Mix again lightly and chill well before serving.

VARIATION
Substitute diced pears for the apple or use half of each—or add 1 sliced banana with the apple.

Lettuce and Orange Salad

Especially good served with chicken, and for those who dislike an oily dressing (Serves 4)

2 oranges
1 lettuce
sugar
1 oz roasted and salted almonds

DRESSING
1 oz butter
1/4 clove garlic, crushed very finely
teaspoon lemon juice

1. Cut the oranges in half lengthways, and each half into four pieces. Remove the pulp with a sharp knife, remove pips and any white pith.

2. Arrange the lettuce in a salad bowl, put the orange pieces on top, sprinkle with a little sugar and add the almonds.

3. For the dressing—melt the butter with the garlic, add lemon juice, mix well and pour into the bowl.

4. Toss the ingredients very lightly.

OMELETTES & OTHER EGG DISHES

Cheese and Ham Omelette

An omelette is perhaps the most popular dish for a snack. It is quick to prepare, light and nourishing. A 2-egg omelette is generally sufficient for 1 person, allow 4 eggs for 2—3 servings.

4 eggs
1 tablespoon water
1/2 teaspoon salt
1/4 teaspoon freshly ground black
 pepper
4 oz ham, cut into fine strips
4 oz cottage cheese, well drained
1/2 oz butter
1 tablespoon oil

1. Beat the eggs, water, salt and pepper until just blended. Add ham and cheese.

2. Heat the butter and oil in an omelette pan. Pour in the egg mixture and cook over medium heat, stirring with a fork, for a few seconds, then lift the eggs to allow the uncooked mixture to run underneath.

3. Fold over and roll out on to a hot dish.

Californian Omelette

3 eggs
1 tablespoon milk
1 tablespoon water
1/2 teaspoon salt
a pinch of black pepper
2 tablespoons diced avocado pear
3—4 tablespoons very finely chopped
 cooked chicken
1 tablespoon finely chopped chives
1/2 oz butter
1 tablespoon oil
1 tablespoon cream

(Serves 2)

1. Beat the eggs lightly, add milk, water, seasoning, avocado, chicken and chives.

2. Heat the butter and oil in an omelette pan, pour in the egg mixture, stir lightly with a fork until the mixture just begins to set.

3. Pour on the cream, cook a minute longer then fold over and serve at once.

Chicken Liver Omelette

FILLING
1.1/2 oz butter
2 tablespoons minced onion
2 oz mushrooms, chopped
1/4 lb chicken livers
1 tablespoon flour
6 fl. oz chicken stock
1 teaspoon tomato paste
a pinch of thyme

OMELETTE
4 eggs
1/4 teaspoon salt
a pinch of black pepper
2 tablespoons cold water
1/2 oz butter

(Serves 2—3)

1. Heat the butter in an omelette pan, sauté the onion, mushrooms and chicken livers until the livers are browned, then remove them from the pan and keep hot.

2. Add the flour to the pan and mix with the pan juices. Add the stock and stir until boiling. Add tomato paste, seasoning and thyme and cook for 5 minutes.

3. Return the livers to the pan and re-heat.

4. Prepare the omelette in the usual way and spread with the liver mixture just before serving.

FILLING
2 tablespoons olive oil
4 tablespoons minced onion
a pinch of minced garlic
3—4 tomatoes, skinned seeded and
  chopped
1/2 teaspoon salt
1/4 teaspoon black pepper
1 tablespoon chopped parsley

OMELETTE
4 eggs
1/4 teaspoon salt
a pinch of pepper
2 tablespoons cold water
1/2 oz butter

Tomato Omelette

(Serves 2—3)

1. Heat the oil in an omelette pan, sauté the onion and garlic for 5 minutes. Stir in tomatoes, salt and pepper and cook over low heat until the tomato is soft. Then add parsley.

2. Prepare the omelette in the usual way. When the eggs are just set, put the tomato mixture in the centre and fold over.

3. Turn out on to a hot dish and serve at once.

Devilled Omelette

(Serves 2—3)

3 eggs
salt, cayenne pepper
1/4 teaspoon dry mustard
a pinch of curry powder
2 tablespoons water
2 tablespoons single cream
2 oz chopped ham
1/2 oz butter

1. Beat the eggs lightly, add seasoning, mustard and curry powder. Stir in water, cream and chopped ham.

2. Heat the butter in an omelette pan, pour in the egg mixture and cook quickly, stirring occasionally with a fork and loosening the omelette from the side of the pan.

3. When the omelette is lightly set on the under side, put the pan under a hot grill to brown the top.

4. Fold over and serve at once.

Cottage Eggs

(Serves 4—5)

6 eggs
1/2 teaspoon salt
1/4 teaspoon pepper
2 tablespoons single cream
4 oz cottage cheese
1 oz butter
4—5 slices hot buttered toast

1. Beat the eggs lightly, season with salt and pepper.

2. Blend the cream with the cottage cheese and stir in the eggs.

3. Heat the butter in a frying pan, pour in the egg mixture and cook lightly as for scrambled eggs.

4. Serve on hot toast.

Scrambled Eggs with Oysters

Canned oysters are excellent for this unusual snack (Serves 4)

6 eggs
dash of Tabasco
1 oz butter
1 teaspoon anchovy paste
1 can oysters
salt, freshly ground black pepper
1 tablespoon finely chopped parsley
croûtons of fried bread

1. Whisk the eggs very lightly with the Tabasco (avoid over-beating).

2. Put the butter and anchovy paste into a small frying pan and when hot pour in the eggs. Stir until just beginning to set, then add the oysters, drained and chopped. Season with salt and black pepper.

3. Finish scrambling the eggs but avoid over-cooking.

4. Put on to hot serving dishes, sprinkle with parsley and serve with croûtons of fried bread or with toast.

Fried Eggs Romano

Eggs fried with bacon and green peppers (Serves 4)

2 tablespoons olive oil
1 onion, peeled and thinly sliced
1 green pepper, seeded and cut into
   strips
4 rashers bacon, cut into pieces
4 eggs

1. Heat the oil in a sauté pan, add onion, green pepper and bacon, and cook over medium heat until the onion is transparent.

2. Break the eggs into the pan carefully, cover with the lid of the pan or with foil and continue to cook for 2—3 minutes or until the eggs are just firm. Add a dash of salt and pepper if desired.

3. Slide carefully on to a hot serving dish.

Eggs Valencia

2 green peppers, seeded and
   chopped
4 fl. oz single cream
1/2 teaspoon salt
3 teaspoons Tabasco
4 eggs
2 oz grated Parmesan cheese

Pre-heat oven to 375°F Mark 5

Eggs cooked in a blend of cream and green pepper with cheese (Serves 4)

1. Blend the peppers and cream in an electric mixer, add salt and Tabasco and pour into a buttered ovenproof baking dish.

2. Break each egg carefully on top, sprinkle with the cheese and cook in a moderate oven until the eggs are set—about 10 minutes.

Bacon Omelette

(Serves 2—3)

1.1/2 oz butter
4 spring onions, sliced
4 eggs
2 tablespoons double cream, whipped
1/2 teaspoon salt
1/4 teaspoon pepper
1 teaspoon prepared mustard
6 rashers crisply fried bacon

1. Melt half the butter in an omelette pan and sauté the onion for 3 minutes. Then remove from the pan.

2. Beat the eggs, cream, salt, pepper and mustard until the mixture is just blended. Add the onion and bacon.

3. Heat the remaining butter in the pan, pour in the egg mixture and cook over low heat, stirring lightly with a fork and lifting the eggs to allow the uncooked mixture to run underneath.

4. When the eggs are just set, fold over and turn out on to a hot dish.

Piperade

An appetizing mixture of eggs and vegetables, originating from the Basque region of France (Serves 4)

3 tablespoons olive oil
1 green pepper, seeded and thinly sliced
1 onion, peeled and finely chopped
1 tomato, peeled, seeded and chopped
1 clove garlic, crushed
1 teaspoon salt
a pinch of freshly ground black pepper
6 eggs

1. Heat the oil in a frying pan, add the green pepper and onion, and sauté until the vegetables begin to soften.

2. Add tomato, garlic and seasoning, and simmer until the ingredients are soft and mushy.

3. Add the lightly beaten eggs and stir just enough to mix with the vegetables. Cook for a few minutes until the eggs are just set.

4. Serve with toast or on thin sautéd slices of ham.

Eggs in Snow

An attractive variation of the simplest of all snacks—eggs on toast (Serves 2)

1. Toast the bread on one side, turn and toast the under side very lightly. Butter the lightly toasted side and keep hot.

2. Separate the eggs, add seasoning and a pinch of nutmeg to the egg whites, and beat until stiff.

3. Spread the egg white over the buttered toast, make a slight indentation in the middle and drop in the egg yolk.

4. Sprinkle with grated cheese and put under a hot grill for a few minutes until the egg yolk has set.

2 slices bread
butter
2 eggs
nutmeg
grated cheese

Golden Buck

A tasty mixture of eggs and cheese served on toast (Serves 4)

1 oz butter
6 oz grated cheese
4 tablespoons beer
1 teaspoon Worcestershire sauce
1 teaspoon lemon juice
salt, cayenne pepper
a pinch of celery salt
4 eggs
4 slices buttered toast

1. Melt the butter in a small frying pan, add cheese, beer, Worcestershire sauce, lemon juice and seasoning. Stir over low heat until smooth and creamy.

2. Beat the eggs lightly and stir into the mixture. Stir until the eggs are lightly set, then spoon on to the hot toast.

Scotch Woodcock

A simple snack of scrambled eggs with anchovies (Serves 4)

2 oz butter
4 slices of bread
anchovy paste
6 eggs
pepper, salt
8 anchovy fillets
capers
cayenne pepper

1. Heat half the butter in a frying pan and fry the bread until crisp. Remove from pan, spread very lightly with anchovy paste and keep hot.

2. Put the rest of the butter into the pan, add the eggs, beaten very slightly with pepper and a small pinch of salt. Stir until just set.

3. Spoon the scrambled egg on to the fried bread and arrange 2 anchovy fillets across each piece. Put a caper into each section, sprinkle sparingly with cayenne and serve at once.

Bacon and Kidney Scramble

Kidney, bacon and eggs cooked together and served on toast (Serves 4)

2 lamb's kidneys
1.1/2—2 oz butter
4 rashers bacon
3 eggs
1 tablespoon cream
black pepper, salt
a pinch of mixed herbs
4 slices hot buttered toast

1. Skin the kidneys, remove the cores and cut into thin slices.

2. Heat the butter in a small frying pan, add kidney, fry for a few minutes, then add the chopped bacon and cook together until the kidney is tender.

3. Beat the eggs lightly, add cream, seasoning and herbs and pour over the kidneys. Stir over low heat until the eggs are lightly set.

4. Serve on hot buttered toast.

Egg and Sweetcorn Savoury

Eggs covered with sweetcorn in a cheese sauce and lightly grilled (Serves 4)

4 eggs
12 oz sweetcorn
milk
2 oz butter
3 tablespoons flour
salt, cayenne pepper
4 oz grated cheese
2 tablespoons breadcrumbs
a little extra butter

1. Boil the eggs for 5 minutes.

2. Drain the sweetcorn, measure the liquid and add sufficient milk to make 12 fl. oz.

3. Make a sauce with the butter, flour, milk and sweetcorn liquid. Add seasoning, most of the cheese, and sweetcorn.

4. Put half this sauce into a buttered baking dish. Shell the eggs and arrange on top. Cover with the remaining sauce.

5. Mix the remaining cheese with breadcrumbs, sprinkle on top and dot with butter.

6. Brown under a hot grill.

Swiss Eggs

A light but nourishing snack of eggs and cheese with cream (Serves 6)

6 eggs
4 oz grated cheese
4 fl. oz single cream
1 teaspoon finely chopped parsley
1 oz butter

Pre-heat oven to 375°F Mark 5

1. Break the eggs carefully into a buttered ovenproof dish and sprinkle with salt and pepper. Cover with half the cheese.

2. Pour the cream on top and sprinkle with the remaining cheese and parsley.

3. Dot with butter and put into a moderately hot oven until the eggs are just set—about 7 to 10 minutes.

CHEESE DISHES & FONDUES

Welsh Rarebit

The Welsh Rarebit available in cans is very good, but if you prefer to make your own it takes only a few minutes. In this recipe the cheese is melted in beer and the curry powder adds piquancy to the flavour (Serves 4)

8 fl. oz beer
2 teaspoons Worcestershire sauce
1/4 teaspoon dry mustard
1/4 teaspoon curry powder
a small pinch cayenne pepper
1 lb grated sharp Cheddar cheese
4 slices toast or crumpets or grilled
**   tomatoes**

1. Combine the beer, Worcestershire sauce, mustard, curry powder and cayenne pepper in a frying pan or chafing dish. Cook over low heat until the ingredients are well mixed and hot.

2. Add the cheese and stir until melted. Serve at once on hot buttered toast or toasted crumpets, or it is very good served on hot grilled tomatoes.

Puffed Cheese Rarebit

(Serves 4)

4 slices bread
butter
3 eggs
4 oz grated cheese
1/4 teaspoon prepared mustard
1—2 tablespoons cream

Pre-heat oven to 400°F Mark 6

1. Toast the bread, spread with butter and arrange the slices in an ovenproof dish.

2. Separate the eggs, beat the yolks, add cheese, mustard, seasoning and cream.

3. Beat the egg whites stiffly and fold into the mixture. Pile onto the slices of toast and put into a moderately hot oven for about 7 minutes or until brown and puffy.

Mushroom Rarebit

A variation of Welsh Rarebit, another good way of serving mushrooms as a snack (Serves 4)

2 oz butter
1 lb mushrooms, sliced
2 tablespoons tomato purée
3 tablespoons stock or water
4 tablespoons grated Parmesan cheese
4 slices toast or crumpets

1. Heat the butter in a frying pan, add the mushrooms and sauté slowly for about 10 minutes.

2. Add seasoning and tomato purée mixed with the stock. Add cheese and continue to cook slowly until the mushrooms are tender—about 5 to 7 minutes.

3. Serve on hot buttered toast or crumpets.

Cheese Puff

A light and airy cheese spread for toast or crumpets

2 egg whites
1/2 teaspoon baking powder
1/4 teaspoon salt
1/4 teaspoon paprika
4 oz grated sharp Cheddar cheese
4 slices hot buttered toast

1. Beat the egg whites until stiff. Stir in the baking powder and salt sifted together. Add paprika and grated cheese and fold in lightly.

2. Spread on the toast about 1/4 inch thick and brown under a hot grill. Serve at once.

Cheese and Ham Toast

(Serves 4)

4 slices ham
4 slices buttered toast
a little chopped mango chutney
4 slices Gruyère cheese
2 tomatoes, peeled and sliced

1. Put a slice of ham on each piece of toast. Spread lightly with chutney and cover with a slice of cheese.

2. Arrange slices of tomato on top and put under a hot grill to heat through.

Cheese and Bacon Slices

(Serves 4)

8 oz grated cheese
1 egg
1 teaspoon Worcestershire sauce
a pinch of prepared mustard
cayenne pepper
1/2 oz butter
4 slices bread
4 rashers bacon
4 black olives

Pre-heat oven to 400°F Mark 6

1. Combine the cheese with beaten egg, Worcestershire sauce and seasonings. Spread on the bread and top with a slice of bacon.

2. Put into a buttered baking tin and bake in a moderately hot oven for 10 minutes.

3. Place an olive on top and serve at once.

Turkey Gratin

Slices of turkey or chicken on toast covered with a piquant cheese sauce (Serves 4)

3/4 oz butter
1.1/2 tablespoons flour
1/4 teaspoon dry mustard
8 fl. oz milk
12 oz grated cheese
1 teaspoon Worcestershire sauce
4 slices toast
8 fairly thick slices turkey
paprika pepper

1. Heat the butter, stir in the flour and mustard. Cook for 2 minutes. Then add the milk gradually and stir until boiling. Add salt and pepper to taste.

2. Add cheese and Worcestershire sauce and stir over low heat until the cheese has melted.

3. Arrange the toast in a shallow baking pan, put the slices of turkey on top and cover with the cheese sauce.

4. Brown under a hot grill and sprinkle with paprika before serving.

Cheese and Anchovy Snack

A hot snack composed of slices of bread and melted cheese topped with anchovy. If you find anchovies a little too salty to your taste, soak them for 10–15 minutes in a little milk and then pat dry before using (Serves 4)

1/4 French loaf
Bel Paese or Cheddar cheese
1 can anchovy fillets
4 oz butter

Pre-heat oven to 400°F Mark 6

1. Cut the bread into slanting slices about 1/4 inch thick. Place a slice of cheese on each and arrange in a baking tin, slightly overlapping. Put into a moderately hot oven until the cheese has melted and the bread is crisp.

2. Mash the anchovy fillets and mix with the butter. Spread over the bread and return to the oven for a few minutes to heat through.

Mexican Cheese

Served on toast, this appetizing mixture of cheese, tomatoes and eggs makes a good snack. For a more substantial dish, try it on boiled rice (Serves 4—5)

2 tablespoons oil
1 green pepper, seeded and chopped
1 onion, finely chopped
1 tablespoon flour
4 fl. oz milk
12 oz grated Cheddar cheese
1 small can (8 oz) tomatoes, drained
1 canned pimento, cut into strips
3 tablespoons chopped black olives
cayenne pepper
3 egg yolks
toast or boiled rice

1. Heat the oil in a pan, add the green pepper and onion and sauté for about 10 minutes.

2. Stir in the flour and milk and stir until boiling.

3. Add cheese and tomatoes and cook over low heat for about 10 minutes. Add pimento, olives and seasoning and cook another few minutes.

4. Add the beaten egg yolks gradually and stir with a fork until the mixture thickens. It should not boil at this stage.

5. Serve on toast or with boiled rice.

Swiss Fondue

*This recipe is for the traditional
Neuchâtel fondue (Serves 4)*

1 clove garlic
12 fl. oz dry white wine
1 teaspoon lemon juice
12 oz grated Emmenthal cheese
12 oz grated Gruyère cheese
2 teaspoons cornflour
2 tablespoons Kirsch
white pepper, cayenne pepper
grated nutmeg, paprika pepper

1. Rub the inside of the fondue
pot with the cut clove of garlic.
2. Put in the wine and lemon
juice, and heat over a low flame.
Add the cheese gradually, stirring
all the time using a figure of
eight motion.
3. When the mixture bubbles add
the cornflour, blended smoothly
with the Kirsch, and cook for
about 3 minutes. Add pepper,
cayenne, nutmeg and paprika to
taste.
4. To serve, spear a piece of bread
on to the fondue fork and dip
into the fondue. If the crust is
left on the bread it is easier to
spear and it is advisable not to
have the bread too fresh, or it
will crumble in the fondue.

Tomato Fondue with Frankfurters

French bread is served separately with this fondue, and small frankfurters are used for dipping (Serves 2—3)

1 clove garlic
8 oz grated Cheddar cheese
2 oz grated Gruyère cheese
4 fl. oz condensed tomato soup
1 teaspoon Worcestershire sauce
3 tablespoons dry sherry
1 small can cocktail frankfurters
French bread

1. Rub the inside of the fondue pot with the cut clove of garlic.

2. Put in the cheeses, tomato soup and Worcestershire sauce, and stir continuously over a low heat until the cheese has melted and the mixture is creamy. Stir in the sherry, and cook 2—3 minutes. Adjust the seasoning before serving.

3. The frankfurters are then speared on to the fondue forks and dipped into the fondue.

4. Serve with plenty of French bread.

English Style Fondue

Beer is used in this recipe instead of wine (Serves 3—4)

8 fl oz beer
8 oz grated Cheddar cheese
1 clove garlic, crushed
1 oz butter
2 tablespoons cornflour
1/2 teaspoon dry mustard
a little extra beer

1. Put the beer, cheese and crushed garlic into the fondue pot and stir over low heat until the cheese has melted.

2. Stir in the butter.

3. Blend the cornflour and mustard smoothly with a little extra beer and stir into the fondue. Continue stirring until the mixture is thick and creamy.

FRIED & TOASTED SANDWICHES & SANDWICH SPREADS

Monte Cristo Sandwich

A crisp fried sandwich of chicken or turkey, ham and cheese (Serves 4)

**8 slices bread
2 eggs
4 fl. oz milk
1/2 teaspoon salt
a pinch of pepper
sliced breast of chicken or turkey
4 slices ham
4 slices Gruyère cheese
prepared mustard
butter for frying**

1. Cut the crusts from the bread.

2. Beat the eggs, milk, salt and pepper together. Dip the slices of bread in the mixture and allow them to soak well, then drain.

3. Arrange some thin slices of chicken on 4 of the slices of bread. Cover with a slice of ham and top with a slice of cheese. Spread lightly with mustard and cover each with another slice of bread. Press down well and cut across diagonally or in half if slices are too large.

4. Heat the butter in a frying pan and fry the sandwiches until brown and crisp, turning once. Serve while hot.

Cheese Fingers

(Serves 3—4)

1. Remove the crusts from the bread, spread with butter and make into sandwiches with the grated cheese. (Spread a little prepared mustard or chopped pickle on one side of the bread if desired.)

2. Cut into neat fingers.

3. Beat the eggs, add milk and seasoning.

4. Dip the fingers quickly in and out of the egg and fry in hot butter until crisp and golden.

9 slices bread
butter
2 oz grated cheese
2 eggs
2 tablespoons milk
butter for frying

Toasted Cheese and Bacon Sandwich

A hearty snack with bacon, cheese and prunes (Serves 4)

1. Cover the prunes with boiling water and let stand about 1 hour.

2. Remove crusts from the bread and butter one side of each slice.

3. Grill the bacon until crisp, set aside 2 rashers and chop the rest coarsely.

4. Remove the stones from the prunes, set aside 4 and chop the remainder.

5. Cover 4 slices of buttered bread with the chopped prunes and bacon. Top with the remaining slices.

6. Toast the sandwiches on one side, turn over and cover the untoasted side with a slice of cheese. Grill until the cheese bubbles and browns.

7. Top each sandwich with half a slice of bacon and a prune. Serve hot garnished with watercress.

12 prunes
8 slices bread
butter
8 rashers bacon
4 slices Gouda or processed cheese
watercress for garnish

Pre-heat grill

Swiss Cheese Snack

Cheese and ham sandwiches fried in butter (Serves 4)

1. Cut the crusts from the bread and spread with butter.

2. Spread a little mustard on half the slices, put a slice of cheese and a slice of ham on top. Cover with the remaining slices of bread and press down firmly.

3. Cut in half crossways and fry in hot butter, turning once.

8 slices bread
butter
prepared mustard
4 slices Gruyère cheese
4 thin slices cooked ham

Chicken Club Sandwich

A club sandwich consists of 3 slices of toast for each sandwich. The filling can vary, but it is generally some kind of poultry or meat and salad. The sandwich should always be served hot (Makes 1 club sandwich)

3 slices bread
butter
mayonnaise (see p. 280)
lettuce
slices of chicken breast
prepared mustard
2 rashers bacon, fried until crisp
1—2 slices tomato or onion
gherkins or stuffed olives for garnish

1. Remove the crusts from the bread, toast and spread with butter.

2. Spread the first slice with a little mayonnaise, cover with 1—2 leaves of lettuce and slices of chicken. Spread a little more mayonnaise on the chicken and cover with the second slice of toast.

3. Spread a very little mustard on the toast and then a little mayonnaise. Cover with the slices of bacon and slices of tomato or onion.

4. Place the third slice of toast on top and press down firmly. Serve at once, garnished with slices of gherkin or stuffed olive.

Sandwich Spreads

Below are a selection of spreads which can be made up for a quick sandwich. In most cases, the sandwiches could be fried or grilled if you prefer a hot snack.

Avocado Spread

4 oz mashed avocado
2 teaspoons minced onion
1 tablespoon lemon juice
1 tablespoon mayonnaise (see p. 280)
a pinch of cayenne pepper
dash of Tabasco

Combine all ingredients and beat until smooth.

Cream Cheese and Orange Spread

3 oz cream cheese
2 tablespoons finely chopped crystallized
   or preserved ginger
2 teaspoons grated orange rind
3 tablespoons orange juice

(see picture, p. 307)

Beat the cream cheese until soft and smooth. Add ginger and orange rind and mix in the orange juice.

Blue Cheese Spread

1/4 lb blue cheese
6 oz cream cheese
2 tablespoons mayonnaise (see p. 280)
2 tablespoons crisply cooked diced
   bacon

Combine the cheeses, and blend until creamy and smooth. Add the mayonnaise and bacon.

Cheese and Pimento Spread

4 oz grated Cheddar cheese
1 canned pimento, drained and
   chopped
3—4 tablespoons mayonnaise
a pinch of paprika pepper

Blend ingredients together to form a spreadable paste.

Ham Sandwich Loaf

Prepare this in advance for a late-night snack—perhaps after the theatre. The loaf is sandwiched with a variety of fillings and needs to be refrigerated for 3—4 hours (Serves 7—8, see picture, p. 307)

1 loaf uncut bread
1/2 lb ham, chopped
1 can (about 3.1/2 oz) pimentos,
   drained and chopped
mayonnaise (see p. 280)
8 fl. oz sweet pickle
2 hard-boiled eggs
butter
12—16 oz cream cheese

1. Remove all crusts from the loaf and cut lengthways into 4 slices of equal thickness.

2. Combine ham and pimentos, and add enough mayonnaise to make a spreadable paste. Chop the pickle and eggs together and moisten with mayonnaise.

3. Spread one slice of bread with butter, then with half the ham mixture. Butter both sides of the second slice of bread and press over the first slice. Spread with the egg and pickle mixture.

4. Butter both sides of the third slice of bread, press on top of the egg and pickle and spread with the remaining ham and pimento mixture.

5. Butter the bottom of the top slice and press into position.

6. Place the re-shaped loaf on to a serving platter and spread the top and sides with a thick layer of cream cheese. If this does not spread easily, soften it with a little cream or milk. Refrigerate for 3—4 hours and when required cut through in slices.

SNACKS ON TOAST

Turkish Sandwich

1/2 oz butter
1 tablespoon flour
4 fl. oz chicken stock
4 fl. oz single cream
5–6 oz cooked diced chicken
1 oz chopped walnuts
1 teaspoon onion juice
paprika
3 slices hot toast
butter
stuffed olives for garnish

This is an open sandwich of chicken and nuts (Serves 3)

1. Make a sauce with the butter, flour and stock, add cream, chicken and nuts, and season carefully with the onion juice, salt, pepper and paprika.

2. Heat and then pile on to the slices of toast. Brush over with a little melted butter and garnish with rings of stuffed olives. Serve at once.

Sweet – Sour Tuna Snack

4 slices bread
butter
1 can tuna fish (about 7 oz)
2–3 tablespoons mayonnaise (see p. 280)
4 slices drained canned pineapple
4 slices Cheddar or Gruyère cheese

Pre-heat grill

An interesting mixture of tuna fish, pineapple and cheese, served hot on toast (Serves 4)

1. Toast the bread on one side only and lightly butter the untoasted side.

2. Drain and flake the tuna, and add enough mayonnaise to make it spreadable. Spread on the buttered side of the toast, cover with a slice of pineapple and top with a slice of cheese.

3. Put under a hot grill until the cheese has melted.

Cheese and Tomato Sandwich

3 oz grated cheese
1 oz softened butter
1 teaspoon prepared mustard
1 teaspoon Worcestershire sauce
2 tomatoes
4 slices buttered toast
4 rashers bacon

Pre-heat oven to 475°F Mark 9

A savoury mixture of cheese, tomato and bacon on toast, browned in the oven (Serves 4)

1. Combine the cheese, butter, mustard and Worcestershire sauce.

2. Peel the tomatoes, cut across in halves and then cut each half through again, making 8 slices. Place 2 slices on each slice of bread and sprinkle with salt and pepper. Cover with the cheese mixture and top with a slice of bacon.

3. Arrange on a baking tin and cook in a fairly hot oven for 5 to 7 minutes, or until the bacon is crisp and the cheese has melted.

Crabmeat Nippies

A snack of crabmeat and cheese made in minutes (Serves 4)

4 slices bread
butter
1 can (about 6 oz) crab meat
2 teaspoons mayonnaise (see p. 280)
1 teaspoon grated onion
2 oz grated Cheddar cheese

Pre-heat grill

1. Remove the crusts from the bread and toast on one side only. Lightly butter the untoasted side.

2. Flake the crab meat, combine with the mayonnaise and onion, and spread on the buttered side of the toast. Sprinkle generously with cheese.

3. Put under a hot grill for 1—2 minutes until the cheese melts and is lightly browned. Serve at once.

Cream Cheese & Orange Spread and Ham Sandwich Loaf (see pp. 304—5)

Haddock Kedgeree

(Serves 5—6)

2 oz butter
1 lb cooked smoked haddock, flaked
6 oz rice, boiled
3 hard-boiled eggs
lemon juice
5—6 slices hot buttered toast
1 orange or lemon

1. Melt the butter in a pan, add the flaked fish, and sauté for 2—3 minutes. Add the rice, chopped eggs, salt as desired, pepper and a good squeeze of lemon juice. Stir over the heat for a few minutes.

2. Arrange on hot toast and serve with wedges of orange or lemon.

Mussel Savoury

1.1/2 oz butter
1 small onion, peeled and finely
   chopped
1/2 green pepper, finely chopped
1 can (7.1/2 oz) mussels drained and
   chopped
4 oz grated cheese
1 tablespoon tomato purée
1 tablespoon Worcestershire sauce
1 tablespoon sherry
a pinch of cayenne pepper
pickled cucumber (optional)
4—5 slices hot buttered toast

A savoury snack of mussels, grated cheese, green pepper and tomato
(Serves 4—5)

1. Heat the butter in a sauté pan, add onion and green pepper, and sauté for 3 minutes.

2. Add mussels, cheese, tomato purée, Worcestershire sauce, sherry and cayenne pepper, and cook for a few minutes until the cheese has melted, stirring all the time.

3. Put a thin slice of pickled cucumber on each slice of toast and serve the mussel mixture on top.

Chicken à la King

*Cooked chicken, mushrooms and green pepper heated in a creamy sauce.
Serve in pastry cases or on toast or toasted crumpets (Serves 5—6)*

2 oz butter
2 tablespoons finely chopped onion
1/4 lb mushrooms, sliced
1/2 green pepper, diced
4 tablespoons flour
16 fl. oz chicken stock
1 lb diced cooked chicken
**2 pimentos, drained and cut into
    thin strips**
3 tablespoons dry sherry

1. Heat the butter in a frying pan, add the onion, mushrooms and green pepper, and cook for 5 minutes.

2. Stir in the flour, mix well with the vegetables, then gradually add chicken stock and stir until boiling. Add seasoning and stir over low heat for 5 minutes.

3. Add chicken, pimentos and sherry and heat through.

English Monkey

(Serves 4)

8 fl. oz milk
4 oz breadcrumbs
4 oz grated Cheddar cheese
1/2 teaspoon salt
1/4 teaspoon paprika pepper
a pinch of dry mustard
1 teaspoon Worcestershire sauce
1 egg
4 slices hot buttered toast

1. Put the milk, breadcrumbs and cheese into the top of a double saucepan. Stir over hot water until the cheese has melted.

2. Add seasoning, Worcestershire sauce and beaten egg. Cook for 1 minute, stirring all the time, then pour over the toast.

Ham and Pineapple Toast

(Serves 4)

6 oz minced ham
1 teaspoon prepared mustard
a pinch of cayenne pepper
1—2 tablespoons mayonnaise (see p. 280)
4 slices canned pineapple
4 slices hot, lightly buttered toast or
  baps

Pre-heat oven to 400°F Mark 6

1. Season the ham with mustard and pepper and add just enough mayonnaise to bind.

2. Arrange slices of pineapple in an ovenproof dish, pile the ham mixture in a mound on top and heat through in a moderately hot oven for about 5—7 minutes.

3. Serve on lightly buttered hot toast or on halves of toasted baps.

QUICK SNACKS

Marrow and Cheese Pie

A supply of baked pie cases in the deep freeze often solves the problem of a snack meal. The filling for this pie consists of marrow covered with a fluffy cheese sauce, garnished with slices of tomato and bacon rolls (Serves 4)

1 small marrow, cooked and drained
1—8 inch baked pie case
nutmeg
1/2 pint white sauce
4 oz grated cheese
1 egg
2 tomatoes, peeled and sliced
bacon rolls

Pre-heat oven to 400°F Mark 6

1. Cut the well drained marrow into cubes and arrange in the pastry case. Sprinkle with salt, pepper and nutmeg.

2. Make the sauce, add most of the cheese, egg yolk and fold in the stiffly beaten egg white. Pour sauce over the marrow.

3. Arrange slices of tomato around the edge and sprinkle the remaining cheese in the middle.

4. Bake for about 15 minutes in a moderately hot oven.

5. Garnish with grilled bacon rolls.

Egg and Shrimp Pie

Slices of egg arranged in a pie case and covered with a creamy shrimp sauce (Serves 4)

6 eggs
1—8 inch baked pie case
1/2 oz butter
1 teaspoon prepared mustard
8 oz fresh or frozen shrimps
1/4 pint white sauce
1 tablespoon chopped parsley
2 tablespoons grated cheese

Pre-heat grill

1. Boil the eggs for 7 minutes, then shell and slice carefully. Arrange the slices in the pie case and sprinkle with a little salt and pepper.

2. Heat the butter in a small pan, add mustard and shrimps and sauté for a few minutes. Stir in the cream sauce and parsley. Check the seasoning and pour the sauce over the eggs.

3. Sprinkle with cheese and brown under a hot grill.

Sweetcorn and Cheese Pie

(Serves 4—5)

8 oz cottage cheese
2 oz grated Parmesan cheese
1 can (12 oz) sweetcorn
1/4 teaspoon paprika
1 canned pimento, chopped
6 oz cooked peas
1 eight-inch baked pie case
2 tomatoes, peeled and sliced

Pre-heat oven to 375°F Mark 5

1. Combine cottage cheese, Parmesan and drained sweetcorn. Season with salt, pepper and paprika and add pimento and peas. If the mixture is a little stiff, add some of the liquid drained from the sweetcorn.

2. Pour into the pie case and arrange slices of tomato around the edge.

3. Bake for about 15 minutes in a moderate oven.

Kidney and Mushroom Saute

A delicious mixture of kidneys, mushrooms and celery in red wine which takes about 10—15 minutes to cook. For a supper snack serve with a green salad or in a border of boiled rice if you need something a little more substantial (Serves 4)

2 oz butter
2 tablespoons finely chopped shallots
2—3 sticks celery, finely chopped
4 small veal kidneys, skinned and cored
1/4 lb mushrooms, sliced
2 tablespoons finely chopped parsley
4 fl. oz dry red wine
1/4 teaspoon dry mustard
8 fl. oz gravy

1. Heat the butter in a frying pan and sauté the shallots and celery until the shallots begin to soften.

2. Add kidneys, cut into small pieces, and cook quickly until browned —about 5 minutes.

3. Add mushrooms, parsley, the wine mixed with the mustard, seasoning and gravy. Bring to the boil and cook gently for 3—4 minutes.

Glazed Mushrooms and Ham

Mushrooms, glazed in butter and sugar and served with ham (Serves 4)

2 oz butter
2.1/2 oz brown sugar
1 teaspoon flour
1 lb mushrooms, thickly sliced
1/4 teaspoon grated nutmeg
1/4 teaspoon ground mace
4—6 slices ham
3 tablespoons sherry

1. Melt the butter in a pan, add sugar and flour mixed together, and stir over low heat until the sugar has melted.

2. Add mushrooms, nutmeg and mace. Cover and cook very slowly for 5 minutes.

3. Uncover, arrange the ham over the mushrooms and increase the heat just long enough for the ham to heat through.

4. Add the sherry and turn upside down on to a hot serving dish.

Mexican Dip

*A favourite with the young—cold, cooked frankfurters heated in a tangy
tomato dip to make a hot snack (Serves 4)*

3 tablespoons minced or very finely
   chopped onion
3 tablespoons white wine vinegar
4 fl. oz tomato ketchup
1 teaspoon Worcestershire sauce
juice of 1/2 lemon
1/2 teaspoon paprika pepper
black pepper, salt, sugar
frankfurters

1. Put onion and vinegar into a pan, and simmer for 5 minutes.

2. Add tomato ketchup, Worcestershire sauce and lemon juice. Simmer for
a few minutes longer, then add paprika, pepper, salt and sugar to taste.

3. Cut some frankfurters into 2—3 pieces and heat in the dip.

4. Serve with crusty French bread.

Kidneys in Sherry Sauce

*Lamb kidneys sautéed in butter and cooked in stock with sherry. Serve
with toast, salad or, for a more substantial snack, on buttered boiled rice
(Serves 4)*

8 lambs' kidneys
2 oz butter
1 medium sized onion, peeled and
   finely chopped
2 tablespoons flour
1 chicken bouillon cube dissolved in
   8 fl. oz hot water
salt, freshly ground black pepper
2—3 tablespoons dry sherry
chopped parsley
buttered rice, see below

BUTTERED RICE
8 oz long-grained rice
16 fl. oz water
1 teaspoon salt
1/2 oz butter

1. Skin and remove the core from the kidneys and cut in halves.

2. Heat half the butter in a small frying pan, add the kidney and sauté for
2—3 minutes, then remove from the pan.

3. Add the remaining butter to the pan, add the onion and cook until soft
and lightly browned.

4. Replace the kidneys, sprinkle with the flour and blend it carefully with
the fat. Stir in the hot stock and continue stirring until boiling. Simmer
for 5 minutes. Add salt and pepper to taste and the sherry.

5. Serve sprinkled with parsley.

BUTTERED RICE
1. Butter a pan with a tightly fitting lid and put in the rice, water and salt.
Bring to the boil, stir once, put on the lid and simmer over a low heat for
12—15 minutes. Do not stir or remove the lid at this stage.

2. When all the liquid has been absorbed, remove from heat and leave for a
few minutes, then add the butter and toss with a fork.

Cheese Crisp

(Serves 4)

10 digestive biscuits
2 oz potato crisps
3 oz butter
1 oz rice, boiled
8 oz cream cheese
2 tablespoons chopped gherkins
4 tablespoons mayonnaise (see p. 280)
seasoning
1—2 gherkins to garnish
paprika

1. Put the biscuits and potato crisps between greaseproof paper and crush with a rolling pin. Add the melted butter, mix well and press into an 8 inch pie dish. Set aside to chill.

2. Mix the rice, cream cheese and gherkins, add mayonnaise and season to taste.

3. Fill the pie dish. Then garnish with slices of gherkin and sprinkle with paprika.

Note
For variety, try flaked cooked fish instead of cheese.

Sausage and Apple Snack

Apple rings topped with sausage meat patties and garnished with bacon rolls (Serves 6)

1 lb sausage meat
2 tablespoons chopped parsley
1/2 teaspoon curry powder
1/2 teaspoon mixed herbs
2 tablespoons flour
butter
2 dessert apples
6 thin rashers bacon
a few sprigs of parsley
toast

1. Combine sausage meat, parsley, curry powder, herbs and seasoning, and shape into 6 patties.

2. Coat lightly with flour and fry in butter for about 5 minutes on each side. Remove from the pan and keep hot.

3. Core but do not peel the apples, cut each into three slices and fry for about 2 minutes on each side.

4. Roll up the bacon, put on to a skewer and fry or grill.

5. Put the apple slices on to a serving dish and arrange the patties on top. Garnish with the bacon rolls and a little parsley or watercress. Serve with hot toast.

Salmon and Cheese Rolls

(Serves 4)

1 small can salmon
1 packet frozen peas
1 small can evaporated milk
lemon juice
4 baps
butter
4 slices Cheddar or processed cheese

1. Drain and flake the fish. Add peas and evaporated milk and season with salt, pepper and lemon juice. Stir over low heat until the mixture is smooth and creamy.

2. Split the baps, spread with butter and put a slice of cheese on one half of each bap.

3. Pile some of the hot fish mixture on top and cover with the other half of the bap. Serve at once.

Index